Trends in Constraint Programming

Trends in Constraint Programming

Edited by

Frédéric Benhamou
Narendra Jussien
Barry O'Sullivan

First published in Great Britain and the United States in 2007 by ISTE Ltd

ISTE Ltd
6 Fitzroy Square
London W1T 5DX
UK

ISTE USA
4308 Patrice Road
Newport Beach, CA 92663
USA

www.iste.co.uk

Library of Congress Cataloging-in-Publication Data

Trends in constraint programming/edited by Frédéric Benhamou, Narendra Jussien, Barry O'Sullivan.
p. cm.
Includes index.
ISBN 978-1-905209-97-2
1. Constraint programming (Computer science) I. Benhamou, Frédéric. II. Jussien, Narendra. III. O'Sullivan, B. (Barry)
QA76.612.T74 2007
005.1'16--dc22

2007009430

British Library Cataloguing-in-Publication Data
A CIP record for this book is available from the British Library
ISBN 13: 978-1-905-209-97-2

Printed and bound in Great Britain by Antony Rowe Ltd, Chippenham, Wiltshire.

Contents

Introduction

Significant advances in computing power since the 1960s have led to a wealth of research on problem solving in fields such as operations research, numerical analysis, symbolic computing, scientific computing, artificial intelligence and programming languages. Constraint programming is a discipline that gathers, exploits and unifies ideas shared by all of these domains to tackle decision support problems.

Over the last 15 years, constraint programming has become a leading technology for modeling and solving real-life combinatorial problems. It has been successfully used in fields such as production planning, scheduling, timetabling, rostering, supply-chain management, product configuration, diagnosis, molecular biology, robotics, computer security and industrial process control. Moreover, in many application domains it is the technology of choice for solving highly complex problems.

Constraint programming is essentially a declarative paradigm: once the problem has been modeled as a constraint satisfaction problem, a constraint solver calculates a solution for it. The behavior of a constraint solver is guided by a strict separation of concerns, in which individual constraints are responsible for pruning the search space. It is the interaction between these individual behaviors that leads to an efficient search procedure by exploiting sophisticated search space exploration techniques and heuristics.

While the principles behind constraint programming are simple, its practical application can be quite complex. Real life problems are often computationally

---

Introduction written by Frédéric BENHAMOU, Narendra JUSSIEN and Barry O'SULLIVAN.

intractable, so intelligent algorithms and heuristics appropriate to the application domain being considered must be used. In addition, the ideal of fully declarative problem formulation that ensures an efficient search process has not yet been achieved. Constraint programming is therefore an active academic field of research: many research papers are presented not only in constraint programming conferences and journals but also within artificial intelligence and operations research fora.

This book presents trends in the field of constraint programming that not only try to improve the efficiency and utility of constraint-based methods, but also present a variety of important emerging application domains for constraint programming.

Purpose of this book

The International Conference on the Principles and Practice of Constraint Programming (CP) is the premier annual meeting dedicated to developments in the field of constraint programming. It is concerned with all aspects of computing with constraints, including algorithms, applications, environments, languages, models, and systems. Constraint programming is an ever-evolving field and each year the set of workshops that run alongside the conference represent the ongoing trends of the field. Very interesting insights, concepts and results are presented during these workshops.

The objective of this book is to complement the CP 2006 conference proceedings with a volume that reflects the current trends in the field as reflected by the workshop program, and collects these in a thematic way to provide a broad perspective on what is currently being studied in these areas. The organizers of each workshop have contributed either a single chapter reflecting the broad trends within the topic of their workshop, or a collection of short chapters presenting condensed versions of key contributions accompanied with an editorial comment.

The intended audience of this book comprises researchers and practitioners interested in all aspects of constraint programming. Research students should find the book useful as a guide to the topics that are considered to be at the cutting edge of constraint programming research.

Organization of the book

The book is organized into eight parts. Part I focuses on the past, present and future of constraint programming. This is the largest part of the book, comprising six chapters.

Chapter 1 is a transcript of a talk that Pascal Van Hentenryck delivered at CP 2006 when he was awarded the Association for Constraint Programming's Research Excellence Award. The chapter presents the experiences of one of CP's top researchers as he was involved in the development of a series of influential constraint programming systems.

Chapter 2 presents a synthesis of the first CP-Tools workshop, which collected together a variety of constraint programming systems, both commercial and non-commercial. The chapter also reports on two panel discussions: one focusing on technical awareness issues, the other considering future directions for the development of CP systems.

Chapter 3 presents a synthesis of the discussions held as part of the workshop on the subject of "The Next 10 Years of Constraint Programming". During this workshop, over 120 people participated in breakout discussions; each breakout group was chaired by a discussion leader who acted as a facilitator of the discussion. This chapter compiles reports of the major points raised during this event summarized by these discussion leaders.

The remainder of Part I presents chapters that reflect trends in constraint propagation and implementation (Chapter 4), a major component of all constraint reasoning tasks; a chapter on the relationships between satisfiability and constraint programming (Chapter 5); and finally, a chapter on trends in bioinformatics and constraint programming (Chapter 6).

Fundamental issues in constraint programming are addressed in Parts II-IV, each part presenting a collection of papers from three workshops: modeling and reformulation, symmetry breaking, and interval constraint reasoning. The chapters on modeling and reformulation (Part II) address different aspects of the importance of modeling in constraint programming. Other complex issues associated with the constraint modeling problem arise when symmetries are present in the problem being solved. This issue is discussed in detail in Part III. Of course, not all constraint models are specified using finite domains. In Part IV we are given a flavor of the depth and rigor associated with continuous constraint modeling and solving.

Part V presents a selection of papers from the workshop on local search techniques in constraint programming. Local search, while incomplete, has been shown to be a key approach to problem solving that has the capability to tackle real-life problems that are too large for systematic solvers. The development of new local search algorithms continues to provide a very rich and practical domain for cutting-edge constraint programming research.

The importance of reasoning about preferences and soft constraints is considered in Part VI. Solving constraint satisfaction problems involving costs continues to be a very important and productive area of research, as reflected in the introduction to this part.

The two final parts of the book (Parts VII and VIII) focus on two important application domains for constraint programming: software verification, testing and analysis, and graphical applications, respectively. Software verification, testing and analysis is becoming more important with the emergence of safety critical systems and the high level of investment in the development of complex technical systems. Graphical applications provide a rich domain for exploiting constraints technology since it brings together human-computer interaction, visual problem solving, and hybrid finite and infinite domain constraint systems. Even though graphical applications of constraints date back to the 1960s, there remain significant challenges in this area.

Acknowledgements

This book would not have been possible without the coordinated efforts of many people. Firstly, we would like to express our thanks to the organizers of each of the CP 2006 workshops, all of whom participated in this project. Secondly, we would like to thank the individual authors of each of the parts, chapters and chapter sections. It is their scientific contributions to the future of constraint programming that we have set out to show-case in this book. Thirdly, the individual workshops would not have been possible without their hard working programme committees, who enabled the peer-review process that ensures scientific excellence.

Finally, we would like to record a very special mention of two special events that took place during the CP 2006 conference: the workshop on CP-Tools and the workshop on "The Next 10 Years of Constraint Programming". These events enabled the industrial and research communities of constraints researchers and users to come together and take stock of what has been achieved by the community over the last decade, and to reflect upon where our community needs to go over the next 10 years. It was clear from the attendance at both events that these were welcomed and highly regarded.

Contributors

Anbulagan, L&C/NICTA and CSL/ANU, Australia; Carlos **Ansótegui**, DIEI, University of Lleida, Spain; Bonny **Banerjee**, Computer Sc. & Eng., Ohio State Univ, USA; Pedro **Barahona**, Universidade Nova de Lisboa, Portugal; Roman **Barták**, Charles University, Czech Republic; J. Christopher **Beck**, University of Toronto, Canada; Frédéric **Benhamou**, LINA/University of Nantes, France; Bruno **Berstel**, ILOG, MPI, France; Christian **Bessiere**, LIRMM/CNRS, France; Benjamin **Blanc**, CEA/LIST, France; María L. **Bonet**, LSI, Universitat Politècnica de Catalunya, Spain; Lucas **Bordeaux**, Microsoft Research, UK; Ondřej **Čepek**, Charles University and Institute of Finance and Administration, Czech Republic; B. **Chandrasekaran**, Computer Sc. & Eng., Ohio State Univ, USA; Yannick **Chevalier**, IRIT, France; Najah **Chridi**, LORIA-UHP, France; Marc **Christie**, LINA/University of Nantes, France; Alessandro **Dal Palù**, Univ. Parma, Matematica, Italy; Nicolas **Delanoue**, ISTIA/LISA, France; Yves **Deville**, UCLouvain, Belgium; Alastair **Donaldson**, University of Glasgow, UK; Agostino **Dovier**, Univ. Udine, DIMI, Italy; Pierre **Dupont**, UCLouvain, Belgium; François **Fages**, INRIA Rocquencourt, France; Alan M. **Frisch**, University of York, UK; Ian **Gent**, University of St. Andrews, UK; Arnaud **Gotlieb**, IRISA/INRIA, France; Peter **Gregory**, University of Strathclyde, UK; Youssef **Hamadi**, Microsoft Research,UK; Ivan **Heckman**, University of Toronto, Canada; Fred **Hemery**, CRIL, France; Michael **Heusch**, LINA/University of Nantes, France Hiroshi **Hosobe**, NII, Japan; Daisuke **Ishii**, Waseda University, Japan; Erwan **Jahier**, CNRS/VERIMAG, France; Luc **Jaulin**, ENSIETA/E3I2, France; Peter **Jeavons**, Oxford University Computing Laboratory, UK; Chris **Jefferson**, Oxford University, UK; Philippe **Jégou**, LSIS / UPCAM 3, France; Christophe **Jermann**, LINA/University of Nantes, France; Narendra **Jussien**, EMN/LINA, France; Tom **Kelsey**, University of St. Andrews, UK; Mounira **Kourjieh**, IRIT, France; Sébastien **Lagrange**, ISTIA/LISA, France; Michel **Leconte**, ILOG, France; Christophe **Lecoutre** CRIL, France; Jordi **Levy**, IIIA, CSIC, Spain; Chu Min **Li**, LaRIA – University of Picardie Jules Verne, France; Steve **Linton**, University of St. Andrews, UK; Felip **Manyà**, DIEI, University of Lleida, Spain; Joao **Marques-Silva**, University of Southampton, UK; Kim **Marriott**, Monash University, Australia; Bernadette **Martínez-Hernández**, University of York, UK; Pedro **Meseguer**, IIIA/CSIC, Spain; Deepak **Mehta**, University College Cork, Ireland; Claude **Michel**, I3S (UNSA/CNRS), France; Laurent **Michel**, CSE, University of Connecticut, USA; Ian **Miguel**, University of St Andrews, UK; Yehuda **Naveh**, IBM Haifa Research Lab, Israel; Samba Ndojh **Ndiaye**, LSIS/UPCAM 3, France; Robert **Nieuwenhuis**, Technical University of Catalonia, Spain; Jean-Marie **Normand**, LINA/University of Nantes, France; Barry **O'Sullivan**, 4C – University College Cork, Ireland; Gilles **Pesant**, Polytechnique Montréal, Canada; Karen **Petrie**, Oxford University, UK; Duc Nghia **Pham**, SAFE/NICTA, Australia; Steve **Prestwich**,

4C – University College Cork, Ireland; Patrick **Prosser**, Glasgow University, UK; Jean-François **Puget**, ILOG, France; Pascal **Raymond**, CNRS/VERIMAG, France; Jean-Charles **Régin**, ILOG, Sophia-Antipolis, France; Andrea **Roli**, DEIS – Univeristy of Bologna, Italy; Francesca **Rossi**, University of Padua, Italy; Abdul **Sattar**, SAFE/NICTA and IIIS/Griffith University, Australia; Pierre **Schaus**, UCLouvain, Belgium; Thomas **Schiex**, INRA Toulouse, France; Christian **Schulte**, KTH/ICT/ECS, Sweden; Meinolf **Sellmann**, Brown University, USA; John **Slaney**, L&C NICTA and CSL/ANU, Australia; Barbara M. **Smith**, 4C – University College Cork, Ireland; Christine **Solnon**, LIRIS, France; Sébastien **Sorlin**, LIRIS, France; Peter **Stuckey**, University of Melbourne, Australia; Cyril **Terrioux**, LSIS / UPCAM 3, France; Kazunori **Ueda**, Waseda University, Japan; M.R.C. **Van Dongen**, University College Cork, Ireland; Pascal **Van Hentenryck**, Brown University, USA; Laurent **Vigneron**, LORIA-UN2, France; Mark **Wallace**, Monash University, Australia; Toby **Walsh**, NICTA – University of New South Wales, Australia; Wanxia **Wei**, University of New Brunswick, Canada; Sebastian **Will**, ALU Freiburg, Bioinformatics, Germany; Roland **Yap**, National University of Singapore, Singapore; Stéphane **Zampelli**, UCLouvain, Belgium; Harry **Zhang**, University of New Brunswick, Canada.

PART I

The Past, Present and Future of Constraint Programming

Edited by Frédéric BENHAMOU, Narendra JUSSIEN and Barry O'SULLIVAN

Chapter 1

Constraint Programming as Declarative Algorithmics

It is a great honor to receive the second ACP award for research excellence in constraint programming. It is also a humbling experience as I reflect how lucky I have been to meet and work with so many talented people at many stages in my career. As William E. Woodward said, "in the queer mess of human destiny the determining factor is luck. For every important place in life, there are many men of fairly equal capacities. Among them, luck divides who shall accomplish the great work, who shall be crowned with laurel, and who should fall back in obscurity and silence". Jean-Charles Régin expressed it a bit more bluntly when he once told me: "everything you did would have been contributed by someone else anyway." It is obvious that I have been fortunate to be at the right place at the right time many times.

I became interested in research in Brittany. The University of Namur in Belgium had the excellent practice of sending students in their final year abroad for about 4 months. I went to the center for telecommunications (CNET) in Lannion to study software engineering. After two months, my fellow students and I had nothing left to work on, so we started looking for other opportunities in the center. I was told that there were two great researchers I should consider, one in concurrent programming and one in logic programming. Concurrent programming sounded more interesting so I went knocking at the door of this fellow several days in a row without success. I gave up and met Mehmet Dincbas the next day. Mehmet gave me papers and books to read, suggested all kinds of

---

Chapter written by Pascal VAN HENTENRYCK.

programming projects in logic programming, answered all my questions (and there were many) and spent considerable time explaining to me the grand challenges and the folklore of logic programming. As I was about to leave, he told me that he was joining Hervé Gallaire at the European Computer-Industry Research Centre (ECRC) and he asked me whether I was interested in coming along. I became the first PhD student at ECRC in August 1985 where I spent about 4.5 years on the CHIP project. I then joined Brown University in 1990 where I was recruited by Paris Kanellakis. I also had the opportunity to spend time at the University of Marseilles, at MIT, and at the University of Louvain, and to collaborate with Ilog.

In this chapter, I would like to reflect on some of the lessons I have learned in the last 20 years and to illustrate them using several research projects. These lessons are:

1) Find the missing link;
2) Build systems;
3) Be driven by applications;
4) Just do it; then clean up the mess;
5) Strive for the declarative ideal;
6) Find great people to work with.

I do not claim that these lessons are universal. I found them useful for the kind of research I engage in. I also did not invent them. I often learned them the hard way, but I keep coming back to them whenever I come down with the research blues. Finally, they are heavily influenced by the research vision promoted by Hervé Gallaire at ECRC.

1.1. The CHIP project

Find the missing link: when I came to ECRC, I was given Alain Colmerauer's slides on PROLOG III and Jean-Louis Laurière's paper on ALICE. Alain's slides had the slogan:

The Power of PROLOG III = Constraint Solving + Non-determinism

while the ALICE system showed how to use constraints to solve a variety of combinatorial optimization problems. Alain and Jean-Louis lived in Marseilles and Paris respectively and could not be more different. My role at ECRC was to bridge their work. I read a lot of papers in the fall of 1985 but could not see the connection. During my Christmas vacation in Belgium, I sneaked out one morning and went the library at the University of Namur to look for the 1977 paper by Alan Mackworth in the AI journal. I read it there sitting on the floor. This is a beautifully written paper with an amazing footnote and I realized then that I had found the missing link: arc consistency was declarative and could unify the goals of ALICE and PROLOG III: solving complex problems in a declarative language. This is obvious *a posteriori* but, at that time, arc consistency was exotic: there were very few papers on this topic in 1985 and AC-4 was not even published yet. I wrote my first constraint paper "Domains in Logic Programming" which was published at AAAI'86. I gave the talk in the last session of the conference in a remote building and there were two people in the audience besides the speakers and the session chair. But I had the chance to meet Alan who could not have been more encouraging.

Given the research focus in the CP conferences in recent years, it should be mentioned why it was an interesting issue to unify ALICE and Prolog III. ALICE was a back-box solver which limited its applicability. Even Jean-Louis Laurière was not actively working on ALICE, but was focusing on his rule-based system SNARK. The contribution of the CHIP system could be captured by the slogan:

The Power of CHIP = Declarative Filtering + Non-determinism

CHIP allowed us to solve much more complex applications than ALICE by opening the search and the language. I will come back to this issue later in the chapter.

Build systems: After finishing the AAAI-86 paper, Hervé and Mehmet told me to implement the ideas. I really did not see the point: I knew that they would work and I wanted to move to another topic and write more papers. But research, Hervé told me, is not about writing papers: it is about creating and communicating new ideas. System building plays a fundamental role in this process. Systems complement papers in communicating ideas: they often spread the ideas much faster, increase awareness in other communities, and help technology transfer. Systems also drive the research as they tell us what really works in practice and often suggest new algorithmic and complexity issues. Hervé, Alain Colmerauer, and Jean-Louis Lassez constantly reminded me of the value of system building.

Be driven by applications: In preparing this chapter, I wanted to stress the importance of applications for our community. But I was afraid of losing 80% of my audience after seven slides, so I decided to research this topic a bit more. Ron Rivest's Turing award slides gave me the courage to approach this issue as he wrote that his research in cryptography tries "to solve practical applications using computer science theory". In 1986, Helmut Simonis joined ECRC and shared on office with me. This shows Mehmet's talent in recruiting great people. Helmut has no fear: he would try CHIP on every possible application and this often boosted the development of the system tremendously. In fact, ECRC itself was a great place for developing a system as industrials would come and give us applications to solve.

Jean-Philippe Carillon visited ECRC in 1987 and demonstrated a package for warehouse location. The first model I wrote in CHIP for this problem looked like this (using mathematical notations, not CHIP syntax):

$$
\begin{array}{ll}
\text{minimize} & \sum_{w \in W} f_w y_w + \sum_{c \in C, w \in W} t_{c,w} x_{c,w} \\
\text{subject to} & \\
& \forall w \in W : y_w = 0 \rightarrow \forall c \in C : x_{c,w} = 0 \\
& \forall c \in C : \sum_{w \in W} x_{c,w} = 1 \\
& \forall w \in W : y_w \in \{0,1\} \\
& \forall c \in C, w \in W : x_{c,w} \in \{0,1\}
\end{array}
$$

It was basically a traditional MIP model, exploiting some of the CHIP coroutining facilities to link the warehouse variables y_w and the decision variables $x_{c,w}$ assigning the customers to the warehouses. I showed the model to Hervé and you could see he was disappointed by the model and the performance, although he was too diplomatic to say so directly. Hervé always had very high standards, which included coming to ECRC earlier, and leaving later, than anyone else. I then wrote another model which was much more efficient. Using mathematical notations, this model could be written as:

$$
\begin{array}{ll}
\text{minimize} & \sum_{w \in W} f_w y_w + \sum_{c \in C, w \in W} t_{c,x_c} \\
\text{subject to} & \\
& \forall w \in W : y_w = 0 \rightarrow \forall c \in C : x_c \neq 0 \\
& \forall w \in W : y_w \in \{0,1\} \\
& \forall c \in C : x_c \in W
\end{array}
$$

The key is the expression t_{c,x_c} which features the *element* constraint, avoiding the 0/1 decision variables $x_{c,w}$. The warehouse location opened a Pandora's box for us: constraints did not have to be numeric: they could capture any relation and hence preserve the high-level structure of the applications. I gave the talk on the resulting paper at AAAI'88 and Ken McAloon was in the audience (there were more people this time around). He was amazingly encouraging and excited about the benefits of capturing the structure of applications.

After that, we saw *element* constraints everywhere. Helmut started solving the car-sequencing problem and the early part of the model looked like (using OPL syntax):

```
solve {
   forall(o in Options & s in Slots)
```

```
3.        setup[o,s] = option[o,slot[s]];
4.     forall(o in Options & s in 1..nbSlots-cap[o].u+1)
5.        sum(j in s..s+cap[o].u-1) setup[o,j] <= cap[o].l;
6.     ...
7. }
```

Lines 2–3 feature the *element* constraint to link the option and slot variables, while lines 4–5 specify the capacity constraints on the options. However the issue was how to express the demand constraints on the cars. Helmut obviously did not want to introduce 0/1 variables and he asked me if I had another idea (recall that we were separated only by two (bulky) monitors). Pandora's box was open and I told him that it was easy to introduce this cardinality constraint in CHIP. Once again, we had captured another important substructure, simply by considering an interesting application.

The resulting program would quickly solve small instances but would backtrack forever on large ones. Helmut then built a visualization of the program and we spent time looking at the screen and understanding what was going on. We eventually realized that the propagation was only detecting failures very late. We designed redundant constraints (which are sometimes called implied constraints now) to address this pathological behavior and obtained the program described in our ECAI'88 paper which looks like this:

```
1. solve {
2.     forall(o in Options & s in Slots)
3.        setup[o,s] = option[o,slot[s]];
4.     forall(o in Options & s in 1..nbSlots-cap[o].u+1)
5.        sum(j in s..s+cap[o].u-1) setup[o,j] <= cap[o].l;
6.     atmost(slot,demand);
7.     forall(o in Options & i in 1..optionDemand[o])
8.        sum(s in 1..nbSlots-i*cap[o].u)
9.           setup[o,s] >= optionDemand[o] - i*cap[o].l;
10.}
```

Line 6 contains the cardinality constraint, while lines 7–9 describe the redundant constraints. These recognize that only so many cars requiring an option can be produced in a given time window and ensure that the remaining cars are produced beforehand.

The car-sequencing application was an amazing learning experience for us. It led to cardinality constraints, to visualizations, and to redundant constraints.

The modeling itself removes symmetries (cars requiring the same options are interchangeable) and was the motivation for Freuder's paper in 1992 on interchangeability. Jean-François Puget also told me that this paper attracted him to the area.

Other applications had similar effects. For instance, the cutting-stock applications presented at ICLP'88 used the *element* constraint, lexicographic ordering on the variables, and domain splitting. The microcode labeling application, published in the journal of logic programming (JLP) in 1990, introduced what are now called *table constraints*. The scheduling application, also in the JLP paper, taught us the value of flexible search procedures.

Just do it, then clean up the mess: Alan Perlis once wrote that "simplicity does not precede complexity, but follows it". It is indeed difficult to isolate the right concepts or abstractions immediately or to come up with the right design the first time. It is just how science works. We have to see the same patterns several times before recognizing them and determining how important they are. CHIP was sometimes criticized because it was growing in an ad hoc fashion. But we could not see the proper abstractions or did not have the knowledge to simplify the concepts at the time. When I joined Brown in 1990, my goal was to clean up the mess and I started working on the `cc(FD)` system. Ole Madsen, speaking about the BETA programming language said that " there were always two criteria for adding a construct to the language: it should be meaningful from a modeling standpoint as well as from a technical standpoint." Together with Yves Deville and Vijay Saraswat, I took the modeling road and tried to find generic abstractions to build all the ad hoc constraints of CHIP. It led to the cardinality operator, constructive disjunction, reification, and indexicals. Many of the ad hoc constraints of CHIP were now easy to build in the language using logical or cardinality combinators. Nicolas Beldiceanu and Jean-Charles Régin took a more algorithmic road and studied how to increase the algorithmic power of constraints. Jean-Charles' papers were especially elegant because they removed the ad hoc aspects of algorithmically sophisticated constraints. Indeed, Jean-Charles showed how to enforce arc consistency on the *alldifferent* and *global cardinality* constraints and, as I said before, arc consistency is a declarative and natural concept. In preparing this chapter, I read Jean-Charles's paper on *alldifferent* again. It contains the observation that "only limited works have been carried out on the semantics of constraints". It is stunning to see how such a fundamental idea was adopted so slowly, even about 10 years after the start of the CHIP project.

Car sequencing provides another example of the slow nature of progress and the necessity of the "just do it; then clean up the mess" approach. Car sequencing introduced a cardinality constraint in 1988, which led to the cardinality operator in 1991 and to the global sequence constraint by Régin and Puget in 1997. In 2006, van Hoeve, Pesant, Rousseau, and Sabharwal won the best paper award for their work on the sequence constraint more than 18 years after the ECAI'88 paper.

Strive for the declarative ideal: I have mentioned several times already the importance of declarative abstractions. The success of constraint programming comes from its declarative aspects allowing users to be in the realm of modeling, more than programming. The filtering algorithms in constraint programming are typically specified declaratively. They are not just a bag of implementation tricks, but rather they specify the properties enforced when the propagation step converges. This property should ideally be arc consistency, but it has to be relaxed for some constraints whose feasibility problems are NP-complete, such as the edge finder. There are significant benefits in having these declarative specifications. On the one hand, they define an algorithmic problem for which algorithmic and complexity results can be derived. On the other hand, they allow for compiler optimizations and model transformations, as studied by Christian Schulte and Peter Stuckey for instance. Search in constraint programming is also declarative and can be viewed as problem decomposition. As a result, constraint programming offers a compositionality and a separation of concerns that is so important in practical applications which typically features many idiosyncratic constraints that are revealed over time during the acquisition process.

Work with good people: I was lucky at ECRC to meet many researchers who had a lasting impact on my career. I mentioned several of them already but there were many others, too many to list in fact. Pierre Dufresne changed my life when he told me to view debugging as a game, man against machine, in which to surrender is not an option. I learned from Mireille Ducassé that a scientific talk is really a show. I saw her give the first talk, the day after a banquet, in which she said about a debugger: "and you press next" and then (really loudly) "splash, you get everything in your face" (except that she did not use "face" but its slang equivalent. I was stunned but everyone else seemed to love it. Abder Aggoun and Jacques Noyé helped me understand that implementations are scientific objects of their own. Thomas Graf convinced me that academics should spend some time in the US.

I would like to come back to Alain Comerauer who I really wanted to meet at that point. Thomas Graf suggested obtaining a result Alain cared deeply about. So we started working on disequations in linear constraints. The main issue in this problem is to identify all variables forced to take a single value (i.e., fixed variables or hidden constants). Many great scientists were working on the topic: Alain, Jean-Louis Lassez and Ken McAloon, and Peter Stuckey. Thomas thought that we could obtain a purely syntactic form and we eventually did: the first non-zero coefficient of a constraint must be greater than zero. It remained to show that this syntactic form could be preserved by pivoting. We started reading a book by Garfinkel and Nemhauser and it contained the lexicographic pivoting rule which, in fact, maintained our standard form. We had the result and I had no idea that, about 10 years later, I would meet George Nemhauser and start working on stochastic optimization with him.

I met Alain in Jerusalem and he then invited me to Marseilles several times. Meeting Alain was always a stimulating experience. I remembered once explaining some implementation details on the syntactic form and he did not believe the results. I went over the results that night, proving everything again. I waited for him to arrive the next morning. He was smiling when he came and told me: "It is correct but you explained these results very badly". Alain then used our syntactic form in Prolog IV, which gave me great pleasure. Visiting Marseilles was always rejuvenating: Alain and Michel van Caneghem always maintained some sense of excitement about science and always looked at papers in a positive light. Alain also gave me a fundamental criterion for reviewing papers when he told me "if I can keep the paper, I accept it". In 1994, Eugene Freuder wrote a paper about search as decomposition. It was short and I could not really see the contribution at the time. But Gene was passionate about the paper, so I kept it. Moreover, in 2001, this paper helped Laurent Michel and I solve a problem about search strategies for optimization problems.

1.2. The Numerica project

Find the missing link: in the fall of 1993, I started a junior sabbatical, which I spent partly at MIT and partly at Marseilles. My host at MIT was David McAllester and we spent the first couple of meetings trying to find a joint project. David had received a couple of papers by Eldon Hansen on the interval Newton method and I had recently read papers in BNR-Prolog by Older and Vellino. We decided to study how to integrate these ideas and, in particular, how to use interval Newton methods to filter non-linear constraints. David thinks very fast and the discussions on the white board were exciting. We ended up finding a way to prune the variable bounds by using interval Newton methods: the pruning operator was itself a search algorithm. David and I then started a race to implement the ideas, David in Scheme and I in `cc(FD)`. We tested the algorithms on the Broyden banded function and the results were amazing. We could solve very large instances without search: propagation alone was sufficient. Eventually we came to realize that constraint programming and numerical analysis methods were really orthogonal: constraint programming techniques were effective to reduce the search space when far from a solution, while interval Newton methods were excellent close to a solution.

Build systems: once again, we built systems for testing the idea: first the NEWTON system and then NUMERICA, a modeling language for global optimization. Here is the Broyden banded function in NUMERICA:

```
Input:  int n :  Number of variables;
Range:  idx = [1..n];
Set:  J[i in idx] = {j in [max(1,i-5)..min(n,i+1)] | i <> j};
Variable:  x :  array[idx] in [-10e8..10e8];
Body:  solve system all
   [i in idx] :
      0 = x[i] * (2 + 5*x[i]^2)+1 - Sum(k in J[i]) x[k]*(1+x[k]);
```

These systems were key in isolating the limitations of the algorithms, discovering the synergies between constraint programming and interval analysis, and conveying the results.

Be driven by applications: Deepak Kapur was also visiting David that fall and joined the discussions. He introduced us to homotopy methods, the other class of global methods for non-linear equations. Some papers in that area contained many interesting benchmarks in chemical engineering, robotics, and economics to name only a few areas. Jean-François Puget also gave me a very challenging problem in circuit design, which helped drive the algorithmic developments further. This problem solved orders of magnitude more efficiently than before and was described in a joint paper in the journal of global optimization. The University of Aachen also provided some extremely challenging distillation problems. Overall, this was an exciting time involving a lot of scientific progress. John Hooker once said in a panel that global optimization was one of the areas in which constraint programming had the most impact.

Just do it, then clean up the mess: I spent the second part of my sabbatical in Marseilles. I explained our results to Frédéric Benhamou and he was not happy about the description of the techniques: we were not formalizing them clearly enough. We worked together on resolving this issue and came up with the concept of box consistency. Once again, it was a declarative specification of the filtering and it helped subsequent algorithmic developments. Later on Yves Deville and I also captured the best we could have hoped for with algorithms such as these, which also improved our understanding of these techniques and the clarity of the NUMERICA book. Once again, I do not think we would have been capable of isolating these concepts initially: we had to experiment, try different algorithms, and find good trade-offs. Subsequently, it became important to formalize these concepts declaratively to foster progress.

Work with good people: I also met Laurent Michel during that period. Laurent spent four months at Brown working on our GAIA abstract interpreter. He really loved research and, after his stay at Brown, applied to the "fonds national de la recherche scientifique", the Belgian counterpart to the French CNRS. I got lucky: he was rejected and had to choose exile and settle for a PhD at Brown University. Laurent and I have been working together on many projects ever since: NUMERICA, LOCALIZER, OPL, and COMET. Laurent has no fear of trying new technologies, which has helped each of these projects substantially.

Epilogue: I do not want to leave the NUMERICA project without mentioning some of the subsequent developments. Many of the lessons I learned were in fact applied by the constraint group at the University of Nantes: they explored new links with symbolic computations, built new systems such as REALPAVER, branched out to new application areas such as vision, and designed new algorithms and filtering concepts. Very much the same can also be said about the group in Nice. I also worked extensively with Micha Janssen and Yves Deville on ordinary differentiable equations. We obtained surprising results by using constraints to address the wrapping effect, one of the main issues in interval methods for ODEs. Micha and I also designed a precisely $A(\alpha)$-stable one-leg multistep method, improving the stability of existing numerical analysis methods. It is amazing to see how constraint programming enabled us to take a fresh look at an area that had been investigated extensively.

1.3. The OPL project

Find the missing link: the NUMERICA project also opened another Pandora's box: modeling languages. Once I saw the beauty of a modeling language, I could not resist designing a modeling language for constraint programming. The OPL system was thus a side-effect of NUMERICA and it played a fundamental role in exposing constraint programming to the operations research community. As a modeling language, OPL was innovative in several respects. It features a very high-level language for expressing search procedures, promoting a declarative style based on `forall` and `tryall` statements. It also provided default search procedures for constraint programming using some simple analyses of the model. Finally, it was the first modeling language integrating constraint and integer programming.

Build systems: OPL was also a huge engineering effort because I had the opportunity to collaborate with Ilog on this project. Jean-François Puget argued early on for the inclusion of linear and integer programming, while Irv Lustig wanted OPL to subsume AMPL. It was a challenge to design a language under these conditions but I had learned to try to keep things simple from my interactions with Alain. Jean-François also wanted OPL to interface with `C++` and we pioneered code generation of models with OPL as well. Finally, I had learned my lessons from Helmut and I wanted to have OPL to support visualizations automatically. Once again, this was a very exciting time with exceptional researchers. OPL also had interesting side-effects: Jain and Grossman wrote a wonderful paper on logical Benders decomposition using both IP and CP models, demonstrating the potential of this technique. John Hooker also wrote more advanced models in OPL later on. Systems are enabling technologies!

Strive for the declarative ideal: for many years, the slogan for constraint programming has been:

$$\text{The Power of Constraint Programming} = \text{Constraints} + \text{Search}$$

In recent years, there has been a significant push to offer black-box CP systems. As I mentioned earlier, the ALICE system by Laurière was a black-box system. But CHIP was instrumental in solving much more complex applications than ALICE by exploiting symmetries and dominance, writing specialized search procedures, using dedicated constraints or what is now called table constraints. Opening the language and exposing the search significantly enlarged the class of applications we could tackle. It does not mean that developing black-box optimization systems is not an important endeavor: it certainly is. But we are in a position to improve on ALICE now because we have built and experimented with open systems, contributed fundamental advances in modeling, filtering, and search, and delivered intermediate layers that dramatically improve productivity. We may want to remember the adage "He who can do more can do less". A rich, open modeling and search language supports the building of sophisticated black-box systems. Observe also that the declarative ideal plays a fundamental role here. Model transformations, the discovery of symmetries, and the derivation of search procedures are greatly facilitated by the declarative nature of constraint programming.

1.4. The Comet project

Find the missing link: I will conclude the system descriptions with the COMET system. Once again, COMET fills a gap in the repertoire of tools for combinatorial optimization. It demonstrates the feasibility of the slogan:

$$\text{Local Search} = \text{Model} + \text{Search}$$

allowing local search algorithms to be specified at a very high level of abstraction.

Build systems: it took us a long time to get there. Laurent developed Localizer as a first step as part of his thesis and our paper at CP'97 introduced the concept of invariants. However it took us another five years and contributions by many other researchers to articulate the above vision. The first paper on Comet was published at OOPSLA in 2002 but, once again, it was a first step which helped us discover many other abstractions and concepts.

Be driven by applications: Comet benefited from the fact that numerous applications of local search existed. Nevertheless, we spent considerable time reproducing them, sometimes discovering interesting variations on existing algorithms such as the iterative flattening algorithm of Cesta, Oddi, and Smith.

Strive for the declarative ideal: one of the most amazing features of Comet is that it allows local search algorithms to be presented using high-level declarative models. The model of the progressive party problem in Comet

```
var{int} boat[Guests,Periods](m,Hosts);
ConstraintSystem S(m);
forall(g in Guests)
   S.post(2*alldifferent(all(p in Periods) boat[g,p]));
forall(p in Periods)
   S.post(2*knapsack(all(g in Guests) boat[g,p],crew,cap));
forall(i in Guests, j in Guests :  j > i)
   S.post(atmost(1,all(p in Periods)(boat[i,p]==boat[j,p])<=1);
```

is almost identifical to its constraint programming counterpart. The search procedure (omitting the tabu-search management) is also rather elegant:

```
while(S.violations() >0)
   selectMax(g in Guests,p in Periods)(S.decrease(boat[g,p]))
      selectMin(h in Hosts)(S.getAssignDelta(boat[g,p],h))
         boat[g,p] := h;
```

Recently, when looking at the Comet visualization on this example (see Figure 1.1), I realized that the moves of this search procedure did not directly address the knapsack constraints: assigning a new boat to a party would never reduce the violations in some configurations. Consider guest 25 assigned to the third boat in Figure 1.1. Assigning this guest to any other boat will only increase the violations. However, simple swaps would remedy this limitation as guest 25 can be swapped with guest 6 on the fifth boat. The resulting search procedure,

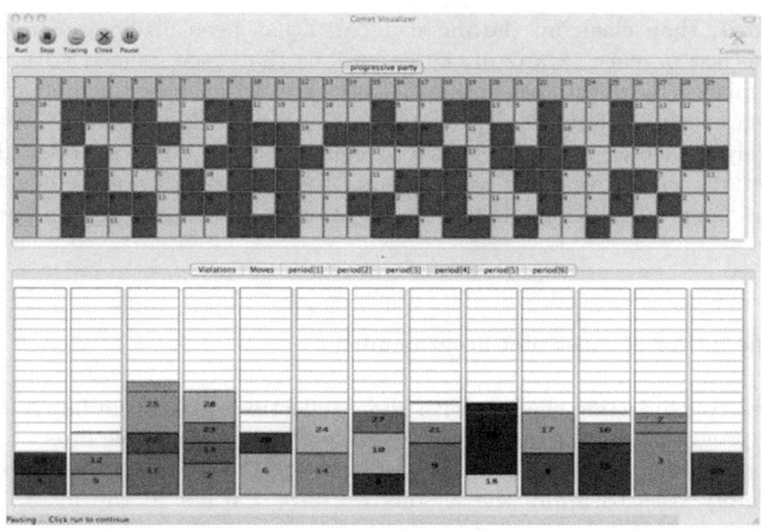

Figure 1.1. *Visualizing the Progressive Party Problem*

```
1. MinNeighborSelector N();
2. while (S.violations() > 0) {
3.   selectMax(g in Guests, p in Periods)(S.violations(boat[g,p]))
4.     selectMin(h in Hosts,d=S.getAssignDelta(boat[g,p],h))(d)
5.       neighbor(d,N)
6.         boat[g,p] := h;
7.     selectMin(g1 in Guests,d=S.getSwapDelta(boat[g,p],boat[g1,p]))(d)
8.       neighbor(d,N)
9.         boat[g,p] :=:  boat[g1,p];
10.  if (N.hasMove()) call(N.getMove());
11.}
```

Figure 1.2. *The Search for the Progressive Party Problem*

once again omitting the tabu-search management, is depicted in Figure 1.2. It is rather elegant in my opinion. It specifies what the neighbors are (lines 3–9), while the neighborhood selector in line 1 specify how to select the neighbor. The fact that this search procedure, combining two kinds of moves, can be expressed in 11 lines is quite satisfying.

Just do it, then clean up the mess: COMET has been evolving significantly over the last 5 years. Many of the extensions that once seemed ad hoc have been replaced by novel abstractions such as constraint-based combinators for local search and differentiable invariants. They probably look obvious retrospectively (which we always take as a compliment). Before we introduced these abstractions, either we could not recognize them or we did not see how to implement them in a reasonable fashion. It is often amazing to realize how slow we are.

1.5. The future of constraint programming

I will conclude this chapter with some reflections about the future of constraint programming. Obviously, there are many other possible directions and this book should give you a flavor about where the field is going. This section simply tries to apply the lessons we have learned to the future. It is important first to acknowledge that CP has great opportunities. The nature of optimization problems induces significant challenges that will not disappear any time soon. Industry needs effective solutions to large-scale and complex problems. Moreover, new telecommunication technologies open considerable opportunities, as optimization is increasingly being applied in operational settings in which decisions are taken online with uncertainty. Finally, CP has not even started branching out yet and has been confined to a small number of application areas.

Find the missing link: CP is an integration technology. It is good at embedding algorithms from many areas and has room to include more advanced algorithms from theoretical computer science, transparently leveraging this wealth of algorithmic knowledge. CP may play an increasingly significant role in reasoning about uncertainty: this is a huge area since most problems are inherently stochastic. Finally, there are intriguing connections between CP and simulation and between CP and machine learning. Exploiting some of these connections would provide new exciting developments in CP. I hope that the community will embrace them, although they will likely lead to publications quite different from your typical CP paper. Hopefully the community will remain open and outward-looking, encompassing new ideas and technologies and a broad view of constraint programming.

Be driven by applications: CP has narrowed in terms of applications in the last decade and has focused on traditional combinatorial optimization. But CP has a role to play in many other areas. Luc Jaulin demonstrated a beautiful application in robotics at CP'07 and I would have loved to have had such applications during our work on ODEs. Graphics and vision have a tradition of using constraints but they have had little or no recognition at the conferences and in the community. Yet I believe that CP may be in a position to contribute to these areas once again. In addition, obviously online applications offer significant challenges in which insights from CP may bring new directions. It seems desirable to have a much more substantial benchmark library to drive the research and to showcase the technology.

Build systems: CP should continue developing increasingly more advanced systems. Providing sophisticated visualization, debugging, and explanation tools, will help users understand complex behaviors and interactions between constraints that are likely to arise in practice. Automatic tuning of CP algorithms would dramatically reduce development time and parallel implementations will boost performance at the time when the speed of processors is leveling off. Artificial intelligence has had significant impact on programming languages in the past thanks to the complexity of the problems it tackled. I believe CP is in a similar position now. Once again, it is important to recognize the need for a proper forum for such research and CP-Tools was introduced with that goal in mind.

Just do it, then clean up the mess: Alan Kay said that "simple things should be simple; complex things should be possible", which is a great guide for the next generation of CP systems. Simple problems should have small models or simple instances should be solved automatically and efficiently. And complex things should be possible by providing open languages with multiple abstraction layers. The regular constraint and differentiable invariants are illustrations of such abstraction layers, but more are needed. The work of Nicolas Beldiceanu on understanding the nature of global constraints is important in that respect.

Strive for the declarative ideal: finally, although my first paper at AAAI'06 was about finite domains, I believe that CP should move on and study constraints over more complex objects such as sets, graphs, trees, and sequences to name but a few. Obviously, the underlying algorithms should exploit these specific structures and should be more than syntactic sugar. As Ole Madsen said: "There were always two criteria for adding a construct to the language: it should be meaningful from a modeling standpoint as well as from technical standpoint".

Acknowledgments I would like to thank the ACP award committee for this recognition and Frédéric Benhamou for inviting me to contribute this chapter. I would also like to thank all my research collaborators who are not acknowledged in the text and all my undergraduate and graduate students. Last but not least, special thanks to Baudouin Le Charlier whose class on programming methodology, although taught with flow charts, showed me the beauty of the declarative ideal early in my studies.

Chapter 2

Constraint Programming Tools

Systems research is and remains a critical element to the success of constraint programming at large. It is through its successes in the field that it has established itself as a potent alternative to other optimization techniques and proved instrumental in several classes of application domain. The continued success largely depends on sustained efforts to perpetuate this tradition and produce the next generation of constraint programming tools that will address the challenges faced today by practitioners at large. CPTOOLS is a series of events meant to foster tool development and create a forum for system researchers to educate the next generation of CPers and expose them to modern tools, trends, and to identify relevant research themes.

2.1. Introduction

Much of the success and recognition of constraint programming stems from constraint programming systems and their successful use to solve practical applications. By providing rich languages and sophisticated implementations, constraint programming tools model complex applications, shorten development time, and produce code that is easier to maintain and extend. Despite this pivotal role for the community and recognition of its importance, existing systems are not as broadly publicized and known and system-oriented research may seem daunting to younger researchers in the field.

Chapter written by Laurent MICHEL, Christian SCHULTE and Pascal VAN HENTENRYCK.

The purpose of the CPTOOLS series (`http://www.cptools.org`) is to foster the development of constraint programming tools, to showcase their applications, to educate young researchers in the use and development of such tools and to encourage cross-fertilization in tool developments. CPTOOLS'06 was the first event in the series with a dual objective.

The first intent was to round up all the systems actively developed and maintained to give to prospective users of the technology an opportunity to discover a broad set of tools along with their strengths, specificities and current use.

The second intent was to give a forum where academics, industrialists, technology users and application developers with a vested interest in system-oriented research could present their respective positions as well as discuss potential research themes and directions that tools are exploring today, or are poised to explore in the near future.

This chapter synthesizes the points of view presented throughout the course of the event.

From an academic standpoint, it first relates the importance of approaching system-oriented research like any other scientific endeavor. Specifically, it argues in favor of system research as a systematic exploration of the design space in which each design decision taken must be informed. It also points out that the key to success as an academic is to effectively communicate not only the outcome of the research but the design process, relative importance, and rationale supporting the decisions so that others can benefit from this knowledge and integrate it in a principled fashion rather than arbitrarily or out-of-habit.

The chapter also details the concerns and objectives of an industrial player (Ilog). Specifically, it argues that industrial applications have a fundamentally different flavor from traditional academic benchmarks like CSPs and that the success of the technology largely hinges on the combination of multiple techniques that include a finite domain solver but also encompass a scheduler engine, a vehicle-routing solver and linear and integer programming solvers. It also reports that, in large part because of its extreme flexibility, constraint programming is becoming a victim of its own success as users turn to CP tools when everything else fails and cooly expect that it will be easy to use and save the day. Industrials are facing a new challenge wherein the technology must become significantly easier to use and where arduous tasks ought to be automated in order to meet the needs of 90% of users while retaining the strength of CP: its flexibility.

Section 2.3 also recounts the presented systems, their specificities, strengths and areas of application. Note that the systems range from libraries (e.g.,

ILOG SOLVER, GECODE, MINION, CHOCO, JACoP and DISOLVER), to modeling (e.g., G12 and BORDERWIJK) and programming languages (e.g., ECLIPSE, SICSTUS-FD and COMET) with some focusing exclusively on finite domain constraint solving while others emphasize modeling or both constraint solving and modeling. While most systems offer tools squarely aimed at finite domain techniques, some (e.g., COMET, ECLIPSE and DISOLVER) are meant to support different solving techniques like local search, integer programming, linear programming or any hybrids.

Finally, the chapter briefly summarizes the panel discussions that often echoed the points made throughout the day.

2.2. Invited talks

An important aspect of the workshop has been to contrast an academic approach to research in systems with the development of an industrial Constraint Programming tool. The invited talks at the workshop reflect this: the first talk, by Jean-François Puget, describes the development of an industrial Constraint Programming tool (section 2.2.1), whereas the second talk, by Christian Schulte, reflects the importance of taking informed design decisions in system research (section 2.2.2).

2.2.1. *The development of an industrial CP tool (Jean-François Puget)*

The development of ILOG Solver as an industrial constraint programming tool has to take particular demands into account. The first and foremost difference to academic systems is that commercial systems do not have *users* but *customers*. Customers pay for a commercial tool and expect a return on their investment. In particular, customers do not want to invest in understanding the underlying technology but expect the technology to be readily usable. An additional aspect is that the development is entirely driven by the need of customers and not by the research interests of the developers.

For ILOG Solver, the needs of the customers have resulted in giving priority to the development on scheduling, vehicle routing, configuration, cooperation with CPLEX, and OPL as a modeling tool. As a corollary, little effort has been spent on the actual solving core of ILOG Solver since 1998.

For commercial tools in particular but also constraint programming in general, the real challenge is that constraint programming is used when other methods do not work. This is due to the fact that constraint programming is both flexible and extensible. While being a reason for using constraint programming, it also poses a major challenge: constraint programming might not be used in an expert fashion and hence might provide for a frustrating experience. Research in constraint programming must address this challenge by aiming at tools that allow users to use constraint programming tools as black boxes: there is no need for custom constraints and the tool uses good default search.

2.2.1.1. *Design goals*

The design goals in ILOG Solver as a commercial tool have been as follows.

Robustness The key features of a robust commercial tool are graceful exits, correctness, and no regressions. A robust commercial system must always gracefully exit by reporting an exception. It is unacceptable to customers that a system produces a core dump but no further information. Correctness implies that no solution is reported when there is none, and that no solutions are missed. In general, ILOG Solver is almost bug free.

Performance ILOG Solver has been the undisputed leader in performance for the last decade, where it is important to consider speed as well as memory consumption. The latter is particularly important for real life applications. For example, an application triggered the inclusion of BagVars in order to save memory and be able to run several sessions (up to 40) of ILOG Solver for an application on the same server.

An interesting recent development has been the advent of systems such as Gecode and Minion that offer competitive performance compared to ILOG Solver. However, an important aspect is the choice of examples used for comparing systems. Examples that have been used in 1995 to assess ILOG Solver's performance included n-queens, Golomb rulers, magic series, crypt-arithmetic puzzles, project scheduling (Bridge) and square packing. Interestingly, only Golomb rulers are used today; the other examples are not.

When comparing ILOG Solver with Minion, a scalability test using 1,000-queens reveals that ILOG Solver is considerably faster and that memory usage for Minion does not scale. The other examples mentioned above can not be expressed in Minion as it lacks the required constraints and only supports static variable ordering. For Boolean problems, ILOG Solver is slower than Minion, however the future version, called ILOG CP, will be faster than Minion.

The comparison with Gecode reveals that ILOG Solver is one order of magnitude faster than Gecode for BIBD problems and uses one order of magnitude less memory. For all other examples, both the performance and the memory footprint of Gecode and ILOG Solver are similar.

Flexibility The flexibility of ILOG Solver is defined by support for many different variable types (Boolean, integer, float, set, multi set, activities, and resources) that can be mixed freely in constraints, by a large variety of global constraints (arithmetics, alldifferent, cardinality, discrete resources, just to name a few), and various search constructs (tree search, local search, and large neighborhood search).

Extensibility A major motivation for making ILOG Solver extensible right from the start has been the fact that not enough resources were available to develop all global constraints available in competing tools. For this reason, ILOG Solver supports custom search and custom constraints that can be programmed using documented ways of how to build goals (for search) and propagators (for constraints). In retrospect, it is unclear whether the amount of extensibility is too much.

Easy to embed ILOG Solver is provided as a C++ library which makes it easy to embed compared to full languages (such as CLP languages) or full applications. For example, SAP has developed the dominant supply chain solution using ILOG Solver, Scheduler, Dispatcher, and CPLEX.

Little C++ knowledge One of the key design goals of ILOG Solver has been to provide abstractions in C++ that avoid common pitfalls, such as for example hiding the peculiarities of memory allocation. However, due to its very nature of being a C++ library, much of the difficulties coming from C++ are inherent.

2.2.1.2. *The future*

The advent of new academic tools with competitive performance is a good development for constraint programming in general as efficient tools will help to promote constraint programming. It is also a good development for ILOG as it forces ILOG to focus again on core performance which will help ILOG's customers.

The future at ILOG will be to develop ILOG CP that will replace ILOG Solver and ILOG Scheduler. ILOG CP will have considerable performance improvements, will increase usability by supporting black box search, and will increase accessibility by being available from Java, .NET, and OPL. A first beta was released in December 2006.

2.2.2. *System design: taking informed decisions (Christian Schulte)*

The creation of a system is a complex process that must be approached methodically to be successful. System research is not different from any other type of research and success is contingent on the ability to explore the design space systematically and evaluate design alternatives according to specific quality criteria to produce and publish informed decisions with all the supporting evidence. The impact of system research is broader than the actual system implementation. It also includes the design decisions and architectural choices, the rationale supporting them to the benefit of others who can integrate the outcomes in their tools in a meaningful way. This section illustrates the informed decision processes that supported design choices for three key components of Gecode, namely: search engines, constraint propagation and finite domain variables.

2.2.2.1. *Search*

Whether it is user-visible, customizable or hidden, non-deterministic search is of paramount importance to finite domain solvers and several design choices present themselves when contemplating an actual implementation. Each design strikes a different trade-off between computational cost, space overhead, invasiveness and orthogonality to heuristics (e.g., variable and value ordering) and search strategy (e.g., DFS, LDS). Note that while computational cost and space overhead can be evaluated objectively, judging how invasive or orthogonal an implementation is, is far more subjective. Gecode considered four alternatives: trailing, copying, re-computations and a re-computation-copying hybrid. In each case, the algorithmic complexity of the technique (with and without optimizations) was considered and the trail-based option was rejected in favor of the hybrid on the grounds of how invasive trailing is and the natural orthogonality of copying and re-computation which remain confined to the search and do not affect propagation. Yet, the actual implementation efforts revealed that the chosen approach is equally intrusive and leads to complicated implementation for the search routines.

2.2.2.2. *Constraint propagation*

Scheduling The order in which constraints are propagated cannot affect the outcome of the propagation (the fix-point solution, i.e., the actual domains of the variables) but does affect the number of iterations and thus propagations required to reach the fix-point and therefore the running time. Gecode considered three design options based on a LIFO (i.e., a stack), a FIFO (i.e., a queue) and a cost-based policy (i.e., an array of queues or stacks) to order the constraints propagation. To inform the decision process, the designer defined several different cost granularities initially based on algorithmic complexity and measured both the number of propagations *and* runtime for the various combinations (pure LIFO, pure FIFO, costs of various granularities with either LIFO or FIFO).

The outcome was a design decision that favored a medium cost granularity with a FIFO policy and *dynamic cost*[1] based on the observation that despite an increase in the number of propagation, this choice delivered the shortest running times and an increase in robustness against pathological benchmarks.

Combination For most global constraints, researchers have defined several filtering algorithms with different levels of consistency and computational costs. This reveals another design decision: How can several filtering algorithms be effectively combined for the same constraint?

Specifically, the strongest filtering could be run alone or a combination with weak first and strong second could be run in the hope that the weakest algorithm alone may prove sufficient and alleviate the cost of the strong filtering. Even for a combined approach, it is still necessary to decide whether to implement it with several "independent" propagators or with a staging scheme in which a state machine decides which stage to run next based on the outcome of the previous stage. The Gecode designers implemented all the alternatives and chose the stage-based combination based on the absence of memory overhead and the largest reduction in running time over a set of representative benchmarks.

2.2.2.3. *Variables*

Representation The domain representation for finite domain variables is critical to the runtime of the propagation algorithms that operate on these domains. Specifically, filtering algorithms rely on the ability to quickly iterate over the elements present in the domain, to get or set bits of the domain through direct access and finally to access the cardinality of the domain. Multiple implementation choices exist ranging from simply linked lists, to doubly linked lists with cardinality and bounds or even bit vectors. Gecode's choice was, in this case, not based on an informed decision process but an attempt to yield a small memory footprint with good performance. It is worth noting that adaptive representation selection may offer even more advantages at the expense of simplicity.

Events Constraint propagators depend on their variables and should be awoken when a relevant variable event occurs. The management of the triggering events and the dependencies is instrumental in the efficiency of a solver. Gecode explored several decisions ranging from dependencies

1. The cost of a propagator is a function of the *stage* the propagator is about to run next.

representation to the distinction between variable events and the conditions under which any such event should trigger a propagation. The informed decision process for the granularity of propagation conditions and their relationship to variable events, various combinations were tried ranging from propagating only when a variable was fixed and when the domain changed to discerning propagation conditions that distinguish bounds, lower bounds and upper bounds conditions. The evaluation revealed that refining the granularity of propagation conditions usually led to an increase in space requirement, a dramatic decrease in the number of propagations *but little to no effects on the actual runtime!*[2].

2.3. System presentations

The following section briefly reviews each system presented during CP-TOOLS.

2.3.1. ECL^{i}PS^e

ECL^{i}PS^e is a Constraint Logic Programming System designed primarily to support problem solving within a constraint logic paradigm as well as to facilitate the development and hybridization of solvers. ECL^{i}PS^e consists of a runtime environment, a control language, libraries, interfaces with external solvers and an integrated development environment. The central objective behind ECL^{i}PS^e is to integrate, within a single system, techniques that are often used in isolation to support hybrid solving techniques that draw from traditional finite domain solvers, linear programming, integer programming and local search. The core language (prolog) is open and has been extended with modeling facilities like logical loops and arrays as well as control mechanisms such as attributed variables, suspension and priority mechanisms to let programmers write their own solvers directly or write interfaces to external ones like CPLEX, XPRESS-MP or even the GAP package (a computational algebra system).

More information on ECL^{i}PS^e is available from `http://eclipse.crosscoreop.com/eclipse`.

2.3.2. *SICStus FD*

SICStus FD is a constraint programming module hosted in a prolog language. It offers both global constraints and indexicals and therefore offers the

2. In one case, it even *adversely affects* the running time.

opportunity to implement the constraint filtering algorithm directly in prolog. The system supports several debuggers that let programmers analyze the behavior of their constraint models. Its modeling language is expressive and covers traditional arithmetic, logical and meta-constraints as well as global constraints.

More information on SICStus FD is available from `http://www.sics.se/isl/sicstuswww/site/index.html`.

2.3.3. *G12*

G12 is a constraint programming platform for modeling and solving large scale optimization problems. One of its key features is the separation between the modeling and the solving technologies and the use of a mapping language to rewrite declarative models into solver-specific representations. ZINC is the modeling language used to write technology neutral models. ZINC models can be compiled into executables via CADMIUM, a mapping language responsible for rewriting the model. Finally, the executable obtained from CADMIUM can be executed inside an interpreter linked against any one of several solvers ranging from ILOG SOLVER, MERCURY or XPRESS-MP to name a few. At the moment, the CADMIUM compiler targets the MERCURY platform as it provides several solvers.

Important future work includes the ability to specify search procedures, templates or mechanisms via CADMIUM as well as the construction of mapping mechanisms so that debugging and reasoning on the ZINC program and behavior remains possible even when the execution environment, and thus all the traces, are at the lower level of abstraction of the implementation language.

More information on G12 is available from `http://www.g12.cs.mu.oz.au/Summary.html`.

2.3.4. *DiSolver*

DiSolver is a system developed by Microsoft Research to solve scheduling, planning and configuration problems as well as test-case generation. Designed from the ground up for naturally distributed problems, it is capable of automatically distributing the search space and works for both local and global search strategies. Its organization is independent of the underlying architecture and runs on everything from multi-core CPUs to clusters or grids through a combination of libraries that cover C++,C#, MPI and the globus grid. Its modeling language is expressive and covers arithmetic, logical and global constraints.

The tree search supports depth-first search, restarts and branch&bound while the local search engine supports Tabu search, Simulated Annealing and Min-conflicts.

Perhaps the most interesting aspect of the design is an information sharing layer responsible for cooperative searches involving both global and local search modules. The critical parameters of the search that are useful to the cooperation are stored in finite domain variables that can be constrained by the solver to alter or guide the cooperation process. For instance, it can affect the load-balancing strategy of a computing node to decide whether to suspend the current work and switch to incoming problems or to carry on with the current sub-problem.

More information on DiSolver is available from `http://research.microsoft.com/~youssefh/DisolverWeb/Disolver.html`.

2.3.5. *MINION*

MINION is a general-purpose constraint solver that relies on a matrix-oriented modeling language which supports a lean and optimized implementation. The ultimate objective is to rely on an external modeling language like ESSENCE to automatically generate a MINION model from a high-level specification. By design, MINION is a black-box solver offering very few options. In particular, it does not support the programming of the search and relies exclusively on static variable and value ordering heuristics. This combination of performance and the complete absence of search is an attempt at building an *easy to use* solver that more closely resembles what mathematical programming users are accustomed to. MINION is meant to be a research platform to experiment with new ideas and therefore it is not encumbered with backward compatibility concerns typically found in commercial products.

More information on MINION is available from `http://minion.sourceforge.net/`.

2.3.6. *Choco*

Choco is a constraint programming solver provided as a Java library supporting several variable domains (such as integers, intervals and sets) and numerous search algorithms. Search is based on backtracking, implementing a model of different worlds for search. One of Choco's most distinguishing features is the support for explanations. Explanations can be used for providing additional insight to users as well as for sophisticated search algorithms. Due to explanations, Choco supports in addition to basic backtracking search also advanced search algorithms such as CBJ (conflict-directed backjumping), DBT (dynamic backtracking), and Benders-decomposition.

An important aspect of Choco is its extensibility. Choco provides powerful interfaces for adding new search heuristics, new variable domains, and new constraints. The support for adding new variable domains is particularly powerful. This allows users to go beyond current standard variable domains and add more structured domains, such as two-dimensional variables for geometric reasoning, for example.

More information on Choco is available from `http://choco-solver.net/`.

2.3.7. *Gecode*

Gecode (Generic Constraint Development Environment) is an open, free, portable, accessible and efficient environment for developing constraint-based systems and applications. In more detail, Gecode is:

Open Gecode is radically open for programming and can be interfaced with other systems. It supports the programming of new propagators (as implementation of constraints), branching strategies, and search engines. New variable domains can be programmed at the same level of efficiency as finite domain and integer set variables that come predefined with Gecode.

Free Gecode is distributed under a BSD-style license and is listed as free software by the FSF. All of its parts including documentation, implementations of global constraints, and examples are available as source code for download.

Portable Gecode is implemented in C++ that carefully follows the C++ standard. It can be compiled with modern C++ compilers and runs on a wide range of machines (including 64bit machines).

Accessible Gecode comes with extensive reference documentation that allows it to focus on different programming tasks with Gecode.

Efficient Gecode offers competitive performance with respect to both runtime and memory usage.

Gecode features a generic kernel on top of which modules such as search, finite domain integer constraints, and so on are provided.

Kernel Gecode's kernel provides a comprehensive programming interface to construct new variable domains (including propagators as implementations of constraints and branchings) and search engines. It is slim (around 1000 lines of code) and requires no modification or hacking to add new variable domains or search engines.

Search Search in Gecode is based on re-computation and copying. Advanced techniques include adaptive (speeds up further search) and batch re-computation (drastically reduces propagation during re-computation). Currently, Gecode supports search for some solutions, optimization (branch-and-bound), and limited discrepancy search. Parallel thread-based search is currently under development.

Finite domain constraints Gecode comes with finite domain constraints implemented on top of the generic kernel. It offers standard constraints such as arithmetics, Boolean, linear equations, and global constraints such as: distinct (alldifferent, both bounds and domain consistent), global cardinality (both bounds and domain consistent), element, cumulatives, regular, sortedness, and lex. The library can be extended with new constraints and branchings.

Finite set constraints Gecode also provides finite integer set variables. The standard set relations and operations are available as constraints, plus some specialized constraints such as convexity, global reasoning for distinctness of sets, selection constraints, weighted sets, and constraints connecting finite domain and finite set variables. This part of the library can also be extended with new constraints and branchings.

Basic modeling support Even though Gecode has been designed to be easy to interface with and not to be easy to model with, it comes with some basic modeling support. This supports expressing linear and Boolean constraints in the standard way as expressions built from numbers and operators.

The main goal for Gecode is to provide a free and open platform for research, education, and deployment. More information on Gecode is available from `http://www.gecode.org`.

2.3.8. *Comet*

COMET is a system supporting Constraint-Based Local Search. Its purpose is to bring to the local-search paradigm the same level of expressiveness and ease of use that is typically associated with traditional finite domain solvers and tools. The mantra of COMET is "*Local Search = Model + Search*", i.e., it argues that writing a local search program should boil down to writing a declarative model capturing the constraints and optimality criteria that solutions must satisfy and combining it with a search procedure to explore the search space. To support this mantra, the architecture of COMET is organized into three layers. The innermost layer supports incremental variables and invariants as primitives for the upper layers. Invariants are particularly innovative in how they let programmers specify what must be maintained incrementally and leave to the system the more arduous task of deriving efficient incremental algorithms to maintain them. The second layer focuses on differential objects, namely constraints and objective functions. Differential objects are declarative and compositional. They let modelers focus on the specification of their constraints and rely on numerical, logical, reified and combinatorial constraints and combinators. Operationally, differential objects support an efficient assessment of the violation degree of constraints as well as a way to find out which variables are most responsible under changes to the decision variables, i.e., *gradients*. Differential objects are thus instrumental in defining the heuristics and metaheuristics that guide iterative refinement of a local search. The third layer of COMET leverages a few core concepts like events, closures and continuations to deliver sophisticated control primitives for non-determinism, a reactive programming style and controllers to decouple orthogonal aspects like search strategies or even distributed and parallel computing techniques.

COMET offers these advances for local search in a completely open object-oriented programming language where new invariants, differentiable objects and controllers can be written directly in COMET itself or alternatively can be written in dynamically loadable shared libraries. The net result is a platform particularly suitable for experimentation and research.

For a slightly more detailed introduction, the reader is encouraged to refer to Chapter 18 where the evolution of COMET is highlighted. More information on the system itself is available from `http://www.comet-online.org`.

2.3.9. *JaCoP*

JaCoP provides support for finite domain constraint programming as a library implemented in Java. It offers the standard set of arithmetic and logical constraints (including reified versions thereof) and a set of global constraints (several variants of alldifferent, cumulative, circuit, element and some others). Search is based on backtracking and offers programmable support for branching. JaCoP is freely available as a JAR file for research and education.

JaCoP is available upon request from Krzysztof Kuchinski (`kris@cs.lth.se`) or Radoslaw Szymanek (`radsz@4c.ucc.ie`).

2.3.10. *Borderwijk*

Borderwijk is provided as a simply-typed, high-level constraint programming environment in the style of OPL [VAN 99] where its modeling language is based on Galileo [BOW 90]. Borderwijk supports finite domains, functions, extensional and intensional constraints, backtracking search with user-defined orders for values and variables, and user-defined libraries.

Currently, constraint propagation in Borderwijk is based on AC3 [MAC 77]. While AC3 has non-optimal time complexity, its use in Borderwijk allows for the quick solution of many benchmark problems involving binary constraints. A key point in Borderwijk is a careful selection of data structures requiring little memory. This has been taken into account for the representation of the constraint graph and variable domains, but also the selection of AC3 that can solve extensionally defined problems with the same space complexity it takes to represent the problems. A witness to the modest memory requirements is the possibility of successfully representing and solving bounded-model checking problems translated from SAT without thrashing (for example, the `bmc-ibm` problem suite involves 2,800–5,100 variables and 4,000—368,000 constraints). Search maintains arc consistency during backtracking where stronger consistency levels (such as singleton arc consistency, weak k-singleton arc consistency, and inverse consistency) can be used before search.

Future plans for Borderwijk include global constraints and specialized hyper-arc consistency algorithms for some constraints, debugging and visualization, and parallelism through threads and distribution.

More information on Borderwijk is available from `http://www.cs.ucc.ie/~dongen/mac/bordewijk/bordewijk.html`.

2.4. Panels

Two panels were held during the course of the day. One panel focused on "Open Issues in Future System Research" while the other addressed "Technical Awareness". The panelists included R. Bartak, L. Bordeaux, M. Carlsson, J.F. Puget, B. O'Sullivan, C. Schulte, M. Wallace and R. Yap. This section summarizes the major points discussed during both forums.

Usability Usability was raised repeatedly by different people. A particularly interesting position was articulated around the idea that there are two kinds of problems: large and easy or small and hard. Constraint programming excels with small and hard, *because* it is flexible and for this class of problem, flexibility and expertise will always be needed. However, for large and easy problems, constraint programming is completely absent. There are no tools that automatically tackle this class of problem. It would be therefore most valuable for constraint programming to look forward to relatively easy but large scale problems. It was noted that industrial players are moving in that direction with attempts to automate the search as much as possible. Taking this point to the extreme, the MINION developers chose to completely do away with search and sacrifice flexibility altogether.

Benchmarks Benchmarking is often perceived as unreliable, irreproducible or not systematic. A repository of standard benchmarks was identified as a shortcoming, however there was little consensus on how to define a constraint programming problem and which problems would be worthy of being in the repository. Incidentally, it was also mentioned that some problems that were used a decade ago have been surprisingly shunted aside by some experimental work while prototypical hybrid problems seen in industrial settings remain conspicuously absent. The absence of a standard language for describing benchmarks as well as a divergence in opinions on what would be a suitable language certainly hinders the establishment of such a repository. Two extreme positions co-exist in this respect: either a structure poor (pure CSP) or structure rich (global constraints) format. It was also noted that it becomes increasingly important to approach benchmarking in a more systematic and scientific way to ease reproducibility and report variations, number of nodes versus wall-clock time, actual heuristics used by the search procedure and detailed models.

Visibility The absence of books focusing on modeling with modern constraint programming tools is universally perceived as a shortcoming that ought to be addressed.

Impact Tools are useful to solve the real problems of real people. The impact of a proposed new method, algorithm or constraint should follow more easily if it is integrated inside a "large" system used by many. Yet, this type of impact requires a lot of work to move ideas beyond a toy prototype into a full-blown robust implementation. Even though publications can follow the experimentation on a toy example, true impact will only be felt if the hard-work of integration into a real system takes place. This cannot be under-estimated.

Support Constraint programming tools are seriously lacking in supporting technologies and the situation is worrisome both for libraries and languages. For instance, debugging tools are at the wrong level of abstraction and do not offer any insights into what is going on in the constraint system. Explanations could be helpful, but people are not taking advantage of them. Visualization would be a boon to understand search and propagation behavior. Yet there is no automation or any form of architectural support to facilitate their use.

Analysis To some, the availability of a simple modeling language with very few primitives is a positive state of affairs as it makes it hard to write bad models. To others, the outstanding results of constraint programming are a by-product of its ability to exploit the sub-structures of a problem that are explicitly expressed by the modeler thanks to a rich modeling language. It appears that the ability to reformulate, decompose, aggregate or otherwise strengthen existing formulation (whether from a poor or a rich modeling language) may be valuable, yet it raises significant challenges when one must deal with real-life complex and heterogenous models.

2.5. Conclusion

It is useful to conclude this chapter with a broader view of CP-Tools'06. The event was a success with a large attendance throughout the day and more than 90 registered participants. It was also a lively event with some spirited discussions on various scientific and "social" topics. The invited talks and panels, in particular, articulated various avenues for future constraint programming tools. These directions were often orthogonal, recognizing the different needs or goals for academics, vendors, and classes of users and applications. Thanks to this diversity, the atmosphere during the day captured some of the passion and excitement of the people involved and the acknowledgment that the impact of constraint programming will continue to come from innovative, high-performance, and robust CP systems. It was also rejuvenating for many participants to see how active this area still is and how many exciting developments are likely to take place in the coming years. Hopefully, the CP'Tools series will be a channel to sustain these efforts and to promote discussions and debates that rarely take place inside the main conference.

Acknowledgments

The authors of this chapter are grateful for the generous monetary support for organizing the event described in this chapter provided by the Cork Constraint Computation Center (Ireland) and the Swedish Institute of Computer Science. Of course, special thanks also go to Frédéric Benhamou for being an early believer in CPTools and Narendra Jussien for making it happen.

2.6. References

[BOW 90] BOWEN J., O'GRADY P., SMITH L., "A constraint programming language for life-cycle engineering", *Artificial Intelligence in Engineering*, vol. 5, num. 4, p. 206–220, 1990.

[MAC 77] MACKWORTH A., "Consistency in networks of relations", *Artificial Intelligence*, vol. 8, p. 99–118, 1977.

[VAN 99] VAN HENTENRYCK P., *The OPL Optimization Programming Language*, The MIT Press, Cambridge, MA, USA, 1999.

Chapter 3

The Next 10 Years of Constraint Programming

The workshop on *The Next 10 Years of Constraint Programming* was a special event organized 10 years after an influential ACM Workshop on Strategic Directions for Computing Science, which was part of the celebrations of the 50th anniversary of the ACM in 1996, and which included the first track of discussions on the future of constraint programming[1]. The 1996 workshop had taken place while the CP community was still at an early stage, and the community has since grown considerably in size and scientific impact, accumulating a number of successes. The goal of the 2006 workshop was to look back at these achievements and to discuss the challenges and opportunities facing CP for the next decade. The workshop was a half-day event; it was very well-attended, with active discussions at each of 12 tables, and consisted of two parts:

– an open discussion, in which all CP participants could freely discuss in groups of about 8 people, moderated by a leading researcher;

– a panel, with invited talks by Hassan Aït-Kaci, Eugene Freuder, Carla Gomes, Jean-Charles Régin, and Mark Wallace[2].

Chapter written by Lucas BORDEAUX, Barry O'SULLIVAN and Pascal VAN HENTENRYCK.

1. See [VAN 96] for the group report, as well as *ACM Computing Surveys* Vol. 28 (1996) and *Constraints* Vol. 2 (1997) for a number of individual position papers from workshop participants.

2. John Hooker contributed to the debate by sending detailed statements, but could not be present. His position will be included in the special issue devoted to the panel.

The positions presented in the second part will form the basis of a forthcoming special journal issue, consisting of invited papers by the panelists. This chapter provides a record of the first part. Each section summarizes the views of one discussion group and is written by its moderator. These sections are therefore *not* personal statements but they represent each moderator's attempt to reflect the viewpoints expressed at their tables.

The discussion topics involved the past, present, and future of constraint programming: what CP has achieved in the last 10 years, what are the challenges it is facing today, where will CP be in 10 years, and, of course, what really is constraint programming. As will become clear, the summaries offer some fundamentally different assessments and views of CP and it is instructive to contrast a few of them in this introduction. This will highlight the degree of diversity, and sometimes of consensus, in our community, provide some broader perspective and spark some early interest.

With regard to the past CP contributions, one group concludes that "if CP went on strike for a whole day, the result would likely be very disruptive", others implicitly suggest that CP is not "competitive with MIP and SAT", while some quantified more precisely the application areas where CP has been most successful. It is interesting however to see such different perceptions of the contributions of CP.

Concerning what CP really is, the word "declarative" seems ubiquitous when trying to define constraint programming. What is interesting, as one group notices, is that the applications of CP have narrowed down in the last 10 years, focusing almost exclusively on combinatorial optimization. Some groups acknowledge this explicitly, suggesting that CP was intended to be more inclusive, some are simply happy with the narrower focus, while some forcefully argue that CP should broaden to avoid "sclerosis". Interestingly, some of the CP definitions provided in the summaries are quite broad, which contrasts with the field narrowing.

John Hooker, in a CP'05 panel, asked whether CP was science or engineering, a question we listed as a discussion topic. Most groups agree that CP has aspects of both and that they mutually strengthen each other. However, several tables question why some of the "scientific" advances have not found their way into the carefully "engineered" solvers, suggesting that applications may provide the missing link.

Interestingly, there is significant agreement about what challenges CP is facing today: increasing visibility, simplicity of use, richer modeling and computational methods, the need for benchmarks, standard formats and applications. However, of course, the various groups do not necessarily agree on how to address them.

These are a few topics that you will read about in this chapter, which will give you interesting and contrasted snapshots of constraint programming. These statements are like good songs: they grow on you and get better with time. You may violently disagree with some of them, strongly approve of a few and dismiss the others, but each of them captures a glimpse of the area now and opens a window into the future. This is raw material, uncensored and unplugged, but we believe that many of us will return to them many times over the next few years. And we also believe that this diversity is a strength of constraint programming that should be carefully cherished.

3.1. Pedro Barahona

What is CP?

In our group we started discussing the nature of constraint programming (CP). Clearly CP aims at adopting computational methods for solving combinatorial problems in various domains, not only finite domains, but also continuous domains, although more focus has gone on the former. It was also agreed that at the heart of CP is the clear separation between modeling a problem by means of declarative constraints and the procedures that should be available in the constraint solvers to implement search. Nowadays, constraint programming is reaching maturity given the variety of existing algorithms that are implemented in the solvers, namely local and general purpose constraint propagation, more specific propagation methods for specific global constraints, local search, that although incomplete is often a better choice than backtracking variants (some of which are incomplete) including nogood learning and restarts, hybrid solvers that take advantage of the hybridization of different inference and search techniques (e.g. mixed integer programming and constraint propagation, local search and backtrack search).

As to the nature of constraint programming – is it science or engineering – we agreed that there are different views to this (false) dichotomy. Clearly, given the algorithms and computational methods available many engineering issues arise. On the one hand, the integration of these methods in CP tools require significant programming and engineering skills. On the other hand, solving complex applications, arising in real life problems, also demand such programming skills (although at a higher level) in order to fully exploit the potential of the tools, and even go beyond it with proper adaptation and interaction between different CP tools and between other programming modules. But CP is also a topic of research, namely the identification of specific classes of problems and the study of their complexity, as well as the rigorous characterization of the algorithms being used.

From the above, someone remarked that CP should be regarded as a science for scientists and as engineering for computer and programming engineers.

Research issues

After the characterization of CP, we had a discussion on some issues that in our view should drive current research. Firstly, we found that one major strength of CP, a clear separation of a declarative specification of constraints and the underlying control mechanisms to solve them, may also become one of its weaknesses, especially in complex applications, where efficiency is important.

In a way, the vision of "black box" constraint solvers is quite appealing – the user should only be concerned about the constraint specification. But the complexity and diversity of existing constraints require explicit knowledge regarding the mapping of constraint models into the particular solvers available. This is also related to another research issue regarding the development of new paradigms for solver implementation, with a higher level of abstraction, as currently illustrated by global constraint solvers regarded as graph properties, invariants that should hold during search, automata specification of constraint solvers, etc.

Explicit constraint knowledge should also be researched not only to map constraints to solvers, but also to identify when and how different CP solvers should cooperate in particular settings, so as to maintain their individual efficiency and obtain an improved joint efficiency.

Visibility of CP

On a more institutional view, we realized that the research issues that we discussed (and others we had no time to discuss) can only be successfully addressed if a number of research groups exist and strengthen their sense of scientific community. This should also be an advantage for increasing the much needed visibility of CP, so as to attract:

– companies that should be aware of the potential of CP to solve some of their problems;

– funding agencies that, together with the companies, should support research in this area;

– universities that should increase CP topics in their curricula; and finally

– interest from students who must inject new blood into the CP community.

Of course these efforts should go together with the study of new application areas for CP (e.g. bioinformatics). Moreover, the CP community should not work in isolation and should strengthen its links with other communities, and not only the obvious links with operations research and artificial intelligence that have been significantly exploited in the past and present.

Many topics researched in CP, namely algorithms and their availability in various tools, are significant to other areas of computer science (algorithms, languages or theoretical computer science). But scientific communities have some points of contact with CP that should be exploited. For example, the complexities of reasoning (with constraints), and in particular the exploitation of symmetries, a hot topic in current CP research, could attract the interest of the cognitive science community.

3.2. Christian Bessiere

Our table was composed of people from quite different areas and with different backgrounds. There were people from the SAT community, people who use CP for applications in other fields, people who build CP solvers, and pure academics working on CP on a more theoretical basis.

The discussion started with an analysis of what had happened in CP since the 1996 ACM workshop on Strategic Directions for Computer Science. However, we quickly moved to what is missing from CP now, and then, naturally, to what the future should be. I present the topics as they were raised in the discussion, chronologically.

A first concern about the current state of constraint solvers is that it is difficult to move a CP model from one solver to another. Different solvers do not provide the same set of predefined constraints. They do not provide the same sophisticated enumeration techniques. A consequence of this is the high variance in performance for a model from one solver to another. Another point that was discussed about current solvers is that they provide better debugging tools than 10 years ago. However, visualization features remain very limited.

We then moved the discussion to the topic of global constraints. Someone pointed out that in the workshop notes of the 1996 ACM workshop, only one paper mentioned global constraints whereas they have become the main trend in the last ten years. We discussed the impact of this great success of global constraints. Do we need more global constraints or should we try to improve the mechanisms for composing solvers? It seems that many global constraints that are published every year are not driven by their practical usefulness but because of the nice algorithmic features they contain.

We discussed the interest of dynamic programming (DP) approaches for solving a constraint problem. Some problems are easily solved using DP techniques whereas standard CP solvers fail to solve them. In spite of this observation, this topic of research evolves quite separately from the area of CP solver implementation. The only way DP comes in solvers is through the implementation of global constraints encapsulating a dynamic program.

We generalized the previous question a little and asked why search (or AI) techniques are not more extensively included in the current generation of CP solvers. The SAT community transfers the benefits of theoretical results into SAT solvers extremely quickly. Examples are phase transition, heavy tail, backbones, restart, nogood learning, etc. Why can CP not do this? It seems that there is no methodology, even if we have the tools. We are stuck in a standard branch+propagate mechanism that we are not eager to modify. We concluded this never-ending discussion by saying that in a close future, it would be nice if CP solvers were at least as fast as the SAT translation of the CP model.

We quickly pointed out the strong need for a common set of benchmarks for CP. They would help compare (and then improve?) solvers.

Someone wondered why CP is not used in embedded systems. Its concurrent aspects would fit in real-time systems well. We came more generally to the problem of the slow spread of CP technology in other communities.

We discussed a promising direction for CP: using its formalism as a formal way to represent flat data. There are direct uses in configuration, but other fields are candidates, such as formalizing communications in multi-agent systems or describing robot motion, where the laws of physics are extremely complex to represent using differential equations.

We observed that existing solvers dealing with continuous domains show interesting performances. Why is this topic not used and studied more often?

We finished rapidly by speaking about AI extensions to the constraint satisfaction problem: Quantified CSP, Dynamic CSP, Valued CSP, etc. How do we integrate these frameworks in solvers? Someone said that we need a killer application using these frameworks. Then, builders of solvers will insert them.

3.3. Peter Jeavons

Our panel explored the issue of the role of *theory* in CP research, and its relation to practice. Are these two strands of research feeding and supporting each other, or are they largely ignoring each other? Are there steps we can take to improve the synergy between them in the next ten years?

We raised the question of whether there are areas of theory that can now be considered "finished" and that ought to be a standard part of the education of all constraint programmers (or even of programmers in general). For example, it was pointed out that the current fashion for Sudoku puzzles has led many people to rediscover the fact there are efficient propagation rules for the all-different constraint - surely this should be part of a body of common knowledge by now? If we can identify the key foundational results that have been achieved in constraints research, then in the next ten years we can try to drive that knowledge down into the education system. The recent Handbook of Constraint Programming seems to be a step in the right direction here by collecting together the key established results across a range of topics. We identified a key goal for the next ten years of moving the most fundamental and important ideas of constraint programming into undergraduate education.

It seemed to us that theory has a distinctive role to play in establishing general abstract frameworks that can be communicated clearly in precise mathematical terms between different communities. At the theoretical level it is clear that there are strong links between CP and many other more established research areas: operations research, graph theory, satisfiability, scheduling, databases, discrete optimization. Papers on constraint satisfaction are now starting to appear at general theory conferences (such as STOC and FOCS) and this will surely help to promote more exchange of ideas beyond the established community of CP researchers. As one example, it is becoming clear that there are deep mathematical problems regarding the complexity of constraint satisfaction which can draw in mathematicians and theoreticians to extend our understanding of the fundamental computational issues we are up against. A second key goal we identified for the next ten years is to build stronger links with the research communities in other areas, to get a clearer picture of the common problems we face and what is distinctive about the approach in each area, including CP.

Finally we spent some time discussing libraries and benchmarks. It seems obvious that we urgently need a set of benchmark problems that can be used to assess the progress of new algorithms and techniques. For example, the attraction of any global constraint that is proposed as a useful tool would be much greater if it can be shown to be of benefit for real problem instances that have shown themselves to be challenging. Properly constructed benchmarks can challenge and stimulate progress, provide a way to measure it, and provide a means to demonstrate and publicize successes. We haven't managed to build up a widely-accepted set of benchmarks in the CP community so far – surely this should be a goal for the next ten years too?

3.4. Pedro Meseguer

In our table most participants were from the world of academia, with some people from industry. All came from very different geographical areas. We considered the following four points: the past of CP, the future of CP, the impact of CP on society and CP challenges.

Firstly, we focused on the developments that CP has achieved in the last 10 years. The most obvious points were about the improvements in performance of constraint technology, amongst which we pointed out:

Global constraints: constraints with specific semantics, exploited in their local consistency propagators, have largely enhanced the power of CP;

Symmetry breaking: breaking symmetries before or during search has caused an impressive improvement of CP when solving symmetrical problems;

SAT solvers: the performance of SAT solvers has increased dramatically in the last years; some of these techniques are still to be applied to CP solvers.

In addition, we noticed the introduction of new models in the CP realm, as well as new solving strategies, amongst which we underlined:

Soft constraints: the inclusion of soft constraints has significantly increased the expressiveness of the classical CSP model;

Local search: these methods provide a real alternative to the classical approach based on systematic search.

We also pinpointed the progress on solving real problems of combinatorial nature. As weak points, we identified the absence of effective learning and concurrency in current CP solvers. The relationship between OR and CP was also discussed.

Secondly, about the future of CP, we considered a number of topics that should be addressed. They are the following:

Automatic modeling: currently, constraint modeling is done manually and requires considerable expertise. Automating this phase, partially or totally, would be a large step towards the popularization and accessibility of constraint technology.

Preferences: CP solvers should be enhanced to support, in a natural form, soft constraints, and more sophisticated forms of preferences and uncertainty. This is a must for the near future.

Learning: while learning has been very successful in the SAT community, leading to substantial improvements in performance, it remains to be fully exploited in CP. It is reasonable to expect that learning could bring similar benefits to constraint reasoning.

Integrating CP into larger systems: embedding constraint technology into larger systems (typically decision-support) seems to be a natural step forward in the maturation and dissemination process of this technology.

Accessibility of constraint technology: currently the use of CP is restricted to computers engineers. Making it accessible to general computer users would enlarge the range of benefits caused by this technology.

Single format: the existence of a common format (like in the SAT community) would be a major point for the effective exchange of problems among different CP solvers; it is expected that competition among solvers would bring benefits in terms of capability and performance.

Benchmark portability/scalability: although some effort has been invested in a benchmark repository (CSPLib), more work is required on this, especially on portability and scalability.

Bioinformatics: given the type of problems considered in bioinformatics, it is a natural target for constraint reasoning; the size of these problems is a real challenge for CP.

Industrial applications exhibition/track: most work at CP conferences is of an academic nature; however, given the success of CP in industry, an industrial exhibition or application track is needed.

Our third topic of discussion was the impact of CP on society, and we considered the following points:

Visibility: this technology is not well known in society. Even in academia, CP is taught inside AI, OR, computer science or mathematics courses. Some effort to enhance visibility is needed.

Security applications: using CP for security issues could be beneficial for software engineering. Some work is needed to disseminate this technology among the software engineering community.

Finally, on CP challenges for the future, we agreed that the simplicity of use of this technology is a kind of *global* challenge that the community has to face if it wants to continue its success in the future.

3.5. Gilles Pesant

Our group, self-dubbed The French Connection because its members were all French-speaking, was predominantly composed of academics (PhD students and professors) but included some members from industry. About half worked in Europe and the other half in North America. We discussed three of the themes proposed.

What is constraint programming?

We first attempted to define constraint programming. The proposals were:

A. *A problem-solving approach integrating orthogonal aspects in a modular and flexible way.* This definition recognizes the building-block nature of CP and, by using the term "problem-solving", its growing affinity with the field of operations research. It mentions key features of CP: its modularity, through a clear separation of modeling and search but also within modeling by offering constraints each encapsulating its own inference algorithm; its flexibility, which is an advantage when addressing realistic and evolving problems.

B. *Pragmatic aspects of solving a particular logic system.* Such a definition emphasizes the formal aspects of constraint programming, its foundation in logic dating back to the early days of constraint *logic* programming. Logic programming itself is seen as a pragmatic reading of a fragment of first-order logic. As one participant put it, "[with constraint programming] we know what we are computing".

C. *A collection of techniques and methods based on constraints allowing declarative modeling and efficient solving.* Perhaps a more inclusive effort here, despite the growing focus on finite domain constraints, there are many more computational domains that caught the attention of constraint programmers, the common thread being declarative yet efficient programming.

We then asked ourselves what specificities made CP what it is? Is it the modularity, both for the user who selects and assembles the key elements to perform the task at hand, and for the researcher who can easily concentrate on one seemingly small aspect of CP knowing that it will likely impact the whole of the field because of easy integration? Is it its potential to empower AI research through efficient algorithms? Or is it its ability to reason at a high level, building declarative abstractions of the world around us? And what makes it not CP? Is a relative newcomer such as constraint-based local search out of scope or, at best, a hybrid living on the fringe? Or is it instead pushing back the frontier by inventing new ways of using constraints while preserving their key features? Twelve years ago, when "constraint logic programming" was the accepted term, one of the fathers of logic programming, Alain Colmerauer, asked whether the word "logic" was still necessary since most of the related research efforts at the time concentrated on constraint domains and programming languages. That word has since been dropped but the essence of "constraint programming" remains and this move probably stimulated the growth of the field. We may be called to do the same yet again.

Finally we reflected on the goals of constraint programming. Broadly speaking, we agreed that it was to advance science and technology. Some suggested that CP was about solving applied, real-life problems. Others proposed a more theoretical path: achieve a better understanding of the structures used to solve problems. On a more pragmatic side, we could aim at being better than others at solving problems, meaning more efficient, less time-consuming in development, and easier to adapt.

How has CP impacted on society?

Moving on to the impact on society, our discussions took on a more political flavor. CP hardly ever makes the news and remains largely unknown in society. To its defense, our field suffers from the same affliction as other fields which work behind the scenes. For example, many applications in the area of scheduling use CP internally. If CP went on strike for a whole day the result would likely be very disruptive.

In any case, visibility should be increased. Constraint programming should systematically be an important part of any undergraduate AI course, especially considering that a third or a quarter of papers presented at international AI conferences fall in the area of CP. Not only should it be taught but also talked about within the government agencies providing research funds. There is a need for lobbying at this level.

What are the grand challenges of CP?

Some of the challenges we identified are:

– The new holy grail, a Universal Solver, offering an integration of different solution techniques (constraint programming, SAT solver, integer programming, local search, etc.) and a smart way of deciding which one(s) to use.

– The related challenge of better interaction and synergy with neighboring communities (artificial intelligence, operations research, satisfiability, discrete algorithms, etc.). There have been past efforts such as conference collocations, interdisciplinary workshops such as CP-AI-OR, and CP sessions in related conferences such as INFORMS, but was this enough?

– A problem description standard to facilitate experimental comparisons between constraint systems, languages, models, or algorithms. Having an expressive modeling language is clearly an advantage for CP but it also keeps it at a distance from any kind of normal form. This is much easier to accomplish for more rigid formalisms like linear programs or SAT clauses. Such experimental comparisons should also be carried out with other approaches such as MIP solvers and SAT solvers.

– Another standardization effort would be the establishment of just a few CP systems for teaching and industry.

– To accentuate the modularity asset of CP by improving its compositional machinery.

– To design an open system that you can instantiate in several possible closed systems.

– To resist the temptation of overspecializing CP for finite domains and combinatorial problems, for deterministic off-line problems. There are other constraint domains to (re)discover, other applications areas to investigate, e.g. with real-time requirements, uncertainty, and the growing availability of parallel computers.

3.6. Francesca Rossi

The table consisted of the following people: M. Carlsson, E. Freuder, B. Gutkovich, F. Laburthe, S. Prestwich, F. Rossi (facilitator), P. Stuckey, R. Szymanek, V. Telerman.

Main goal of CP

Our table started by trying to define the main goal of constraint programming, which was finally defined as follows: to build technology for efficiently solving real-life combinatorial problems in a declarative framework. On a less technical level, the goal should be to help people make decisions.

Specificities of CP

The table then passed on to point out the main specificities of constraint programming, which were found to be:

– building systems and reusable components rather than building solutions;

– the almost ubiquitous use of local techniques such as constraint propagation;

– the preference of using inference as much as possible rather than search.

Open issues

The main open issues in constraint programming were identified to be: scalability, modeling beyond finite domains, automatization, handling uncertainty, integration with other techniques (OR, case-based reasoning, etc.), acquisition/explanation, and in general tools that improve the interaction with users, and robustness.

Science vs. engineering

On the science vs. engineering issue, the table agreed that constraint programming has an engineering goal. However, this goal needs the development of new science to be achieved. If the constraint programming research community focuses only on one of these two aspects, there will be little improvement. So we need to be both scientists and engineers.

The last 10 years

If we look at the progress made since the 1996 workshop on strategic directions of constraint programming, much work has been done, especially in areas such as the integration of CP and OR methods, declarativity, debugging and visualization. However, some research lines which were active at that time have almost disappeared, such as constraint databases. We believe that the reason is that the database companies are not flexible enough to allow new external technology to enter. In terms of disciplines used within CP, with respect to ten years ago we can see more AI, OR, theoretical computer science, embedded systems, and software engineering, but fewer programming languages and databases.

The main achievements of the past ten years have been identified in the development of the first CP-based industrial solutions, the vast development of global constraints and hybrid methods, and the solution of some open problems in areas like job-shop scheduling. CP is currently present in many conferences outside the most related ones (such as CP, CP-AI-OR, AAAI, IJCAI, and ECAI). This is a sign that CP is also perceived as a useful technology by other computer science areas.

Next main applications

The table indicated the following as some of the next main applications in CP: networking, distributed scheduling, mixed domain problems, automated vehicles, hybrid control theory, engineering design via geometric constraints, games, smart buildings, service industry, electronic commerce, biology problems, health care, e-government, and CAD. The funding agencies do not really care about the technology used to achieve a certain result, so currently when we ask for funds we usually hide CP. What is needed to convince the funding agencies to fund constraint-based projects is to show successful applications.

The impact that CP has on society could be larger if CP were taught more at universities. A measure of such an impact could be the number of job advertisements in the field of CP posted every year.

Application papers

The CP conference usually receives very few application papers. To attract such papers, the community should produce free and good constraint-based tools. Moreover, it could start a best application paper prize. Finally, it could start an application/engineering track with a separate program committee (a sort of parallel conference co-located with CP), structured by industrial sector or by applications.

Some grand challenges

We identified some grand challenges for CP as the following:

- be competitive with MIP and SAT;
- define a universal interchange format for problems;
- integrate with simulation;
- understand failure.

3.7. Thomas Schiex

On the definition of CP itself, no clear definition emerged but there was a consensus that "declarativity" is a core characteristic of CP. As it was said, CP should allow people to "just state the problem and the machine will take care of the rest". People agreed that we are still far from this.

Concerning science vs. engineering, people considered that CP is both science and engineering. The science aspect lies for example in the study of NP-complete problems, how they can be solved and characterized. The engineering lies in the development of techniques to solve actual instances and languages to express them, and their application to real problems. Each should benefit from the other.

Considering open problems, even if there are a lot of results on frameworks enabling us to express preferences or uncertainty, the algorithmic results are apparently less visible. They are not available in existing CP languages. More work is needed to integrate existing algorithms that deal with "soft constraint problems", over-constrained problems and uncertainty (and not necessarily only complete problems) into existing languages.

Several people pointed out that CP is probably too closed on the "hard" science aspects. The community is oriented towards formal results and complete methods. If it has partly opened itself up to "ILP" in OR, it should open up for example to incomplete methods such as local search and also be more open to applications. The creation of a dedicated application submission track in CP has been repeatedly cited as a necessary step in avoiding the sclerosis of CP.

Concerning applications, the strategy of just trying to "attract" people that develop applications to CP was considered as necessary but insufficient. Part of the community should actively move towards applications and not passively hope that people will come to use CP. The best tool for anybody is usually the one he already knows, unless someone proves to him that there is a technology worth the effort of moving. We have to prove this on (preferably hot) applications. Beyond the usual industrial problems, bioinformatics is an expanding area of application were CP should probably be more visible.

An important area where effort can be made to boost CP success is teaching. CP should be taught more often in universities, and not only as part of computer science. It would be good to share teaching documents, exercises, etc. This is already being done in France (C. Solnon is organizing this in the context of the French association for constraint programming, the AFPC).

Considering the past achievements, several successes of CP were identified. The most important successes cited were scheduling, the successful introduction of global constraints, the success of SAT in EDA (in our group SAT was considered to be part of CP; which might be a controversial point of view) and the most visible success in "society" cited was the generation of Sudoku puzzles (in France produced for *Le Monde* by a CP company called Koalog for example). For SAT, the success in EDA was connected to the existence of a large collection of well formalized benchmarks, expressed in a simple language (CNF) together with competitions for black box solvers. Therefore, it was stressed that some similar mechanisms should be put into practice in the CP case. The difficulty of defining a closed and normalized language for CP is clear. An open definition, with possible evolutions, was considered as the best approach here.

3.8. Christian Schulte

Much of our discussion was centered around the topic of global constraints (a rather specific area), where the discussion was conducted in two parts:

The past

One of the essential questions was: why was the significance of global constraints not recognized in 1996? Some reasons that were mentioned and discussed included: the scope of subproblems which can be captured was not easy to understand at that time, much focus of research was concentrated on programming languages and combination mechanisms, the effect of strong reasoning was grossly underestimated.

The future

A general theme in the discussion was that global constraints are indeed essential as they are the cornerstone of capturing structure in problems and exploiting it to reason efficiently and strongly on this structure. For the future the following issues were discussed:

– how to discover and manage structure: should the detection of structure be left to the programmer and/or modeler?

– how to systematize the plethora of global constraints: abstraction of known constraints to more powerful families such as range/roots; using powerful models to define the semantics of propagation performed by global constraints exactly (here it was mentioned that approaches using automata, formulae, or graph properties will play an essential role);

– how to choose the best implementation for a particular constraint? This will need quite some attention as the choice is difficult and not even the seasoned modelers would be able to do it by hand;

– what will the role of global constraints in modeling be? It was put forward that the future of global constraints will be more concerned with finding substructures that are good for modeling rather than good for solving;

– extensions such as costs and softness for global constraints will play a major role in extension of current modeling practice;

– a conjecture put forward by Willem-Jan van Hoeve: "global constraints are algorithms now, but will be a tool for automatic modeling of problem substructures in the future".

Other topics

Other topics that were discussed can be summarized as follows:

– Black box solvers versus white box solvers: the discussion revealed that it is expected that in the future both approaches will receive attention, where the focus for black box solvers will be on usability and for white box solvers on research. It has been mentioned that a key approach to successful black box solvers will be an incremental better understanding of problem classes that can be successfully handled by them.

– Standard modeling notation: it has been stressed in the discussion that a key development that is currently missing is a standard notation for models. Particularly challenging aspects for the future which were mentioned are: how to deal with global constraints (how to use models for different systems with different capabilities), what can a framework to describe models and solvers be (first-order languages versus higher-order languages), how rich should the language be in general, how to design languages that do not lock in the development of constraint programming to the current state-of-the-art, how should the semantics be described and captured (just declaratively or also operationally).

3.9. Meinolf Sellmann

Our discussion was structured in three parts: an assessment of past developments, the current state of affairs, and an outlook on promising future directions.

How we got here?

The first observation we made was that, since 1996, CP research has opened to a much wider range of methods while, at the same time, the range of CP applications has narrowed dramatically. In particular, CP has successfully incorporated methods from local search, algorithm theory, operations research, and artificial intelligence. However, in application domains like databases, visualization, or time tabling where it used to play a role, CP is not visible anymore. Furthermore, with a few exceptions, today CP research is almost exclusively focusing on finite domain applications.

The second trend that we identified is the fact that the introduction of global constraints has somewhat compromised the declarative principle of constraint programming. In contrast to SAT or IP, CP users cannot model their problems easily anymore, they need to know which constraints are available and often they need to hand-tune search organization (like branching variable/value selection or the choice of the search method like LDS) to achieve an efficient solution approach. Sophisticated methods like symmetry breaking complicate the modeling process further.

Finally, we stated that many promising young researchers have entered the field, which can be attributed at least in part to the successful introduction of the CP doctoral program.

Where we are now?

With the growing number of young minds working on CP and the wide spectrum of methods that CP researchers have integrated in their work, the field has great potential to grow scientifically. However, CP research is currently detached from the world of real-world applications. Users have great difficulties exploiting CP technology, and the lack of automation is a real obstacle to a broader impact of CP technology. Consequently, the visibility of CP in many relevant areas is limited. As a final side note, it was mentioned by one participant that the quality of reviewing for the CP conference had declined.

Where to go next?

Based on our assessment of the past and current state of affairs, we identified four action points that we hope will be addressed by CP researchers and/or the ACP(EC).

Connect: to increase visibility, CP as a field needs to venture out to other research areas, such as for example, security, data bases, or planning. We need ambassadors that represent CP and make it recognizable, both in research and in academia. Another way to achieve more visibility is to invite practitioners to the conference. A permanent application track at CP would be desirable.

Target: CP research needs to address the *relevant* research issues. There is a large body of CP research that appears to be entirely academic with respect to real-world applications. For instance, we urgently need to address the currently lacking ease of use. Automation should therefore be identified as a hot topic that could also be given priority in the selection of papers at CP. Additionally, we could consider a special track or workshop where CP systems are presented and users can be educated in the technology while they themselves provide feedback to the system designers.

Control: to ensure a high standard of reviewing at CP, we agreed that returning to (potentially virtual) Programme Committee (PC) meetings would be desirable. All papers should be discussed by all PC members, and not just by the selected reviewers for each paper. Another way to hold reviewers to high standards would be to introduce a feedback channel where authors can answer the reviews before a final decision is made.

Foster: we need to bring CP to the classroom. We need courses that integrate topics on CP. We need to actively attend to the careers of the younger members of our community, both in academia and in industry. Finally, we need to actively work on a broader visibility of CP, also outside of Europe, and particularly in North America.

3.10. Mark Wallace

The discussion group comprised a majority of participants working in industry as well as some academics (like myself). In particular there were people from Bouygues, ILOG, Cadence and Interactive Research. However the following report is my own, and in no way claims to represent the views of these companies. These are companies that all use CP, so they at least reflect the success of CP over the last 10 years!

What is CP?

The initial question – "What is constraint programming?" – motivated and focused the discussion.

Constraint programming has to date been used to identify:
- a class of problem models; and
- a class of algorithmic techniques for solving problems.

Problem modeling: our view for the future is a consolidated concept of constraint problem modeling that is shared by academia and industry. This concept is, naturally, broader than that of a Constraint Satisfaction Problem (CSP). The CSP is too restricted for modeling real industrial problems. From an industrial point of view we are also keen to establish a stable concept that is not too open-ended. Much has been said about the advantages of stable but limited modeling formalisms such as integer/linear programming. Nevertheless this formalism shares the disadvantage of the CSP formalism, that integer/linear constraints can't fully capture real problems.

The following were identified as key modeling requirements for CP:

- data structures: records, lists, arrays, sets, etc.;
- soft constraints: absolute and relative preferences, multiple preference criteria, measures of violation, etc.;
- continuous variables;
- dynamic problems: problems that must be solved repeatedly and where the change in the solution should reflect the change in the problem.

Most industrial problems involve all four of these modeling requirements.

Problem solving: there has been a view that CP is an approach based on tree search with intelligent reasoning (propagation) carried out at each node. Large scale industrial problems require a much broader armory, and it was agreed that CP should not in future be associated with any restricted set of solving methods.

Benchmarks

An important connection between industry and academia is through benchmarks. Benchmarks both drive forward research and provide a measure of its success. From an industrial perspective benchmarks should be simple and abstract enough to inspire and motivate a substantial amount of research, but remain close enough to the real problem that an algorithm that performs well on the benchmark could be adapted to perform well on the application itself.

Such benchmarks stretch the modeling and solving facilities of CP beyond its "comfort zone": CSP problems do not do this! Industrial benchmarks naturally include data structures, soft constraints, continuous variables and dynamic problems.

The first challenge is to assemble a body of benchmarks that industry really cares about. Examples might include an abstract crew scheduling problem, an abstract configuration problem, an abstract minimal perturbation problem, interleaving problem changes and rescheduling.

The second challenge is to establish a standard problem modeling formalism both simple enough for non-specialists to grasp and flexible enough to express the full range of CP problems, and in particular benchmarks.

Usability

The demand for usability has been repeated many times within the CP community, but has been too often sacrificed in favor of other priorities. The group identified two areas of usability which are most urgent for users of CP technology:

- explanations;
- support for algorithm development.

Automation of algorithm development has been called the "holy grail" of our community, and support for algorithm development is already a target for many research groups.

The requirement for explanations can be broken down into three different needs:

Minimal conflict sets and "nogoods": these are explanations of why a particular set of choices cannot yield a good result: they can be reused to narrow down the search for solutions, or even to contribute to a proof that there is no solution.

Performance debugging: this is a form of analysis of the behavior of an algorithm, rather than its outputs. This is essential for recognizing algorithm deficiencies and focusing the search for the best algorithm to solve a problem.

Meaningful feedback: the joke goes "How many Prolog programmers does it take to change a light bulb? Answer: No ". Too often CP systems also behave like this. When things go wrong, an ability to explore why there wasn't a solution, or why the solution wasn't better, is extremely important for the end user. This is a more informal kind of explanation than the others, but it is just as necessary.

3.11. Toby Walsh

Although the goal of the workshop was to celebrate past successes and identify future directions, our panel spent little time celebrating the past and most of its time looking to the future.

In terms of the past, as one participant put it, "... Scheduling may be one of our only achievements. More than half of our successful applications are scheduling ...". After this, there come applications in areas like resource allocation, transportation and configuration.

In terms of the future, we discussed a number of directions, some of which are promising and others of which ought to be promising.

Solver robustness: constraint programming is too brittle compared to OR methods like integer programming. Small changes to the model can change the performance dramatically, and it is hard to predict what will help and what will hinder performance. If we want CP to be more widely adopted, we perhaps need to make it more of a black box, push button technology.

Uncertainty: no constraint toolkit supports uncertainty yet dealing with uncertainty is central to many business problems. One promising direction may be to combine CP with simulation.

More realistic and useful models: surprisingly CP has resisted extension. There are many proposed extensions to make CP more realistic and useful (e.g. soft constraints, stochastic constraints). However, these extensions are not in the toolkits. Why is this so?

Symbolic and algebraic reasoning: we have constraints with rich semantics so there is much we could reason about them. Why then did we lose touch with this community?

New territories: there are also many new application areas like e-commerce, e-government, and bioinformatics where CP could play a role. How do we get people in these areas to take up our technology?

Science or engineering: a major problem is that CP involves both science and engineering. However, an event like the CP conference is a scientific meeting. How then can we document and reward engineering achievements? Why don't more industry people attend CP? What happened to the practical applications and user group conferences?

3.12. Roland Yap

Our discussion group was heterogenous including academics, people working in industry and also researchers from cross disciplines such as databases. We spent some time discussing the specific features of CP i.e. what makes it CP.

What is CP? We discussed what makes CP different. For example, in contrast to an MIP solver, CP solvers not only focus on the core algorithms but are also characterized by open architectures that take into account the software engineering aspects of dealing with multiple solvers and extensibility. Other related points are below.

What are the specificities of CP research? A basic principle in CP is that it is based on inference. Thus, it is not only about algorithms but includes taking into account dealing with general mechanisms of exploiting inference such as managing and communicating between specific solvers, for example, using propagation to manage interaction between MIP and SAT solver and other user defined propagators.

CP is also different as it tries to exploit the structure of the problem both from a modeling as well as a solving perspective.

We discussed the issue of impact of CP on society and industrial applications together. One problem we discussed was that while CP might be an important component of many critical and important applications, it stays in the shadows so that it cannot be visible. Thus while CP might have an impact on the actual application, this might not be evident to a broader audience or user base. From an educational perspective, CP also might not be very well known since it would not be considered as a core requirement in curricula like databases would be. There is also the issue that the CP conferences do not have many industrial applications presented in the technical program. Perhaps on that front, specific efforts to attract industrial applications with papers might be one direction.

Another idea we had was maybe to have more specifically invited industry application papers or speakers.

The discussion on grand challenges and future directions echoed some of the discussions in CP-Tools:

How can the use of CP be increased? CP is not as easy to use as other technologies such as MIP solvers or even databases which are more like black box technologies. This leads to the challenge of how to broaden the applicability and use of CP technology? Some of the new directions towards more black box solvers may make CP more successful in this regard.

New areas for CP: CP is being used in areas outside the traditional CP and AI communities. An example where CP seems to be of increasing importance is in satisfiability modulo theories where it is used in model checking. Perhaps more attention needs to be paid to new areas as this does not appear much in the CP conferences.

3.13. References

[VAN 96] VAN HENTENRYCK P., SARASWAT V., "Strategic Directions in Constraint Programming", *ACM Computing Surveys*, vol. 28, num. 4, p. 701-726, 1996.

Chapter 4

Constraint Propagation and Implementation

Constraint propagation is an essential part of many constraint programming systems. Sitting at the heart of constraint solvers, it consumes a significant portion of the time that is required for problem solving. The *Third International Workshop on Constraint Propagation and Implementation (CPAI'06)* was convened to study the design and analysis of new propagation algorithms as well as any related practical issues. The implementation and evaluation of constraint propagation is studied in contexts ranging from special purpose solvers to programming language systems.

For this third workshop, seven papers were submitted, carefully reviewed and selected for publication in the proceedings. Interestingly, the high quality of these papers attracted a lot of people during the half-day workshop. Consequently, we intend to organize a fourth workshop in a few years.

Below, you will find extended abstracts for four papers which were presented orally at the workshop as well as two shorter abstracts. They correspond to a brief description of the lastest developments in both generic (see sections 4.2, 4.3 and 4.4) and specific (see sections 4.1, 4.5 and 4.6) approaches to filtering. We hope that reading this will incite you to get the full version of these papers, available at: `http://cpai.ucc.ie/`.

Also, note that, in conjunction with this workshop, a second competition for CSP solvers has been organized. This year, it was possible to register a solver for CSP and Max-CSP, for binary and non-binary instances, and for constraints

---

Chapter edited by Marc VAN DONGEN and Christophe LECOUTRE.

represented in extension and in intention. Fifteen contestants participated in this event. All results are available at: `http://www.cril.univ-artois.fr/CPAI06/`.

4.1. Filtering algorithms for precedence and dependency constraints (by Roman Barták and Ondřej Čepek)

4.1.1. *Problem description and related works*

Precedence constraints play a crucial role in planning and scheduling problems. The *precedence constraint* $A \prec B$ specifies that activity A must be before activity B in the schedule. Many real-life scheduling problems are "oversubscribed", that is, the scheduler should decide which activities are included in the schedule without violating the precedence constraints, that is, without a cycle between the selected activities. We call the activities that are selected to be in the schedule *valid activities*; the omitted activities are called *invalid activities*. Frequently, the activities are also connected via so called dependency constraints. The *dependency constraint* $A \Rightarrow B$ specifies that if activity A is valid then activity B must be valid as well. This is one of the dependency constraints proposed in the general model for manufacturing scheduling [NUI 03]. The task is to decide about the (in)validity of the activities and to find a set of valid activities satisfying the precedence and dependency constraints. Usually, the problem is formulated as an optimization problem, where the task is to find a feasible solution in the above sense that maximizes the number of valid activities.

Though our motivation is mainly in the area of scheduling, the above problem is also known as a log-based reconciliation problem in databases. The straightforward constraint model for this problem was proposed in [FAG 01]. The model uses n integer variables $p_1, \ldots, p_n$ which give the absolute positions of activities in the schedule (n is the number of activities). The initial domain of these variables is $1, \ldots, n$. There are also n Boolean (0/1) variables $a_1, \ldots, a_n$ describing whether the activity is valid (1) or invalid (0). The precedence constraint between activities i and j is then described using the formula:

$$(a_i \wedge a_j) \Rightarrow (p_i < p_j) \text{ or equivalently } (a_i * a_j * p_i < p_j).$$

The dependency constraint between activities i and j can be formulated as:

$$a_i \Rightarrow a_j \text{ or equivalently } (a_i \leq a_j).$$

The solver uses standard constraint propagation over the above described constraints combined with an enumeration of the Boolean variables a_i. Note also, that the log-based reconciliation problem is NP-hard [FAG 01].

4.1.2. *Filtering rules for precedence and dependency constraints*

Our approach is different from existing techniques by integrating reasoning on both precedence and dependency constraints. The main idea is to incrementally maintain a transitive closure of the precedence graph while doing some logical reasoning on dependencies. We say that a precedence graph G with optional activities is transitively closed if for any two arcs A to B and B to C such that B is a valid activity and A and C are valid activities there is also an arc A to C in G.

To simplify implementation in existing constraint solvers, we propose an innovative data model for the precedence graph. We index each activity with a unique number from the set $1, \ldots, n$, where n is the number of activities. For each activity we use a 0/1 variable Valid indicating whether the activity is valid (1) or invalid (0). If the activity is undecided (not yet known to be valid or invalid) then the domain of Valid is $\{0, 1\}$. The precedence graph is encoded in two sets attached to each activity. CanBeBefore(A) is a set of indices of activities that can be before activity A. CanBeAfter(A) is a set of indices of activities that can be after activity A. For simplicity reasons we will write A instead of the index of A. Figure 4.1 explains how this data model describes the precedence graph, for details see [BAR 06]. Notice also that as the arcs are added to the graph (for example using our filtering rules), only the two sets CanBeBefore and CanBeAfter shrink. This corresponds to domain filtering by removing inconsistent values.

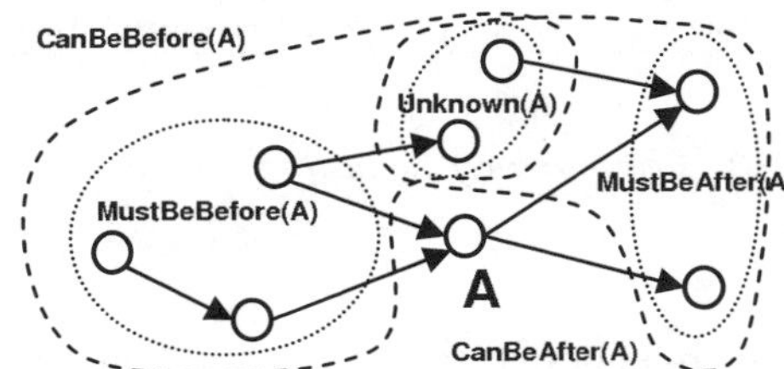

Figure 4.1. *Representation of the precedence graph*

Our filtering rules add new arcs to the precedence graph to keep its transitive closure. They can also deduce that some activities are valid or invalid. Note that the transitive closure of the precedence graph simplifies detection of inconsistency of the graph. The precedence graph is inconsistent if there is a cycle of valid activities. In a transitively closed graph, each such cycle can be detected by finding two valid activities A and B such that $A \prec B$ and $B \prec A$. Our filtering rules prevent cycles by making the last undecided activity in each cycle invalid. This propagation is realized by using an exclusion constraint. As soon as a cycle $A \prec B$ and $B \prec A$ is detected, the following exclusion constraint can be posted:

$$\text{Valid}(A) = 0 \vee \text{Valid}(B) = 0.$$

This constraint ensures that each cycle is broken by making at least one activity in the cycle invalid. Instead of directly posting the constraint to the constraint solver, we propose keeping the set Ex of exclusions. The above exclusion constraint is modeled as a set $\{A, B\} \in Ex$. Now, the propagation of exclusions is realized explicitly – if activity A becomes valid then all activities C such that $\{A, C\} \in Ex$ are made invalid. In addition to precedence constraints, there are also dependency constraints in the problem. The dependency $A \Rightarrow B$ can be easily described using the constraint:

$$(\text{Valid}(A) = 1) \Rightarrow (\text{Valid}(B) = 1).$$

As with the exclusions, we propose keeping the set Dep of dependencies instead of posting the above constraints, and realizing the propagation of dependencies explicitly. In particular, if activity A becomes valid then all activities C such that $(A \Rightarrow C) \in Dep$ are made valid. On the other hand, if activity A becomes invalid then all activities C such that $(C \Rightarrow A) \in Dep$ are made invalid. Keeping the exclusions and dependencies explicit has the advantage of stronger filtering, which is formally described in Table 4.1.

Condition	**Effect**
$\{A, B\} \in Ex \wedge (A \Rightarrow B) \in Dep$	$\text{Valid}(A) = 0$
$\{A, B\} \in Ex \wedge (C \Rightarrow A), (C \Rightarrow B) \in Dep$	$\text{Valid}(C) = 0$

Table 4.1. *Reasoning on exclusions and dependencies*

We propose two incremental filtering rules working with the precedence and dependency relations. The first rule is evoked each time the validity status of the activity becomes known. If the activity becomes invalid then it is disconnected from the graph by removing it from all sets CanBeBefore and CanBeAfter. If the activity becomes valid then the arcs to keep a transitive closure are added and possible cycles are detected. If a new exclusion constraint is generated (to break a cycle) then logical reasoning described by Table 1 is realized. If implemented properly, the worst-case time complexity of the filtering rule including all possible recursive calls is $O(n^3)$, where n is the number of activities.

The second filtering rule reacts to new arcs added to the graph either by the user, by the scheduler/planner (as a decision), or by other filtering rules (arcs added by the above rule do not need to be handled there because full filtering is done by that rule). If a new arc is added then the corresponding sets CanBeBefore and CanBeAfter are updated, the arcs, which are to keep a transitive closure are added (if any end point of the added arc is valid), and possible cycles are detected. Moreover, we can add more arcs using information about dependencies – this is useful for earlier detection of possible cycles. We assume that arc $A \prec B$ has been added. If $(B \Rightarrow A) \in Dep$ then all predecessors of A can be connected to B as in the case when A is valid. This is sound because if B becomes valid then A must be valid as well and such arcs will be added anyway and if B becomes invalid then any arc related to B is irrelevant. For the same reason, if there is any predecessor C of A such that $(C \Rightarrow A) \in Dep$ then C can be connected to B. The same reasoning can be applied to successors of B. Again, if a new exclusion constraint is generated (to break a cycle) then logical reasoning based on Table 1 is realized. Note that the propagators for new arcs are evoked after the propagator of the current rule finishes. The worst-case time complexity of the filtering rule including all recursive calls is $O(n^3)$, where n is the number of activities.

4.1.3. *Summary*

In this section we proposed new incremental filtering rules for precedence and dependency constraints. These rules were based on maintaining a transitive closure of the precedence graph with optional activities. As opposed to existing approaches, we proposed using information about dependency constraints within the filtering rules for the precedence constraints rather than propagating dependencies separately. Full technical details including proofs of soundness and time complexity are given in [BAR 06] where we also proposed a filtering rule that uses information about the requested number of valid activities in the precedence graph. Though we focused on a particular form of dependencies, we believe that our approach is extendable to other dependency constraints, for example, those in [NUI 03] where existence of an activity forces removal of another activity.

This research is supported by the Czech Science Foundation under contract no. 201/04/1102.

4.2. A study of residual supports in arc consistency (by Christophe Lecoutre and Fred Hemery)

It is well-known that arc consistency (AC) plays a central role in solving instances of the constraint satisfaction problem (CSP). Indeed, the MAC algorithm, i.e., the algorithm which maintains arc consistency during the search of a solution, is still considered to be the most efficient generic approach to cope with large and hard problem instances. Furthermore, AC is at the heart of a stronger consistency called singleton arc consistency (SAC) which has recently attracted a lot of attention (e.g., [BES 05a, LEC 05]).

For more that two decades, many algorithms have been proposed to establish arc consistency. Today, the most referenced algorithms are AC3 [MAC 77] because of its simplicity and AC2001/3.1 [BES 05b] because of its optimality (while not being too complex). The worst-case time complexities of AC3 and AC2001 are respectively $O(ed^3)$ and $O(ed^2)$ where e denotes the number of constraints and d the greatest domain size. The interest of an optimal algorithm such as AC2001 resides in its robustness. This means that, in some instances, AC2001 can largely be faster than an algorithm such as AC3 whereas the reverse is not true. This situation occurs when the tightness of the constraints is high, as is the case for the equality constraint (i.e. constraint with the form $X = Y$). Indeed, as naturally expected, AC3 then admits a practical behavior which is close to the worst-case, and the difference by a factor d between the two theoretical worst-case complexities becomes a reality.

In this section, we are interested in residues for AC algorithms. A residue is a support that has been stored during a previous execution of the procedure which determines if a value is supported by a constraint. The point is that a residue is not guaranteed to represent a lower bound of the smallest current support of a value. The basic algorithm AC3 can be refined by exploiting residues as follows: before searching a support for a value from scratch, the validity of the residue associated with this value is checked. We then obtain an algorithm denoted AC3r, and when multi-directionality is exploited, an algorithm denoted AC3rm. In fact, AC3r is an algorithm which can be advantageously replaced by AC2001 when AC must be established as stand-alone on a given constraint network. However, when AC has to be maintained during search, MAC3r which corresponds to mac3.1residue [LIK 04] becomes quite competitive. On the other hand, AC3rm is interesting on its own as it exploits *multi-directional* residues just as with AC3.2 [LEC 03].

We prove in this section that AC3r and AC3rm, contrary to AC3, admits an optimal behavior when the tightness of the constraints is high. Next, we analyze the cost of managing data structures with respect to backtracking. On the one hand, it is easy to embed AC3, AC3r or AC3rm in MAC and SAC algorithms as these algorithms do not not require any maintenance of data structures during MAC search and SAC inference. On the other hand, embedding an optimal algorithm such as AC2001 entails an extra development effort, with, in addition, an overhead at the execution. For MAC2001, this overhead is $O(\mu ed)$ per branch of the binary tree built by MAC as we have to take into account the re-initialization of a structure (called $last$) which contains the smallest supports found. Here, μ denotes the number of refutations of the branch. MAC3r(m) then admits a better worst-case time complexity than MAC2001 for a branch of the binary search tree when either $\mu > d^2$ or $\mu > d$ and the tightness of any constraint is low or high.

On the practical side, we have run a vast experimentation including MAC and SAC-1 algorithms on binary and non-binary instances. The results that we have obtained clearly show the interest of exploiting residues as AC3r(m) (embedded in MAC or SAC-1) were almost always the quickest algorithms (only beaten by AC3.2 on some non-binary instances). We also noted that GAC3rm was more robust than GAC3r on non-binary instances and constraints of high tightness.

Finally, we want to emphasize that implementing (G)AC3r(m) (and embedding it in MAC or SAC) is quite easy as no maintenance of data structures upon backtracking is required. It should be compared with the intricacy of fine-grained algorithms which requires a clever use of data structures, in particular when applied to non-binary instances. The simplicity of AC3r(m) offers another scientific advantage: the easy reproducibility of the experimentation by other researchers. A revised version of this work has been accepted for publication [LEC 07].

4.3. Maintaining singleton arc consistency (by Christophe Lecoutre and Patrick Prosser)

In this section, we study three partial forms of SAC for CNs (constraint networks). The first is Bound-SAC where the first and last values in the domains of variables are SAC, and all other domain values are arc-consistent. The second level of SAC follows on immediately and we call it First-SAC, where the first value in the domain of a variable is SAC and all other values are AC. Finally we present Existential-SAC ($\exists$-SAC), where we guarantee that some value in the domain is SAC and all others are AC. These different levels of consistency can then be maintained on different sets of variables within a problem. For example when modeling a problem we might maintain SAC on one set of variables, Bound-SAC on another set of variables, and AC on the remaining variables. That is, we might use varying levels of consistency across different parts of a problem, attempting to find a good balance between inference and exploration.

It is natural to conceive algorithms to enforce First-SAC, Last-SAC and Bound-SAC on CNs. Indeed, it suffices to remove all values detected as arc inconsistent and bound values (only the minimal ones for First-SAC and the maximal ones for Last-SAC) detected as singleton arc inconsistent. When enforcing a CN P to be First-SAC, Last-SAC or Bound-SAC, one then obtains the greatest sub-network of P which is First-SAC, Last-SAC or Bound-SAC. But this is not true for Existential-SAC. Indeed, enforcing Existential-SAC on a CN is meaningless. Either the network is (already) Existential-SAC, or the network is singleton arc inconsistent. It is then better to talk about checking Existential-SAC. An algorithm to check Existential-SAC will have to find a singleton arc consistent value in each domain. As a side-effect, if singleton arc inconsistent values are encountered, they will be, of course, removed. However, we have absolutely no guarantee about the network obtained after checking Existential-SAC due to the non-deterministic nature of this consistency.

4.3.1. *Mixed consistency*

The different levels of consistency (AC, SAC, Bound-SAC, First-SAC, etc.) can be applied selectively across different sets of variables in a problem by the constraint programmer, allowing the programmer to control the blend of mixed-consistency maintained during search.

We performed experiments on 15 of the Lawrence Job-Shop scheduling instances. For each instance, we have two distinct sets of variables: a set of 0/1 variables that control disjunctive precedence constraints on resources and a set of start times attached to operations. Consequently, this is a good model to explore the effects of mixed-consistency. The results of four of our experiments are shown in Table 4.2. The first experiment used MAC (all variables were maintained arc-consistent). The second experiment used Bound-SAC on the 0/1 decision variables and MAC on all other variables, and this is column B-SAC$_{dn}$. Experiment three maintains Bound-SAC on the start times of operations, and this is column B-SAC$_{st}$. Finally, in experiment four, all variables are made Bound-SAC, and this is column B-SAC. What we see is that Bound-SAC can indeed be beneficial, allowing us to frequently find better solutions than just using MAC on its own. In particular, the B-SAC$_{dn}$ results show that more often than not Bound-SAC on the decision variables alone results in significantly lower makespans than with MAC. However, too much SAC appears to be a bad thing. In experiments B-SAC$_{st}$ and B-SAC we see that too much time

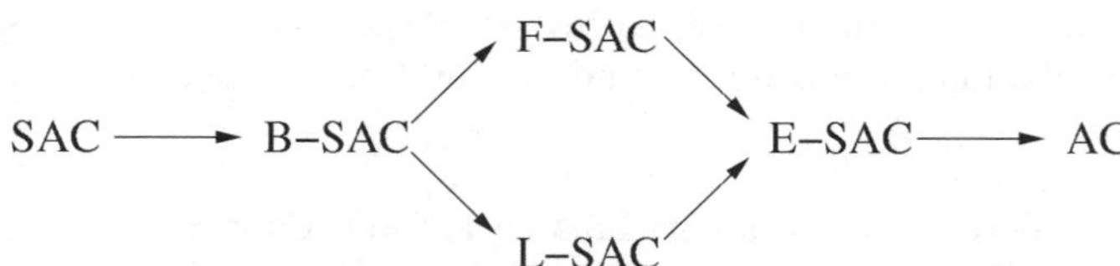

Figure 4.2. *Relationships between consistencies. $A \rightarrow B$ means consistency A is stronger than B*

is spent in SAC processing compared to time spent in search. Consequently solution quality suffers. In fact, as instance size increases from la11 onwards no solutions were found as all the CPU time was spent in SAC and none in search.

In [PRO 00], experiments were performed on Golomb rulers. In particular, given the length l of the shortest ruler with t ticks (or marks), the objective is to find that ruler and prove it optimal. The study showed that SAC preprocessing and restricted SAC preprocessing could lead to a modest reduction in run-times. We repeat those experiments, but now maintain a mix of SAC during the search process. The problem was represented using n *tick* variables with enumerated domains whose values range from 0 to l, and, in addition $t(t-1)/2$ $diff$ variables with similar domains. Again we have a problem with two obviously different sets of variables, the *tick* variables and the $diff$ variables, and this again gives us an opportunity to investigate the effects of blending mixed-consistency. The results of the experiments are given in Table 4.3 which clearly shows that maintaining Bound-SAC on the *tick* variables (denoted B-SAC$_{tk}$) dominates MAC, whereas maintaining SAC on the *tick* variables (denoted SAC$_{tk}$) is far too expensive. We also experimented with maintaining restricted Bound-SAC on the *tick* variables (denoted RB-SAC$_{tk}$), i.e. only a single pass is made over the variables as proposed in [PRO 00]. Table 4.3 shows that this results in our best performance.

4.3.2. *Checking existential-SAC*

In [LEC 05], an original approach to establish SAC was proposed. The principle of this is to perform several runs of a greedy search, where at each step arc-consistency is maintained. Using a greedy approach to check Existential-SAC seems to be quite appropriate, and, in particular, it is straightforward to

		Maintaining		
Instance	MAC	B-SAC$_{dn}$	B-SAC$_{st}$	B-SAC
la07	1214	897	1336	1359
la08	1161	1084	1400	1393
la09	1498	1049	1527	1520
la10	1658	972	1192	1259
la11	1453	1787	–	–
la12	1467	1504	–	–
la13	2899	2310	–	–
la14	1970	1784	–	–
la15	2368	2200	–	–

Table 4.2. *Best solution found for Lawrence scheduling instances, given 10 minutes CPU*

		Maintaining		
Instance	MAC	SAC_{tk}	B-SAC_{tk}	RB-SAC_{tk}
5/11	0.01 (5)	0.12 (3)	0.08 (3)	0.08 (3)
6/17	0.1 (18)	0.27 (5)	0.14 (5)	0.14 (5)
7/25	0.47 (116)	0.81 (6)	0.30 (7)	0.34 (11)
8/34	3.6 (904)	14.6 (19)	1.8 (23)	1.6 (3 3)
9/44	29.1 (5,502)	136 (62)	11.3 (68)	9.6 (103)
10/55	217.3 (30,097)	1,075 (218)	68.8 (245)	59 (479)
11/72	7,200 (773,560)	—	5,534 (11,742)	4,645 (20,056)

Table 4.3. *The runtime in seconds (and in brackets number of nodes visited) to find and prove optimal a Golomb ruler t/l, with n ticks of length l*

adapt algorithm SAC3 [LEC 05] to guarantee ∃-SAC. We have thus developed an algorithm called ∃-SAC3. The time complexity of ∃-SAC3 is that of SAC3, that is $O(bed^2)$ where b denotes the number of branches built by the algorithm, e the number of constraints of the CN and d the maximum domain size. In the best case, only one branch is built (leading then directly to a solution), and then we obtain $O(ed^2)$ whereas, in the worst-case, we obtain $O(en^2d^3)$. Finally, when no inconsistent value is detected, the worst-case time complexity of ∃-SAC3 is $O(end^2)$.

We believe that it is worth studying the effect of maintaining ∃-SAC on satisfiable instances using ∃-SAC3, as due to greedy runs solutions can be found at any step of the search. This is illustrated in Table 4.4 with some instances of the n-queens problem. We also show results for forward checking (FC), maintaining arc consistency (MAC), First-SAC (F-SAC), Bound-SAC (B-SAC), and SAC maintained using the SAC1 algorithm. It is interesting to note that, for all these satisfiable instances, maintaining SAC3 or ∃-SAC3 explores no more than 2 nodes. However, one could expect to find less impressive results with unsatisfiable instances. To check this, we have tested, some difficult (modified) unsatisfiable instances of the Radio Link Frequency Assignment Problem (RLFAP). In Table 4.4, it appears that maintaining SAC3 or ∃-SAC3 really limits the number of nodes that have to be visited. It can be explained by the fact that both algorithms learn from failures (of greedy runs) as the employed heuristic is *dom*/*wdeg*.

4.3.3. *Conclusion*

From an abstract point of view, we have shown that rather than using the same level of inference (maintaining arc-consistency) all the time (during search) everywhere (over all the variables) we can often do much better by varying the level of inference (AC, SAC, Bound-SAC, First-SAC, etc.) and

Instance	FC	MAC	Maintaining				
			F-SAC	B-SAC	SAC1	SAC3	∃-SAC3
100-queens (sat)	0.5 (194)	4.2 (118)	267 (101)	421 (101)	–	17.4 (0)	18.9 (2)
110-queens (sat)	–	–	–	–	–	37.9 (0)	22.7 (1)
120-queens (sat)	–	1636 (323K)	–	–	–	16.7 (0)	47.3 (2)
scen11-f12 (unsat)	69.1 (18K)	3.6 (695)	63.3 (60)	110 (48)	1072 (41)	418 (5)	48.3 (30)
scen11-f10 (unsat)	131 (34K)	4.4 (862)	84.4 (70)	140 (55)	1732 (52)	814 (8)	38.3 (25)
scen11-f8 (unsat)	260 (66K)	67.8 (14K)	1660 (2K)	–	–	–	290 (213)

Table 4.4. *CPU time (and number of visited nodes) for instances of the n-queens and the RLFAP, given 30 minutes CPU*

doing this over only parts of the problem (a subset of the variables). We have also introduced a simple and efficient implementation of an algorithm that checks ∃-SAC. Empirical results suggest that this represents a promising generic approach.

4.4. Probabilistic singleton arc consistency (by Deepak Mehta and Marc van Dongen)

Local consistency algorithms, also known as constraint propagation algorithms are used to reduce the search space of constraint satisfaction problems (CSPs). Establishing a higher level of consistency can remove more inconsistent values and thus can avoid much unfruitful exploration of the search tree. However, as the level of consistency increases, the time required to establish it, also increases. Moreover, on many occasions, despite removing more inconsistent values, establishing higher levels of consistency may not be beneficial when the overall solution time is taken into account. The most widely used local consistency technique before and during search is arc consistency because of its low overheads. However, recently there has been a surge of interest in applying singleton arc consistency (SAC) before search. Various algorithms such as SAC-1 [DEB 97], SAC-2 [BAR 04], SAC-SDS [BES 05a], SAC-OPT [BES 05a], SAC-3 [LEC 05] and SAC-3+ [LEC 05] have been proposed.

Singleton arc consistency is a meta-consistency that enhances the pruning capability of arc consistency. It guarantees that the network can be made arc consistent after assigning a value to any variable. Establishing singleton arc consistency can prune more inconsistent values from the domains as compared to establishing arc consistency. However, it may consume more time and can be a huge overhead, especially for loose problems. Removing more values at the expense of increase in overall time required to solve the problem is not beneficial. The advantage arises only when the impact of removing more values reduces the search effort to an extent such that the overall time required to solve the problem reduces. This may not always happen. The basic problem is to optimize the tradeoff between the time required to detect and remove singleton arc inconsistent values and that required during search. One way to overcome this problem is to reduce ineffective constraint propagation in the underlying arc consistency algorithm of an SAC algorithm.

A coarse-grained arc consistency algorithm such as AC-3 [MAC 77], AC-2001 [BES 05b] repeatedly carries out revisions, which require support checks for identifying and deleting all unsupported values from the domain of a variable. In many revisions, *some* or *all* values successfully find some support, that is to say, ineffective constraint propagation occurs. In fact, in the worst case, such a coarse-grained arc consistency algorithm can perform $O(ed - nd)$ ineffective revisions (when not a single value is deleted from a domain), where e is the number of constraints, n is the number of variables and d is the maximum domain size. One can envisage more ineffective constraint propagation in SAC. For example, establishing SAC in SAC-1 style equipped with a coarse-grained arc consistency algorithm can perform $O(n^2d^2(ed-nd))$ ineffective revisions in the worst-case. This comes from the fact that SAC-1 can invoke the underlying arc consistency algorithm n^2d^2 times in the worst-case scenario. Thus, applying it before search can be expensive and maintaining it during search can be even more expensive. However, if we can reduce the ineffective constraint propagation then a considerable amount of work can be saved.

We propose *probabilistic support inference* to resolve when to seek support and when not to. This probabilistic support inference is to *avoid the process of seeking a support, when the probability of its existence is at least equal to some, carefully chosen, threshold.* At the CPAI'2005 workshop, [MEH 05] presented such an approach and studied it with respect to arc consistency when maintained during search on random problems. More specifically, the notions of a *probabilistic support condition* (PSC) and a *probabilistic revision condition* (PRC) were introduced. The PSC holds if, and only if, the probability of having some support for a value is at least equal to some, carefully chosen, threshold. If the PSC holds, then the process of seeking a support is avoided. The PRC holds if, and only if, the probability of having some support for each value in a given domain, is at least equal to the threshold. If the PRC holds, then the corresponding revision is avoided. Both PSC and PRC can be embodied in any coarse-grained arc consistency algorithm.

When PSC or PRC holds while making the problem arc consistent, the existence of a support is not always guaranteed. It depends on the threshold value used. Thus, using PSC and PRC may not always allow full arc consistency to be achieved which in turn may not always allow full singleton arc consistency to be achieved. Sometimes it may be less, depending on the threshold. As a consequence, *probabilistic singleton arc consistency (*PSAC*)* may leave some singleton arc inconsistent values in the domains of the variables and we can expect more nodes in the search tree. However, this need not necessarily be less efficient. Even though there are more nodes in the search tree, they may be the result of significantly less work done before search which may result in overall saving of time

Our experimental results demonstrate that enforcing probabilistic SAC almost always enforces SAC but that it requires significantly less time than SAC.

Likewise, maintaining probabilistic singleton arc consistency requires significantly less time than maintaining singleton arc consistency. In summary, inferring the existence of a support with a high probability slightly affects the pruning capability of SAC, but allows a lot of time to be saved. An extended version of this work [MEH 07] has also been accepted for publication.

4.5. Simplification and extension of the SPREAD constraint (by Pierre Schaus, Yves Deville, Pierre Dupont and Jean-Charles Régin)

Many constraint satisfaction problems like the Balanced Academic Curriculum Problem (BACP, problem 30 of CSPLib) require the solution to be balanced. The goal of BACP is to assign periods to courses such that the academic load of each period is balanced, i.e. as similar as possible. The most balanced solution will depend on the chosen criterion. Given a set of variables $X = \{x_1, ..., x_n\}$, a first criterion used in [HNI 02] to solve BACP is to minimize the largest deviation from the mean: $\max_{x \in X} |x - \mu|$. An alternative one is to minimize the sum of square deviations from the mean: $\sum_{x \in X}(x - \mu)^2$. The minimization of one criterion does not imply the minimization of the second one. Nevertheless, the sum of square deviations probably corresponds better to the intuitive notion of balance measure and is commonly used in statistics. SPREAD recently introduced by Pesant and Régin [PES 05] constraints the mean and the sum of square deviations of a set of variables. The particular case of SPREAD with a fixed mean is considered here. Given a set of finite domain (discrete) variables $X = \{x_1, ..., x_n\}$, one value μ and one interval variable π, SPREAD(X, μ, π) holds if $n.\mu = \sum_{i=1}^{n} x_i$ and $\pi = \sum_{i=1}^{n}(x_i - \mu)^2$. For the constraint to be consistent, $n.\mu$ must be an integer. As a consequence $n^2.\pi$ is also an integer. Pesant and Régin [PES 05] propose a filtering algorithm of π from X and μ, and of X from $\pi^{\max}$. We extend these results and describe a simpler filtering algorithm on X with the same $O(n^2)$ complexity achieving bound-consistency with respect to $\pi^{\max}$ and μ. Section 4.5.1 recall the filtering of π [PES 05] and section 4.5.2 describes the filtering on X.

4.5.1. *Filtering of* π

Let S_μ denote the set of tuples x satisfying the following constraints:

$$\sum_{i=1}^{n} x_i = n.\mu \qquad [4.1]$$

$$x_i^{\min} \leq x_i \leq x_i^{\max}, \quad \forall i \in [1, .., n] \qquad [4.2]$$

The filtering of π is based on the optimal values $\underline{\pi} = \min\{\sum_{i=1}^{n}(x_i - \mu)^2 \ : x \in S_\mu\}$ and $\overline{\pi} = \max\{\sum_{i=1}^{n}(x_i - \mu)^2 \ : x \in S_\mu\}$. Computing $\overline{\pi}$ can be shown to be $\mathcal{NP}$-hard. Instead of the exact value, an upper bound $\overline{\pi}^{\uparrow}$ can be used to perform filtering. An upper bound obtained from the relaxed problem without the mean constraint [4.1] is $\overline{\pi}^{\uparrow} = \sum_{i=1}^{n} \left(\max\left(|x_i^{\max} - \mu|, |x_i^{\min} - \mu|\right)\right)^2$. The filtering on the domain of π is $Dom(\pi) \longleftarrow Dom(\pi) \cap [\underline{\pi}, \overline{\pi}^{\uparrow}]$. The rest of this section describes the algorithmic solution from Pesant and Régin [PES 05] to calculate $\underline{\pi}$.

It can be shown that an optimal tuple in the problem of finding $\underline{\pi}$ is a v-centered assignment on each variable: $x_i := x_i^{\max}$ if $x_i^{\max} \leq v$, $x_i := x_i^{\min}$ if $x_i^{\min} \geq v$ and $x_i := v$ otherwise. The optimization problem is now reduced to finding a value v such that the v-centered assignment on every variable $x \in X$ respects constraint [4.1]. The value v can be anywhere in $[\min_X x^{\min}, \max_X x^{\max}]$. A splitting of this interval into a set of $\mathcal{O}(n)$ contiguous intervals $\mathcal{I}(X) = \{[I_1^{\min}, I_1^{\max}], [I_2^{\min}, I_2^{\max}], ...\}$ enables us to find v by iterating once over this set. The construction of this set is described below.

Let $B(X)$ be the sorted sequence of bounds of the variables of X, in non-decreasing order and with duplicates removed. Define $\mathcal{I}(X)$ as the set of intervals defined by a pair of consecutive elements of $B(X)$. The kth interval of $\mathcal{I}(X)$ is denoted by I_k. For an interval I_k, $prev(I_k) = I_{k-1}$ $(k > 1)$ and $succ(I_k) = I_{k+1}$. For example, let $X = \{x_1, x_2, x_3\}$ with $x_1 \in [1, 3]$, $x_2 \in [2, 6]$ and $x_3 \in [3, 9]$ then $\mathcal{I}(X) = \{I_1, I_2, I_3, I_4\}$ with $I_1 = [1, 2]$, $I_2 = [2, 3]$, $I_3 = [3, 6]$, $I_4 = [6, 9]$ and $prev(I_3) = I_2$, $succ(I_3) = I_4$.

Let us assume that the value v of the optimal solution lies in the interval $I \in \mathcal{I}(X)$. Sets $R(I)$ and $L(I)$ are defined as $R(I) = \{x | x^{\min} \geq \max(I)\}$ and $L(I) = \{x | x^{\max} \leq \min(I)\}$. The optimal solution is a v-centered assignment, hence all variables $x \in L(I)$ take value $x^{\max}$ and all variables in $R(I)$ value $x^{\min}$. It remains to assign the variables subsuming I denoted by $M(I) = \{x | I \subseteq I_D(x)\}$ and the cardinality of this set by $m = |M(I)|$. In a v-centered assignment with $v \in I$, the variables in $M(I)$ must take a common value

v. Sum constraint [4.1] can be reformulated with the notations introduced as $\sum_{x\in R(I)} x^{\min} + \sum_{x\in L(I)} x^{\max} + \sum_{x\in M(I)} v = n.\mu$ or more simply as $v^* = (n.\mu - ES(I))/m$ where $ES(I) = \sum_{x\in R(I)} x^{\min} + \sum_{x\in L(I)} x^{\max}$. The value v^* is admissible only if $v^* \in I$. This constraint is satisfied if $n.\mu \in V(I) = [ES(I) + \min(I).m, ES(I) + \max(I).m]$. For two consecutive intervals $I_k, I_{k+1} \in \mathcal{I}(X)$, intervals $V(I_k)$ and $V(I_{k+1})$ are also contiguous: $\min(V(I_{k+1})) = \max(V(I_k))$. As a consequence, for every consistent value μ, there exists one interval $I \in \mathcal{I}(X)$ such that $n.\mu \in V(I)$. The procedure to find $\underline{\pi}$ can be easily described and can be calculated in linear time given $\mathcal{I}(X)$ and the x_i sorted according to their bounds [PES 05].

1) Find $I \in \mathcal{I}(X)$ such that $n.\mu \in V(I)$. This interval is denoted I^{μ}.

2) Calculate $v = (n.\mu - ES(I^{\mu}))/m$.

3) The optimal solution is the v-centered assignment uniquely defined by v.

4.5.2. *Filtering of* X

Let $S_{\mu\pi}$ denote the set of tuples x satisfying the following constraints:

$$\sum_{i=1}^{n} x_i = n.\mu$$

$$\sum_{j=1}^{n} (x_j - \mu)^2 \leq \pi^{\max}$$

$$x_i^{\min} \leq x_i \leq x_i^{\max}, \quad \forall i \in [1, .., n]$$

The filtering on X is based on the optimal values $\overline{x}_i = \max\{x[i] \ : \ x \in S_{\mu\pi}\}$ and $\underline{x}_i = \min\{x[i] \ : \ x \in S_{\mu\pi}\}$. We find that $\overline{x}_i$ and $\underline{x}_i$ are symmetrical problems with respect to μ, thus only the former is considered here. The optimal value $\overline{x}_i$ can be found by shifting all the domain of x_i until the minimization of the sum of square deviations gives $\underline{\pi} = \pi^{\max}$. More formally, the maximization problem can be transformed into an equivalent problem by renaming $x_i = x_i^{\min} + d_i$. The objective of this equivalent problem is $\overline{d}_i = \max(d_i)$ with $0 \leq d_i \leq x_i^{\max} - x_i^{\min}$. The algorithm shown on Figure 4.3 calculates $\overline{d}_i$ in $\mathcal{O}(n)$.

The procedure starts from the optimal value $\underline{\pi}$. The problem of finding $\underline{\pi}$ is then modified by increasing all values from the domain of variable x_i by a non-negative value d_i. Let us denote the variable with modified domain by x_i', the

```
Algorithm: FindDMax(x_i, I^μ)
Data: x_i ∈ R(I^μ); I^μ ∈ 𝓘; n.μ ∈ V(I^μ);
Result: d̄_i such that π̲' = π^max with x' = x + d̄_i
if M(I^q) = φ then
  | return FindDMax(x_i, prev(I^μ))
end
Δ = n.μ − min(V(I^μ))
d̄*_i = (−b+√(b²−ac))/a          /* values a, b, c are defined in the text */
if d̄*_i ≤ Δ then
  | return d̄*_i
else
  | if I^μ = I_1 then
  |   | return Δ
  | else
  |   | return Δ+FindDMax(x_i + Δ, prev(I^μ))
  | end
end
```

Figure 4.3. *Algorithm to find $\overline{d}_i$ when $x_i \in R(I^\mu)$*

modified set of variables by X' and the corresponding quantities by $ES'(I^\mu)$ and $V'(I^\mu)$. For a variable $x_i \in R(I^\mu) \cup M(I^\mu)$, the new optimal value $\underline{\pi}'$ increases quadratically with d_i. The procedure of modifying the domain of x_i is repeated at most $\mathcal{O}(n)$ times until $\underline{\pi}' = \pi^{\max}$.

Let us assume first that $x_i \in R(I^\mu)$. After a shift of d_i, $ES'(I^\mu) = ES(I^\mu)+d_i$ and $V'(I^\mu) = V(I^\mu)+d_i$. If $d_i \leq \Delta = n.\mu - \min(V(I^\mu))$, the value v' of the v-centered assignment remains in I^μ but becomes $v' = v - d_i/m$. Consequently, the new optimal value becomes $\underline{\pi}' = \left(\sum_{x_j \in L(I^\mu)}(x_j^{\max})^2\right) + \left(\sum_{x_j \in R(I^\mu)}(x_j^{\min})^2\right) + d_i^2 + 2.d_i.x_i^{\min} + \left(\sum_{x_j \in M(I^\mu)}(v - \frac{d_j}{m})^2\right) - n.\mu^2 = \underline{\pi} + d_i^2 + 2.d_i.x_i^{\min} + m\left(\frac{d_i^2}{m^2} - 2\frac{d_i}{m}v\right)$. Recall that the problem is to find $\overline{d}_i$ such that $\underline{\pi}' = \pi^{\max}$. Hence, $\overline{d}_i^*$ is the positive solution of the second degree equation $a.d_i^2 + 2.b.d_i + c = 0$, where $a = (1 + \frac{1}{m})$, $b = x_i^{\min} - v$ and $c = \underline{\pi} - \pi^{\max}$. We have $\overline{d}_i = \overline{d}_i^*$ only if $\overline{d}_i^* \leq \Delta$ because otherwise the v-centered assignment does not remain in I^μ. If $\overline{d}_i^* > \Delta$ then x_i can be shifted by Δ so that the value of the v-centered assignment lies in $prev(I^\mu)$, and repeat the procedure on the new problem. The process stops when I_1 is reached or if $\overline{d}_i^* \leq \Delta$. Complete algorithm is shown on Figure 4.3 and runs in $\mathcal{O}(n)$ since there are at most $|\mathcal{I}(\mathcal{X})| < n$ recursive calls and that the body executes in constant time.

Finding $\overline{d}_i$ for $x_i \in M(I^\mu)$ reduces easily to the previous case. When x_i is increased by d_i, the optimal assignment does not change while $d_i \leq v - x_i^{\min}$. For $d_i = v - x_i^{\min}$ two new intervals are created replacing I^μ. These are $I_j = [\min(I^\mu), v]$ and $I_k = [v, \max(I^\mu)]$ with $n.\mu = \max(V'(I_j)) = \min(V'(I_k))$. For this new configuration, the optimal assignment is the same but now $n.\mu \in V'(I_j)$ and $x'_i \in R(I_j)$. Hence $\overline{d}_i = v - x_i^{\min} + FindDMax(x'_i, I_j)$ where $x'_i = x_i + v - x_i^{\min}$.

4.5.3. *Conclusion*

SPREAD is a balancing constraint for the criterion of sum of square deviations from the mean. Filtering algorithms associated with it have been proposed by [PES 05]. We have shown that simpler filtering algorithms with the same efficiency can be designed when the mean is fixed. We currently work on an implementation of SPREAD.

4.6. A new filtering algorithm for the graph isomorphism problem (by Sébastien Sorlin and Christine Solnon)

The graph isomorphism problem (GIP) consists of deciding if two given graphs $G = (V, E)$ and $G' = (V', E')$ have an identical structure, i.e., in finding a bijective function $f : V \rightarrow V'$ such that $(u, v) \in E \Leftrightarrow (f(u), f(v)) \in E'$. This problem may be modeled as a constraint satisfaction problem in a very straightforward way, so that one can use constraint programming to solve it. However, generic constraint solvers may be less efficient than dedicated algorithms which take advantage of the global semantic of the original problem to reduce the search space. Hence, we propose a new partial consistency for the GIP and an associated filtering algorithm. We experimentally show that this algorithm makes constraint programming competitive with dedicated algorithms for this problem.

4.6.1. *A global constraint for the graph isomorphism problem*

We have introduced in [SOR 04] the global constraint *gip* to define a GIP by a relation $gip(V, E, V', E', L)$ where:

– $G = (V, E)$ and $G' = (V', E')$ are two graphs,

– L is a set of couples which associates one different variable of the CSP to each different value of V.

Semantically, the global constraint $gip(V, E, V', E', L)$ is consistent if and only if there exists an isomorphism function $f : V \rightarrow V'$ between G and G' such that for each couple $(x_u, u) \in L$ there exists a value $u' \in D(x_u)$ so that $u' = f(u)$.

We have also defined in [SOR 04] a partial consistency, called label consistency, that strongly reduces the search space. However, achieving label-consistency implies the computation of the shortest path between every pair of vertices of the graphs and as a consequence, it is time expensive.

4.6.2. *ILL-consistency and ILL-filtering*

We now introduce another filtering algorithm for the *gip* constraint. The main idea is to label every vertex with respect to its neighbourhood. This labeling is "isomorphic-consistent", i.e. two vertices that may be associated by an isomorphism function necessarily have a same label, so that it can be used to narrow the domains of the variables: only vertices having the same label can be matched together. These labels are built iteratively: starting from an empty label, each label is extended by considering the labels of its adjacent vertices. This labeling extension is iterated until a fixed point is reached. This fixed point corresponds to a new partial consistency for the GIP. Our vertex labeling is similar to the refinement functions used to canonically label a graph with Nauty [MCK 81].

Definition. A *labeling function* is a function denoted by α that, given a graph $G = (V, E)$ and a vertex $v \in V$, returns a label $\alpha_G(v)$. A labeling function α is *isomorphic-consistent* if it always associates the same labels to vertices that can be matched in an isomorphism function.

For example, the labeling function that labels each vertex by its degree is isomorphic-consistent as isomorphism functions only match vertices that have a same number of adjacent vertices.

Definition. A labeling function α is *stronger* than another labeling function α' if it allows a stronger or equivalent narrowing, i.e., if $\forall(u, v) \in V^2, \alpha'_G(u) \neq \alpha'_G(v) \Rightarrow \alpha_G(u) \neq \alpha_G(v)$.

Definition. Given a graph $G = (V, E)$ and a labeling function α^i_G for G, we define the new labeling function $\alpha^{i+1}_G : V \rightarrow image(\alpha^i_G) \times \wp(N^* \times image(\alpha^i_G))$ as follows: $\forall v \in V, \alpha^{i+1}_G(v) = \alpha^i_G(v) \cdot \{(k, l), k = |\{u \in V, (v, u) \in E \wedge \alpha^i_G(u) = l \wedge k > 0\}|\}$.

Theorem 1. Given an isomorphic-consistent labeling function α^i, the labeling function α^{i+1} is also an isomorphic-consistent labeling function.

Theorem 2. Given a graph $G = (V, E)$ and a labeling function α^i, the function α^{i+1} is stronger than α^i.

A direct consequence of theorems 1 and 2 is that, when relabeling the vertices of two graphs G and G' with α^{i+1}, the domain of each variable x_v of the CSP corresponding to a GIP always has a size less than or equal to the domain of x_v when the vertices are only labeled by α^i.

The relabeling step can be iterated until a fixed point is reached, i.e., until the number of different labels is no longer increased. Starting from an initial isomorphic-consistent labeling α^0, we define a sequence α^1, α^2, ... of labeling functions such that each step k of this sequence corresponds to a relabeling of the vertices from the labels given at the step $k-1$. Theorem 1 and 2 states that each labeling function $\alpha^k + 1$ is isomorphic-consistent and stronger than the previous one α^k. We can then easily show that this sequence reaches a fixed point in at most $|V|$ steps.

Definition. The global constraint $gip(V, E, V', E', L)$ corresponding to a graph isomorphism problem between $G = (V, E)$ and $G' = (V', E')$ is iterated-local-label consistent (ILL-consistent) if, and only if: $\forall (x_u, u) \in L$, $\forall u' \in D(x_u), \forall k \in N, \alpha^k_G(u) = \alpha^k_{G'}(u')$ where α^0 is the labeling function that associates the same label $\emptyset$ to each vertex.

To make the *gip* constraint ILL-consistent, we just have to calculate the sequence α^1, α^2, ... of labeling functions for each graph G and G' until the fixed point α^{max} is reached and to filter the variable domains with the labeling function α^{max}.

At each step of the sequence, the vertex labels become larger and comparing such labels can be costly in time and in memory. However, these labels can be renamed after each relabeling step, provided that the same name is associated with identical labels in the two graphs. As a consequence, at the end of each relabeling step, labels are renamed with unique integers in order to keep the cost in memory and in time constant at each step of the sequence.

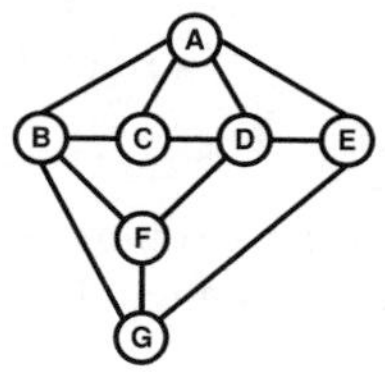

Figure 4.4. *A graph* $G = (V, E)$

In the worst case, achieving the ILL-consistency can be done in $\mathcal{O}(|V| \times |E|)$ for each graph $G = (V, E)$, the same as for filtering based on labels [SOR 04].

However, the average complexity of establishing label-consistency is much more expensive than establishing ILL-consistency.

Complete example. We propose here a complete example of our relabeling procedure on the graph G of Figure 4.4. At each step i of the sequence, the vertices are renamed by labels $l_{i,j}$. For reasons of space, we shall write $\alpha_G^k(S)$ when $\forall(u,v) \in S^2, \alpha_G^k(u) = \alpha_G^k(v)$.

At step 0, the vertex labels are all initialized to $\emptyset$: $\alpha_G^0(\{A,B,C,D,E,F,G\}) = \emptyset$

At step 1 and 2:

$$
\begin{array}{lcrcl}
\alpha_G^1(\{A,B,D\}) & = & \emptyset.\{(4,\emptyset)\} & \Rightarrow & l_{1,1} \\
\alpha_G^1(\{C,E,F,G\}) & = & \emptyset.\{(3,\emptyset)\} & \Rightarrow & l_{1,2} \\
\\
\alpha_G^2(A) & = & l_{1,1}.\{(2,l_{1,1}),(2,l_{1,2})\} & \Rightarrow & l_{2,1} \\
\alpha_G^2(\{B,D\}) & = & l_{1,1}.\{(1,l_{1,1}),(3,l_{1,2})\} & \Rightarrow & l_{2,2} \\
\alpha_G^2(C) & = & l_{1,2}.\{(3,l_{1,1})\} & \Rightarrow & l_{2,3} \\
\alpha_G^2(\{E,F\}) & = & l_{1,2}.\{(1,l_{1,2}),(2,l_{1,1})\} & \Rightarrow & l_{2,4} \\
\alpha_G^2(G) & = & l_{1,2}.\{(1,l_{1,1}),(2,l_{1,2})\} & \Rightarrow & l_{2,5}
\end{array}
$$

We note that, at step 2, three vertices (A, C and G) have unique labels. As a consequence, we do not need to relabel these vertices during the next steps. The vertex A (resp. C and G) keeps the label $l_{2,1}$ (resp. $l_{2,3}$ and $l_{2,5}$).

$$
\begin{array}{lcrcl}
\alpha_G^3(B) & = & l_{2,2}.\{(1,l_{2,1}),(1,l_{2,3}),(1,l_{2,4}),(1,l_{2,5})\} & \Rightarrow & l_{3,1} \\
\alpha_G^3(D) & = & l_{2,2}.\{(1,l_{2,1}),(1,l_{2,3}),(2,l_{2,4})\} & \Rightarrow & l_{3,2} \\
\alpha_G^3(E) & = & l_{2,4}.\{(1,l_{2,1}),(1,l_{2,2}),(1,l_{2,5})\} & \Rightarrow & l_{3,3} \\
\alpha_G^3(F) & = & l_{2,4}.\{(1,l_{2,5}),(2,l_{2,2})\} & \Rightarrow & l_{3,4}
\end{array}
$$

From step 3, all the vertices have different labels. As a consequence, any GIP involving the graph G of Figure 4.4 will be solved by our filtering technique.

4.6.3. *Experimental results*

In order to evaluate the ability of ILL-consistency to find a perfect labeling of the graph vertices (i.e., such that all vertices have a unique label), we have considered randomly generated non-automorphic graphs having between 200 and 10,000 vertices and three different edge densities: 1%, 5% and 10%. Except for very few instances (less than 1%) having less than 400 vertices and a low density, both label-consistency [SOR 04] and ILL-consistency are able to give a unique label to each vertex and, as a consequence, always solve the problem.

We have also compared CPU times spent in solving GIP by using ILL-filtering and Nauty [MCK 81]. We have performed experiments on graphs with different edge densities (ranging from 1% to 50%) and different sizes (ranging from 1, 000 to 10, 000 vertices). These experiments showed us that ILL-filtering and Nauty exhibit the same scale-up properties, but Nauty is generally 3 times as fast as ILL-consistency. The same experiments on label-consistency show that label-consistency is an order of magnitude more expensive than ILL-consistency.

4.7. References

[BAR 04] BARTÁK R., ERBEN R., "A New Algorithm for Singleton Arc Consistency", *Proceedings of FLAIRS'04*, p. 257–262, 2004.

[BAR 06] BARTÁK R., ČEPEK O., "Incremental Filtering Algorithms for Precedence and Dependency Constraints", *Proceedings of ICTAI'06*, p. 416–423, 2006.

[BES 05a] BESSIERE C., DEBRUYNE R., "Optimal and Suboptimal Singleton Arc Consistency Algorithms", *Proceedings of IJCAI'05*, p. 54-59, 2005.

[BES 05b] BESSIERE C., RÉGIN J., YAP R., ZHANG Y., "An optimal coarse-grained arc consistency algorithm", *Artificial Intelligence*, vol. 165, num. 2, p. 165-185, 2005.

[DEB 97] DEBRUYNE R., BESSIÈRE C., "Some practical filtering techniques for the constraint satisfaction problem", *Proccedings of IJCAI'97*, p. 412–417, 1997.

[FAG 01] FAGES F., "CLP versus LS on log-based reconciliation problems for nomadic applications", *Proceedings of ERCIM/CompulogNet Workshop on Constraints*, Praha, 2001.

[HNI 02] HNICH B., KIZILTAN Z., WALSH T., "Modelling a Balanced Academic Curriculum Problem", *Proceedings of CP-AI-OR'02*, 2002.

[LEC 03] LECOUTRE C., BOUSSEMART F., HEMERY F., "Exploiting multidirectionality in coarse-grained arc consistency algorithms", *Proceedings of CP'03*, p. 480–494, 2003.

[LEC 05] LECOUTRE C., CARDON S., "A greedy approach to establish Singleton Arc Consistency", *Proceedings of IJCAI'05*, p. 199-204, 2005.

[LEC 07] LECOUTRE C., HEMERY F., "A study of residual supports in Arc Consistency", *Proceedings of IJCAI'07*, 2007.

[LIK 04] LIKITVIVATANAVONG C., ZHANG Y., BOWEN J., FREUDER E., "Arc Consistency in MAC: a new perspective", *Proceedings of CPAI'04*, p. 93-107, 2004.

[MAC 77] MACKWORTH A., "Consistency in Networks of Relations", *Artificial Intelligence*, vol. 8, p. 99–118, Elsevier Science Publishers B.V., 1977.

[MCK 81] MCKAY B., "Practical graph isomorphism", *Congressus Numerantium*, 1981.

[MEH 05] MEHTA D., VAN DONGEN M., "Maintaining Probabilistic Arc Consistency", *Proceedings of CPAI'05*, p. 49–64, 2005.

[MEH 07] MEHTA D., VAN DONGEN M., "Probabilistic Consistency Boosts: MAC and SAC", *Proceedings of IJCAI'07*, 2007.

[NUI 03] NUIJTEN W., BOUSONVILLE T., FOCACCI F., GODARD D., LE PAPE C., "MaScLib: Problem description and test bed design", 2003.

[PES 05] PESANT G., RÉGIN J., "SPREAD: A Balancing Constraint Based on Statistics", *Lecture Notes in Computer Science*, vol. 3709, p. 460-474, 2005.

[PRO 00] PROSSER P., STERGIOU K., WALSH T., "Singleton Consistencies", *Proceedings of CP'00*, p. 353-368, 2000.

[SOR 04] SORLIN S., SOLNON C., "A global constraint for graph isomorphism problems", *Proceedings of CP-AI-OR'04*, p. 287–301, 2004.

Chapter 5

On the First SAT/CP Integration Workshop

SAT and CP techniques are two problem solving technologies which share many similarities, and there is considerable interest in cross-fertilizing these two areas. The techniques used in SAT (propagation, activity-based heuristics, conflict analysis, restarts, etc.) constitute a very successful combination which makes modern DPLL solvers robust enough to solve large real-life instances without the heavy tuning usually required by CP tools. Whether such techniques can help the CP community develop more robust and easier-to-use tools is an exciting question. One limitation of SAT, on the other hand, is that not all problems are effectively expressed in a Boolean format. This makes CP an appealing candidate for many applications, like software verification, where SAT is traditionally used but more expressive types of constraints would be more natural.

The goal of the CP'2006 first workshop on SAT and CP integration was to boost the discussions between the SAT and CP communities by encouraging submissions at the border of these two areas [HAM 06]. This chapter gives a high level overview of the event with a special focus on the questions addressed to the participants during the panel session.

In the following, section 5.1 gives an overview of the technical program. Section 5.2 summarizes the discussion of the panel and section 5.3 gives a general conclusion along expected directions for the SAT and CP thematic.

Chapter written by Youssef HAMADI and Lucas BORDEAUX.

5.1. The technical program

The day event started with one invited talk followed by eight 25 minute technical presentations. Robert Nieuwenhuis, the invited speaker presented SMT as a possible connection between SAT and CP. The morning session presented works related to pseudo-Boolean, interval constraints, interpolant-based decision procedure and local search. The afternoon session, presented works related to CSP and CP. This section quotes the summaries of each presentation. The full papers can be accessed in [HAM 06].

5.1.1. *The invited talk*

R. Nieuwenhuis, SAT Modulo Theories: A Possible Connection between SAT and CP

First we give an overview of SAT Modulo Theories (SMT) and its current state of the art. For this, we use our framework of Abstract DPLL and Abstract DPLL modulo Theories, which enables practical SMT algorithms to be expressed easily and enables us to formally reason about them. After this, we explain our DPLL(T) approach to SMT, a modular architecture for building SMT systems that has now been adopted in several state-of-the-art SMT tools. Experimental results and applications are given within the Barcelogic SMT system. In particular, we discuss its use for CP (including optimization) problems, thus going beyond the typical hard/software verification SMT applications.

5.1.2. *Contributions related to SMT and solver integration*

Shuvendu K. Lahiri and Krishna K. Mehra, Interpolant-based Decision Procedure for Quantifier-Free Presburger Arithmetic

Recently, off-the-shelf Boolean SAT solvers have been used to construct ground decision procedures for various theories, including Quantifier-Free Presburger (QFP) arithmetic. One such approach (often called the eager approach) is based on a satisfiability-preserving translation to a Boolean formula. Eager approaches are usually based on encoding integers as bit-vectors and suffer from the loss of structure and sometimes very large size for the bit-vectors. In this section, we present a decision procedure for QFP that is based on alternately under and over-approximating a formula, where Boolean interpolants are used to calculate the over-approximation. The novelty of the approach lies in using information from each phase (either under-approximation or over-approximation) to improve the other phase. Our preliminary experiments indicate that the algorithm consistently outperforms approaches based on eager and very lazy methods on a set of verification benchmarks.

Belaid Benhamou, Lionel Paris, and Pierre Siegel, Dealing with SAT and CSPs in a Single Framework

We investigate in this work a generalization of the known CNF representation which allows an efficient Boolean encoding for n-ary CSPs. We show that the space complexity of the Boolean encoding is identical to the one of the classical CSP representation and introduce a new inference rule whose application until saturation achieves arc-consistency in a linear time complexity for n-ary CSPs expressed in the Boolean encoding. Two enumerative methods for the Boolean encoding are studied: the first one (equivalent to MAC in CSPs) maintains full arc-consistency on each node of the search tree while the second (equivalent to FC in CSPs) performs partial arc-consistency on each node. Both methods are experimented and compared on some instances of the Ramsey problem and randomly generated 3/4-ary CSPs and promising results are obtained.

Martin Franzle, Christian Herde, Stefan Ratschan, Tobias Schubert, and Tino Teige, Interval Constraint Solving using Propositional SAT Solving Techniques

In order to facilitate automated reasoning about large Boolean combinations of non-linear arithmetic constraints involving transcendental functions, we extend the paradigm of lazy theorem proving to interval-based arithmetic constraint solving. Algorithmically, our approach deviates substantially from *classical* lazy theorem proving approaches in that it directly controls arithmetic constraint propagation from the SAT solver rather than completely delegating arithmetic decisions to a subordinate solver. From the constraint-solving perspective, it extends interval-based constraint solving with all the algorithmic enhancements that were instrumental to the enormous performance gains recently achieved in propositional SAT solving, such as conflict-driven learning combined with non-chronological backtracking.

5.1.3. *Contributions related to the use of SAT techniques to improve CSP/CP solvers*

Christophe Lecoutre, Lakhdar Sais and Julien Vion, Using SAT Encodings to Derive CSP Value Ordering Heuristics

In this section, we address the issue of value ordering heuristics in the context of a backtracking search algorithm that exploits binary branching and the adaptive variable ordering heuristic dom/wdeg. Our initial experimentation on random instances shows that (in this context), contrary to general belief, following the fail-first policy instead of the promise policy is not really penalizing. Furthermore, using SAT encodings of CSP instances, a new value ordering heuristic related to the fail-first policy can be naturally derived from the well-known Jeroslow-Wang heuristic. This heuristic, called min-inverse, exploits the bi-directionality of constraint supports to give a more comprehensive picture in terms of domain reduction when a given value is assigned to (resp. removed from) a given variable. An extensive experimentation on a wide range of CSP instances shows that min-inverse can outperform the other known value ordering heuristics.

Christophe Lecoutre, Lakhdar Sais, Sebastien Tabary, and Vincent Vidal, Nogood Recording from Restarts

In this section, nogood recording is investigated for CSP within the randomization and restart framework. Our goal is to avoid the same situations occurring from one run to the next one. More precisely, nogoods are recorded when the current cutoff value is reached, i.e. before restarting the search algorithm. A set of nogoods such as this is extracted from the last branch of the current search tree and managed using the structure of watched literals originally proposed for SAT. Interestingly, the number of nogoods recorded before each new run is bounded by the length of the last branch of the search tree. As a consequence, the total number of recorded nogoods is polynomial in the number of restarts. Experiments over a wide range of CSP instances demonstrate the effectiveness of this approach.

Guillaume Richaud, Hadrien Cambazard, Barry O'Sullivan, and Narendra Jussien, Automata for Nogood Recording in Constraint Satisfaction Problems

Nogood recording is a well-known technique for reducing the thrashing encountered by tree search algorithms. One of the most significant disadvantages of nogood recording has been its prohibitive space complexity. In this section we attempt to mitigate this by using an automaton to compactly represent a set of nogoods. We demonstrate how nogoods can be propagated using a known algorithm for achieving generalized arc consistency. Our experimental results on a number of benchmark problems demonstrate the utility of our approach.

5.1.4. *Other contributions*

Colin Quirke and Steve Prestwich, Constraint-Based Sub-search in Dynamic Local Search for Lifted SAT Problems

Many very large SAT problems can be more naturally expressed by quantification over variables, or *lifting*. We explore implementation, heuristic and modeling issues in the use of local search on lifted SAT models. Firstly, adapting existing local search algorithms to lifted models creates overheads that limit the practicality of lifting, and we design a new form of dynamic local search for lifted models. Secondly, finding a violated clause in a lifted model is an NP-complete problem called *subsearch*, and we show that subsearch benefits from advanced constraint techniques. Thirdly, lifting provides the opportunity for using SAT models that would normally be ignored because of their poor space complexities, and we use alternative SAT-encodings of a constraint problem to show that such lifted models can give superior results.

Jan-Georg Smaus, Representing Boolean Functions as Linear Pseudo Boolean Constraints

A linear pseudo-Boolean constraint (LPB) is an expression of the form $a_1 l_1 + ... + a_m l_m >= d$, where each l_i is a literal (it assumes the value 1 or 0 depending on whether a propositional variable xi is true or false) and the $a_1, ..., a_m$, d are natural numbers. The formalism can be viewed as a generalization of a propositional clause. It has been said that LPBs can be used to represent Boolean functions more compactly than the well-known conjunctive or disjunctive normal forms. In this section, we address the question: how much more compactly? We compare the expressiveness of a single LPB to that of related formalisms, and we give a statement that outlines how the problem of computing an LPB representation of a given CNF or DNF might be solved recursively. However, there is currently still a missing link for this to be a full algorithm.

5.2. The panel session

In an attempt to have a lively and controversial discussion, a list of questions, sometimes provocative, was addressed to the workshop participants. We present here for each question the starting viewpoints taken by the workshop organizers along with a summary of the standpoints taken by the most active participants. Each standpoint comes with the name of these participants who were asked to redevelop their own ideas in a short paragraph.

5.2.1. *Are SAT and CP different or similar?*

In order to support this interrogation, two different views were offered to the participants.

– The first view was taken by a reviewer commenting on [BOR 06]:

> *The two approaches could not be more different. SAT is a black-box using a minimal language; CP is a white-box with rich search and constraint languages. Both have advantages and drawbacks.*

– The second view came from a colleague commenting on the SAT/CP workshop:

I think the frontier between SAT/CSP/ILP (and Max-SAT/Max-CSP) is becoming increasingly loose and permeable[1].

[**M. Leconte**] CP contains SAT as it is easy to express a SAT problem for a CP Solver. In CP, we could implement a global constraint handling SAT problems the very same way SAT Solvers perform unit-propagation. The issue is then to let inferences from this SAT constraint benefit other constraints. The DPLL(T) architecture of SMT (Sat Modulo Theory) can be seen as an extension of the CLP(X) schema but, as far as CP finite domain solvers are concerned, constraints communicate only via their domains seen as a set of possible values. This is called non-relational domain in the Abstract Interpretation field and one can wonder whether such communication channels would be enough for effective cooperation between the global SAT constraint and the usual CP ones. This makes SAT and CP very different as SAT uses clauses to record nogoods whereas finite domain CP is restricted to removing possible values for variables.

[**J. Marques-Silva**] SAT and CP differ extensively. CP provides rich modeling features, SAT does not. SAT algorithms can be extremely simple, CP algorithms cannot. CP has a number of strategic application areas, whereas SAT has other, mostly orthogonal, strategic application areas. It does not seem possible for SAT to easily replace CP in applications where CP has shown results. Similarly, CP is unlikely to replace SAT in the most well-known applications of SAT.

[**P. Stuckey**] SAT and CP are in my opinion very similar. Both have interest in complete and local search methods for tackling their problems. I'll concentrate on complete methods. In these terms search DPLL SAT is almost an instance of CP, unit propagation is one particular choice of propagators, and a particular type of search (selecting a literal to enforce). The perceived difference arises from the convergence of complete SAT solvers to a common set of particular techniques: restarts, nogoods and activity based search heuristics. All of these have been explored in the CP community, but since the problem space is broader, it it is less easy to see it converging to a single *best* solution. CP will converge with SAT by reinvestigating the SAT techniques that have been successful. The other lesson CP takes from SAT, is the importance of standard input language, a problem the CP community clearly admits, and the resulting engineering achievements that can be made once a standard is available. SAT is converging toward CP as well. Higher level modeling is clearly important to both communities and SMT drives SAT to effectively a form of global constraints. The more eager the communication between DPLL and theory T, the more it becomes analogous with propagation. The difference is

1. D. Le Berre, personal communication.

the concentration on learning. I am confident that with better understanding of complete approaches CP and SAT we will end in a single algorithmic toolbox for both classes.

[R. Yap] CP has more issues than SAT. For SAT, usually the modeling is not an important component, one assumes one already has an SAT model, i.e. in CNF form. In CP, the model itself might be the issue. The development of global constraints is driven by such modeling questions since global constraints are usually for specific kinds of uses.

5.2.2. *Why has SAT succeeded in reducing the tuning issue?*

Two possible answers were proposed:

– SAT researchers have just tried harder: whereas ease of use was never a fundamental concern in the design of CP tools, the SAT community has from the very beginning aimed at finding a universal SAT algorithm integrating many techniques in a transparent way (activity-based heuristics, restarts, learning, etc.); furthermore, by using large sets of real-life instances, the SAT community was very effective at evaluating and comparing the robustness of the algorithms;

– SAT researchers have *cheated*: the claim that SAT solvers are universal reasoning tools is over-stated, because they focus on particular classes of applications (essentially verification and transition systems), and their instances have a very specific structure (low tree-width; unsatisfiable instances have a small core, *etc.*).

[M. Leconte] Since SAT models are at a lower level than the CP ones, it is more difficult for the user to indicate an efficient search strategy to an SAT solver than a CP solver. This is because the variables of the original problem are generally not directly represented in the SAT formalism whereas they correspond to decision variables in CP. In a sense, this makes a specific search strategy much harder to express on a SAT model than on a CP model. This shows that generic solving is crucial for SAT solvers; this is a reason for the focus and the success of the SAT community in reducing the tuning issue. Note that the same story happened in the MIP community: modern MIP solvers are efficient enough to be used without specific tuning. We can hope for and believe that CP will follow this path.

[J. Marques-Silva] SAT solvers are solving a much simpler problem. This makes SAT solvers much easier to tune. The availability of representative problem instances contributed decisively to the development of optimized SAT solvers. I do not think SAT researchers have *cheated*! The performance results of modern SAT solvers are indeed impressive, but this is for problem instances from concrete application domains (e.g. model checking, etc.). In a good number of application areas SAT is not effective, and this is known.

[R. Nieuwenhuis] SAT researchers have not cheated. The restricted formalism of SAT has made it possible, after a lot of research, to come up with several key ideas:

a) good general-purpose heuristics based on literal activity. I see this as locally working from one constraint *cluster* at a time (extracting the right lemmas from it);

b) the right conflict analysis mechanism (called *1UIP*), that allows us to backjump and at the same time provides the lemmas (nogoods in the form of new clauses) that work well with the heuristic; cheap enough ways of generating smaller – and hence in principle stronger – lemmas are known, but tend to perform worse;

c) refined data structures for unit propagation (two-watched literals), clause representation, and bookkeeping for the heuristics.

For most real-world problems admitting a reasonable-sized reduction to SAT, this black-box setting works impressively well, and most attempts at problem-specific tuning only worsen the performance. This is also the case for problems from new application domains that keep coming up.

I believe that CP's generality and diversity makes it difficult to achieve something similar. Another disadvantage for CP is the fact that the community has been – and still is – being mislead by artificial problems. Even nowadays most CSP solver competition problems are artificial or are translations from artificial problems. SAT experts know very well that random or handcrafted SAT is completely different from real-world SAT. For example, in random SAT lemma learning is useless and the heuristics are completely different.

[B. O'Sullivan] The advantage of SAT is that it is based on a standard simple input language. The solvers tend to be regarded as black-boxes that can be tuned. This has provided a common basis for specifying industrial benchmarks in a standard way. Therefore, the solvers tend not to focus on modeling and reformulation concerns, but on how to tune the solver to best solve the instance. Researchers are therefore provided with an opportunity to focus on developing good solvers and not on developing a complex input language which has been challenging for CP. Of course, there are advantages with having a complex input language. Specifically, in CP we can be true to the actual structure of the problem and formulate a model that is more natural for humans to interpret and debug.

[T. Walsh] SAT is such a simple language. We typically only consider sets of clauses. The problem is coming up with an encoding into SAT that works well. Once we have a set of clauses, the language is very flat and uniform. The SAT competitions have also allowed us to come up with good uniform parameter settings, default heuristics, etc. This contrasts with CSP where we have a very rich language and tuning is correspondingly more difficult. In addition, CP has not had a long running competition so default heuristics are still relatively primitive (e.g. fail first, domain/degree).

5.2.3. *How long can the current generation of SAT solvers evolve?*

This question was illustrated by a recent statement from an SAT colleague:

> *I think that we found the right combinations of components for successful SAT solvers*[2].

It is also interesting to note for instance that, among the 37 papers presented in the technical tracks of the SAT 2006 symposium [BIE 06], very few presented direct improvements of the state-of-the-art DPLL architecture. The topics this year were: *proofs and cores*, *heuristics and algorithms*, *applications*, *Satisfiability Modulo Theories*, *structure*, *Max-SAT*, *local search and survey propagation*, *Quantified Boolean Formulas* and *counting and concurrency*. The *heuristics and algorithms* session included 4 papers, some related to resolution-based solvers or non-clausal formulas, and essentially *one single* paper proposed improvements to a central component of the standard DPLL solvers, namely the *restarts* aspect.

There are signs that DPLL with the standard combination (propagation based on 2-watched literals, conflict analysis based on variants of 1-UIP, activity-based heuristics and restarts) are the last word on complete, search-based SAT solvers. On the one hand this would be a considerable achievement; on the other hand this is a worrying sign of stagnation. Stagnation which may come from the propinquity effect generated by yearly SAT-competitions.

The question is therefore whether this situation is temporary, and new techniques will be found, or whether one can predict that the performance of SAT solvers will essentially remain stable during the next years.

[I. Gent] In 1993, I sat on a panel at a DIMACS workshop. I remember saying that I had been impressed how much SAT solvers had improved just in the last year or two, and I thought that might continue and so enable us

2. K. Sakallah, personal communication.

to solve much larger instances. I got the impression that few agreed with me, based on the obvious argument of the combinatorial explosion. In one sense I was wrong, since I was mainly thinking of Random 3-SAT instances, and for now the record is only at about 700 variables for a complete solver. However, I was right in the bigger picture, as SAT solvers have become technologically marvelous.

This is a long winded way of saying *maybe*. First of all, something surprising might come along and revolutionize the way we build SAT solvers. I think there was a slight feeling of stagnation before Chaff revolutionized SAT solvers around 2000, so some advance of that scale would get the field going again. Another answer is that the scale of effort needed may be increasing, which is a good thing and a bad thing. It is a good thing if the field is mature with well-known techniques which can be built on by a large team, and researchers should continue to go after the difficult big wins after the easy big wins have been achieved. On the other hand, it is a bad thing if researchers with good ideas have no chance of competing with the top teams.

I think it is a common experience amongst communities with competitions that they can lead to diminishing returns over a few years. It may be necessary to think of ways of avoiding this, for example running competitions on instances which current SAT solvers are bad at, to encourage experimentation. The problem with this is obviously that of getting successful entries!

[**M. Leconte**] Let us look at MIP solvers. Their expressive power is only between SAT and CP. As black-boxes, their efficiency is also only between these two. It took quite a long time for the MIP community to recognize the value of presolving. The common belief was that presolving techniques were useful only on bad models, and globally useless. As long as the efficiency of MIP solvers improved, the solved models became bigger and presolve gained more and more impact. Nowadays, all modern MIP solvers have a presolve phase. This is mainly what SAT solvers are missing compared to MIP solvers. Presolving could be the next subject to be (re)investigated.

[**J. Marques-Silva**] Recent years have not seen a dramatic improvement in SAT solvers. This suggests that improvements to the current organization of conflict-driven clause learning SAT solvers will become difficult to identify and justify. There is always the possibility of another paradigm shift in SAT solver technology, but performance data from the past couple of years suggests that the performance of SAT solvers is not improving significantly.

[**R. Nieuwenhuis**] I believe that there is still room for improvement, especially for finding models, i.e., for satisfiable problems. This is closely related to the issue of restarts, which appear to be not completely understood. There is of course also a lot of work to be done in extensions, such as Max-SAT and other optimization problems, all-SAT, proof generation, unsatisfiable cores, or, of course, SAT modulo theories.

5.2.4. *Were performance issues correctly addressed by CP?*

The CSP/CP community addressed performance issues by pushing on the inference side and by completely avoiding intelligent look-back techniques or nogood-recording strategies. The heavy commitment to global constraints is part of this quest for more inference, sometimes only possible when a whole sub-problem is analyzed at once by a specific method.

A legitimate question is whether this focus on propagation, was justified: is it the case that conflict analysis, activity-based heuristics and other techniques that are so useful in SAT simply do not pay for CP? Or has the CP community neglected these techniques because the standards it followed for evaluating algorithms was different (and admittedly *poorer*) from the ones used in SAT?

[C. Bessiere] Conventional wisdom on conflict-directed techniques differs in SAT and CP essentially because of the inherent differences in the encoding of problems and in the characteristics of standard solvers.

Let us recall that an encoding (or model) for a problem is a SAT formula or a constraint network that makes a number of nogoods explicit via its clauses or constraints. These explicit nogoods subsume many other nogoods that are implicit. Implicit nogoods can cause thrashing if they are not detected early by the search procedure. Inference (or constraint propagation) and conflict-directed techniques are two orthogonal methods of trying to avoid thrashing. Inference uses explicit nogoods to detect implicit ones *before* committing to inconsistent subspaces. Conflict-directed techniques use information contained in a dead-end to extract a culprit nogood and to use it to discard future subspaces inconsistent because of this nogood. SAT and CP solvers all use some form of inference. The standard level of inference, called unit propagation in SAT and arc consistency in CP, is to remove a value v for variable X (unary nogood) only if there exists a clause/constraint c for which all valid assignments of the variables of c containing v for X are forbidden by c. Now, a SAT clause represents a single nogood whereas a CP constraint is a compilation of several nogoods. As a result, in most cases, standard inference prunes more inconsistencies in CP than in SAT. Since conflict-directed techniques are useful only if inference has missed a nogood, there are more chances that they improve a DPLL-like search procedure in SAT than an arc consistency-based backtracking in CP. This can explain in part the discrepancy between the respective conventional wisdom in SAT and CP about conflict-directed techniques. Furthermore, in CP, if we increase the number of nogoods considered jointly during propagation (by propagating more than arc consistency or by using global constraints), we increase the amount of implicit nogoods found by CP solvers. The CP community observed that the more we increase the level of propagation during search, the smaller the number of problems on which conflict-directed techniques pay off [BES 96, CHE 01]. However, it was shown in [JUS 00] that we can build instances of problems on which standard arc consistency always thrashes whereas adding some form of backjumping allows a smooth solving.

There are other characteristics of SAT solvers that can explain the success of conflict-directed techniques such as nogood learning. Recent SAT solvers use the *restart* technique. Restart has been shown to combine extremely well with nogood learning. The fact that nogood learning can greatly pay off when maintained over several searches was observed in dynamic constraint problems, where the problem is repeatedly solved after small changes in the constraints [SCH 93]. However, it has not been applied to standard CP solvers. One reason for this is perhaps that non-unary nogoods are much easier to handle in SAT than in CP. A nogood is extremely easy to express as a clause to be used by a SAT solver. On the contrary, non-unary nogoods are not constraint objects that can easily be handled by the current generation of CP solvers.

[I. Gent] There is certainly a lot of research on backjumping and learning in CP. However, there is one important reason it has not yet taken off in practical solvers. Whenever a constraint propagates in a backjumping system, it is required to provide a conflict set responsible for the propagation. In SAT, this is trivial: when a unit clause is created the conflict set is the other literals in the original version of that clause. In CP, propagators can be very complicated and (even worse) the global nature of some makes it hard to construct a useful conflict set, i.e. of a size much less than the number of variables being searched on. This does not mean that backjumping and learning is doomed, but making it pay off in practice is hard.

I agree that the CP community has very low standards in benchmarking, and I have been guilty of this as many others have. I do not agree that the standard in SAT is necessarily better. SAT does have advantages of a standard input format and a large number of instances in that format, but this still allows for poor experiments poorly done, just as CP practitioners can perform good experiments very well.

It is true that it has been perceived to be hard to construct an outstanding constraint solver, and this has inhibited the number of world-class solvers constructed by research teams. In fact this perception is false, as we recently showed with the Minion constraint solver, the first version of which (almost all by Chris Jefferson) was the result of only a few man-months of work. A major lesson we have learned is that people can build high-performance solvers just as we did, and we would encourage people to do so if it would help them incorporate novel techniques and prove their worth. If they don't want to spend the time building their own solver, they can add code to one of the other open source solvers: not just Minion but also Gecode, Choco or Eclipse.

[**M. Leconte**] In the early days, performance issues of *automatic* systems such as Alice from J-L. Laurière in 1978 were addressed by *opening the box*. Ten years later, the *white-box* approach or *control on search*, was first highlighted by the CHIP system from ECRC. Still for efficiency reasons, to let users implement global constraints, the glass-box approach or *implementing your own constraints* was introduced by ILOG in 1995. These answers effectively bring efficiency to CP systems but at the cost of user-specified control. Use of CP systems became more and more difficult as well as time-consuming. ILOG have been working on the ease of use of our CP solver for a few years. The next ILOG CP solver (due out in 2007) provides an efficient default search strategy generic enough to remove (or reduce) the need for specific tuning. We have been trying to repeat the MIP solvers' story which also succeeded in reducing the tuning issue while maintaining good performances. The next step, as in MIP, would be to incorporate presolving techniques such as model reformulations or simplifications.

[**J. Marques-Silva**] In the early 1990s the evaluation of CP solvers was not convincing, with some emphasis on randomly generated problem instances. This may in part justify the emphasis on propagation/inference observed in CP. I believe things have changed over the last few years. The CP competition is a good example, and has been important for motivating the development of better CP tools. In contrast, from the mid 1990s the development of SAT solvers was motivated by concrete applications (e.g. test pattern generation, circuit delay computation, hardware model checking, software testing and model checking, etc.). This enabled the selection of the best techniques for solving these concrete problems.

[**P. Stuckey**] I suspect performance issues have always been of interest to the CP community, but a CP solving engine (here I mean for complete search) is a large software undertaking. A competitive SAT solver may be less than a thousand lines of code. Hence SAT performance is an easier thing to investigate, by an order of magnitude. A standard language for specifying CP problems is obviously missing, but this won't fundamentally change the problem that investigating design choices for performance in CP will always be much harder work than in SAT. The focus on propagation has been justified I think, by large industrial CP/MIP solutions, where while the MIP solver is doing the majority of the solving, the propagation of CP is key to modeling and solving some parts of the problem. Many of these industrial solutions do not have large search trees, but involve substantial work at each node, so conflict analysis and other techniques have less of a role to play.

[**T. Walsh**] CP researchers have not agreed on a common input language format (unlike SAT where everyone accepts DIMACS). Therefore comparing different solvers is difficult. This must be fixed in the near future if CP is to progress rapidly.

CP has also neglected issues like nogoods, learning and non-chronological backtracking. This is partly technological. The older solvers around today were engineered before we had understood these methods and it would be difficult to re-engineer them with nogoods. However, it is also because the research community was misled by looking at random problems. With random problems, techniques like nogood learning are of limited value. The SAT community missed out this trap as nogoods are clearly of great value in domains like hardware verification.

[**R. Yap**] The CP community has not addressed the performance issues as seriously as in SAT. This is related to question 1. We do not even have agreement on common benchmarks, different solvers support different constraints, etc. Thus, it is less clear how to even carry out proper benchmarking.

5.2.5. *Was CP too ambitious?*

Modern CP toolkits come from a long tradition of *General Problem Solving*, a quest that was pursued from the early days of AI (see e.g., [NEW 60]). It is worth remembering that all attempts at general problem solving failed, because they were too ambitious.

Constraint programming's response to the apparent impossibility of building a completely general and automatic general problem solver was to open the solver and to let the user have some control: with this *glass-box* approach, CP allows the user to tailor the system to their application space – generality is preserved, but not the full automation. The approach of the SAT community was different: by focusing on a restricted language and on a restricted class of applications for which this language is a natural fit, SAT solvers follow the dream of being fully automated, but abandon the dream of being fully general.

The question is therefore whether there is a way to reconcile these apparently orthogonal approaches, whether some of the original ambition of CP should be given-up, whether the dream of general problem solving is still worth pursuing, and, if so, whether CP or SAT is the best candidate.

[C. Bessiere] The best candidate for a general problem solver is neither SAT nor CP, it is AI.

This is true that all the attempts at a general problem solver have failed in the past. SAT has a limited expressiveness but thanks to its simplicity, it is good at automatically adapting the model to improve the search. Thanks to its very high expressiveness CP allows representations very close to the nature of the problem, but the rigid separation between modeling and solving forces the user to go back and forth from modeling to solving to improve their model. The positive side is that these strengths and weaknesses are now quite well understood in both communities. There has been some work in SAT to integrate into the model some of the lost structure of the problem [KAS 90, KAU 99, GEN 02]. In CP, there were preliminary attempts at adapting the solver to the instance to be solved [LOB 98, EPS 01]. If the general problem solver exists, it will need help from other AI fields. Case-based reasoning, machine learning, or knowledge compilation can certainly be used to draw lessons from previously solved instances, for self-adaptivity of the solver to the instance, or for model reformulation.

[J. Marques-Silva] Generality often comes at a price. Work on SAT has always been quite focused. In contrast, the CP quest for general problem solving may have come at a cost. Nevertheless, I do not think that SAT will ever be a strong candidate for general problem solving. In contrast, SMT solvers are much more general than SAT solvers, and may well successfully challenge CP in the near future.

5.2.6. *Do we still need CP?*

With this provocative question we wanted to stress the fact that several important research fields consider SAT solvers as trouble-free problem solvers, e.g. knowledge representation [GIU 06], biology [LYN 06], planning [KAU 92], etc.

On the contrary, few application domains naturally consider using CP. One possible explanation is that people understand more easily what solvers for the famous SAT problem are about. After all, propositional logic is widely known; building a modeling on it and using a solver able to understand it may look like an easy path for many end-users. Another possible explanation is that people assume (perhaps wrongly) that CP is less efficient, or more difficult to use.

An interesting indicator of this fact is the current interest of the computer aided verification community for satisfiability modulo theories (SMT). This is an application domain where people need to solve problems that have a large

Boolean part, but also include constraints on other domains, such as integers and arrays. The most successful attempts to build solvers for this large class of problems started from an SAT solver and extended it with other theories [NIE 07]. Another natural approach would be to start from a CP solver and specialize or adapt it. This approach has simply not been considered by the CAV community. This may come from their long-time commitment to DPLL solvers, and to the importance of the Boolean part in their formulations.

It is therefore important for the CP community to assess its position against SAT: which advantages does CP offer, in which cases should it be used, and why is it not considered in more of the aforementioned application areas?

[J. Marques-Silva] I am not sure the CP community should assess its position against SAT. SAT technology is useful in a number of contexts, CP in other contexts. CP is more general, SAT is more focused. In contrast, the CP community should probably pay more attention to the work being done in SMT. SMT solvers can be extremely general, and so could compete with CP in a number of contexts. I believe the contributions of CP justify the future of CP. I would like to see CP people involved in the development of the next generation of SMT solvers. This might be beneficial for both communities.

[B. O'Sullivan] A significant difference between constraint programming and SAT is that the former tends to focus more on optimization problems. Typically, in constraint programming we wish to differentiate between alternative solutions in terms of some measure of overall cost, reliability or cost. These can be incorporated more easily, in some sense, in a constraint-based approach since we can exploit the structure of the problem to give good bounds on the objective function. Also, there are many tools available to hybridize with traditional operations research techniques. Systematic SAT approaches have typically focused on verification and satisfiability checking, but there are specialized optimization problems such as Max-SAT that can be solved well in this framework. Local search techniques give rise to new opportunities for optimization in both SAT and CP. However, CP offers greater opportunities for expressing the real structure in an optimization problem which is lost in the traditional CNF encodings used in SAT. Therefore, in the case of optimization I would argue that CP is a more appropriate technology.

[R. Yap] The work in SMT could be thought of as an extension of SAT. However, I think it seems to be quite analogous to the development of CLP. Constraints were the natural way of making the logic programming languages and formalism more powerful. So SMT also uses CP in the same way.

5.3. Summary, future directions and conclusion

In any new thematic, low-hanging fruits represent the first catches, and this SAT/CP event verified this traditional saying. Not surprisingly, the first wave of SAT/CP integration research tried to blend some of the most successful SAT techniques into current CSP/CP frameworks. We can see this in some of the sections presented here [HAM 06] but also in some recently published conference papers [GEN 06]. In this respect it is interesting to remark that in SAT it is not a particular technique *in isolation* that explains the success of current DPPL solvers, but the miraculous alchemy between the fast 2-watch propagation (which is not slowed-down too much when clauses are added, thus making clause-learning practical), the 1UIP conflict-analysis (which uses the fact that the *implication graph* can be recovered cheaply from the data-structures used for propagation), and the activity-based heuristics (which is nourished by the learning), and the other components (e.g. restarts). It is fair to say that we are still far from such a finely-tuned integration of techniques in CP, and that finding the right alchemy will be much more challenging than in SAT.

It seems reasonable to forecast the integration of a SAT solver as part of a CP engine. We see two potential consequences on the future of CP tools:

– The impressive achievements of the SAT community will very probably impact the CP community positively: the next generation of CP tools will be able to handle the Boolean part of CP problems much more efficiently thanks to the lessons learned from SAT solvers. Many combinatorial problems include a significant Boolean part together with other types of constraints. It was long assumed in CP that the Boolean part could be handled just as the rest (a Boolean variable is just a normal discrete variable with domain 0/1, it is propagated using the general-purpose propagation techniques of the solver). There is now every evidence, as shown by Minion, that specialized methods to deal with the Boolean part do make a difference.

– If the integration of SAT techniques within CP is successful, one can conceive that the interest for purely Boolean solvers will diminish. At the time of writing, using a general CP tool to solve a purely Boolean problem is out of question: the performance would simply not be acceptable compared to a specialized SAT solver. If CP solvers reach a performance that is reasonably competitive to SAT on purely Boolean instances, then many more users might feel tempted to consider CP solvers as their default problem solving tool. This would, in our opinion, improve on a situation which is currently paradoxical: in too many cases, problems are nowadays encoded to SAT even though part of their constraints are originally non-Boolean. The reason is twofold: first SAT solvers are so easy to use compared to CP tools that the effort of encoding the non-Boolean part into CNF appears acceptable; second, the speed-up on the Boolean part is so considerable that it often outweighs the possible slow-down incurred by the non-natural encoding of the non-Boolean part. In a sense, the success of SAT has been a lesson whose positive outcome for CP might be that it would force us to analyze why SAT solvers are used for problems where CP solvers would appear to be more natural candidates, and how we can correct that.

Another interesting thing to come of this first workshop is the growing importance of the satisfiability modulo theories formalism and its potential connection with existing CLP/CP research. It seems reasonable to forecast a possible integration CP/SMT where existing CP results would be reused in specific SMT theories. We can think of specific propagators for constraints over integers, lists, reals, which have been well studied in CLP/CP. One possible challenge in using these CP results for SMT is that in SMT the algorithms for each theory do not communicate solely by propagation. In CP, the communication between constraints is typically done by deductions of only one form: *variable x cannot be assigned to value v.* In most existing frameworks for satisfiability modulo theories, such as the traditional Shostak and Nelson-Oppen methods or the recent DPLL(X) framework [NIE 07], the decision procedures typically exchange richer information, for instance equalities (each decision procedure is able to generate deductions of the form *variables x and y are equal*) or proofs (each decision procedure is able to generate an explanation of which hypothesis was really used to produce a particular deduction). In his invited talk, R. Nieuwenhuis explained the need for this rich information exchange by saying that [each component] *guides* the search instead of only *validating* it. For many types of constraints considered in CP, such a rich communication remains to be studied. In addition to improving the impact of CP results on SMT, the philosophy summarized by R. Nieuwenhuis might inspire new perspectives in solver cooperation for CP itself.

The workshop was the first event devoted specifically to the issues of cross-fertilization between SAT and CP; it can be safely predicted that it will not be the last, and that more papers on this issue will also be published in mainstream conferences in the near future. Our personal guess is that the contributions related to the advancement of SAT/SMT from a CP perspective will be among the most exciting of these forthcoming contributions.

5.4. References

[BES 96] BESSIERE C., RÉGIN J., "MAC and combined heuristics: two reasons to forsake FC (and CBJ?) on hard problems", *Proc. of Int Conf. on Principles and Practice of Constraint Programming (CP)*, p. 61-75, 1996.

[BIE 06] BIERE A., GOMES C., *Theory and Applications of Satisfiability Testing - SAT 2006, 9th International Conference*, LNCS 4121, Springer, 2006.

[BOR 06] Bordeaux L., Hamadi Y., Zhang L., "Propositional Satisfiability and Constraint Programming: a Comparative Survey", *ACM Computing Surveys*, vol. 38, num. 4, p. 1-54, 2006, Article 12.

[CHE 01] Chen X., van Beek P., "Conflict-directed backjumping revisited", *J. of Artificial Intelligence Research*, vol. 14, p. 53–81, 2001.

[EPS 01] Epstein S., Freuder E., "Collaborative learning for constraint solving", *Proc. of Int Conf. on Principles and Practice of Constraint Programming (CP)*, p. 46–60, 2001.

[GEN 02] Gent I., "Arc consistency in SAT", *Proc. of European Conf. on Artificial Intelligence (ECAI)*, p. 141-145, 2002.

[GEN 06] Gent I. P., Jefferson C., Miguel I., "Watched Literals for Constraint Propagation in Minion.", *Proc. of Int Conf. on Principles and Practice of Constraint Programming (CP)*, p. 182-197, 2006.

[GIU 06] Giunchiglia F., "Managing Diversity in Knowledge", *Proc. of European Conf. on Artificial Intelligence (ECAI)*, Page 4, 2006.

[HAM 06] Hamadi Y., Bordeaux L., Proceedings of the First Workshop on the Integration of SAT and CP techniques, Report num. MSR-TR-2006-153, Microsoft Research, Nov 2006.

[JUS 00] Jussien N., Debruyne R., Boizumault P., "Maintaining arc consistency within dynamic backtracking", *Proc. of Int Conf. on Principles and Practice of Constraint Programming (CP)*, p. 249–261, 2000.

[KAS 90] Kasif S., "On the Parallel Complexity of Discrete Relaxation in Constraint Satisfaction Networks.", *Artificial Intelligence*, vol. 45, num. 3, p. 275-286, 1990.

[KAU 92] Kautz H. A., Selman B., "Planning as Satisfiability", *Proc. of European Conf. on Artificial Intelligence (ECAI)*, p. 359-363, 1992.

[KAU 99] Kautz H., Selman B., "Unifying SAT-based and Graph-based Planning", *Proc. of Int. Joint Conf. on Artificial Intelligence (IJCAI)*, p. 318-325, 1999.

[LOB 98] Lobjois L., Lemaître M., "Branch and Bound Algorithm Selection by Performance Prediction", *Proc. of Nat. Conf. on Artificial Intelligence (AAAI)*, p. 353-358, 1998.

[LYN 06] Lynce I., Marques-Silva J., "SAT in Bioinformatics: Making the Case with Haplotype Inference", *Proc. of Int. Symp. on Theory and Applications of Satisfiability Testing (SAT)*, p. 136-141, 2006.

[NEW 60] Newell A., Shaw J. C., Simon H. A., "Report on a general problem-solving program", *Proc. of IFIP World Computer Congress*, UNESCO, p. 256-264, 1960.

[NIE 07] Nieuwenhuis R., Oliveras A., Tinelli C., "Solving SAT and SAT Modulo Theories: From an Abstract Davis-Putnam-Logemann-Loveland Procedure to DPLL(T)", *J. of the ACM*, 2007, forthcoming.

[SCH 93] Schiex T., Verfaillie G., "Nogood recording for static and dynamic CSPs", *Proc. of Int. Conf. on Tools for Artificial Intelligence (ICTAI)*, IEEE, p. 48-55, 1993.

Chapter 6

Constraint-Based Methods for Bioinformatics

Bioinformatics is a challenging area of research where every serious contribution can have thousands of positive effects in medicine, agriculture, or industry. Biology, in general, is a source of extremely interesting and computationally expensive tasks. Most of the typical problems can be effectively formulated by using declarative languages and constraints. Constraints on finite domains (and on reals) are applied for predicting spatial conformation of polymers, concurrent constraint programming can be used for simulations of biological systems, and constraints on strings are employed for the analysis of DNA sequences.

The WCB06 workshop was organized with the aim of sharing new theoretical and practical results in the area and of summarizing new challenging problems for the declarative programming and constraint community. The workshop is the successor of the workshops *Constraints and Bioinformatics/Biocomputing* colocated with CP'97 and CP'98, and of the WCB05 workshop colocated with ICLP 2005.

The workshop benefited from the excellent invited talk of François Fages about *Using temporal logics with constraints to express biological properties of cell processes* (section 6.1) and from the presentation of seven contributed papers. The contribution by Bortolussi and Policriti (section 6.2) also belongs to the field of *Systems Biology*. In the area of *Structural Prediction* we had four contributions: by Krippahl and Barahona; Elisabetta De Maria et al., Dal

---

Chapter edited by Alessandro DAL PALÙ, Agostino DOVIER, François FAGES and Sebastian WILL.

Palù et al., and Will and Mann (section 6.4–6.6). A work on suffix array by Zytnicki et al. (section 6.7) and a paper by Prosser on Supertree Construction (section 6.8) concluded the contributions to the workshop. In the rest of this chapter we report the abstract of the invited talk written by François Fages (section 6.1) whom we would like to thank again, and our short summaries of the seven contributed papers (section 6.2–6.8).

The interest of the constraint community in bioinformatics and biology is shown by the considerable number of participants (35) even though the workshop was run in parallel with other extremely interesting workshops. During the final discussion, we decided to apply for co-location of WCB07 at the next ICLP07 in Porto, Portugal, where we are confident of receiving another strong contribution to this research area by the Logic Programming community. Other information, the proceedings and some pictures from the workshop can be found in the WCB06 website `http://www.dimi.uniud.it/dovier/WCB06`. We conclude by acknowledging all the PC members, the external referees, and all the participants. Particular thanks to the CP workshop chair Barry O'Sullivan, and to the two other editors of this book, Frédéric Benhamou and Narendra Jussien.

6.1. On using temporal logic with constraints to express biological properties of cell processes (by François Fages)

One promise of systems biology is to model biochemical processes on a sufficiently large scale so that the behavior of a complex system can be predicted under various conditions in *in silico* experiments. The language approach to systems biology aims at designing formal languages for describing biochemical mechanisms, processes and systems at different levels of abstraction, and for providing automated reasoning tools to assist the biologists [FAG 04a].

The pioneering use of the π-calculus process algebra for modeling cell signaling pathways in [REG 01], has been the source of inspiration for numerous works in the line of process calculi and of their stochastic extensions. The biochemical abstract machine BIOCHAM[1] [FAG 04b] has been designed as a

1. BIOCHAM is a free software implemented in Prolog and distributed under the GPL license. It is downloadable on the web at `http://contraintes.inria.fr/BIOCHAM`. The BIOCHAM project is a joint work with Nathalie Chabrier-Rivier, Sylvain Soliman and Laurence Calzone, with contributions from Sakina Ayata, Loïc Fosse, Lucie Gentils, Shrivaths Rajagopalan and Nathalie Sznajder. In addition, support from the EU STREP project April-II and the EU Network of Excellence REWERSE are warmly acknowledged.

simplification of the process calculi approach to model biological processes, using a language of reaction rules that is both more natural to the biologists, and well suited to considering different dynamics and using model-checking techniques.

In BIOCHAM, the rule-based language is used for modeling biochemical networks at three abstraction levels:

1) the *Boolean semantics*, where a Boolean variable representing its presence or absence in the system is associated with each object (protein, gene, etc.), and the reaction rules are interpreted by a highly non-deterministic *asynchronous transition system* representing competition between reactions;

2) the *concentration semantics*, where a real number representing its concentration is associated with each object, and the reaction rules are interpreted with their kinetic expressions by a set of non-linear ordinary differential equations (ODE);

3) the *stochastic semantics*, where an integer representing the number of molecules in the system is associated with each BIOCHAM object, and the rules are interpreted as a continuous time Markov chain.

One striking feature of this multi-level approach is that in the three cases, temporal logics can be used to formalize the biological properties of the system, and verify them by different model-checking techniques. The thesis is that, to a large extent, the following identifications can be made:

$$\begin{aligned} \textit{biological model} &= \textit{transition system}, \\ \textit{biological property} &= \textit{temporal logic formula}, \\ \textit{biological validation} &= \textit{model-checking}. \end{aligned}$$

At the Boolean level, the *Computation Tree Logic* CTL [CLA 99] allows *qualitative properties* about the production of a particular protein (reachability), the checkpoints for its production, the stability or oscillations for its presence, etc. to be expressed. These properties are known from biological experiments in wild-life or mutated organisms. Some of the most commonly used CTL formulae are abbreviated in BIOCHAM as follows:

- `reachable(P)` stands for $EF(P)$;
- `steady(P)` stands for $EG(P)$;
- `stable(P)` stands for $AG(P)$;
- `checkpoint(Q,P)` stands for $!E(!Q\ U\ P)$;
- `oscil(P)` stands for $AG((P \Rightarrow EF\ !P) \wedge (!P \Rightarrow EF\ P))$.

In this setting, such properties can be checked with state-of-the-art symbolic model checkers such as NuSMV using binary decision diagrams. The performances obtained on a large model of the mammalian cell cycle control according to Kohn's map [KOH 99], involving 800 rules and 500 variables, have been shown to be of the order of a few tenths of a second to compile the model, and check simple CTL formulae.

At the concentration level, a first-order fragment of Linear Time Logic (LTL) is used with *arithmetic constraints* containing equality, inequality and arithmetic operators ranging over the real values of concentrations and their derivatives. For instance `F([A]>10)` expresses that the concentration of `A` eventually gets above the threshold value 10. `G([A]+[B]<[C])` expresses that the concentration of C is always greater than the sum of the concentrations of A and B. Oscillation properties, abbreviated as `oscil(M,K)`, are defined as a change of sign of the derivative of M at least K times in the time horizon:

```
F((d[M]/dt > 0) & F((d[M]/dt < 0) & F((d[M]/dt > 0)...)))
```

The abbreviated formula `oscil(M,K,V)` adds the constraint that the maximum concentration of M must be above the threshold V in at least K oscillations.

Under the hypothesis that the initial state is completely defined, numerical integration methods (such as Runge-Kutta or Rosenbrock methods) provide a discrete simulation trace. This trace constitutes a linear Kripke structure in which LTL formulae with constraints can be interpreted and model-checked [CAL 06]. Since constraints refer not only to concentrations, but also to their derivatives, we consider traces of the form $(\langle t_0, x_0, dx_0/dt\rangle, \langle t_1, x_1, dx_1/dt\rangle, \dots)$ where at each time point, t_i, the trace associates the concentration values of the x_i and the values of their derivatives dx_i/dt.

Beyond making simulations, and checking properties of the models, the temporal properties can also be turned into specifications and temporal logic constraints for automatically searching and learning modifications or refinements of the model when incorporating new biological knowledge. This is implemented in BIOCHAM by a combination of model-checking, search and machine learning techniques in the three abstraction levels.

For instance, in a simple continuous model of the cell cycle after Tyson [TYS 91], the search of parameter values for kinetic parameters k_3 and k_4, so that the concentration of the cyclin `Cdc2-Cyclin p1` oscillates three times in the time horizon 150, can be formalized as follows:

```
biocham: learn_parameters([k3, k4], [(0, 200), (0, 200)], 20,
```

```
                    oscil(Cdc2-Cyclin~{p1},3),150).
First values found that make oscil(Cdc2-Cyclin~{p1},3) true:
parameter(k3,_).
parameter(k4,_).
```

The system finds the parameter values $k_3 = 10$ and $k_4 = 70$ satisfying the specification. However, the corresponding curve depicted in Figure 6.1 on the left exhibits damped oscillations. The specification can be further refined by imposing a constraint of period equal to 35 time units, `period(Cdc2-Cyclin~{p1},35)`. This produces the curve depicted in Figure 6.1 on the right which is close to the original model.

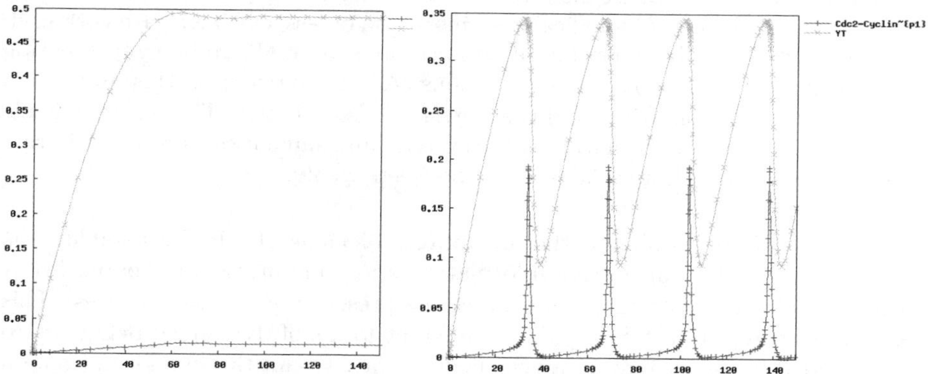

Figure 6.1. *Concentration experimental results*

These first results implemented in BIOCHAM are quite encouraging and motivate further research in the direction of the formal specification of biological systems and in the improvement of the search algorithms. A coupled model of the cell cycle and the circadian cycle is under development along these lines in BIOCHAM with applications to cancer chronotherapies.

6.2. Modeling biological systems in stochastic concurrent constraint programming (by Luca Bortolussi and Alberto Policriti)

In this work the authors show how stochastic concurrent constraint programming (sCCP—[BOR 06]) can be used for modeling biological systems. sCCP is based on CCP [SAR 93], a process algebra where agents interact by posting constraints on the variables of the system in the constraint store.

Computational systems biology is a field in which different modeling techniques are used to capture the intrinsic dynamics of biological systems. Some of them are based on *differential equations*, mostly ordinary, and therefore they represent phenomena as *continuous and deterministic*. On the other side there are *stochastic and discrete* models, that are usually simulated with *Gillespie's algorithm* [GIL 77]. In the middle, there are hybrid approaches like the *Chemical Langevin Equation*, a stochastic differential equation that partially bridges these two opposite formalisms.

In the last few years *stochastic process algebras* (SPA) have emerged [PRI 01]. They are based on the parallel between molecules and reactions on one side and processes and communications on the other side. SPA have been used to model biological systems (e.g., biochemical reactions and genetic regulatory networks). Stochastic modeling of biological systems works by associating a rate with each active reaction (or, in general, interaction); rates are real numbers representing the frequency or propensity of interactions. All active reactions then undergo a (stochastic) race condition, and the fastest one is executed. These rates encode all the quantitative information of the system, and simulations produce discrete temporal traces with a variable delay between events.

In the author's opinion, the advantages of using sCCP are twofold: the presence of both quantitative information and computational capabilities at the level of the constraint systems and the presence of functional rates. This second feature, in particular, allows different forms of dynamical behaviors to be encoded in the system, in a very flexible way. Quantitative information, on the other hand, allows a more compact representation of models, as some of the details can be described in relations at the level of the store.

At high level, biological systems are composed of two ingredients: (biological) entities and interactions among those entities. For instance, in biochemical reaction networks, the molecules are the entities and the chemical reactions are the possible interactions. In gene regulatory networks, instead, the entities are genes and regulatory proteins, while the interactions are production and degradation of proteins, and repression and enhancement of the gene's expression. In addition, entities fall into two separate classes: measurable and logical. Measurable entities are those present in a certain quantity in the system, like proteins or other molecules. Logical entities, instead, have a control function, hence they are neither produced nor degraded. Note that logical entities are not real world entities, but rather they are part of the models.

Measurable entities are associated exactly with stream variables (unbounded tail lists of time varying variables). Logical entities, instead, are represented as processes actively performing control activities. In addition, they can use variables of the constraint store either as control variables or to exchange information. Finally, each interaction is associated with a process modifying the value of certain measurable stream variables of the system. Associating variables with measurable entities means that they are represented as part of the environment, while the active agents are associated with the different action capabilities of the system. These actions have a certain duration and a certain propensity to happen: a fact represented here in the standard way, i.e. associating a stochastic rate with each action.

Constraints maintain information about the biological entities. This leads to the definition of a general purpose library of processes that can be used in the modeling phase. However, this is only a part of the general picture, as there are more complex classes of biological systems that need to be modeled, like transport networks and membranes. In addition, all these systems are strongly interconnected, and they must be modeled altogether in order to extract deep information about living beings. The authors believe that the flexibility of constraints makes sCCP a powerful general purpose language that can be programmed simply, extended with libraries, and used to model all these different classes of systems in a compact way.

Biochemical reactions can be challenging to model, because proteins can form very big complexes that are built incrementally. Therefore, the cell is populated by a huge number of sub-complexes. Usually, these networks are described by biologists with diagrams, like Kohn maps, that are very compact, because they represent complexes and sub-complexes implicitly. Constraints can be used to encode the calculus elegantly, by representing complexes implicitly, i.e. as lists of basic constituents.

Functional rates can be used in enzymatic reactions to represent more complex kinetic dynamics, allowing a more compact description of the networks. In this direction, the authors need to analyze the relationship between these different kinetics more in the context of stochastic simulation, in order to characterize the cases where these different kinetics can be used equivalently. Notice that the use of complex rates can be seen as an operation on the Markov chain, replacing a subgraph with a smaller one, hiding part of its complexity in the expression of rates. Finally, the authors plan to implement a more powerful and fast interpreter for the language, also using all available tricks to increase the speed of stochastic simulations. Moreover, the authors plan to tackle the problem of distributing the stochastic simulations of programs written in sCCP efficiently.

6.3. Chemera: constraints in protein structural problems (by Pedro Barahona and Ludwig Krippahl)

Chemera is a molecular modeling software package that includes the algorithms BiGGER (bimolecular complex generation with global evaluation and ranking), for modeling protein interactions and protein complex structures [KRI 05], and PSICO (processing structural information with constraint programming and optimization), to integrate experimental and theoretical data to solve protein structures [KRI 02]. The authors' contribution to the workshop focuses on the constraint programming aspects of Chemera, namely *constrained docking*, which allows the user to restrict the search for protein-protein complex models in a manner consistent with the ambiguity of some experimental data, and the processing of structural constraints to generate approximate models of protein structures from heterogenous data (e.g. spectroscopy, site-directed mutagenesis, homology models, secondary structure prediction, reaction mechanisms).

Protein-protein interactions play a central role in biochemical reactions. Modeling software provides useful tools to help researchers elucidate protein interaction mechanisms. A common trend in these approaches is to try to model interactions using only knowledge derived from the structure and physicochemical properties of the proteins involved.

In modeling the structure of a protein, the common approaches have been either theoretical, to try to predict the structure from the physical properties of the amino acid sequence in the protein, possibly using homologies with other known structures, or experimental, specializing on the processing of data from specific techniques like nuclear magnetic resonance (NMR) spectroscopy. PSICO aims at bringing the two approaches together by providing a flexible framework for processing geometrical constraints and thus integrate information from all relevant sources in the modeling of a protein structure. NMR data can be modeled as distance constraints [KRI 02] or as torsion-angle constraints [KRI 05], homology or secondary structure prediction data can be modeled as rigid-group constraints [KRI 05], energy functions can be included in the local-search optimization stage, and amino acid properties relevant for protein folding, such as hydrophobicity, can be part of the enumeration heuristics during constraint processing.

The core of protein docking algorithms is the representation of the protein shapes and the measure of surface contact. The former is a straightforward representation using a regular cubic lattice of cells. In BiGGER the cells do not correspond to numerical values, but each cell can be either an empty cell, a surface cell, or a core cell. The surface cells define the surface of the structure, and the overlap of surface cells measures the surface of contact. BiGGER also models side-chain flexibility implicitly by adjusting the core grid representation and allows for hard or soft docking simulations depending on the nature of the interaction to model. Furthermore, this representation and the search algorithm can take advantage of information about the interaction to simultaneously improve the results and speed up the calculations.

Grids are composed of lists of intervals specifying the segments of similar cells along the x coordinate. The fact that core cells can not overlap induces a powerful constraint that is able to prune the relative shifts between the two structures. Moreover, a branch and bound search is applied in order to optimize the overlap of surface cells, and restrict the search to those regions where this overlap can be higher than that of the lowest ranking model to be kept.

In some cases there is information about distances between points in the structures, information that can be used to restrict the search region. The most common situation is to have a set of likely distance constraints of which not all necessarily hold. To cope with this, the program supports the constraint of the form: *at least K atoms of set A must be within R of at least one atom of set B*, where set A is on one protein and set B on the other, and R is a distance value.

There are several sources of information that can help model the structure of a protein. First of all, the amino acid sequences of the protein chains determines most chemical bonds, restricting interatomic distances in many atom pairs, angles formed by atom triplets, of even larger groups of atoms that are effectively rigidly bound together by the chemical bonds. NMR data provides several types of distance constraints by showing that two atoms must be close enough, by limiting the angles of rotation around some chemical bonds, by suggesting limits for relative special orientations of groups of atoms. Furthermore, homology with known structures or modeling secondary structure can provide detailed information of the structure of parts of the protein being modeled. This information identifies three types of constraints implemented in the program: distance constraints between two atoms, group constraints that fix the relative positions of a group of atoms in a rigid configuration, and torsion angle constraints that restrict the relative orientation of two groups joined together by a chemical bond.

Chemera is the interface to all BiGGER and PSICO calculations and includes tools for handling *Electrostatics* (Figure 6.2–A), *Clustering and Scoring* (Figure 6.2–B) and *Web Services* — interface with several web services, to assign secondary structure elements, identify domains, display sequence conservation along the protein structure (Figure 6.2–C).

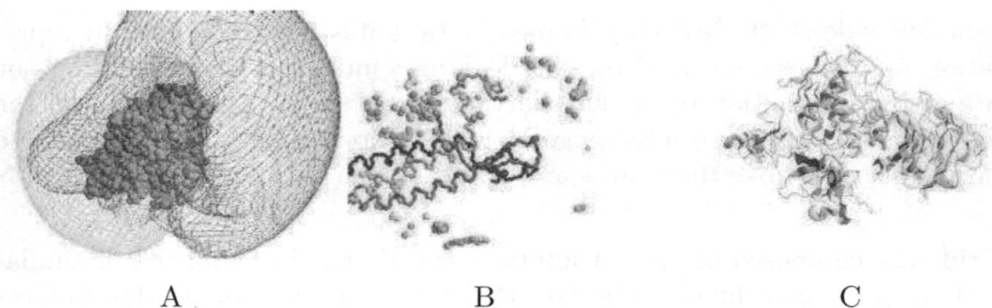

Figure 6.2. *Visualization possibilities in Chemera. See text for details*

Constraint programming techniques in Chemera are seamlessly integrated into a general molecular modeling package. This is an important aspect because research and development in this area is very dependent on a close interaction with the end users in the biochemistry community. The authors' experience and work currently in progress on several protein interactions (e.g. Aldehyde Oxidoreductase and Flavodoxin, Ferredoxin NADP Reductase and Ferredoxin, Fibrinogen and Gelatinase A) demonstrate this for the BiGGER docking algorithm, which is currently available in Chemera 3.0 `http://www.cqfb.fct.unl.pt/bioin/chemera/`.

6.4. Exploiting model checking in constraint-based approaches to the protein folding problem (by Elisabetta De Maria, Agostino Dovier, Angelo Montanari and Carla Piazza)

In this section the authors show how *model checking* could be used to drive the solution search in the protein folding problem encoded as a constraint optimization problem. The application of the model checking techniques allows the authors to distinguish between meaningful and bad protein conformations. This classification of conformations could be exploited by constraint solvers to significatively prune the search space of the protein folding problem. Furthermore, the approach seems promising in the study of folding/energy landscapes of proteins.

The authors consider foldings (i.e., self-avoiding walks) of proteins on 2D discrete lattices. If the first two points are set (w.l.o.g., the authors set $\omega(0) = (n, n)$ and $\omega(1) = (n, n+1)$), then a folding on this lattice can be uniquely represented by a sequence of directions with respect to the preceding one: left (l), forward (f), and right (r) (see Figure 6.3 for an example).

The authors exploit their analysis using the HP energy model (although the method can be employed on richer energy models such as the 20×20 contact

Figure 6.3. *The folding* frrfll *on* $\mathbb{Z}^2$ *lattice (left). Contacts and energy contributions of the string HHPHHHPH w.r.t. the same folding (right)*

energy table used in [Dal 04]). A model such as this reduces the 20-letter alphabet of amino acids to a two-letter alphabet $\{H, P\}$, where H (resp., P) represents a hydrophobic (resp., polar) amino acid. The energy function states that the energy contribution of a *contact* between two non-consecutive amino acids is -1 if both of them are H amino acids, 0 otherwise (see Figure 6.3–right).

The authors then introduce the notion of valid transformations among foldings. Roughly speaking, a valid transformation of a given folding f consists of selecting at random a position in f and performing a rotation of the part of f between this position and the ending position (*pivot move*). Precisely, let $f = f_1 \dots f_n$, with $f_i \in \{l, f, r\}$ for all $2 \leq i \leq n$, be a folding of a sequence s. A folding f' of s is obtained from f through a *pivot move* with pivot k if $f'_i = f_i$ for all $i \neq k$ and $f'_k \neq f_k$. As an example, consider the 6 pivot moves from folding *lfl* in Figure 6.4. It is possible to show that pivot moves are ergodic, namely, they allow coverage of the entire folding space.

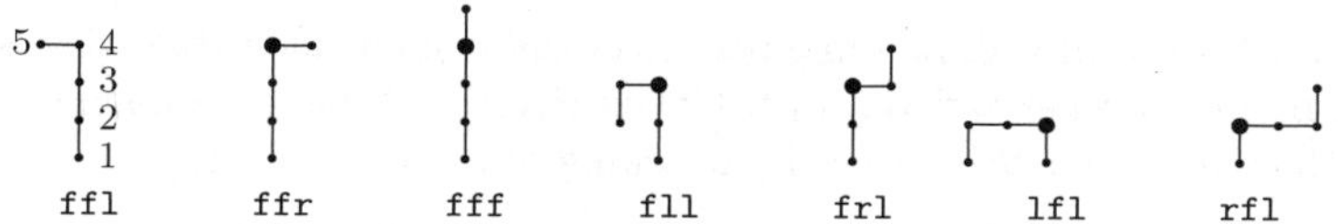

Figure 6.4. *The 6 pivot moves from string* `fll`. *Large bullets are the pivots*

The authors then define the notion of *2D Protein Transition System* of a string P of length n over $\{H, P\}$ as a tuple $M_P = (Q, T, L)$, where

– Q is the set of all foldings of length n on the $2n \times 2n$ 2D lattice;

– $T \subseteq Q \times Q$ is the set of pairs of states (q_1, q_2) such that q_2 can be obtained from q_1 by a pivot move;

– $L : Q \rightarrow 2^{AP}$ is a labeling function over the set AP of atomic propositions which consists of the following predicates: $2nd\_l, 2nd\_f, 2nd\_r, \ldots, nth\_l, nth\_f, nth\_r$, plus the following three predicates: min_en, $inter\_en$, max_en, where for all $2 \leq i \leq n$, the predicate ith_l (resp., ith_f, ith_r) holds at a state q if the i-th segment of q has a *left* (resp., *forward, right*) orientation and min_en (resp., $inter\_en$, max_en) holds at a state q if the energy of q is minimum (resp., intermediate, 0).

Given a 2D protein transition system $M_P = (Q, T, L)$ and a temporal logic formula f expressing a particular desirable property of the system, the *model checking problem* consists of finding the set of all states in Q satisfying f [CLA 99]. When a state does not satisfy a formula, model checking algorithms produce a counter-example that falsifies it, thus providing an insight to understand failure causes and important clues for fixing the problem. The authors restrict their attention to two well-known fragments of the *computation tree logic* CTL*, namely, the *branching time* logic CTL and the *linear time* logic LTL.

The authors then show how meaningful properties of 2D protein transition systems can be encoded in both CTL and LTL. Here two of them are reported:

F1: Is there a path of length k at most that reaches a state with minimum energy?
CTL: $\bigvee_{i=0}^{k} E_1 X_1 \ldots E_i X_i min\_en$.
LTL (actually, it expresses $\neg F1$): $A(\bigwedge_{i=0}^{k} X_1 \ldots X_i \neg min\_en)$.
F2: Is this the minimum amount of energy? Alternatively, if energy is at maximum, is it possible to reach a state with minimum energy without passing through states with intermediate energy?
CTL, LTL: $A(max\_en\ U\ min\_en)$.

The authors finally show some results of the tests of the properties described using a model checker written in SICStus Prolog. A faster implementation of the method using *on-the-fly* model checking is under analysis.

6.5. Global constraints for discrete lattices (by Alessandro Dal Palù, Agostino Dovier and Enrico Pontelli)

Constraint solving on discrete lattices has gained momentum as a declarative and effective approach to solve complex problems such as protein folding determination. In particular, [Dal 05] presented a comprehensive constraint-solving platform (COLA) dealing with primitive constraints in discrete lattices.

The authors discuss some preliminary ideas on possible global constraints that can be introduced in a constraint system like COLA. Various alternatives are presented and preliminary results concerning the computational properties of the different global constraints are reported.

Discrete finite lattices are often used for approximated studies of 3D conformations of molecular structures. These models are used, in particular, to calculate reasonable approximations of foldings of protein structures in 3D space [SKO 04]. Polymers are laid out in particular subsets of $\mathbb{N}^3$. These subsets are often described by the vectors that specify the set of neighbors of each point. Lattice models like FCC and chess knight are among them.

The protein structure prediction in the context of discrete lattice structures has been studied as a *constraint optimization problem* in the FCC lattice, using simplified energy models [BAC 06, Dal 04]. In these approaches, each point P of the lattice is identified by a triplet of *finite domain variables* (P_x, P_y, P_z). It is proved that mantaining an independent variable for each point coordinate limits the power of *propagation* w.r.t. an approach (as in COLA) where a point is considered as a whole.

The authors propose a study targeting the problem of dealing with *global* constraints in the general context of constraint solvers on lattice domain. Global constraints are proven constructs that facilitate the declarative encoding of problems; at the same time, they allow the programmer to express knowledge about relationships between variables, that can be effectively employed by the search algorithm to prune infeasible parts of the solution search space. The authors introduce different global constraints, and they study the complexity of their satisfiability and the associated propagation process. For each global constraint C (with variables $X_1, \ldots, X_n$) analyzed, the authors are interested in verifying two properties:

– *consistency (CON):* $C \neq \emptyset$

– *generalized arc consistency (GAC):* $\forall i \in \{1, \ldots, n\} \, \forall a_i \in D^{X_i}$

$$\exists a_1 \in D^{X_1} \cdots \exists a_{i-1} \in D^{X_{i-1}} \exists a_{i+1} \in D^{X_{i+1}} \cdots \exists a_n \in D^{X_n} \ (a_1, \ldots, a_n) \in C$$

• The `alldifferent` global constraint is used to describe that all the variables must assume different points. It is well known that consistency and propagation of `alldifferent` is polynomial.

• The `contiguous` global constraint is used to describe the fact that a list of variables represent lattice points that are adjacent (in terms of positions in the lattice graph) and has the form:

$$\texttt{contiguous}(X_1, \ldots, X_n) = (D^{X_1} \times \cdots \times D^{X_n}) \setminus \{(a_1, \ldots, a_n) : \exists i. \ (1 \leq i < n \wedge (a_i, a_{i+1}) \notin E)\}$$

where E is the set of edges in a lattice, and $X_1, \ldots, X_n$ is a list of variables (respectively, with domains $D^{X_1}, \ldots, D^{X_n}$).

The authors prove that verifying CON and GAC are in P.

• The saw constraint is used to require that each assignment to the variables $X_1, \ldots, X_n$ represents a self-avoiding walk (SAW) in the lattice and has the form:

$$\texttt{saw}(X_1, \ldots, X_n) = \texttt{contiguous}(X_1, \ldots, X_n) \cap \texttt{alldifferent}(X_1, \ldots, X_n)$$

The saw constraint can be used, for example, to model the fact that the primary sequence of a protein cannot create cycles when placed in the 3D space. The authors prove that CON of saw global constraint is NP-complete, and, consequently, GAC is NP-hard. saw can be replaced by a set of binary constraints. AC filtering on them is a trivial polynomial approximation for GAC filtering. Iterating alldifferent and contiguous GAC filtering is a second polynomial filtering. However, these polynomial filterings have weaker propagation than saw GAC filtering.

• The alldistant constraint formalizes the fact that different amino acids of a protein have a specific volume occupancy. Given n variables $X_1, \ldots, X_n$, with respective domains $D^{X_1}, \ldots, D^{X_n}$, and n numbers $c_1, \ldots, c_n$, admissible solutions $X_1 = p_1, \ldots, X_n = p_n$ are searched such that p_i and p_j are located at distance at least $c_i + c_j$, with $1 \leq i, j \leq n$. More formally:

$$\texttt{alldistant}(X_1, \ldots, X_n, c_1, \ldots, c_n) = (D^{X_1} \times \cdots \times D^{X_n}) \setminus \{(a_1, \ldots, a_n) : \exists i, j.\ 1 \leq i < j \leq n \wedge ||a_i - a_j||_2 < (c_i + c_j)\}$$

Note that alldistant with $c_1 = \frac{1}{2}, \ldots, c_n = \frac{1}{2}$, is equivalent to alldifferent. The authors prove that the CON and GAC test are both NP-complete.

The authors also introduce and study the *rigid block constraint* and prove that CON and GAC are in P. Future work is needed for fast implementation of the polynomial time algorithms and efficient approximations of the NP-complete tests and filtering.

6.6. Counting protein structures by DFS with dynamic decomposition (by Sebastian Will and Martin Mann)

The authors introduce depth-first search with dynamic decomposition for counting all solutions of a binary CSP. In particular, they use their method for computing the number of minimal energy structures for a discrete protein model.

The number of minimal energy structures of proteins in a discrete model is an important measure, which is strongly related to protein stability. The enumeration of optimal and suboptimal structures has applications in the study of protein evolution and kinetics [REN 97, WOL 06]. Even the prediction of protein structures in simplified protein models is a complex, NP-complete combinatorial optimization problem that has received lots of interest in the past. Importantly for the presented work, it can be successfully modeled as constraint satisfaction problem (CSP) [BAC 01, BAC 06]. Recently, counting solutions of a CSP in general and related problems gained a lot of interest over considering only satisfiability [ROT 96]. This is partly due to the increased complexity of counting compared to deciding on satisfiability [PES 05]. For general CSPs and in particular for protein structure prediction, solving is NP-complete. However, the counting of CSP solutions is an even harder problem in the complexity class #P. This class is defined as the class of counting problems associated with non-deterministic polynomial time computations.

Standard solving methods in constraint programming like depth-first search (DFS) combined with constraint propagation are well-suited for determining one solution, but leave room for saving redundant work when counting all solutions. Here, the authors present a method that is especially tailored for this case. Applied to the CSP formulation of structure prediction, it improves exhaustive counting and enumeration of optimal protein structures.

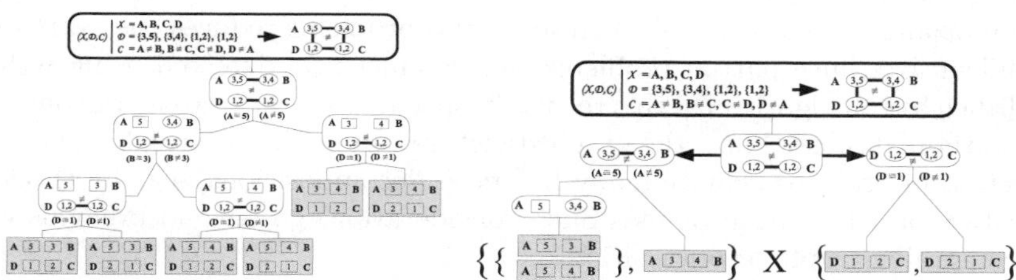

Figure 6.5. *Search tree traversed by DFS (left) and DDS (right) search*

In a few words, the new method *dynamically* decomposes the constraint (sub-)problems that emerge during the search into independent partial problems along connected components of the problem's associated constraint graph. Separate counting in the partial problems still allows to infer the number of solutions of the complete problem. Figure 6.5 illustrates the new decomposing strategy. For a simple example CSP, the standard non-decomposing search yields a search tree Figure 6.5(left). For the same problem, dynamically decomposing search yields the search tree in Figure 6.5(right). Even for the small example the tree is much reduced. Note that at the same time it yields a sort of compressed representation of the solution space.

Instead of *statically* exploiting only properties of the initial constraint graph, dynamic strategies analyze the emerging constraint graphs during the search and employ their features. The authors believe this is a major advantage in many constraint problems. In particular, if the initial constraint network is very dense (as in the structure prediction problem), static methods do not make an impact.

Decomposing into connected components and, more generally, utilizing the special structure of the constraint graph has already been discussed for a long time. As their main contribution, Will and Mann demonstrate that the ideas of employing the graph structure dynamically are applicable to binary CSPs, even including certain global constraints, and are useful for constraint programming. In particular, this enables the strategy to be used in the complex problem of protein structure counting. Furthermore, they discuss several ideas going beyond previous approaches. For example, dynamic decomposition can yield a more compact representation of the solution space.

The section shows that the introduced method can be generalized such that even global constraints can be used. As shown the strategy of dynamically decomposing the (sub-)problems into partial problems reduces the search tree significantly. Since partial problems can be efficiently detected using well established graph algorithms, this results in speeding up the search. Beyond this, the authors discussed how the graph structure can guide the variable and value selection in order to achieve many balanced decompositions, e.g. by the identification of articulation points. Such considerations go beyond previous work on constraint graph decomposition.

The application of dynamically decomposing search (DDS) to the CPSP problem shows the large capabilities of the method. First results with a prototypic implementation already show a significant speedup. Improving the ability for counting and enumerating optimal structures has important implications for the investigation of protein evolution and the folding process.

The section gives evidence that the more general approach of dynamically analyzing the constraint graph during the search and employing its special structure has a large potential for solution counting in constraint programming. To the authors conviction, exploring these possibilities even further is an interesting field for future research.

6.7. Suffix array and weighted CSPs (by Matthias Zytnicki, Christine Gaspin and Thomas Schiex)

The authors describe a new constraint that uses the data structure suffix array, well-known in pattern matching. They show how it helps answering the question of non-coding RNA detection (ncRNA), and more precisely, finding the best hybrid in a duplex constraint. A ncRNA is usually represented by a sequel of letters, or *nucleotides*: A, C, G and T and it also contains *interactions*—mainly A–T and C–G—that are essential to its biological function.

The authors work under the assumption that the *structure* (namely, the set of information located on an ncRNA that discriminates for a given biological function) is known. The aim of the work is to answer the following question: how can I get all the candidates matching a given structure in a sequence that may contain several billions of nucleotides?

One of the main approaches to solving this problem uses statistical information in a context-free grammar that describes this structure [EDD 94]. However, some complex ncRNA families cannot be described within this formalism and [VIA 04] showed that only NP-hard formalisms may correctly describe them. This favors a CSP model of the problem.

However, usual queries give hundred of thousands of solutions and, in practice, it is impossible to exploit this huge amount of solutions.

This is why the authors use the weighted CSP (WCSP) [LAR 04] formalism to solve the ncRNA detection problem In WCSP a cost can be associated with each domain value in order to express preferences. A *valuation structure* $\mathcal{S} = \langle E, \oplus, \leq \rangle$ specifies the costs, where: $E = [0..k] \subseteq \mathbb{N}$ is the *set of costs.* The highest cost k can possibly be ∞, and it represents an *inconsistency.* $\leq$ is the usual operator on $\mathbb{N}$ and $\oplus$, the *addition* on E, is defined by $\forall(a, b) \in \mathbb{N}^2, a \oplus b = \min\{a + b, k\}$. A WCSP is a tuple $\mathcal{P} = \langle \mathcal{S}, \mathcal{X}, \mathcal{D}, \mathcal{C} \rangle$, where: $\mathcal{S}$ is the valuation structure; $\mathcal{X} = \{x_1, \ldots, x_n\}$ is a set of n *variables*; $\mathcal{D} = \{D(x_1), \ldots, D(x_n)\}$ is the set of possible *values* of each variable, or *domain*, and the size of the largest one is d; $\mathcal{C} = \{c_1, \ldots, c_e\}$ is the set of e soft constraints. Assignments, which are defined as usual, can now not only be permitted or forbidden by a (soft) constraint but also be admissible with a certain cost. The cost of an assignment is the sum of costs over all constraints.

In the model, the variables represent the *positions* on the sequence of the elements of structure. The initial domain of the variables will therefore be equal to the size of the sequence. The constraints enforce the presence of the desired elements of structure between the specified variables. Within this model, a solution is a position for each variable, such that all the structural elements

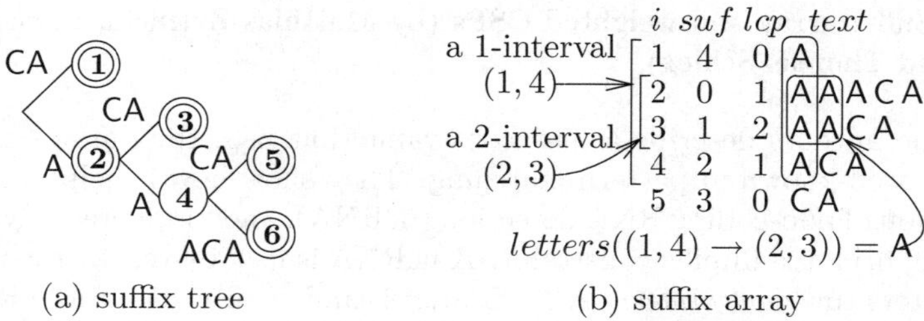

Figure 6.6. *Two representations of the suffixes of AAACA*

specified by the constraints can be found. The aim is to find all the solutions of the problem, i.e. assignments with a cost less than a maximum cost k.

The authors focus on the duplex constraint. This constraint ensures that there exists a set of interactions between one sequence (the *main sequence*) and another given sequence (the *target sequence*). It has two parameters: the target sequence and the maximum number of errors in the interaction set. Similarly to the edit distance, the number of errors of a hybridization is the number of nucleotides that do not interact with any other nucleotide, plus the number of pairs of nucleotides associated through a non-allowed interaction. This will be the cost given by the constraint. The duplex constraint involves four variables: x_i, x_j, y_k and y_l. x_i represents the start position of the main stem, x_j represents its end position, whereas y_k and y_l represent the start and end positions of the target stem. To solve the problem, the authors use a depth-first branch-and-bound algorithm that maintains an extension of 2B-consistency adapted to soft constraints, called *bound arc consistency* (BAC*, [ZYT 06]).

The main contribution of the section is to develop an algorithm for maintaining bound arc consistency for the duplex constraint. The algorithm uses the data structure of suffix arrays. Suffix arrays have several advantages over the more widely known suffix trees. The *suffix tree* is a tree with edges labeled with words. This data structure has been widely used in pattern matching algorithms. Given a text, the paths from the root node of its suffix tree and its terminal nodes enumerate all the suffixes of this text (see Figure 6.6(a)) for the string AAACA). Basically, a *suffix array* is an array where all the suffixes of a text are sorted through lexicographic order (see Figure 6.6(b)), which can be used to simulate a suffix tree. Both data structures allow fast lookup of sub-sequences.

The algorithm takes as an input the suffix array S, a word w of size n and a maximum edit distance $maxErr$. It returns the minimum distance between w and any subsequence of T, or $maxErr + 1$ if this distance is greater than *maxErr*. It uses a hybridization cost matrix c_{hyb}, that, given two nucleotides, returns the hybridization penalty (0 being a perfect hybridization). c_{ins} is the penalty cost for a non-hybridized nucleotide.

After introducing a version of their algorithm the authors discuss several optimizations, which save redundant work and take advantage of information in the WCSP about already reduced domains. In the future, the authors are going to compare their method with other existing ones, and provide for an empirical evaluation of their approach. An implementation is available at `carlit.toulouse.inra.fr/Darn/index.php`.

6.8. Supertree construction with constraint programming: recent progress and new challenges (by Patrick Prosser)

One goal of biology is to build the *Tree of Life* (ToL), a representation of the evolutionary history of every living thing. To date, biologists have catalogued about 1.7 million species, yet estimates of the total number of species ranges from 4 to 100 million. Of the 1.7 million species identified only about 80,000 species have been placed in the ToL [PEN 03]. There are applications for the ToL: to help understand how pathogens become more virulent over time, how new diseases emerge, and how recognizing species at risk of extinction. One approach to building the ToL is to combine smaller trees into "supertrees". Phylogenetic trees have been created for relatively small sets of species (see `www.treebase.org`). These trees are then combined together into supertrees.

The problem of supertree construction is combining leaf labeled species trees, where there is an intersection in the leaf labels of those trees. The trees must be combined whilst respecting all the arboreal relationships in each tree. One of the first techniques for supertree construction is the OneTree algorithm [NG 96]. Using the same terminology, in Figure 6.7 there are the triples $(ab)c$, $(ac)b$, and $(bc)a$[2] and the fan (abc).

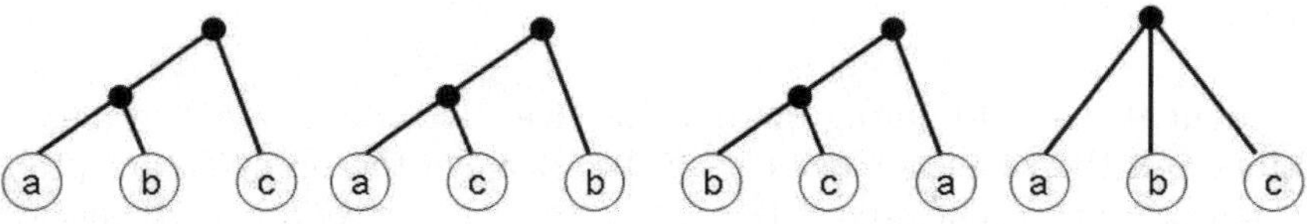

Figure 6.7. *The four possible relationships between three leaf nodes in a tree*

2. Where $(xy)z$ can be read as "x is closer to y than z".

The constraint programming model for this problem [GEN 03] is based on the observation that any rooted species-tree is *ultrametric.* Ultrametric trees can be uniquely constructed from ultrametric matrices. In such matrices M, the ultrametric condition holds, i.e. for any triplet i, j, k the distances $M_{i,j}$, $M_{i,k}$, and $M_{k,j}$ are either all equal or two of them are equal and the remaining one is smaller [GUS 97]. Given an ultrametric tree T and its ultrametric matrix M, it holds that the most recent common ancestor $mrca(i, j)$ of two leaf nodes i and j in T has depth $M_{i,j}$.

The constraint encoding starts by producing an $n \times n$ matrix M of constrained integer variables, each with a domain $1..n-1$. Amongst the trees to be combined there are exactly n species and each species is mapped to an integer. The array M is symmetric such that $M_{i,j}$ is the same constrained integer variable as $M_{j,i}$ and all diagonal elements $M_{i,i}$ are preset to zero. An ultrametric constraint is blanketed across the array. This means that for all i, j, k where $1 \leq i < j < k \leq n$ the following constraint is posted

$$M_{i,j} < M_{i,k} = M_{j,k} \vee M_{i,k} < M_{i,j} = M_{j,k} \vee$$
$$M_{j,k} < M_{i,j} = M_{i,k} \vee M_{i,j} = M_{i,k} = M_{j,k}$$

The species trees are then broken up, using the BreakUp algorithm [NG 96], into triples and fans. These triples and 3-fans are then used to break disjunctions in the above constraint. The M variables are used as decision variables for finding a solution.

After describing the basics, Prosser applies the model for constructing a supertree of sea birds. Furthermore, the author incorporates the ancestral divergence dates into the constraint model. The idea follows the RANKEDTREE algorithm [BIN 04], which takes as input two species trees where interior nodes are assigned integer values such that if the divergence of species A and B predates the divergence of species X and Y then the most recent ancestor of A and B will be assigned a value less than the most recent common ancestor of species X and Y.

The model is self-limiting by its cubic size. There are $O(n^3)$ ternary constraints and the same number of variables for the the optimization problem (minimizing fans). The largest trees that were built have about 70 species. A next step is to make this model more compact, and this might be done by implementing a specialized ultrametric constraint that involves three variables. This constraint might propagate more efficiently than as at present (using toolkit primitives) and each of the constraints might take less space. To reduce the number of constraints, an n-ary ultrametric constraint that takes as arguments the $n \times n$ array M could be introduced.

The model is available at `www.dcs.gla.ac.uk/~pat/superTrees`. The author shows the versatility of the constraint programming technology, by taking a model that essentially does the same as OneTree. Then he modified it to take a forest as input, dealt with ancestral divergence dates, managed to produce all solutions compactly, and addressed an optimization problem (although this might not be biologically sound). However, the model is limited in what it can do by its sheer size, and this should be addressed soon. The author believes that constraint programming will be the technology to retrieve the common information that is carried in all these supertrees.

6.9. References

[BAC 01] Backofen R., Will S., "Fast, Constraint-based Threading of HP-Sequences to Hydrophobic Cores", *CP2001*, vol. 2239 of *LNCS*, p. 494–508, 2001.

[BAC 06] Backofen R., Will S., "A Constraint-Based Approach to Fast and Exact Structure Prediction in Three-Dimensional Protein Models", *Constraints*, vol. 11, num. 1, p. 5–30, 2006.

[BIN 04] Bininda-Emonds O., *Phylogenetic Supertrees: Combining Information to Reveal the Tree of Life*, Springer, 2004.

[BOR 06] Bortolussi L., "Stochastic Concurrent Constraint Programming", *4th International Workshop on Quantitative Aspects of Programming Languages*, 2006.

[CAL 06] Calzone L., Chabrier-Rivier N., Fages F., Soliman S., "Machine Learning Biochemical Networks from Temporal Logic Properties", *Transactions on Computational Systems Biology*, vol. 4220 of *LNCS*, 2006.

[CLA 99] Clarke E. M., Grumberg O., Peled D. A., *Model Checking*, The MIT Press, 1999.

[Dal 04] Dal Palù A., Dovier A., Fogolari F., "Constraint Logic Programming Approach to Protein Structure Prediction", *BMC Bioinformatics*, vol. 5, num. 186, 2004.

[Dal 05] Dal Palù A., Dovier A., Pontelli E., "A New Constraint Solver for 3D Lattices and Its Application to the Protein Folding Problem", *LPAR 2005*, vol. 3835 of *LNCS*, p. 48–63, 2005.

[EDD 94] Eddy S., Durbin R., "RNA Sequence Analysis using Covariance Models", *Nucleic Acids Research*, vol. 22, p. 2079–2088, 1994.

[FAG 04a] Fages F., "From Syntax to Semantics in Systems Biology - Towards Automated Reasoning Tools", *Converging Sciences*, vol. 3939 of *LNCS*, 2004.

[FAG 04b] Fages F., Soliman S., Chabrier-Rivier N., "Modelling and Querying Interaction Networks in the Biochemical Abstract Machine BIOCHAM", *Journal of Biological Physics and Chemistry*, vol. 4, p. 64–73, 2004.

[GEN 03] Gent I. P., Prosser P., Smith B. M., Wei C. W., "Supertree Construction with Constraint Programming", *CP2003*, vol. 2833 of *LNCS*, p. 837–841, 2003.

[GIL 77] Gillespie D., "Exact Stochastic Simulation of Coupled Chemical Reactions", *J. of Physical Chemistry*, vol. 81, num. 25, 1977.

[GUS 97] GUSFIELD D., *Algorithms on Strings, Trees, and Sequences*, Cambridge University Press, 1997.

[KOH 99] KOHN K. W., "Molecular Interaction Map of the Mammalian Cell Cycle Control and DNA Repair Systems", *Molecular Biology of the Cell*, vol. 10, p. 2703–2734, 1999.

[KRI 02] KRIPPAHL L., BARAHONA P., "PSICO: Solving Protein Structures with Constraint Programming and Optimization.", *Constraints*, vol. 7, num. 3–4, p. 317–331, 2002.

[KRI 05] KRIPPAHL L., BARAHONA P., "Applying Constraint Programming to Rigid Body Protein Docking.", *CP2005*, vol. 3079 of *LNCS*, p. 373–387, 2005.

[LAR 04] LARROSA J., SCHIEX T., "Solving Weighted CSP by Maintaining Arc-consistency", *Artificial Intelligence*, vol. 159, p. 1–26, 2004.

[NG 96] NG M. P., WORMALD N. C., "Reconstruction of Rooted Trees from Subtrees", *Discrete Applied Mathematics*, vol. 69, p. 19–31, 1996.

[PEN 03] PENNISI E., "Modernizing the Tree of Life", *Science*, vol. 300, p. 1692–1697, 2003.

[PES 05] PESANT G., "Counting Solutions of CSPs: A Structural Approach", *IJCAI2005*, p. 260–265, 2005.

[PRI 01] PRIAMI C., REGEV A., SHAPIRO E. Y., SILVERMAN W., "Application of a Stochastic Name-passing Calculus to Representation and Simulation of Molecular Processes", *Inf. Process. Lett.*, vol. 80, num. 1, p. 25–31, 2001.

[REG 01] REGEV A., SILVERMAN W., SHAPIRO E. Y., "Representation and Simulation of Biochemical Processes using the pi-calculus Process Algebra", *Proceedings of the sixth Pacific Symposium of Biocomputing*, p. 459–470, 2001.

[REN 97] RENNER A., BORNBERG-BAUER E., "Exploring the Fitness Landscapes of Lattice Proteins", *2nd. Pacif. Symp. Biocomp.*, Singapore, 1997.

[ROT 96] ROTH D., "On the Hardness of Approximate Reasoning", *Artif. Intelligence*, vol. 82, num. 1–2, p. 273-302, 1996.

[SAR 93] SARASWAT V. A., *Concurrent Constraint Programming*, MIT press, 1993.

[SKO 04] SKOLNICK J., KOLINSKI A., "Reduced Models of Proteins and their Applications", *Polymer*, vol. 45, p. 511–524, 2004.

[TYS 91] TYSON J. J., "Modeling the Cell Division Dycle: cdc2 and cyclin Interactions", *Proceedings of the National Academy of Sciences*, vol. 88, p. 7328–7332, 1991.

[VIA 04] VIALETTE S., "On the Computational Complexity of 2-interval Pattern Matching Problems", *Theoretical Computer Science*, vol. 312, p. 223–249, 2004.

[WOL 06] WOLFINGER M., WILL S., HOFACKER I., BACKOFEN R., STADLER P., "Exploring the Lower Part of Discrete Polymer Model Energy Landscapes", *Europhysics Letters*, vol. 74, num. 4, p. 725–732, 2006.

[ZYT 06] ZYTNICKI M., SCHIEX T., GASPIN C., "A New Local Consistency for Weighted CSP Dedicated to Long Domains", *SAC2006*, p. 394–398, 2006.

PART II

Constraint Modeling and Reformulation

Edited by Ian MIGUEL and Steven PRESTWICH

Introduction

Constraint programming offers a powerful and efficient means of solving complex combinatorial problems that are ubiquitous in both academia and industry. Examples include scheduling, design, planning, configuration and supply-chain optimization. To solve a problem using constraint programming it must first be characterized or *modeled* as a set of constraints on a set of decision variables. Since constraints provide a rich language, there are often many possible models for a given problem. The choice of model has a substantial effect on the efficiency of the subsequent search for a solution or solutions. Formulating an *effective* model (one that is efficiently solvable in practice) is difficult, typically requiring a great deal of experience. Hence, there exists a modeling *bottleneck* preventing the truly widespread adoption of constraint programming.

For constraint programming to be used by non-experts more research effort is needed to support the modeling process. Over several years, researchers and practitioners have developed effective models for a wide range of problems. It is now an appropriate time to generalize and codify the lessons learnt from these case studies. The development of a general, principled understanding of modeling would help to guide the manual or automatic formulation of models, and the choice among alternative models. As well as helping modeling novices, an improved understanding of modeling issues can aid experts to obtain greatly improved performance from constraint solvers, and thus to solve larger and more difficult problems.

The International Workshop on Constraint Modeling and Reformulation series has run alongside the International Conference on Principles and Practice of Constraint Programming for the past five years. Together with related workshops co-located with the major conferences on artificial intelligence, it aims to realize these goals of generalizing and codifying constraint modeling expertise.

The 2006 workshop continued the traditions of attracting both an excellent set of submissions addressing a wide variety of modeling issues, and a good attendance at the workshop itself. To summarize briefly the papers presented at the workshop: Bessiere, Quinqueton and Raymond aim to automate the modeling process, by using existing solutions to related problems to build "viewpoints" of the problem; Bessiere and Verger extend quantified constraint satisfaction Problems (QCSPs) to strategic CSPs, allowing many two-player games to be modeled more easily; Frisch, Grum, Jefferson, Martinez-Hernandez and Miguel further describe, and clarify misconceptions about, the ESSENCE abstract constraint specification language; Martinez-Hernandez and Frisch automatically generate redundancy and channeling constraints for constraint models; Prestwich automatically removes constraints in order to improve local search performance; Puget and Smith present a new and more efficient model for the graceful labeling of graphs, obtaining several new results; Razgon, O'Sullivan and Provan formulate network flow-based global constraints in terms of a tractable problem; and Soto and Granvilliers consider software engineering aspects of constraint programming languages.

All these papers make useful contributions, but we have selected the two that received the best reviews from our programme committee to represent the workshop. These two papers, reproduced here in their entirety, are "Improved Models for Graceful Graphs" by Jean-Francois Puget and Barbara Smith, and "The Automatic Generation of Redundant Representations and Channeling Constraints" by Bernadette Martinez-Hernandez and Alan Frisch. The latter is a revision of the paper presented at the workshop. We hope that these very interesting chapters will stimulate further research into constraint modeling, and encourage further submissions to future workshops.

Chapter 7

Improved Models for Graceful Graphs

The problem of finding a graceful labeling of a graph, or proving that the graph is not graceful, has previously been modeled as a CSP. A new and much faster CSP model of the problem has been recently proposed. This model was inspired by a mathematical proof. We present a third model that is in some sense a combination of the previous two, but is much more efficient than either. We give several new results for graphs whose gracefulness was previously unknown. The possibility to generalize the use of the modeling techniques presented here is discussed.

7.1. Introduction

The problem of finding graceful labeling of a graph has been investigated in the CP community because these are good test beds for symmetry breaking methods, and because several open problems seem to be easily solved using constraint programming.

A labeling f of the nodes of a graph with q edges is *graceful* if f assigns each node a unique label from $\{0, 1, ..., q\}$ and when each edge xy is labeled with $|f(x) - f(y)|$, the edge labels are all different. (Hence, the edge labels are a permutation of 1, 2, ..., q.)

Gallian [GAL 05] gives a survey of graceful graphs, i.e. graphs with a graceful labeling, and lists the graphs whose status is known; his survey is frequently

---

Chapter written by Jean-François PUGET and Barbara SMITH.

updated to include new results. Graceful labeling were first defined by Rosa in 1967, although the name was introduced by Golomb [GOL 72] in 1972. Gallian lists a number of applications of labeled graphs; however, the study of graceful graphs has become an active area of research in its own right. The survey lists several classes of graph for which it is known that every instance is graceful, for instance the wheel graph W_n, consisting of a cycle C_n and an additional node joined to every node of the cycle. However, the only general result given by Gallian is that if every node has even degree and the number of edges is congruent to 1 or 2 (mod 4) then the graph is not graceful. For example, the cycles C_{4n+1} and C_{4n+2} are not graceful, although C_{4n} and C_{4n+3} are graceful for all n. There is a long-standing conjecture that all trees are graceful and although this has been proved for several classes of tree (including paths), and for all trees with at most 27 nodes, the general case remains unproven.

Given a graph whose gracefulness is so far unknown, in general there is no way to tell whether it is graceful or not, except by trying to label it. Constraint programming is thus a useful tool to use in investigating graceful graphs.

7.2. A direct model

A simple CSP model was introduced in [LUS 01]. It has two sets of variables: a variable for each node, $x_0, x_1, ..., x_{n-1}$ each with domain $\{0, 1, ..., , q\}$ and a variable for each edge, $d_0, d_1, ..., d_{q-1}$, each with domain $\{1, 2, ..., , q\}$. The value assigned to x_i is the label attached to node i, and the value of d_k is the label attached to the edge k.

The constraints of the problem are: if edge k joins nodes i and j then $d_k = |x_i - x_j|$, for $k = 1, 2, ..., q$; $x_0, x_1, ..., x_{n-1}$ are all different; $d_0, d_1, ..., d_{q-1}$ are all different (and form a permutation).

Let us consider graph $K_3 \times P_2$ depicted in Figure 7.1. There are 6 variables x_i corresponding to the vertices of the graph, and 9 variables d_j corresponding to the edges.

There are two kinds of symmetry in the problem of finding a graceful labeling of a graph: first, there may be symmetry in the graph. For instance, if the graph is a clique, any permutation of the node labels in a graceful labeling is also graceful, and if the graph is a path, P_n, the node labels can be reversed. The second type of symmetry is that we can replace the value v of every node variable x_i by its complement $q - v$. We can also combine each graph symmetry with the complement symmetry. For instance, the graceful labeling (0, 3, 1, 2) of P_4 has three symmetric equivalents: reversal (2, 1, 3, 0); complement (3, 0, 2, 1); and reversal + complement (1, 2, 0, 3).

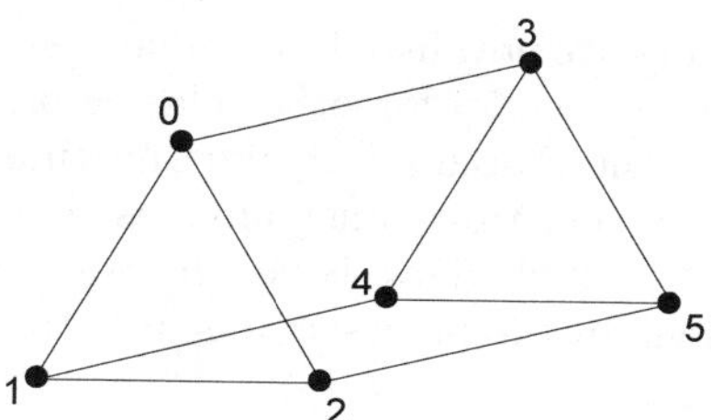

Figure 7.1. *The graph $K_3 \times P_2$*

If the graph is symmetric, it is essential to eliminate all or most of the symmetry in the CSP in order to avoid wasted search, especially if all graceful labelings are required or the graph is not graceful. In terms of the CSP model described above, the symmetry of the graph leads to variable symmetries in the CSP affecting the node variables $x_1, x_2, ..., x_n$; each symmetry maps an assignment of a value l to a variable x_i to an assignment of the same value to a variable x_j. Following the procedure introduced by Crawford *et al.* [CRA 96], variable symmetries can be eliminated by adding a lexicographic ordering constraint for each symmetry. Although in general this may not be practicable, we showed in [PUG 05a] that when there is an allDifferent constraint on the variables, the symmetry can be eliminated by at most $n-1$ binary constraints.

The symmetries of the graph in Figure 7.1 are, firstly, any permutation of the 3-cliques which acts on both in the same way, for instance, transposing nodes 1 and 2 and simultaneously nodes 4 and 5. Secondly, the labels of the first clique (nodes 1, 2, 3) can be interchanged with the labels of the corresponding nodes (nodes 4, 5, 6) in the second. A possible set of constraints to eliminate the graph symmetry is $x_1 < x_2$, $x_2 < x_3$, to exclude permutations within the cliques and $x_1 < x_4$, $x_1 < x_5$, $x_1 < x_6$ to exclude swapping the cliques and permuting both. Since the constraints imply that $x_1 = 0$, this constraint together with $x_2 < x_3$ is sufficient.

We have shown in [PUG 06a] that combinations of value symmetries with variable symmetries could be broken by a combination of lexicographic ordering constraints and element constraints. We state one such constraint for each combination of the complement symmetry with one variable symmetry.

The model just described, which will be called the *node model* in the rest of the chapter, is adequate to find all graceful labelings of the graph in Figure 7.1, and allow us to investigate slightly larger graphs as well, e.g. the related graphs $K_4 \times P_2$, $K_5 \times P_2$ and $K_6 \times P_2$. $K_5 \times P_2$ is graceful, and has a unique graceful labeling, apart from symmetric equivalents, whereas $K_6 \times P_2$ is not graceful; these new results are now listed in Gallian's survey [GAL 05]. Results that we obtained with this model for other classes of graph are summarized in [SMI 03a]. However, the search effort and run time increase rapidly with problem size, so that it is very time-consuming, as shown below, to prove that $K_7 \times P_2$, with 14 nodes and 49 edges, is not graceful; $K_8 \times P_2$ is out of reach within a reasonable time. In the next sections, a better model of the problem is introduced.

7.3. The edge-label model

A more efficient model has recently been introduced in [SMI 03b]. We summarize it here. Its roots are in a search algorithm by Beutner & Harborth [BEU 02]. They use a backtracking search procedure, based on the approach in the proof, to find graceful labelings or prove that there are none. They focus on the edge labels, considering each label in turn, from q (the number of edges) downwards. Each edge label has to be used, and appear somewhere in the graph, and they construct a labeling, or prove that there is no labeling, by trying to decide, for each edge label in turn, which node labels will appear at either end of the edge. The classes they consider are nearly complete graphs, with specific kinds of sub graph removed from a clique; for instance, they show that $K_n - e$, i.e. an n-clique with one edge removed, is graceful only for $n \leq 5$ and that any graph derived from K_n by removing 2 or 3 edges is not graceful for $n > 6$.

The edge-label model has a variable e_i for each edge label i, which indicates how this edge label will be formed. The value assigned to e_i is the smaller node label forming the edge labeled i, i.e. if $e_i = j$, the edge labeled i joins the nodes labeled j and $j + i$. Hence, the domain of e_i is $\{0, 1, ..., q - i\}$. (Essentially, an edge label is associated with a *pair* of node labels, but since if the edge label and the smaller node label are known, the other node label is also known, we need only associate an edge label with one node label.) Note that the domain of e_q is $\{0\}$. The domain of e_{q-1} is initially $\{0, 1\}$ but this can be reduced either to $\{1\}$ or to $\{0\}$ arbitrarily, to break the complement symmetry. We choose to set $e_{q-1} = 1$ (although choosing $e_{q-1} = 0$ instead makes little difference).

There is also a variable l_j for each node label j; the value of l_j represents the node to which the label j is attached, provided that this node label is used in the labeling. To allow for the fact that a label may not be used, the domains of these variables contain a dummy value, say $n + 1$. The node label variables must all have different values (unless they are assigned the dummy value).

The link between the two sets of variables is achieved by the constraints: $e_i = j$ if, and only if, the values of l_j and l_{j+i} represent adjacent nodes in the graph ($1 \leq i \leq q$; $0 \leq j \leq q-i$). In ILOG Solver 6.3, this is expressed as a table constraint, using a ternary predicate which uses the adjacency matrix of the graph. GAC is enforced on table constraints, which is relatively slow.

The graph symmetry, if any, has still to be dealt with. In the edge-label model, it appears as value symmetries affecting the node-label variables. If a graph symmetry σ maps the node numbered i to the node numbered $\sigma(i)$, then it maps the assignment $l_j = i$ to the assignment $l_j = \sigma(i)$, whereas in the node model, it maps $x_i = j$ into $x_{\sigma(i)} = j$. Law and Lee [LAW 06] point out that value symmetry can be transformed into variable symmetry acting on the dual variables and then is amenable to the Crawford *et al.* procedure for deriving symmetry breaking constraints.

Hence, a simple way to derive symmetry breaking constraints in the edge-label model is to re-introduce the variables $x_1, ..., x_n$ from the node model. These are the duals of the node label variables $l_1, ..., l_q$. The two sets of variables can be linked by the channeling constraints: $x_i = j$ if, and only if, $l_j = i$ for $i = 1, ..., n$ and $j = 0, ..., q$, or equivalently by the global *inverse* constraint [BEL 00]. As a side-effect, the channeling constraints are sufficient to ensure that every possible node label is assigned to a different node, or else is not used, so that no explicit allDifferent constraint is required.

It was shown in [SMI 03b] that another symmetry breaking technique, SBDS [GEN 00] is more efficient for several classes of graphs. We found that dynamic lex constraints (DLC) [PUG 06b], yet another symmetry breaking technique, are even more efficient than SBDS on these problems. Therefore, we will use DLC for breaking symmetries in the edge-label model.

The search strategy considers the edge labels in descending order; for each one in turn, the search first decides which node labels will make that edge label, and then decides where in the graph to put those node labels. Hence, both the edge label variables $e_1, e_2, ..., e_q$ and the node label variables $l_0, l_1, ..., l_q$ are search variables. The variable ordering strategy finds the largest edge label i that has not yet been attached to a specific edge in the graph. The next variable assigned is e_i, if that has not been assigned; if e_i has been assigned a value j, then the next variable is l_j, if that is not yet assigned, or l_{i+j} (if all three variables have been assigned, the label i is already associated with a specific edge).

Since the domains of the edge label variables increase in size as the labels decrease, at least initially, this variable ordering is approximately equivalent to minimum domain ordering, as far as the edge label variables are concerned. However, limited experiments with choosing the edge label variable with smallest domain, if different from the largest unassigned edge label variable, did not give good results. As in the node model, the value ordering chooses the smallest available value in the domain.

7.4. A combined model

The efficiency of the edge-label model is due in part to its clever search order. The search focuses first on the edges labeled with the largest values. A similar idea can be adapted to the node model: we can try to label first the edge with the largest value. One simple way to do this is to introduce a variable y_j for each edge label, whose value will be the edge labeled with j. These variables are the duals of the node label variables $d_0, ..., d_q$ in the original model. The two sets of variables can be linked by the channeling constraints: $d_i = j$ if, and only if, $y_j = i$ for $i = 0, ..., n$ and $j = 0, ..., q$, or equivalently by the global *inverse* constraint [BEL 00].

Therefore, we consider the following model. It has three sets of variables: a variable for each node, $x_0, x_1, ..., x_{n-1}$ each with domain $\{0, 1, ...,, q\}$, a variable for each edge, $d_0, d_1, ..., d_{q-1}$, each with domain $\{1, 2, ...,, q\}$, and a variable for each edge label $y_1, y_2, ..., y_q$. The value assigned to x_i is the label attached to node i, and the value of d_k is the label attached to the edge k.

The constraints of the problem are: if edge k joins nodes i and j then $d_k = |x_i - x_j|$, for $k = 1, 2, ..., q$; $x_1, x_2, ..., x_n$ are all different; $d_1, d_2, ..., d_q$ are all different (and form a permutation); d_i and y_j are linked by an inverse constraint.

The graph symmetries, if any, need to be dealt with. Any graph symmetry induces a value symmetry for the variables y_j. If edge i is mapped to edge k by a symmetry, then the assignment $y_j = i$ is mapped to $y_j = k$. These value symmetries can be broken using dynamic lex constraints as explained in [PUG 06b]. Therefore we use DLC to break these symmetries.

The complement symmetry does not impact edge labels. Therefore, this symmetry is not broken by the DLC method on the y_j variables. The complement symmetry induces a value symmetry for the x_i variables, exactly as in the original node model. We can break it using a lexicographic constraint and an element constraint as in [PUG 06a].

The search strategy is similar to that used in the edge-label model. It considers the edge labels in descending order; for each one in turn, the search first decides which node labels will make that edge label, and then decides where in the graph to put those node labels. Hence, both the edge label variables $y_1, y_2, ..., y_q$ and the node label variables $x_0, x_1, ..., x_{n-1}$ are search variables.

The variable ordering strategy finds the largest edge label i that has not yet been attached to a specific edge in the graph. The next variable assigned is y_i, if that has not been assigned; if y_i has been assigned a value j then we look at both ends of edge j. Suppose that these are nodes a and b. Then both variables x_a and x_b are eligible as the next search variable. When there are several node variables eligible as the next search variable, the one corresponding to the largest edge label is selected first.

As in the node model and in the edge-label model, the value ordering chooses the smallest available value in the domain.

7.5. Experimental results

All three models have been implemented with ILOG Solver 6.3 [ILO 06]. Experiments were run on a 1.4GHz Pentium M laptop computer. Graph symmetries are calculated automatically using the AUTOM routine [PUG 05b]. Running time includes symmetry detection time.

Several classes of graphs were considered. The class $K_n \times P_2$ was studied in [LUS 01], [PET 03], and [SMI 03b] among others. These graphs are made of two cliques of size n plus n edges linking pairs of nodes, one from each clique. The graph in Figure 1 is the smallest graph in this class. We also considered graphs where the number of cliques is larger than 2. We report for each graph the number of solutions (0 when the graph has no graceful labeling), and for each method the number of backtracks and the running time. Results are given in Table 7.5. It was not previously known that $K_5 \times P_3$ is graceful and that $K_4 \times P_4$ is not.

The results for the $K_n \times P_2$ class clearly show a significant improvement in running times when going from the node model to the edge-label model, and yet another significant improvement when going from the edge-label model to the combined model. However, the edge-label model remains the one that leads to the smallest search tree. When the number of cliques is larger than 2, the node model is faster than the edge-label model, but again the latter model gives the smallest search trees. The combined model is by far the most efficient of the three, in terms of run-time.

We considered a related class, $K_n \times C_m$. Graphs in this class are made of m cliques of size n, where corresponding nodes in each cliques are connected in a cycle of length m. Results are given in Table 7.5. The graphs $K_3 \times C_3$ and $K_5 \times C_3$ are not graceful because of the parity condition given earlier (all nodes are of even degree and the number of edges is $\equiv 1$ or $2 \pmod 4$). However, the

Graph	Solutions	Node model		Edge model		Combined model	
		BT	sec.	BT	sec.	BT	sec.
$K_3 \times P_2$	4	46	0	14	0.01	15	0.01
$K_4 \times P_2$	15	908	0.2	151	0.32	166	0.03
$K_5 \times P_2$	1	22,182	5.48	725	5.26	956	0.31
$K_6 \times P_2$	0	544,549	396	1,559	41	2,538	1.09
$K_7 \times P_2$	0			1,986	140.8	4,080	3.13
$K_8 \times P_2$	0			2,041	325.8	4,620	6.58
$K_9 \times P_2$	0			2,045	668.8	4,690	11.7
$K_3 \times P_3$	284	5,363	0.48	1,833	1.88	1,939	0.33
$K_4 \times P_3$	704	1,248,935	195	155,693	883	183,150	25.1
$K_5 \times P_3$	101					7,049,003	1,974
$K_3 \times P_4$	12,754	1,936,585	205	370,802	964	424,573	37.2
$K_4 \times P_4$	0					416,756,282	76635

Table 7.1. *Results for $K_n \times P_m$ graphs*

Graph	Solutions	Node model		Edge model		Combined model	
		BT	sec.	BT	sec.	BT	sec.
$K_3 \times C_3$	0	5,059	0.74	604	1.08	599	0.14
$K_4 \times C_3$	22	3,104,352	665	47,532	522	51,058	10.8
$K_5 \times C_3$	0					1,184,296	509
$K_6 \times C_3$	0					12,019,060	38,431
$K_3 \times C_4$	0					206,244	24.1
$K_4 \times C_4$	0					169,287,859	40,233

Table 7.2. *Results for $K_n \times C_m$ graphs*

results that there is no graceful labeling for the graphs $K_6 \times C_3$, $K_3 \times C_4$, and $K_4 \times C_4$ are new.

These results show again that the combined model is by far the most efficient one. For these graphs, the size of the search tree for the edge-label model is comparable to that for the combined model. The run-time for the node model and the edge-label model are comparable.

We now consider another class of graphs, double wheel graphs: these consist of a pair of cycles C_n, with each node joined to a common hub. Previous results with the node model are given in [SMI 03a]. Results for all three models are given in Table 7.5.

Graph	Solutions	Node model		Edge model		Combined model	
		BT	sec.	BT	sec.	BT	sec.
DW3	0	198	0.03	20	0.03	21	0.01
DW4	44	4,014	0.54	378	0.6	408	0.11
DW5	1,216	132,632	16.9	14,140	24.7	14,565	1.62
DW6	35,877	6,740,234	1,028	891,351	2,572	916,253	102

Table 7.3. *Results for double wheel graphs*

For this class of graphs, the combined model is again the most efficient. The tree size is comparable for the edge-label model and the combined model. For these graphs, the node model is faster than the edge-label model. This is probably because these graphs are very far from complete graphs, and indeed quite sparse, whereas the edge-label model was derived from an algorithm tailored for almost complete graphs. This explanation may hold for the graphs $K_n \times P_m$ with $m > 2$ as well. Surprisingly enough, the combined model is very efficient on these sparse graphs.

The last class of graphs was studied in [SMI 03b]. These are dense graphs, consisting of m cliques of size n that share a common clique of size r. They are denoted $B(n, r, m)$. Results for this class are given in Table 7.5.

Graph	Solutions	Node model		Edge model		Combined model	
		BT	sec.	BT	sec.	BT	sec.
B(3,2,2)	4	7	0.01	1	0.01	1	0
B(4,2,2)	4	127	0.03	20	0.04	26	0
B(5,2,2)	1	2,552	0.45	75	0.32	88	0.04
B(6,2,2)	0	48,783	18.9	109	2.21	135	0.15
B(7,2,2)	0			120	7.46	161	0.42
B(8,2,2)	0			120	23.4	163	6.22
B(6,3,2)	0	20,698	4.7	102	1.48	141	0.12
B(6,4,2)	0	5,102	1.21	47	0.53	77	0.05
B(6,5,2)	0	470	0.26	11	0.12	16	0.02
B(5,3,3)	5	10,109	1.88	266	1.76	346	0.15
B(6,3,3)	0	996,667	591	1,588	49.7	1,924	1.18
B(7,3,2)	0	49,763	314	135	6.35	193	0.34

Table 7.4. *Results for multi-clique graphs*

We can summarize our experimental results as follows. The combined model is by far the most efficient model, whereas the edge-label model is the one that leads to the smallest search trees. For dense graphs, the edge-label model is much more efficient than the node model, but for sparse graphs, the reverse is true.

7.6. Discussion

We have presented a new model for graceful graphs. It is derived from the classical node model and the recently proposed edge-label model. It reuses the variables and the constraints of the former, and the search strategy of the latter. The resulting model is quite simple, yet much more efficient than both its predecessors. We were able to derive new mathematical results using that model, namely we have shown that $K_5 \times P_3$ is graceful, and found all its graceful labelings, while several other graphs have been shown to have no graceful labeling. These results in themselves are interesting enough. Moreover, some of the following modeling techniques could be useful in other domains.

The first technique is to make more use of duality. Instead of using the original variables (the edge variables d_i in the node model) as search variables, we use their duals (the y_j variables in the combined model). This amounts to selecting first which value to assign to the d_i variables, and then selecting which variable d_i will receive that value. As we show, using the dual variables in this way can improve the performance of the model even when they play no other role. This technique can be applied to any permutation problem; for instance, Régin used a similar idea in solving sports scheduling problems [REG 99].

The second technique is to group variables together in the search. When an edge variable d_i is assigned a value, search proceeds with the variables x_a and x_b corresponding to both ends of the edge. These variables are linked by the constraint $d_i = |x_a - x_b|$. Therefore, the second technique amounts to following the constraint graph during search.

The last technique is quite a general one. Both the edge-label model and the combined model use a clever search strategy. We believe that the search strategy should often be considered as part of the model. Indeed, we tried various other variable ordering strategies, such as smallest domain, most constrained variable, etc., and none of them gave good results. The search strategy that we used is crucial to the efficiency of these models.

Acknowledgment Barbara SMITH is supported by the Science Foundation Ireland under Grant No. 00/PI.1/C075.

7.7. References

[BEL 00] BELDICEANU N., "Global constraints as graph properties on structured network of elementary constraints of the same type", *Technical Report T2000/01, SICS*, 2000.

[BEU 02] BEUTNER D., HARBORTH H., "Graceful labelings of nearly complete graphs", *Results in Mathematics*, 41:34–39, 2002.

[CRA 96] CRAWFORD J., GINSBERG M., LUKS E., A. ROY, "Symmetry-breaking predicates for search problems", in *Proceedings KR'96*, pages 149–159, 1996.

[GAL 05] GALLIAN J.A., "A dynamic survey of graph labeling", *The Electronic Journal of Combinatorics*, 9th edition, 2005.

[GEN 00] GENT I.P., SMITH B.M., "Symmetry breaking during search in constraint programming", in *Proceedings ECAI 2000 – European Conference on Artificial Intelligence*, pages 599–603, 2000.

[GOL 72] GOLOMB S.W., "How to number a graph", in *Graph Theory and Computing*, pages 23–37, Academic Press, 1972.

[ILO 06] ILOG., "ILOG Solver 6.3. User Manual", ILOG, S.A., Gentilly, France, July 2006.

[LAW 06] LAW Y.C., LEE J.H.M., "Symmetry breaking constraints for value symmetries in constraint satisfaction", *Constraints*, 11:221–267, 2006.

[LUS 01] LUSTIG I.J., PUGET J.F., "Program does not equal program: constraint programming and its relationship to mathematical programming", *INTERFACES*, 31(6):29–53, 2001.

[PET 03] PETRIE K.E., SMITH B.M., "Symmetry breaking in graceful graphs", *Technical Report APES-56-2003, APES Research Group*, 2003.

[PUG 05a] PUGET J-F., "Breaking symmetries in all different problems", in *Proceedings IJCAI 2005*, pages 272–277, 2005.

[PUG 05b] PUGET J-F., "Automatic detection of variable and value symmetries", in *Proceedings CP 2005 – Principles and Practice of Constraint Programming*, Springer LNCS 3709, pages 475–489, 2005.

[PUG 06a] PUGET J-F., "An efficient way of breaking value symmetries", in *Proceedings AAAI 2006 – 21st National Conference on Artificial Intelligence*, pages 117–122, 2006.

[PUG 06b] PUGET J-F. "Dynamic lex constraints", in *Proceedings CP 2006 – Principles and Practice of Constraint Programming*, Springer LNCS 4204, pages 453–467, 2006.

[REG 99] RÉGIN J-C. "Constraint programming and sports scheduling problems", *Informs*, 1999.

[SMI 03a] SMITH B.M., PETRIE K. "Graceful graphs: results from constraint programming", http://4c.ucc.ie/~bms/Graceful/, 2003.

[SMI 03b] SMITH, B.M. "Constraint programming models for graceful graphs", in *Proceedings CP2006 – Principles and Practice of Constraint Programming*, Springer LNCS 4204, pages 545–559, 2006.

Chapter 8

The Automatic Generation of Redundant Representations and Channeling Constraints

Constraint modeling is the process of encoding a given problem to be solved by constraint satisfaction technology. Automatic modeling systems aim to reduce the number of decisions human modelers must take. To do so, these systems implement common modeling guidelines and techniques. In this chapter we focus on the automatic addition of redundant information, and most importantly the corresponding channeling constraints to synchronise it. We discuss and formalize a systematic method of generation of both elements; redundancy and channeling constraints. We also provide a new insight on this formalization that aims to clarify and increase previous work on the subject [FRI 05c].

8.1. Introduction

Constraint modeling is the process of encoding a problem into finite domain decision variables and a set of constraints posed over these variables. A model used to solve a constraint satisfaction problem is normally not unique. In many cases, the way we model a problem determines how fast we find a solution or whether we find one at all. Modelers propose and test several alternative models to finally select the most efficient ones to solve the general problem. During the modeling process, alternative models are created by means of formulating the problem with different sorts of variables and constraints.

Chapter written by Bernadette MARTÍNEZ-HERNÁNDEZ and Alan M. FRISCH.

Efficient constraint modeling is a hard task often learnt by novice constraint users from modeling examples. In order to reduce the time spent on modeling, many automatic modeling systems have arisen. The construction of one of these automatic systems requires a good understanding of the modeling process as well as each commonly used modeling technique. One of these frequently used modeling techniques is the addition of *redundant representations* and *channeling constraints*. Channeling constraints (channels) were defined by Cheng [CHE 96] and, although widely used, little has been done to study them thoroughly from a point of view that systematically associates both redundant information and the needed channeling constraint. Previously, we introduced an algorithm of generation of channels [FRI 05c]. This algorithm, even though correct, lacked a clear association with the redundant elements added to the model. We seek to clarify in this chapter this relationship between redundant representations and channels as well as describing the conditions and requirements for adding channeling constraints. In the remainder of this section we explain in more detail what channeling constraints are to then introduce the main channeling issues addressed in this chapter.

Let us now use the well known *n-queens* problem as an example of modeling. To solve this problem we need to find a configuration of n queens on an $n \times n$ board such that no queen is under attack. There are many models to solve this problem and Nadel [NAD 90] has already discussed several of these alternative approaches. We detail as follows two of the models described in his chapter, and afterwards a third *combined* model, composed of the previous two alternatives together with the necessary channeling constraints.

The first approach to be considered uses an array R of n variables to encode the n rows of the chess board. Each variable of the array R has an integer domain $1..n$, that is, each element of the domain corresponds to one of the n columns of the board. Hence, $R[i] = j$ whenever a queen is placed on row i and column j.

The second approach swaps the column-values for the row-variables obtaining the array of n variables C. The variables of the array C also have an integer domain $1..n$, but for this model we say $C[i] = j$ whenever a queen is placed on the column i and row j. Both models impose `alldifferent` constraints as well as other constraints on their arrays of variables to ensure none of the queens is under attack.

The third approach, and the most important one, considers both R and C, however, solving both alternatives simultaneously without any synchronization of the assignments to R and C produces (in many cases) solutions that represent different configurations of the chess board. Propagating a greater number of variables and constraints can only cause overhead if we do not benefit from sharing the information each approach encodes during the search. Therefore, we need to introduce a constraint (or a group of constraints) to propagate the values and assignments pruned from one array of variables to the other (and vice verse).

This connecting constraint, shown below, must ensure simultaneous assignments of values to variables of each model stand for the same "abstract" value in the chess board, that is, the assignment of a queen to the position row i and column j must occur in both R and C at the same time.

$$\forall i{:}1..n \ . \ \forall j{:}1..k \ . \ R[i] = j \Leftrightarrow C[j] = i \qquad [8.1]$$

The consistency between R and C is maintained by the addition of the previous channeling constraint to the combined model. Channels are not restricted to connecting integer matrices of one dimension such as R and C, they can link highly complex structures such as matrices of several dimensions grouping variables of integer or set of integer domains. For example, consider the Sonet problem [FRI 05a] where a network of a certain number of available rings (*nrings*) which can allocate a limited number (*capacity*) of elements from a number of nodes to connect (*nnodes*) needs to be found. A solution to the Sonet problem must satisfy certain connections between nodes besides being an optimal configuration using the smallest number of rings, however, in this reduced example we discard these extra requirements since they are not necessary to generate alternative models of the problem and their corresponding channel.

The first solving approach we review encodes each of the rings in a Boolean array; modeling the Sonet network as a 2-dimensional matrix $rings_1$ indexed by $1..nrings$ and $1..nnodes$. In this encoding a node is said to be in a ring if its value indexes a variable assigned to True, that is, $rings_1[i,j] = True$ if node j is in ring i. Also, to set bounds to the number of nodes in each ring, we impose a constraint on the sum of values of each Boolean array: $\forall\ i \in 1..nrings\ .\ ((\sum j \in 1..nnodes\ .\ rings_1[i,j]) \leq capacity)$.

Each ring can also be encoded by explicitly assigning its node elements to an array of variables. The number of elements of each ring varies but it is limited by the *capacity*; therefore an extra Boolean array can be used to indicate the variables (and nodes) which are to be taken into account. Hence, the second model for the Sonet network uses two 2-dimensional matrices, $rings_2$ and *switch* indexed by $1..nrings$ and $1..capacity$. The domain of each variable in $rings_2$ is $1..nnodes$, whereas variables in *switch* have a Boolean domain. In

X	$=$ *rings*
$D(rings)$	$=$ *multisets (of size nrings) of sets (of maxsize capacity) of 1..nnodes*
C	$= \emptyset$

Figure 8.1. *CSP instance 1 of the rings of the Sonet problem*

this encoding node j is in ring i if there exists a k such that $rings_2[i, k] = j$ and $switch[i, k] = True$.

Both approaches find a correct Sonet network (if any) separately. Solving them simultaneously requires, as in the n-queens problem example, the addition of a channel to maintain the consistency between assignments. We can use the following constraint for that purpose:

$$\forall i \in 1..nrings\ .\ \forall j \in 1..nnodes\ . \qquad [8.2]$$
$$(rings_1[i, j] \Leftrightarrow \exists k \in 1..capacity\ .\ (rings_2[i, k] = j \wedge switch[i, l]))$$

The channeling constraint [8.2] ensures that node j is part of ring i for $rings_1$ ($rings_1[i, j] = True$) if and only if it is also part of ring i for ($rings_2$, $switch$), that is, there is a position k such that $rings_2[i, k] = j$ and the position k is activated by $switch[i, k] = True$. Note this channel enforces the same ring order on both linked models by using the same index i when channeling.

In both examples each of the alternatives were the product of a sequence of modeling decisions, although they were not described when the models were introduced. These decisions, in an implicit way, also provide the guideline to construct the connection between two redundant alternatives. Therefore, to fully describe the correct generation of channeling constraints we start by focusing in the formalization of modeling. As a first step we introduce a definition for representation and alternative representation in section 8.2, using this notion we then define what channels are in section 8.3; to later give an account of the generation of alternative redundant representations in section 8.4. We detail the main topic of this chapter, the automatic generation of channels for alternative representations, in section 8.5; followed by a discussion on the generation of efficient implementations of channels in section 8.6. Finally, conclusions and future work are presented in the last section.

X_1	$= rings_1$
$D_1(rings_1)$	$=$ *2-D matrix of Boolean indexed by 1..nrings and 1..nnodes*
C_1	$= \forall\, i \in 1..nrings\ .\ ((\sum j \in 1..nnodes\ .\ rings_1[i, j]) \leq capacity)$

Figure 8.2. *CSP instance 2 of the rings of the Sonet problem*

8.2. Representations

Any CSP model is formulated to *represent* a problem. A CSP solver finds the solution(s) of a CSP instance, that is, the representation of only *one* instance of the problem. A CSP instance is a triple (X, D, C) composed of a set of variables X, a domain D that maps each variable x in X to a finite set of allowed values for x, $D(x)$, and a group of constraints C over the variables in X. We generate CSP instances from our previous Sonet example if we suppose *nrings*, *nnodes* and *capacity* are given a numeric value; we assume from now on that that is the case. We will now discuss these Sonet CSP instances as an introduction to the intuition of representation.

The first CSP instance, shown in Figure 8.1, consists of the variable *rings*, whose domain is composed of multisets (groups of elements possibly with multiple occurrences) of sets of integers. Current CSP solvers do not support variables of multiset of set domain; however throughout this chapter this implementation is not taken into account when we construct CSP instances. The reason is that this CSP instance and many others describe in a very simple manner the problem instance, that is, all the elements of the domain of the *rings* variable, encode every possible configuration the Sonet network may take if we regard each set as a ring.

The solutions of CSP instance 2 (Figure 8.2) can also reproduce every Sonet network of rings whenever each of the arrays is seen as a ring as previously performed in section 8.1.

Both CSP instances characterize the Sonet problem instance with their solutions; more importantly, each solution of the CSP instance 2 can be mapped into a solution of the CSP instance 1. This mapping between solutions of the instances outlines how CSP instance 2 *represents* CSP instance 1, therefore, the definition of representation we now introduce includes it.

Definition 1 R' ***represents*** R *via* ψ, *if* $R' = (X', D', C')$ *and* $R = (X, D, C)$ *are CSP instances and* ψ *is a partial function from the total assignments of* X' *into the total assignments of* X *such that:*

– for each total assignment w' *of the variables in* X', w' *is a solution of* C' ***if and only if*** $\psi(w')$ *is defined and it is a solution of* C*;*

X_2	$=$ *rings*$_2$, *switch*
$D_2(rings_2)$	$=$ *2-D matrix of 1..nnodes indexed by 1..nrings and 1..capacity*
$D_2(switch)$	$=$ *2-D matrix of Boolean indexed by 1..nrings and 1..capacity*
C_2	$= \forall\ i \in 1..nrings$. `alldifferent`$(rings_2[i])$

Figure 8.3. *CSP instance 3 of the rings of the Sonet problem*

– for each solution w of C, there is at least one solution w' of C' such that $\psi(w') = w$.

*We say that R' **represents** or **is a representation** of R if R' represents R via ψ, for some ψ .*

In our example, CSP instance 2 represents CSP instance 1 via the function ψ from assignments of $rings_1$ to assignments of *rings*, such that each of the rows of the Boolean matrix is transformed into a set composed of the value indexing variables set to *True*.

Our definition of representation is strongly influenced by definition of *variable representation* introduced by Jefferson and Frisch [JEF 05]. Their variable representation has attached the surjective mapping used to preserve the solutions but initially disregards any constraint imposed on any of the variables.

Modelers seek to construct alternative redundant representations, either to combine them or to test on their own. We need then, to understand how two CSP instances can be considered alternative.

8.3. Alternative representations and channels

Constraints provide a rich language that enables a problem to be solved in many different ways. Two CSP instances may look unrelated at first glance, but a more careful analysis may show they are in fact alternative representations of a problem instance and more importantly, how to construct the channel to connect them. In this section, we first show how to identify alternative representations; and second we introduce a definition of channeling constraints and we present a general view of the cases where the addition of channels is necessary.

8.3.1. *Alternative representations*

The CSP instance of Figure 8.3 containing matrices $rings_2$ and *switch*, of integer and Boolean variables respectively, represents CSP instance 1. The mapping transforms each row of values of $rings_2$ activated by the same row in the matrix *switch* into the sets containing those values. Since CSP instance 2 and CSP instance 3 represent CSP instance 1; the two options can be intuitively considered as *redundant.* Also, and because they use different variables we can call them *alternative.* We now present a formal definition of redundancy based on these intuitions.

Definition 2 *The CSP instances R_1 and R_2 are* ***redundant*** *representations with respect to the CSP instance R if R_1 represents R and R_2 represents R. R_1 and R_2 are* ***alternative redundant*** *representations if their set of variables is disjoint.*

Two CSP instances are *equivalent* when they both represent each other. Notice redundancy does not necessarily entail equivalence, for example, CSP 2 and 3 are not equivalent as CSP 2 cannot represent CSP 3. This example shows how limited the scope of equivalent CSP is compared to that of redundant representations as redundant representations describe many more alternatives used by human modelers.

Law and Lee in their Model Induction [LAW 02b] and Algebra [LAW 02a] introduce a different definition of redundancy related to alternative modeling and channeling. This definition labels two CSP instances[1] as redundant only if there is a bijective mapping between them. As well as with the equivalent CSP instances, the existence of a bijective mapping highly restricts the scope of the CSP instances to be considered.

8.3.2. *Constraint-wise quasi-representations and channeling constraints*

Adding channeling constraints to a CSP instance composed of alternative redundant CSP instances is not always necessary. For example, the instance obtained by joining ($\cup$) all the variables, domains and constraints of a group of redundant instances with respect to R also represents the CSP instance R as an extension of any of their mappings can be used to preserve the solutions. Again using our Sonet example, the union of CSP instances 2 and 3 represents CSP instance 1 if function ψ (detailed at the end of section 8.2) is expanded to take assignments of $rings_1$, $rings_2$ and *switch* but returning the same value used when only $rings_1$ was considered.

1. They say *Models.*

The need for channeling constraints arises when the alternatives are representations of one variable, rather than a CSP instance; and these alternative representations have different constraints imposed upon them. To formalize this intuition we introduce two extensions defined as representations which are used later to describe a new construct where separate representations of the constraints of an instance are put together.

Definition 3 ***Variable representation.*** *Let x_R be a variable with a domain defined in D. The CSP instance R* ***represents the decision variable*** *x_R if R represents the CSP instance $(\{x_R\}, D, \{\})$.*

Constraint representation. *Let C_R be a constraint over the variables $x_1, \ldots,$ x_n with domains in D. The CSP instance R* ***represents the constraint*** *C_R if R represents the CSP instance $(\{x_1, \ldots, x_n\}, D, \{C_R\})$.*

The previous definitions relate a single variable (or a constraint) to a CSP instance; the following definition relates to many CSP instances representing sections of another CSP instance. The union of these instances is a composed instance where many alternative redundant representations operate simultaneously.

Definition 4 *Let R be the CSP instance (X, D, C) and $Y \subseteq X$ be the (possibly empty) set of variables outside of the scope of every constraint in C.*

For every constraint c in C, let CSP instance R_c be a representation of c such that for every variable x in the scope of c there is a CSP instance $R_x \subseteq R_c$[2] *representing x.*

For every $y \in Y$, let CSP instance R_y be a representation of y.

For every pair of variables, x and y, $x \neq y$, let the set of variables of any of their representations, R_x and R_y respectively, be ***disjoint.***

The CSP instance $R_{cwq} = (\bigcup_{c \in C} R_c) \cup (\bigcup_{y \in Y} R_y)$ is a ***constraint-wise quasi-representation*** *of CSP instance R. A constraint-wise quasi-representation of R is a* ***constraint-wise representation*** *of R if it represents R.*

2. A CSP instance A is a subset of a CSP instance B if the variables, domains and constraints of A are subsets of the variables, domains and constraints of B.

X	$=$	*rings*
$D(rings)$	$=$	*multisets (of size nrings) of sets (of maxsize capacity) of 1..nnodes*
C	$=$	$C_m(rings), C_p(rings)$

Figure 8.4. *CSP-instance 1a of the rings of the Sonet problem*

X_1	$=$	$rings_1$
$D_1(rings_1)$	$=$	*2-D matrix of Boolean indexed by 1..nrings and 1..nnodes*
C_1	$=$	$\forall\, i \in 1..nrings\ .\ ((\sum j \in 1..nnodes\ .\ rings_1[i,j]) \leq capacity)$ $C'_m(rings_1)$

Figure 8.5. *CSP-instance 2a of the rings of the Sonet problem*

This definition comprises the representations of the constraints of an instance (plus the representations of the unconstrained variables) in one single CSP instance. To exemplify it, let us add to CSP instance 1 two constraints which we shall call $C_m(rings)$ and $C_p(rings)$. Add also to CSP instance 2 some constraint $C'_m(rings_1)$; and to instance 3 some constraint $C'_p(rings_2, switch)$. Let us call these extensions CSP instances 1a, 2a and 3a respectively (see Figures 8.4, 8.5 and 8.6)[3].

Let us assume CSP instance 2a and CSP instance 3a represent constraint $C_m(rings)$ and $C_p(rings)$ respectively. Note that both 2a and 3a contain a representation of the variable *rings*, essentially CSP instances 2 and 3 respectively. The CSP instance (X_{12}, D_{12}, C_{12}), composed by the union of instance 2a and 3a (shown in Figure 8.7), is a constraint-wise quasi-representation of CSP instance 1a.

From definition 4, note that every constraint-wise quasi-representation where there is a unique representation for every variable in X, is a constraint-wise representation. In our example that is not the case; there are two representations of *rings* which would not be synchronized if the constraint-wise quasi-representation were solved. In a nutshell, a solution of CSP instance $2a \cup 3a$ possibly represents two different network configurations, where each configuration satisfies either constraint C_p or C_m, but may not satisfy both. Unlike the simple union of full alternative representations, we may not always easily extend the mapping of one of the alternatives to cover all the solutions. A solution for the problem instance needs to satisfy both constraints, thus we need to connect both representations of the rings to ensure simultaneous solutions

3. To simplify the examples constraints C_m, C'_m, C_p, C'_p remain undefined.

$$
\begin{array}{|lll|}
\hline
X_2 & = & rings_2,\ switch \\
D_2(rings_2) & = & \textit{2-D matrix of 1..nnodes indexed by 1..nrings and 1..capacity} \\
D_2(switch) & = & \textit{2-D matrix of Boolean indexed by 1..nrings and 1..capacity} \\
C_2 & = & \forall\ i \in 1..nrings\ .\ \texttt{alldifferent}(rings_2[i]) \\
 & & C'_p(rings_2, switch) \\
\hline
\end{array}
$$

Figure 8.6. *CSP instance 3a of the rings of the Sonet problem*

$$
\begin{array}{|lll|}
\hline
X_{12} & = & rings_2,\ switch,\ rings_1 \\
D_{12}(rings_1) & = & \textit{2-D matrix of Boolean indexed by 1..nrings and 1..nnodes} \\
D_{12}(rings_2) & = & \textit{2-D matrix of 1..nnodes indexed by 1..nrings and 1..capacity} \\
D_{12}(switch) & = & \textit{2-D matrix of Boolean indexed by 1..nrings and 1..capacity} \\
C_{12} & = & \forall\ i \in 1..nrings\ .\ ((\sum j \in 1..nnodes\ .\ rings_1[i,j]) = capacity) \\
 & & C'_m(rings_1) \\
 & & \forall\ i \in 1..nrings\ .\ \texttt{alldifferent}(rings_2[i]) \\
 & & C'_p(rings_2, switch) \\
\hline
\end{array}
$$

Figure 8.7. *CSP instance 2a ∪ 3a of the rings of the Sonet problem*

represent the same Sonet network and that the configuration satisfies both constraints. Thus, we need to the add the corresponding channels to maintain the consistency between these alternatives, in this case:

$$
\begin{gathered}
\forall i \in 1..nrings\ .occ(rings_1[i], Sonet1) = occ(rings_1[i], Sonet2) \qquad [8.3] \\
\wedge \\
\forall i \in 1..nrings\ .occ((rings_2[i], switch[i]), Sonet2) \\
= occ((rings_2[i], switch[i]), Sonet1)
\end{gathered}
$$

In our example, the channel is shown as a "macro" version which counts the number of occurrences of a ring of nodes in both representations and checks that it is identical. Sonet1 and Sonet2 refer to CSP instances 1 and 2 respectively. The counting of the occurrences shown in the previous constraint is expanded with the constraints below[4]

4. Boolean constraints are reified for counting.

$$\sum j \in 1..nrings\ .\ \forall k \in 1..nnodes\ .\exists l\ .\ rings_1[i,k] = rings_1[j,l] \quad [8.4]$$

$$=$$

$$\sum j \in 1..nrings\ .\ \forall k \in 1..nnodes\ .(rings_1[i,k] \Leftrightarrow$$
$$\exists l \in 1..capacity\ .\ (rings_2[j,l] = k \wedge switch[j,l]))$$

$$\sum j \in 1..nrings\ .\forall l \in 1..capacity\ .\forall k \in 1..nnodes\ . \quad [8.5]$$
$$(rings_2[j,l] = k \wedge switch[j,l]) \Leftrightarrow$$
$$\exists o \in 1..capacity\ .\ (rings_2[i,o] = k \wedge switch[i,o])$$

$$=$$

$$\sum j \in 1..nrings\ .\forall k \in 1..nnodes\ .$$
$$(rings_1[j,k] \Leftrightarrow \exists l \in 1..capacity\ .\ (rings_2[i,l] = k \wedge switch[i,l])$$

Ensuring the solution of each alternative is identical when mapped to the assignment of the variable they represent is the intuitive notion of a channel. We formalize it as follows.

Definition 5 *Let R_1 represent R via ψ_1 and R_2 represent R via ψ_2. Let $vars(R_1)$ and $vars(R_2)$ be disjoint sets of variables. The set of constraints C_h is considered a set of* ***channeling constraints between** R_1 **and** R_2* *if:*

– for each solution x_1 of R_1 there is at least one total assignment x_2 (of the variables in R_2) such that the composed assignment $x_1 \cup x_2$ satisfies the constraints in C_h. Similarly for each solution x_2 there must be an assignment x_1 such that the composed assignment $x_1 \cup x_2$ satisfies the constraints in C_h;

– for all total assignments x_1 and x_2 where the composed assignment $x_1 \cup x_2$ satisfies the constraints in C_h, $\psi_1(x_1)$ and $\psi_2(x_2)$ are either both undefined or take the same value.

We identify then that channels are necessary when a constraint-wise quasi-representations includes multiple representations of one (or many) variable(s), if we want to transform it into a representation.

Lemma 1 *Let R_{cwq} be a constraint-wise quasi-representation of R, where only the variable x of R has two variable representations R_1 and R_2 in R_{cwq}. Let C_h be the correct channeling constraint between R_1 and R_2. Then, the CSP instance $\bigcup R_{cwq} \cup C_h$ represents R.*

This lemma can be extended to cover three or more alternative representations of numerous variables. Thus, as long as we can provide correct channels between alternative representations we can transform constraint-wise quasi-representations into constraint-wise representations. We present in the next section an automatic modeling system that generates constraint-wise quasi-representations using a recursive process called refinement. [FRI 05b].

8.4. Refinement

Modeling a problem can become a big task, and for that reason many researchers have pursued the construction of automatic modeling tools to assist the user by performing the task modelers usually do. These tools are in various stages of development and help in diverse ways, but in this section we focus on a modeling tool called CONJURE giving its capacity of producing constraint-wise quasi-representations. To introduce it we will compare it with other similar tools.

ESRA [FLE 03], Fiona [HNI 03] and CONJURE [FRI 05b] produce one or various models from problem specifications. The specifications taken by each tool differ, while ESRA and Fiona concentrate on containing variables with relation and function domains respectively, CONJURE has a broader scope, also allowing variables of multisets, partitions and unnamed types domain, for example. Also, the complexity of the domains for the specifications of ESRA and Fiona is reduced since domain composition is not allowed in these systems. CONJURE, on the other hand, tackles problem specifications where variables can take highly compound domains, just like the one in our Sonet example: multisets of sets of integers.

Due to the limited number of domains Fiona and ESRA need to deal with, they transform given specifications by applying a succession of replacements that lead to a final model. CONJURE follows a different strategy, partitioning the problem specification into smaller pieces which are *refined*. The refinement engine of CONJURE basically recursively reduces the input until something that can be placed in a CSP model is obtained. The refinement performed by CONJURE is a generalization of the refinement restricted to instances which is explained in this chapter.

X'	$=$	$\{$ *rings*$_1$ $\}$
$D'(rings')$	$=$	*1-D matrix of sets (of maxsize capacity) of 1..nnodes indexed by 1..nrings*
C'	$=$	$\emptyset$

Figure 8.8. *CSP-instance* $1'$ *of the rings of the Sonet problem*

We call a CSP instance *abstract* if it cannot yet be implemented in a current solver. An example of an abstract CSP instance is shown in Figure 8.1 which represents the network of rings of the Sonet problem with a multiset decision variable. Refinement transforms abstract instances into *concrete* CSP instances that can be implemented directly in a solver. In every step of the refinement a level of abstraction is reduced, and a new representation of its predecessor is created. The final output of the refinement, the concrete CSP instance, is also a representation of the abstract initial instance.

CSP instance 2 and 3 are, according to these definitions, concrete representations of CSP instance 1. Concrete instances are often obtained after several refinement steps, overall when the domain of the variable is compound. In our example, CSP instance 1 is initially refined to produce the instance $1'$ of Figure 8.8, and either CSP 2 or CSP 3. Each final representation has a different sequence of representations, the one composed by CSP instances 1, $1'$ and 2; and the one composed of CSP instances 1, $1'$ and 3.

From this brief explanation the refinement process may appear to be a succession of applications of replacement rules to specific parts of the instance, but that is not the case. Instead, the implementation of refinement over CSP instances is a recursive process. Given an input CSP instance R, CONJURE generates constraint-wise quasi-representations of R where each one is generated by independently producing the representations of the constraints and unconstrained variables of R. The sequences of representations generated by the refinement process are produced by recursive application of the *refinement rules*.

To illustrate this let us use our Sonet example again. We feed the *rings* variable (CSP instance 1) to the refinement engine, where the `MultisetOfSizeInToExplicit` rule is applied. The `MultisetOfSizeInToExplicit` rule transforms a multiset variable into its *explicit* representation, that is, a fixed size array of variables where each variable takes the domain of the elements of the multiset. Hence, the multiset variable *rings* is transformed into the array *rings*$'$ as the rule composes the intermediate CSP instance $1'$. Afterwards, each of the sets of the *rings*$'$ variable needs to be refined. At this point two rules can be applied, the `SetOfMaxsizeInToOccurrence` or the `SetOfMaxsizeInToVariableSizedExplicit` rule. Given a set variable of bounded size, the `SetOfMaxsizeInToOccurrence` rule transforms it into a Boolean array where the domain of the elements of the set variable is used to index the array. This array composes the so-called *occurrence* representation where we set a variable to *True* when the indexing value is in the set. This representation includes constraints to bound the number of elements of the set. For the example, this rule transforms the intermediate CSP instance 1′ into CSP instance 2. On the other hand the `SetOfMaxsizeInToVariableSizedExplicit` transforms CSP instance 1′ into CSP instance 3, an explicit representation ($rings_2$) together with a group of Boolean arrays to indicate the active variables (*switch*).

As in our example, on many occasions there are various rules that can be applied each time. Therefore, refinement returns a set of representations with all the possibilities obtained during the recursion. Regardless of how a constraint is processed the transformations on variables are always recorded using tags called *representation annotations*. These tags do not contain any information about the rule used for the generation but they contain the associated variables and a *name* specifying the sort of representation constructed by the rule for a specific domain. For non-recursive rules the annotation directly links the variables fed to the rule with those of the representation constructed inside the rule. Otherwise, the annotations added by the rule connect the variables fed to the rule with the variables of the intermediate representation. During the refinement of the intermediate representation more annotations are added within the system at each call to a recursive rule, the last one connecting the final and concrete representation. By ordering the annotations using the variables they associate with, we can create sequences of annotations from the variables in the specification to their final representations. In essence, these sequences detail the sequence of representations the refinement process produce. For example, for the refinements of CSP instances 2 and 3 of CSP instance 1 we have the respective sequences

$$\begin{aligned}&[\texttt{represent}(exp, rings, rings'),\\ &\forall i \in 1..nrings.\texttt{represent}(occ, rings'[i], rings_1[i])]\end{aligned} \qquad [8.6]$$

$$\begin{aligned}&[\texttt{represent}(exp, rings, rings'),\\ &\forall i \in 1..nrings.\texttt{represent}(varexp, rings'[i], (rings_2[i], switch[i]))]\end{aligned} \qquad [8.7]$$

Note both sequences are also produced when refining CSP instance 1a and obtaining the union of instances 2a and 3a. In general we use the notation $R[rep]$ to indicate the sequence of representation annotations in R.

The refinement performed by CONJURE is a process that produces a constraint-wise quasi-representation from a CSP instance. The aim of this automatic modeling tool is, however, to produce a representation of the given CSP instance. Thus, in the cases where there are alternative redundant representations of the problem variables we need to introduce channels according to the reasoning over constraint-wise quasi-representation of the previous section. In the next section we detail the generation of the needed channels, which is based on the information recorded in the representation annotations.

8.5. Systematic generation of channeling constraints

Redundancy between two alternative representations is defined with respect to a third instance which connects the two CSP instances without actually describing the way their solutions mutually correspond. The task of channels is to maintain this correspondence, and for that reason the knowledge of the direct relation between each of the alternatives and the instance they both represent is an aid to constructing correct channels. For that reason, keeping an accurate record of the various variable representations in annotations becomes essential for the process of generation

These representation annotations can also help us distinguish some equivalent representations, such as two representations of a variable whose only difference in their respective sequences of annotations is that the name of the variables are alphabetic variants[5]. These alphabetic variants can be unified in one representation, and obviously, do not need to be considered for channeled purposes.

In essence, the method generates candidates to channeling constraints via a second refinement. It selects the adequate candidates with the information provided by the annotations. The algorithm of generation is presented as follows.

Postprocessing algorithm of generation of channels

Let `R` be the given problem instance. Let `R'` be one of the constraint-wise quasi-representations obtained from the refinement.

```
1 For each variable X in R
```

5. The name of the variables heading the sequences must be identical. The rest of the elements of the sequence, including the quantifiers, must be identical except for the name of the variables.

```
2   For each pair of alternative representations RX1 and RX2 of X in R'
3     Let X' be a fresh variable with domain identical to X
4     Substitute X' for X in RX2
5     For each Rc refinement of X = X'
6       Let RX1' and RX2' be the representations in Ch of X and X' resp.
7       If (RX1'[rep] is an alphabetic variant of RX1[rep]
8           and RX2'[rep] is an alphabetic variant of RX2[rep])
9         Substitute X for X' in Ch and RX2
10        Unify the variable names in Ch with respect to RX1 and RX2
11        Return Ch as a channel between X1 and X2
```

The algorithm generates channels for every pair of alternative representations (lines 1, 2). The generation is based on the refinement of a (possibly abstract) channeling constraint: equality (line 5). Note `X = X'` satisfies the definition of a channeling constraint if we consider `X` and `X'` to be alternative representations of `X`. A refinement of `X = X'` fulfils the properties of a representation, and for that reason, whenever it contains the expected representations of the variables `X` and `X'` we can declare it a channel. To select the right channel (or channels since many correct alternative channels can be returned) we use the annotations (lines 7, 8).

Let us now show an example of the postprocessing algorithm of generation of channels:

1) for our Sonet example we start by creating *ringsdummy*; a variable whose domain is, as well as the *rings* variable, composed of multisets of sets;

2) we modify one of the sequences of annotations to assign a path conducting the dummy variable to an alternative representation. In our example we change only the sequence of [8.7] into:

$$[\texttt{represent}(exp, ringsdummy, ringsdummy'),\\ \forall i \in 1..nrings.\texttt{represent}(varexp, ringsdummy'[i], (rings_2[i],\\ switch[i]))] \qquad [8.8]$$

3) refine $rings = ringsdummy$;

4) channel [8.3] is produced.

As expected, this process is based fully on storing the information that shows the transformations that composed a representation disregarding the set of rules that were applied. The correctness of this generation technique of channels is ensured by the following theorem:

Theorem 1 *The postprocessing algorithm of generation of channels transforms a constraint-wise quasi-representation with multiple redundant alternative representations into a constraint wise representation.*

Proof. This theorem can be proved considering lemma 1 and the fact that the equality constraint satisfies the definition of a channeling constraint as well as any of its representations.

8.6. Producing the best alternative for channeling

Consider the channeling constraint [8.1]. Direct implementation of this channel attempts to propagate over an extensive set of constraints that may not give the most efficient pruning. Some of the most common constraints over groups of variables have been identified and implemented with particular propagators (global constraints). Some global constraints are already strongly associated with channeling constraints (see [BEL 05]).

In our *n-queens* example, channel [8.1] could be expressed with the global constraint[6]:

$$\texttt{inverse}(C, R) \qquad [8.9]$$

The automatic generation technique of channels presented in the previous section is able to generate the most common global constraints used for channels between two alternative redundant representations of a variable. This production is achieved by including rules in the refinement system that refine the equivalence to the needed global constraint. Notice that these global constraints are always imposed to representations that do not need to be refined again; frequently, variables with uncompound domains.

Another method to improve a channeled representation is the deletion of redundant constraints on variables. One of the most widely known examples of this sort of deletion is the removal of the `alldifferent` constraint in a permutation problem [WAL 01], if the primal and the dual representation are combined through channeling constraints[7]. Many well documented deletions like this one can be included in a postprocessing system working over the generated instances that pattern-match the cases.

The real challenge is to compile a big number of reduction rules, including some representations of variables with compound domains. The main difference between the process of reduction and refinement is that during reduction the

6. The syntax of this constraint may vary from solver to solver.

7. Note this strategy is useful only when a competitive implementation of the channel is at hand, since enforcing GAC on `alldifferent` is stronger.

rules must account for all elements of the instance to validate the reduction, whereas during the refinement every part of the instance is treated separately. For example in section 8.2 the channeling constraint [8.3] between CSP instances 2 and 3 of the Sonet ring variable differs from the simpler constraint [8.2] shown in section 8.1. The reason for this is that the order on which the elements of the multiset are arranged is considered to be different for each representation. Assuming all the representations of the network of the Sonet problem have the same order we can ensure it is safe to replace constraint [8.3] with [8.2]. This replacement has several consequences, we discard some solutions for each representation as only the cases with equivalent order satisfy the channel. Nevertheless, the combined representation with the new constraints preserves the solutions of the initial variable. In addition to the case of the construction of the refinement rules, we need to carefully compose these reduction rules in order to guarantee the preservation of solutions.

8.7. Conclusions and future work

In this chapter, we introduced the definitions of CSP instance, variable and constraint representation. We also introduced the definition of constraint-wise quasi-representation, a structure helpful in describing the transformation method to generate representations used by the refinement process. We showed that the cases where recursive refinement may fail to produce a correct representation are reduced to those presenting alternative representations of the same variable. To ensure the preservation of solutions after the refinement we must introduce channeling constraints to synchronize the alternatives.

In section 8.5 we discussed a technique to automatically generate the channeling constraints needed. This technique makes use of the very same refinement process, thus dispensing with the extra burden of implementing an additional subsystem for the generation. Generating the final (and most efficient) implementation of a channel can be made via refinement or reduction. As discussed in section 8.6, common global constraints can be produced by adding the respective refinement rules. For some novel representations some known propagators can be adapted or new ones need to be constructed to suit global constraints for channels of novel representations, for example, the channels for the *variable sized explicit* representation introduced by Jefferson et al [JEF 05]. Also, as pointed out in the previous section, most of our future work is related to the generalization of redundancy reduction rules.

8.8. References

[BEL 05] BELDICEANU N., CARLSSON M., RAMPON J.X., "Global Constraint Catalog", *Technical report, Swedish Institute of Computer Science*, 2005.

[CHE 96] CHENG B.M.W., LEE J.H.M., WU J.C.K., "Speeding up Constraint Propagation by Redundant Modeling", in *CP 1996*, 91–103, 1996.

[FLE 03] FLENER P., PEARSON J., ÅGREN M. "Introducing ESRA, a Relational Language for Modeling Combinatorial Problems", in *CP 2003*, 971, 2003.

[FRI 05a] FRISCH A.M., HNICH B., MIGUEL I., SMITH B.M., Walsh T., "Transforming and Refining Abstract Constraint Specifications", in *Proceedings SARA 2005 – 6th International Symposium on Abstraction, Reformulation and Approximation*, Springer LNAI 3607, pages 76–91, 2005.

[FRI 05b] FRISCH A.M., JEFFERSON C., MARTÍNEZ-HERNÁNDEZ B., MIGUEL I., "The Rules of Constraint Modeling", in *Proceedings IJCAI 2005 – Nineteenth Int. Joint Conf. on Artificial Intelligence*, pages 109–116, 2005.

[FRI 05c] FRISCH A.M., MARTÍNEZ-HERNÁNDEZ B., "The Systematic Generation of Channelling Constraints", in *Proceedings Fourth International Workshop on Modeling and Reformulating Constraint Satisfaction Problems*, pages 89–101, 2005.

[HNI 03] HNICH B., "Function Variables for Constraint Programming", PhD thesis, Computer Science Division, Department of Information Science, Uppsala University, 2003.

[JEF 05] JEFFERSON, C., FRISCH A.M., "Representations of Sets and Multisets in Constraint Programming", in *Proceedings Fourth International Workshop on Modeling and Reformulating Constraint Satisfaction Problems*, pages 102–116, 2005.

[LAW 02a] LAW Y.C., LEE J.H.M., "Algebraic Properties of CSP Model Operators", in *Proceedings International Workshop on Reformulating Constraint Satisfaction Problems: Towards Systematisation and Automation*, pages 57–71, 2002.

[LAW 02b] LAW Y.C., LEE J.H.M., "Model Induction: a New Source of CSP Model Redundancy", in *Proceedings AAAI 2002 – Eighteenth National Conference on Artificial Intelligence*, pages 54–60, 2002.

[NAD 90] NADEL B.A., "Representation Selection for Constraint Satisfaction: a Case Study using n-queens", in *IEEE Expert* 5:16–23, 1990.

[WAL 01] WALSH T., "Permutation Problems and Channelling Constraints", in *Proceedings LPAR*, pages 377–391, 2001.

PART III

Symmetry in Constraint Satisfaction Problems

Edited by Alastair DONALDSON, Peter GREGORY and Karen PETRIE

Introduction

The following two chapters are revised versions of papers which appeared in the proceedings of SymCon'06, the Sixth International Workshop on Symmetry and Constraint Satisfaction Problems.[1] The workshop, held in conjunction with the Twelfth International Conference on Principles and Practice of Constraint Programming (CP'06), marked the sixth in a successful series of workshops on the topic. SymCon'06 follows earlier workshops at CP '01 in Paphos, Cyprus, at CP '02 in Ithaca, NY, USA, at CP '03 in Cork, Ireland, at CP '04 in Toronto, Ontario, Canda, and at CP '05 in Barcelona, Spain.

Of the eight papers included in the proceedings, six were invited for presentation at the workshop. The contributions investigated a range of problems relating to symmetry breaking, such as automatic symmetry detection, exploiting symmetry in not-equals binary constraint networks, breaking *almost-symmetries* in CSPs, and combining symmetry breaking and random restarts.

The contribution of Jefferson *et al.*, revised and presented as Chapter 9, introduces GAPLex, a new symmetry breaking technique which aims to retain the best features of static symmetry breaking in a dynamic framework based on computational group theory. Their approach takes advantage of recent results in computational group theory which allow the minimum image of a set of integers with respect to a permutation group to be efficiently calculated. They present the GAPLex algorithms, together with experimental results showing that GAPLex can be effectively combined with incomplete static symmetry breaking methods.

Chapter 10 is a revised version of a contribution to SymCon'06 by Zampelli *et al.* This work extends existing symmetry breaking techniques for subgraph

---

1. The proceedings are available online: http://www.cis.strath.ac.uk/~pg/symcon06/.

matching problems. They show how (global and local) variable and value symmetries of a subgraph matching CSP can be automatically detected and broken, using standard algorithms to calculate graph automorphisms. In order to effectively break local symmetries, they extend existing techniques for symmetry breaking using restricted search trees. Experimental results show that a larger set of benchmark problems can be solved when symmetries are broken using their methods.

We would like to thank all the authors who submitted papers to SymCon'06, the members of the Programme Committee, and the CP'06 Workshop and Tutorial chair Barry O'Sullivan. We also thank Chris Jefferson for help in reviewing papers.

December 2006

Alastair F. Donaldson
Peter Gregory
Karen E. Petrie
(SymCon'06 Programme Chairs)

Programme Committee

Rolf Backofen,
Belaïd Benhamou,
Alan Frisch,
Ian Gent,
Warwick Harvey,
Tom Kelsey,
Zeynep Kiziltan,
Steve Linton,
Derek Long,
Igor Markov,
Pedro Meseguer,
Ian Miguel,
Michela Milano,
Alice Miller,
Steve Prestwich,
Jean-François Puget,
Colva Roney-Dougal,
Meinolf Sellmann,
Pascal van Hentenrych,
Toby Walsh.

Chapter 9

GAPLex: Generalized Static Symmetry Breaking

We introduce GAPLex, a novel method for breaking symmetries in constraint satisfaction problems. The idea behind GAPLex is to take advantage of recent advances in computational group theory that allow us to efficiently decide whether a set of numbers is minimal with respect to a set of permutations (and, of course, with respect to an ordering relation on the numbers). We apply this decision procedure during the search for solutions to constraint satisfaction problems: any partial assignment can be thought of as a set of literals (a literal is a variable-value pair), and each such assignment is either lex-minimal with respect to the group of symmetries acting on literals, or it isn't. We describe how GAPLex allows us to safely backtrack away from non-minimal assignments and provide information on "near-misses" that allows us to further prune the search tree. We believe that GAPLex combines the best aspects of breaking symmetries by lex-ordering – simplicity and effective propagation – with the best aspects of dynamic, computational group theory-based symmetry breaking methods – general applicability, soundness and completeness. Empirical evidence to support this belief is provided and discussed, along with an outline of future avenues of related research.

Chapter written by Chris JEFFERSON, Tom KELSEY, Steve LINTON and Karen PETRIE.

9.1. Background and introduction

Constraint satisfaction problems (CSPs) are often highly symmetric. Given any solution, there are others which are equivalent in terms of the underlying problem. Symmetries may be inherent in the problem, or be created in the process of representing the problem as a CSP. Without symmetry breaking (henceforth SB), many symmetrically equivalent solutions may be found and, in some ways more importantly, many symmetric equivalent parts of the search will be explored. An SB method aims to avoid both of these problems.

Most SB algorithms fall into one of two groups. The first, known as static SB algorithms, decide before search which assignments will be permitted and which will be forbidden, and are therefore independent of search ordering. The second group, known as dynamic symmetry breaking methods, instead choose which assignments will be permitted during search.

Existing static symmetry breaking methods work by adding extra constraints to the CSP. This typically involves constraints that rule out solutions by enforcing some lexicographic-ordering on the variables of the problem [CRA 96, FRI 02]. STAB [PUG 03] is an SB algorithm for solving balanced incomplete block designs (BIBDs) which avoids adding an exponential number of constraints at the start of search by adding constraints during search on the row of the BIBD currently being assigned.

Dynamic symmetry breaking methods operate in a number of ways, including posting constraints that rule out search at states that are symmetrically equivalent to the current assignment [BAC 99, GEN 00], building the search tree such that symmetric nodes are avoided [RON 04] or backtracking from nodes that are symmetrically equivalent to root nodes of subtrees that have previously been fully explored [FAH 01, FOC 01, PUG 03]. These methods, especially in the case that symmetries are represented by permutation groups, are related to a class of algorithms first described in [BRO 88].

The major weakness of static SB methods, compared to dynamic methods, is that they can increase the number of search nodes visited [GEN 02], whenever the first solution which would have been found is forbidden by the symmetry breaking constraints. The major advantage of static symmetry breaking methods is that ad hoc problem-specific simplifications often perform very well, and powerful implied constraints can be derived from these constraints [FRI 04]. Moreover, since static SB does not depend on previously encountered search nodes, it can be used when searching in parallel on multiple machines.

Other methods of breaking symmetry exist, for example a CSP can be reformulated so that either the number of symmetries is reduced, or a bespoke SB approach can be applied more effectively [KEL 04, MES 01], or both. However, these methods are largely problem-specific, and we are concerned with general methods that can be applied to any formulation of a class of CSPs.

Permutation groups are the mathematical structures that best encapsulate symmetry. Many powerful algorithms for investigating group-theoretic questions are known, and have been efficiently implemented in systems such as GAP [GAP 00] and MAGMA [BOS 93]. We describe the symmetries of a CSP as a permutation group of the literals (variable-value pairs) of the CSP, and obtain information regarding symmetric equivalence of search states from the GAP Computational Group Theory (CGT) system.

Using literals in this way has been successful, but it is easy to lose sight of the fact that each variable can only take one value. Our generalized static symmetry breaking methodology is motivated by the potential for efficiencies induced by the use of this basic concept. We therefore address the open research question: can we implement lex-ordering with a CGT approach in such a way that we retain the best features of static symmetry breaking while gaining the speed and flexibility of a general group-theoretic framework? Our contribution is twofold. We first describe a novel SB method, GAPLex, which involves both ordering constraints and symmetry information regarding the current state of search to break as many solution symmetries of a CSP as are required. We also demonstrate that GAPLex can be combined with previous fast – but incomplete – static lex-orderings to provide fast and complete SB. We are not aware of any existing SB method that effectively combines static and dynamic approaches, although Harvey has made an interesting initial attempt [HAR 04].

Puget [PUG 93] proved that whenever a CSP has symmetry, it is possible to find a "reduced form", with the symmetries eliminated, by adding constraints to the original problem and showed such a form for three CSPs. Following this, the key advance was to show a method whereby such a set of constraints could be generated. Crawford, Ginsberg, Luks and Roy showed a general technique, called "lex-leader", for generating such constraints for any variable symmetry [CRA 96]. In later work, Aloul *et al.* also showed how the lex-leader constraints for symmetry breaking can be expressed more efficiently [ALO 03]. This method was developed in the context of Propositional Satisfiability (SAT), but the results can also be applied to CSPs.

The idea behind lex-leader is essentially simple. For each equivalence class of assignments under our symmetry group, we choose one to be canonical. We then add constraints before search starts which are satisfied by canonical assignments and not by any others. We generate canonical assignments by choosing an ordering of the variables and representing assignments as tuples under this variable ordering. Any permutation of variables g maps tuples to tuples, and the lexicographically least of these is our canonical assignment. This gives the set of constraints

$$\forall g \in G,\ V \preceq_{\text{lex}} V^g$$

where V is the vector of the variables of the CSP, $\preceq_{\text{lex}}$ is the standard lexicographic ordering relation, defined by $AD \preceq_{\text{lex}} BC$ if, and only if, either $A < B$ or $A = B$ and $D \leq C$, and V^g denotes the permutation of the variables by application of the group element.

9.1.1. *Group theory for CSPs*

DEFINITION.– *A CSP L is a set of constraints $\mathcal{C}$ acting on a finite set of variables $\Delta = \{A_1, A_2, \ldots, A_n\}$, each of which has finite domain of possible values $D(A_i)$ (denoted D_i). A* solution *to L is an instantiation of all of the variables in Δ such that all of the constraints in $\mathcal{C}$ are satisfied.*

Constraint logic programming systems typically model CSPs using constraints over finite domains. The usual search method is depth-first, with values assigned to variables at choice points. After each assignment a partial consistency test is applied: domain values that are found to be inconsistent are deleted, so that a smaller search tree is produced.

Statements of the form (*Var* = *val*) are called *literals*, so a partial assignment is a conjunction of literals. We denote the set of all literals by χ, and denote variables by Roman capitals and values by lower case Greek letters.

DEFINITION.– *Given a CSP L, with a set of constraints $\mathcal{C}$, and a set of literals χ, a* symmetry *of L is a bijection $f : \chi \rightarrow \chi$ such that a full assignment A of L satisfies all constraints in $\mathcal{C}$ if and only if $f(A)$ does.*

We denote the image of a literal $(X = \alpha)$ under a symmetry g by $(X = \alpha)^g$. The set of all symmetries of a CSP form a *group*: that is, they are a collection of bijections from the set of all literals to itself that is closed under composition of mappings and under inversion. We denote the symmetry group of a CSP by G.

DEFINITION.– *Let G be a group of symmetries of a CSP. The* stabilizer *of a literal $(X = \alpha)$ is the set of all symmetries in G that map $(X = \alpha)$ to itself. This set is itself a group. The* orbit *of a literal $(X = \alpha)$, denoted $(X = \alpha)^G$, is the set of all literals that can be mapped to $(X = \alpha)$ by a symmetry in G. The orbit of a node is defined similarly.*

Given a collection $\mathcal{S}$ of literals, the *pointwise* stabilizer of $\mathcal{S}$ is the subgroup of G which stabilizes each element of $\mathcal{S}$ individually. The *setwise* stabilizer of $\mathcal{S}$ is the subgroup of G that consists of symmetries mapping the set $\mathcal{S}$ to itself.

9.1.2. *Using GAP to break CSP symmetries*

There have been three successful implementations of SB methods which use GAP to provide answers to symmetry-related questions during search. All three combined GAP with the constraint solver ECL^{i}PS^e [WAL 97]. GAP-SBDS [GEN 02] is an implementation of symmetry breaking during search: at each search node, constraints are posted which ensure that no symmetrically equivalent node will be visited later in search. The overhead comprises maintenance (in GAP) of a stabilizer chain of the symmetry group, the search for group elements which map the current state to a future state (also in GAP), and the posting of the SB constraints. Enough pruning of the search tree is made, in general, to make GAP-SBDS more efficient than straightforward search. The number of SB constraints is linear in the size of the group, making GAP-SBDS unattractive for groups of size greater than about 10^9.

GAP-SBDD [GEN 03] uses GAP to check that the next assignment is not equivalent to a state which is the root of a previously explored sub-tree. Again, the overhead of finding (or failing to find) these group elements is usually more than offset by the reduction in search due to early backtracking. Larger groups – up to about 10^{25} – can be dealt with, simply because the answer from GAP is a straight yes or no to the dominance question; the overhead of passing constraint information is not present. GAP also reports literals that can be safely deleted because setting them would have led to dominance. Provided that the cost of computing these safe deletions is low enough, the domain reductions are a gain over not making them. We follow the same idea in this chapter; we search for literals that, if set, would have lead to a non-lex-least assignment.

The third use of GAP is the building of search trees that, by construction, have no symmetrically equivalent nodes and contain a member from each solution equivalence class: GE-trees [KEL 04]. In the event that all the symmetries act only on variables (either by suitable formulation or the use of channeling constraints from an unsuitable formulation), these trees can be constructed in low-degree polynomial time per node. This is due to pointwise stabilizers being polynomial time obtainable, whilst setwise stabilizers (the general case) are not known to be obtainable in polynomial time.

In this chapter we aim to build upon the strengths of these existing frameworks by using lex-ordering as the main SB technique, using GAP to decide if the current partial assignment is lex-smallest of the orbit of the assignment under the symmetry group.

9.2. GAPLex

9.2.1. *Motivation and rationale*

Both lex-ordering and CGT-based SB methods are effective and attractive options for breaking symmetries in CSPs. Our aim is to implement lexicographic static symmetry breaking using the CGT methods used in GAP-SBDS and GAP-SBDD, thus combining useful features of both approaches.

We want to enforce a lex ordering on the literals of a CSP so that only solutions that are minimal in the ordering are returned after complete backtrack search with propagation. Moreover, we want this to work with any symmetry structure induced by the formulation of the CSP.

The key idea is that we can calculate the minimum image, under a symmetry group G, of those literals that represent the ground variables in any branch of the search tree. By minimum image, we mean the lex-least ordered list of literals that can be obtained by applying group elements (symmetries) to our set of ground literals. If the minimum image of our current partial assignment is lex-smaller than that assignment, then it is safe to backtrack from the current search node: further search will either fail to find a solution or return a solution that is not the lex-smallest in its equivalence class.

Clearly, the cost of computing minimum images is crucial to our methodology: we are no better off if the time taken is not offset by the induced reduction in search for solutions to CSPs. Recent advances in algorithms for finding minimal images have lead to dramatic improvements in both worst-case and apparent average-case time complexities [LIN 04]. We use these more efficient CGT methods to obtain the minimal images and decide the ordering predicate. As a useful extension to the main technique, we can also use CGT to identify those literals involving non-ground variables that, if taken as assignments, would result in failure of the lex-smaller test. The assignments of any such literals can be ruled out immediately by deleting the values from their respective domains. These domain deletions, together with the propagation of the domain deletion decisions, reduce the search required to find solutions (or confirm that no solutions exist) for the CSP. This process is analogous to the deletion of "near misses" in GAP-SBDD, as discussed in [FOC 01, GEN 03].

Since the cost of computing minimal images and comparing lists is generally outweighed by the reduction in search due to early backtracking and early domain deletion, our method is a useful and generic extension of lex-ordering as a symmetry breaking technique.

9.2.2. *Motivating example*

Suppose that we wish to solve

$$\frac{A}{10B+C}+\frac{D}{10E+F}+\frac{G}{10H+I}=1$$

where each variable takes a value from 1 to 9. There are 3! permutations of the summands which preserve solutions. Suppose now that during search for all solutions we have made the partial assignment $PA: A=2$, $B=3$, $C=8$, $D=2$, $E=1$. This is mapped by the group element $(DAG)(EBH)(FCI)$ as a sequence to $G=2$, $H=3$, $I=8$, $A=2$, $B=1$; or, in sorted order, $A=2$, $B=1$, $G=2$, $H=3$, $I=8$.

Under the variable ordering $ABCDEFGHI$, this is lexicographically smaller than PA (since $B=1$ is smaller than $B=3$) so we would backtrack from this position. Notice that although we map a state which includes $A=2$ into a smaller state we *can't* do it by mapping the literal $A=2$ to itself.

Even if we can't immediately backtrack, there are often safe domain deletions that can be made. For example if we have only assigned $A=7$, it is safe to remove values 1 through 6 from the domains of D and G, since making any of these assignments would lead to an immediate backtrack. This combination of early backtrack and domain reduction provides the search pruning needed to offset the overhead of computing and comparing images of assignments.

9.2.3. *The GAPLex algorithms*

We have a CSP and a symmetry group, G, for the CSP. G acts on the set of literals (variable-value pairs) of the problem, written as an initial subset of the natural numbers. The set of literals forms a variables × values array, so that the literals of the lex-least variable are $1, 2, \ldots, |dom(V_1)|$, etc. The GAPLex method, applied at a node N in search, proceeds as follows:

Require: $PA \leftarrow$ current partial assignment
Require: $var \leftarrow$ next variable w.r.t. any fixed choice heuristic
Require: $val \leftarrow$ next value w.r.t. lex-least value ordering
set $Var = val$ and propagate
add $Var = val$ to PA
$T \leftarrow$ literals involving unassigned variables
pass PA and T to the GAPLex CGT test
if the test returns **false then**
    backtrack
else

  the test returns **true** and a list of literals, D
  for $(X = \alpha) \in D$ **do**
    remove α from the domain of X and propagate
  end for
  continue search
end if
if $Var = val$ does not lead to a solution **then**
  set $Var \neq val$ and propagate
  if a solution is obtained **then**
    check that the solution is not isomorphic to any previous solution
  else
    move to next search node
  end if
end if

There are several points of interest. We assume that some consistency heuristics are in place, which propagate search decisions, backtracking away from nogoods and either stopping at the first solution or continuing search until all solutions are found. Every time we assign a variable during search, the consistency heuristics can provide additional domain reductions. The list T passed to the CGT test contains only those literals that involve the current domains of non-ground variables, as opposed to the domains before search. In this sense T is the smallest list we can pass, making the CGT test as efficient as possible. The method – if applied at every node in search – is sound, since we only backtrack away from solutions that are not lex-least, and we make no domain deletions involving lex-least solutions. This method is very much in the spirit of GAP-SBDD; the aim is to replace dominance detection by the power and simplicity of lex-ordering SB heuristics. Another way of looking at the method is as a propagator for (unposted) lex-ordering SB constraints. The method backtracks and reduces domains in line with the constraints that a static lex-ordering would have posted before search. Indeed, this conceptualization motivates the notion that we can *combine* GAPLex with static lex-ordering constraints. The combination will be sound, since the same constraints apply, with only the order of their posting or propagation affecting the dynamics of CSP search.

As in other CGT-based SB methods, we can only expect a win if the cost of the CGT test is less than the cost of performing the search needed without early backtracking and early domain deletions provided by the test. By using highly efficient implementations of powerful permutation group algorithms, we can achieve this goal. The GAPLex CGT test, written in GAP, is specified as follows:

Require: G – a symmetry group for a CSP

```
Require: PA and T – as ordered lists of literals
if PA is not lex-least in its orbit under G then
    result = false
else
    D ← t ∈ T if added to PA would make PA not lex-least
    result = true and D
end if
```

The test proceeds by recursive search, similar to that described in [LIN 04], terminating when either the elements of *PA* have been exhausted, or the group at the bottom of the stabilizer chain consists only of the identity permutation. This stabilizer chain is the sequence stabilizer of the literals involving the decisions made above the current node during search. More precisely, a recursive routine with the following specification is applied:

```
Require: G – a permutation group
Require: SOURCE and EXTRA – as ordered lists of points
Require: TARGET – an ordered list of points
if ∃g ∈ G : g(SOURCE) ≺_lex TARGET then
    result = false
else
    D ← {t ∈ EXTRA : ∃g ∈ G : g(SOURCE ∪ {t}) ≺_lex TARGET}
    appropriate subset of D is added to a global list DL
    result = true
end if
```

Calling this routine with the same G, and with *SOURCE* and *TARGET* both equal to *PA* and *EXTRA* equal to T clearly achieves the specification above. The implementation of this routine is:

```
GAPLexSearch(G, SOURCE, TARGET, EXTRA)
if TARGET is empty then
    return true
end if
x ← TARGET[1]
for y ∈ SOURCE do
    if ∃g ∈ G : g(y) < x then
        return false
    else
        if ∃g ∈ G : g(y) = x then
            G′ ← the stabilizer of x in G
            S′ ← SOURCE \ {y}
            T′ ← TARGET \ {x}
            res ← GAPLexSearch(G′, S′, T′, EXTRA)
```

```
            if res = false then
                return false
            end if
        end if
    end if
end for
for y ∈ EXTRA do
    if y ∉ DL and ∃g ∈ G : g(y) < x then
        add y to DL
    end if
end for
return true
```

9.3. Empirical evaluation

Our implementation uses the GAP–ECL^{i}PS^e system, with CSP modeling and search performed in ECL^{i}PS^e, and with GAP providing black-box answers to symmetry questions. We have tested our implementation on two classes of CSP. The first is Balanced Incomplete Block Designs (BIBDs), problem class 28 in *csplib*[1]. This class was chosen to be a stern test of the effectiveness of GAPLex, with a large number of symmetries and small domains. We would therefore expect the search for lex-inspired early backtracks to be expensive, with not many useful domain deletions being returned. This expectation is realized in our results given in Table 9.1. The better results for GAP-SBDD are in part because GAP-SBDD has special support for problems with Boolean variables. We tried posting the complete set of lexicographic lex-leader constraints on each BIBD instance, but the number of constraints was too great.

					GAP-SBDD		GAPLex		Double-Lex		GAPLex no prop		Combined	
V	B	R	K	λ	□	○	□	○	□	○	□	○	□	○
7	7	3	3	1	3	470	3	1,150	3	20	21	1,389	3	1,150
6	10	5	3	2	4	869	29	80,100	5	30	29	80,100	4	50,340
7	14	6	3	2	13	502,625	-	-	30	110	-	-	-	-
9	12	4	3	1	12	451,012	-	-	30	120	-	-	-	-
11	11	5	5	2	11	68,910	-	-	20	140	-	-	-	-
8	14	7	4	3	14	219,945	-	-	143	720	-	-	-	-

- > 2 hours □ Number of Backtracks ○ Total runtime in ms

Table 9.1. *GAP-SBDD vs GAPLex. Problem class: BIBDs modeled as binary matrices*

1. http://www.csplib.org.

The second problem class is graceful graphs, a graph labeling problem described in [PET 03]. The symmetries that arise are any symmetries of the graph, combined with symmetries of the labels. In this class the domains are larger, and, in general, there are fewer symmetries. The results for this class of problems (given in Table 9.2) are, as expected, more encouraging. We see that, in contrast to BIBDs, GAPLex provides fewer backtracks but performs faster than GAP-SBDD. GAPLex performs as well as GAP-SBDS on these problems. We also tested the heuristic observation that no GAPLex tests will fail (resulting in a backtrack) until the first search-related backtrack occurs, although propagation may occur. The test involved simply turning GAPLex tests off until the first (if any) backtrack occurred in normal search. Our results for this heuristic are inconclusive for this class of problems.

	GAP-SBDS				GAP-SBDD			
Instance	□	Φ	△	○	□	Φ	△	○
$K_3 \times P_2$	9	290	110	400	22	310	180	490
$K_4 \times P_2$	165	1,140	3,590	4,730	496	3,449	8,670	12,110
$K_5 \times P_2$	4,390	35,520	166,149	201,669	17,977	174180	501,580	675,760
	GAPLex				Partial GAPLex			
Instance	□	Φ	△	○	□	Φ	△	○
$K_3 \times P_2$	10	160	100	260	12	150	130	280
$K_4 \times P_2$	184	1,550	4,020	5,570	202	670	4,980	5,650
$K_5 \times P_2$	4,722	47,870	176,200	224,070	5,024	18,820	224,310	243,130

□ Number of Backtracks Φ GAP Time in ms
△ Eclipse time in ms ○ Total runtime in ms

Table 9.2. *Comparison of symmetry breaking methods. Partial GAPLex is where GAPLex checks do not commence until after the first backtrack*

9.3.1. *Combining GAPLex with incomplete static SB methods*

Much research has concentrated on symmetry-breaking constraints for *matrix models*, a constraint program that contains one or more matrices of decision variables, which occur frequently as CSPs. The prime example of this body of work is "double-lex", which imposes that both the rows and the columns are lexicographically ordered [FLE 02]. This does *not* break all the compositions of the row and column symmetries.

Frisch *et al.* introduced an optimal algorithm to establish generalized arc-consistency for the $\preceq_{\text{lex}}$ constraint [FRI 02]. This gives an attractive point on the tradeoff: a linear time to establish a high level of consistency on constraints which often break a large proportion of the symmetry in matrix models. The algorithm can be used to establish consistency in any use of $\preceq_{\text{lex}}$, so in particular is useful for any use of lex-leader constraints.

					Double-Lex		GAPLex no Prop				Combined			
V	B	R	K	λ	□	○	□	Φ	△	○	□	Φ	△	○
7	7	3	3	1	3	20	21	1,330	59	1,389	3	1,130	20	1,150
6	10	5	3	2	5	30	29	79,970	130	80,100	4	50,290	50	50,340
7	14	6	3	2	30	110	-	-	-	-	-	-	-	-
9	12	4	3	1	30	120	-	-	-	-	-	-	-	-
11	11	5	5	2	20	140	-	-	-	-	-	-	-	-
8	14	7	4	3	143	720	-	-	-	-	-	-	-	-

- > 2 hours □ Number of Backtracks Φ GAP Time in ms
△ Eclipse time in ms ○ Total runtime in ms

Table 9.3. *Static double-lex vs GAPLex with no search for safe deletions vs combined GAPLex and double-lex. Problem class: all solutions of BIBDs modeled as binary matrices*

Our approach is straightforward. We add static double-lex constraints before search. At each node in the search tree we run GAPLex, *without* supplying the list of candidate domain deletions. This clearly means that the test is computationally more efficient: the final for-loop in the CGT algorithm isn't performed. We justify this with the hypothesis that any safe deletion found would almost certainly be already ruled out by the static double-lex constraints.

The results set out in Table 9.3 show that GAPLex does not perform as well as simply posting double-lex constraints before search. However, GAPLex returns the correct number of solutions, whilst double-lex returns many symmetrically equivalent solutions. It seems that combining GAPLex with double-lex is an advantage over just using GAPLex. These results are not unexpected, as GAPLex was shown to behave poorly on this formulation of BIBDs in Table 9.1. We feel that the proof of concept is, however, interesting and useful.

9.3.2. *Combining GAPLex with Puget's all-different constraints*

Puget recently presented a method of implementing lex-leader constraints for variable symmetries in CSPs with all-different constraints [PUG 05] in linear time. In problems with both variable and value symmetries, these can be usefully combined with GAPLex. Our approach is the same as for double-lex: we post the static all-different constraints before search, and run the GAPLex test at each search node.

Our results, given in Table 9.4, show that GAPLex performs slightly better than static constraints, and that combining the two methods is better than using either in isolation. These encouraging results are made better by noting that, for this class of problems, using only static constraints results in twice as many solutions being returned as necessary.

Instance	Constraints		GAPLex no Prop				Combined			
	□	○	□	Φ	△	○	□	Φ	△	○
$K_3 \times P_2$	16	800	12	150	130	280	10	140	100	240
$K_4 \times P_2$	369	4,530	202	600	5,140	5,740	188	510	3,300	3,810
$K_5 \times P_2$	9,887	297,880	5,024	19,010	224,740	243,750	4,787	14,820	188,820	203,640

□ Number of Backtracks Φ GAP Time in ms
△ Eclipse time in ms ○ Total runtime in ms

Table 9.4. *Static symmetry breaking all-different constraints vs GAPLex with no search for safe deletions vs combined GAPLex and static constraints. Problem class: all solutions of Graceful Graphs in the standard model*

9.4. Conclusions and future work

We have used and extended recent advances in computational group theory to add lex-ordering to the class of symmetry breaking techniques that can be effectively implemented by using a CGT system to provide black-box answers to symmetry related questions. Our implementation, GAPLex, is competitive with GAP-SBDS and GAP-SBDD. The choice of which method to use for which class of CSPs appears to be an interesting research question. Answers to this question could provide insight into yet more symmetry breaking methods. Indeed, the CGT algorithms used are still new and based on experience with GAP-SBDD may improve by orders of magnitude with further investigation.

We have, moreover, demonstrated the first combination of static and search-based symmetry breaking methods that is (for certain classes of CSP) more efficient than using either the static or search-based method in isolation. This result is important, since the successful combination of symmetry breaking methods is taxing and open area of CSP research, with great potential benefits attached to positive answers.

More work is needed in two areas. Firstly, we must address the questions relating to why a particular symmetry breaking approach works better for some CSPs than others. Secondly, we need to investigate other potentially successful combinations of symmetry breaking techniques.

9.5. References

[ALO 03] Aloul F. A., Sakallah K. A., Markov I. L., "Efficient Symmetry Breaking for Boolean Satisfiability", Gottlob G., Walsh T., Eds., *IJCAI-03, Proceedings of the Eighteenth International Joint Conference on Artificial Intelligence, Acapulco, Mexico, August 9-15, 2003*, Morgan Kaufmann, p. 271-276, 2003.

[BAC 99] BACKOFEN R., WILL S., "Excluding Symmetries in Constraint-Based Search", JAFFAR J., Ed., *Principles and Practice of Constraint Programming – CP'99, 5th International Conference, Alexandria, Virginia, USA, October 11-14, 1999, Proceedings*, vol. 1713 of *Lecture Notes in Computer Science*, Springer, p. 73-87, 1999.

[BOS 93] BOSMA W., CANNON J., Handbook of MAGMA Functions, Sydney University, 1993.

[BRO 88] BROWN C. A., FINKELSTEIN L., JR. P. W. P., "Backtrack Searching in the Presence of Symmetry", MORA T., Ed., *Applied Algebra, Algebraic Algorithms and Error-Correcting Codes, 6th International Conference, AAECC-6, Rome, Italy, July 4-8, 1988, Proceedings*, vol. 357 of *Lecture Notes in Computer Science*, Springer, p. 99-110, 1988.

[CRA 96] CRAWFORD J., GINSBERG M. L., LUCK E., ROY A., "Symmetry-Breaking Predicates for Search Problems", AIELLO L. C., DOYLE J., SHAPIRO S., Eds., *KR'96: Principles of Knowledge Representation and Reasoning, Cambridge, Massachusetts, USA*, p. 148–159, Morgan Kaufmann, November 1996.

[FAH 01] FAHLE T., SCHAMBERGER S., SELLMANN M., "Symmetry Breaking", Walsh [WAL 01], p. 93-107, 2001.

[FLE 02] FLENER P., FRISCH A. M., HNICH B., KIZILTAN Z., MIGUEL I., PEARSON J., WALSH T., "Breaking Row and Column Symmetries in Matrix Models", Hentenryck [HEN 02], p. 462-476, 2002.

[FOC 01] FOCACCI F., MILANO M., "Global Cut Framework for Removing Symmetries", Walsh [WAL 01], p. 77-92, 2001.

[FRI 02] FRISCH A. M., HNICH B., KIZILTAN Z., MIGUEL I., WALSH T., "Global Constraints for Lexicographic Orderings", Hentenryck [HEN 02], p. 93-108, 2002.

[FRI 04] FRISCH A. M., JEFFERSON C., MIGUEL I., "Symmetry Breaking as a Prelude to Implied Constraints: A Constraint Modelling Pattern", DE MÁNTARAS R. L., SAITTA L., Eds., *Proceedings of the 16th European Conference on Artificial Intelligence, ECAI'2004, including Prestigious Applicants of Intelligent Systems, PAIS 2004, Valencia, Spain, August 22-27, 2004*, IOS Press, p. 171-175, 2004.

[GAP 00] GAP GROUP T., GAP – Groups, Algorithms, and Programming, Version 4.2, 2000, (http://www.gap-system.org).

[GEN 00] GENT I. P., SMITH B. M., "Symmetry Breaking in Constraint Programming", HORN W., Ed., *ECAI 2000, Proceedings of the 14th European Conference on Artificial Intelligence, Berlin, Germany, August 20-25, 2000*, IOS Press, p. 599-603, 2000.

[GEN 02] GENT I. P., HARVEY W., KELSEY T., "Groups and Constraints: Symmetry Breaking during Search", Hentenryck [HEN 02], p. 415-430, 2002.

[GEN 03] GENT I. P., HARVEY W., KELSEY T., LINTON S., "Generic SBDD Using Computational Group Theory", Rossi [ROS 03], p. 333-347, 2003.

[HAR 04] HARVEY W., "A Note on the Compatibility of Static Symmetry Breaking Constraints and Dynamic Symmetry Breaking Methods", HARVEY W., KIZILTAN Z., Eds., *Fourth International Workshop on Symmetry and Constraint Satisfaction Problems, (in conjunction with the Tenth International Conference on Principles and Practice of Constraint Programming), Toronto, Proceedings*, p. 42-47, September 2004.

[HEN 02] HENTENRYCK P. V., Ed., *Principles and Practice of Constraint Programming – CP 2002, 8th International Conference, CP 2002, Ithaca, NY, USA, September 9-13, 2002, Proceedings*, vol. 2470 of *Lecture Notes in Computer Science*, Springer, 2002.

[KEL 04] KELSEY T., LINTON S., RONEY-DOUGAL C. M., "New Developments in Symmetry Breaking in Search Using Computational Group Theory", BUCHBERGER B., CAMPBELL J. A., Eds., *Artificial Intelligence and Symbolic Computation, 7th International Conference, AISC 2004, Linz, Austria, September 22-24, 2004, Proceedings*, vol. 3249 of *Lecture Notes in Computer Science*, Springer, p. 199-210, 2004.

[LIN 04] LINTON S., "Finding the smallest image of a set", GUTIERREZ J., Ed., *Symbolic and Algebraic Computation, International Symposium ISSAC 2004, Santander, Spain, July 4-7, 2004, Proceedings*, ACM, p. 229-234, 2004.

[MES 01] MESEGUER P., TORRAS C., "Exploiting Symmetries within Constraint Satisfcation Search", *AI*, vol. 129, p. 133-163, 2001.

[PET 03] PETRIE K. E., SMITH B. M., "Symmetry Breaking in Graceful Graphs", Rossi [ROS 03], p. 930-934, 2003.

[PUG 93] PUGET J.-F., "On the Satisfiability of Symmetrical Constrained Satisfaction Problems", KOMOROWSKI H. J., RAS Z. W., Eds., *Methodologies for Intelligent Systems, 7th International Symposium, ISMIS '93, Trondheim, Norway, June 15-18, 1993, Proceedings*, vol. 689 of *Lecture Notes in Computer Science*, Springer, p. 350-361, 1993.

[PUG 03] PUGET J.-F., "Symmetry Breaking Using Stabilizers", Rossi [ROS 03], p. 585-599, 2003.

[PUG 05] PUGET J.-F., "Breaking symmetries in all different problems", KAELBLING L. P., SAFFIOTTI A., Eds., *IJCAI-05, Proceedings of the Nineteenth International Joint Conference on Artificial Intelligence, Edinburgh, Scotland, UK, July 30-August 5, 2005*, Professional Book Center, p. 272-277, 2005.

[RON 04] RONEY-DOUGAL C. M., GENT I. P., KELSEY T., LINTON S., "Tractable symmetry breaking using restricted search trees", DE MÁNTARAS R. L., SAITTA L., Eds., *Proceedings, 16th European Conference on Artificial Intelligence: ECAI-04*, IOS Press, p. 211–215, 2004.

[ROS 03] ROSSI F., Ed., *Principles and Practice of Constraint Programming - CP 2003, 9th International Conference, CP 2003, Kinsale, Ireland, September 29 – October 3, 2003, Proceedings*, vol. 2833 of *Lecture Notes in Computer Science*, Springer, 2003.

[WAL 97] WALLACE M. G., NOVELLO S., SCHIMPF J., "ECLiPSe: A Platform for Constraint Logic Programming", *ICL Systems Journal*, vol. 12, num. 1, p. 159–200, May 1997.

[WAL 01] WALSH T., Ed., *Principles and Practice of Constraint Programming - CP 2001, 7th International Conference, CP 2001, Paphos, Cyprus, November 26 – December 1, 2001, Proceedings*, vol. 2239 of *Lecture Notes in Computer Science*, Springer, 2001.

Chapter 10

Symmetry Breaking in Subgraph Pattern Matching

A symmetry of a constraint satisfaction problem (CSP) is a bijective function that preserves CSP structure and solutions. Symmetries are important because they induce symmetric subtrees in the search tree. If the instance has no solution, failure has to be proved for equivalent subtrees regarding symmetries. If the instance has solutions, and all solutions are required, many symmetric solutions will have to be enumerated in symmetric subtrees. The detection and breaking of symmetries can thus speed up the solving of a CSP. Symmetries arise naturally in graphs as automorphisms. However, although a lot of graph problems have been tackled [BEL 05, CAM 04, SEL 03] and a computation domain for graphs has been defined [DOO 05], and despite the fact that symmetries and graphs are related, little has been done to investigate the use of symmetry breaking for graph problems in constraint programming.

This work aims to extend and implement symmetry breaking techniques for subgraph matching. We show how to detect and handle global variable and value symmetries as well as local value symmetries.

Related works

Handling symmetries to reduce search space has been a subject of research in constraint programming for many years. Crawford *et al.* [CRA 96] showed that computing the set of predicates breaking the symmetries of an instance

---

Chapter written by Stéphane ZAMPELLI, Yves DEVILLE and Pierre DUPONT.

is NP-hard in general. Different approaches exist for exploiting symmetries: symmetries can be broken during search either by posting additional constraints (SBDS) [GEN 01b] or by pruning the tree below a state symmetrical to a previous one (SBDD) [GEN 03]; by taking account of the symmetries in the heuristic [MES 01]; by constraints to the initial problem at its root node [CRA 96, GEN 01a]; and by re-modelling the problem [SMI 01].

Dynamic detection of value symmetries (also called local value symmetries or conditional value symmetries) and a general method for detecting them has been proposed in [BEN 94]. The general case for such a detection is difficult. However in not-equal binary CSPs, some value symmetries can be detected in linear time [BEN 04] and dominance detection for value symmetries can be performed in linear time [BEN 06].

Research efforts have been geared towards defining, detecting and breaking symmetries. Cohen et al. [COH 06] define two types of symmetries, solution symmetries and constraint symmetries and prove that the group of constraint symmetries is a subgroup of the group of solution symmetries. Gent et al. [GEN 05b] rediscovered local symmetries defined in [BEN 94] and evaluated several techniques to break local symmetries. However the detection of local symmetries remains a research topic. Symmetries have been shown to produce stronger forms of consistency and more efficient consistency algorithms [GEN 05a]. Finally, Puget [PUG 05a] shows how to detect symmetries automatically, and that, for the case of injective problems, all variable symmetries can be broken with a linear number of constraints [PUG 05b].

Graph pattern matching is a central application in many fields [CON 04]. Many different types of algorithms have been proposed, ranging from general methods to specific algorithms for particular types of graphs. In constraint programming, several authors [LAR 02, RUD 98] have shown that subgraph matching can be formulated as a CSP, and argued that constraint programming could be a powerful tool to handle its combinatorial complexity. Within the CSP framework, a model for subgraph monomorphism has been proposed by Rudolf [RUD 98] and Valiente et al. [LAR 02]. Our modeling [ZAM 05] is based on these works. Sorlin and Solnon [SOR 04] propose a filtering algorithm based on paths for graph isomorphism and part of our approach can be seen as a generalization of this filtering. The same authors recently proposed a new filtering algorithm for graph isomorphism based on iterative labelling of nodes using local neighborhood structure [SOR 06]. A declarative view of matching has also been proposed in [MAM 04]. In [ZAM 05], we showed that the CSP approach is competitive with dedicated algorithms over a graph database representing graphs with various topologies.

Objectives

This work aims to develop symmetry breaking techniques for subgraph matching modeled as a CSP in order to increase the number of tractable instances of graph matching. Our first goal is to develop specific detection techniques for the classical variable symmetries and value symmetries, and to break such symmetries when solving subgraph matching. Our second goal is to develop detection and breaking techniques, for local symmetries, that can be easily handled for subgraph matching.

Results

– We show that all global variable symmetries can be detected by computing the set of automorphisms of the pattern graph, and how they can be broken.

– We show that all global value symmetries can be detected by computing the set of automorphisms of the target graph, and how they can be broken.

– Experimental results compare and analyze the enhancement achieved by global symmetries and show that symmetry breaking is an effective way to increase the number of tractable instances of the subgraph matching problem.

– We show that local value symmetries can be detected by computing the set of automorphisms on various subgraphs of the target graph. The GE-Tree method [RON 04] can be extended to handle these local symmetries.

Outline

Section 10.1 provides the necessary background in subgraph matching and in symmetry breaking. It also describes a CSP approach for subgraph matching. Sections 10.2 and 10.3 present variable symmetries and value symmetries in subgraph matching. Section 10.4 describes experimental results for global symmetries. Local value symmetries are discussed in section 10.5. Finally, section 10.6 concludes this work.

10.1. Background and definitions

Basic definitions for subgraph matching and symmetries are introduced.

A *graph* $G = (N, E)$ consists of a *node set* N and an *edge set* $E \subseteq N \times N$, where an edge (u, v) is a pair of nodes. The nodes u and v are the endpoints of the edge (u, v). We consider directed and undirected graphs. A *subgraph* of a graph $G = (N, E)$ is a graph $S = (N', E')$ where N' is a subset of N and E' is a subset of E such that for all $(u, v) \in E'$, $u, v \in N'$.

A *subgraph monomorphism* (or subgraph matching) between G_p (the *pattern* graph) and G_t (the *target* graph) is a total injective function $f\colon N_p \to N_t$

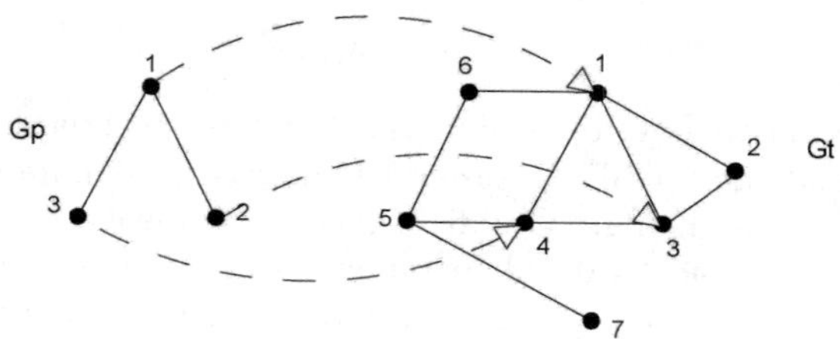

Figure 10.1. *Example solution for a monomorphism problem instance*

respecting the monomorphism constraint: $(u, v) \in E_p \Rightarrow (f(u), f(v)) \in E_t$. Figure 10.1 shows an example of subgraph monomorphism.

The CSP model of subgraph matching should represent a total function $f : N_p \rightarrow N_t$. This total function can be modeled with $X = x_1, \ldots, x_n$ where x_i is an FD variable corresponding to the ith node of G_p and $D(x_i) = N_t$. The injective condition is modeled with the global constraint $\texttt{alldiff}(x_1, \ldots, x_n)$. The monomorphism condition is translated into a set of constraints $MC_l(x_i, x_j) \equiv (x_i, x_j) \in E_t$ for all $(i, j) \in E_p$. This set of constraints can be turned into a global constraint $MC(x_1, \ldots, x_n) \equiv \bigwedge_{(i,j)\in E_p} MC_l(x_i, x_j)$. Implementation, comparison with dedicated algorithms, and extension to subgraph isomorphism and to graph and function computation domains can be found in [ZAM 05, DEV 05]. A CSP instance is a triple $< X, D, C >$ where X is the set of variables, D is the universal domain specifying the possible values for those variables, and C is the set of constraints. In the sequel, $n = |N_p|$, $d = |D|$, and $D(x_i)$ is the domain of x_i. A symmetry over a CSP instance P is a bijection σ (with domain and target sets discussed below) mapping solutions to solutions, and hence non-solutions to non-solutions [PUG 05a]. Since a symmetry is a bijection where domain and target sets are the same, a symmetry is a permutation. A *variable symmetry* is a bijective function $\sigma : X \rightarrow X$ mapping a (non-) solution $s = ((x_1, d_1), \ldots, (x_n, d_n))$ to a (non-) solution $\sigma s = ((\sigma(x_1), d_1), \ldots, (\sigma(x_n), d_n))$. A *value symmetry* is a bijective function $\sigma : D \rightarrow D$ mapping a (non-) solution $s = ((x_1, d_1), \ldots, (x_n, d_n))$ to a (non-) solution $\sigma s = ((x_1, \sigma(d_1)), \ldots, (x_n, \sigma(d_n)))$. A *value and variable symmetry* is a bijective function $\sigma : X \times D \rightarrow X \times D$ mapping a (non-) solution $s = ((x_1, d_1), \ldots, (x_n, d_n))$ to a (non-) solution $\sigma s = ((\sigma(x_1), \sigma(d_1)), \ldots, (\sigma(x_n), \sigma(d_n)))$. A *global symmetry* of a CSP is a symmetry holding on the initial problem. A *local symmetry* of a CSP P is a symmetry holding only in a subproblem P' of P. The conditions of the symmetry are the constraints necessary to generate P' from P [GEN 05b] [BEN 94]. A *group* is a finite or infinite set of elements together with a binary operation (called the group operation) that satisfies the four basic properties of closure, associativity, the identity property,

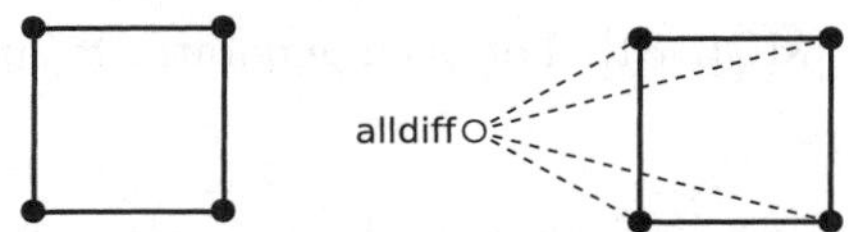

Figure 10.2. *Example of symbolic graph for a square pattern*

and the inverse property. An *automorphism of a graph* is a graph isomorphism with itself. The set of automorphisms $Aut(G)$ defines a finite group of permutations.

10.2. Variable symmetries

In this section, we show that the set of global variable symmetries of a subgraph monomorphism CSP is the set of automorphisms of the pattern graph. Moreover, we show how existing techniques can be used to break all global variable symmetries.

10.2.1. *Detection*

We now show that global variable symmetries of a subgraph matching problem are the automorphisms of the pattern graph and do not depend on the target graph. It has been shown that the set of all variable symmetries of the CSP is the automorphism group of a *symbolic graph* [PUG 05a]. The pattern G_p is easily transformed into a symbolic graph $S(G_p)$ where $Aut(S(G_p))$ is the set of variable symmetries of the CSP. The graph $S(G_p)$ is the same as G_p, except that there is an additional, distinctly colored node typed with label a, representing the *alldiff* constraint. There is an arc (a, x_i) in $S(G_p)$ for each $x_i \in N_p$, the node set of G_p.

Figure 10.2 shows a pattern transformed into its symbolic graph. Clearly the group $Aut(S(G_p))$ is equal to $Aut(G_p)$ when restricted to N_p. Thus only $Aut(G_p)$ has to be calculated in order to get all variable symmetries of the problem.

10.2.2. *Breaking*

Two existing techniques are relevant to our particular problem. The first technique is an approximation and consists of breaking only the generators of the symmetry group [CRA 96]. Those generators are obtained by using a tool such as NAUTY [MCK 81]. For each generator σ, an ordering constraint $s \leq \sigma s$ is posted.

The second technique breaks all variable symmetries of an injective problem by using a Schreier-Sims algorithm [BUT 91], provided that the generators of the variable symmetry group are known [PUG 05a]. Puget showed that the number of constraints to be posted is linear with the number of variables. The Schreier-Sims algorithm calculates a base and a strong generating set of a permutation group in $O(n^2 log^3|G| + t.n.log|G|)$, where G is the group, t the number of generators and n is the degree of G.

10.3. Value symmetries

In this section we show how all global value symmetries can be detected and how existing techniques can be extended to break them.

10.3.1. *Detection*

In subgraph matching, global value symmetries are automorphisms of the target graph and do not depend on the pattern graph.

THEOREM.– *Given a subgraph monomorphism instance (G_p, G_t) and its associated CSP P, each $\sigma \in Aut(G_t)$ is a value symmetry of P.*

Proof Suppose that f is a subgraph monomorphism between G_p and G_t, and $f(i) = v_i$ for $i \in N_p$. Consider the subgraph $G = (N, E)$ of G_t, where $N = \{v_1, \ldots, v_n\}$ and $E = \{(i, j) \in E_t \mid (f^{-1}(i), f^{-1}(j)) \in E_p\}$. This means that there exists a monomorphic function f' matching G_p to σG. Hence $((x_1, \sigma(v_1)), \ldots, (x_n, \sigma(v_n)))$ is a solution. ■

10.3.2. *Breaking*

Breaking global value symmetries can be performed by using the GE-Tree technique [RON 04]. The idea is to modify the distribution by avoiding symmetrical value assignments. Suppose a state S is reached, where $x_1, \ldots, x_k$ are assigned to $v_1, \ldots, v_k$ respectively, and $x_{k+1}, \ldots, x_n$ are not assigned yet. The variable x_{k+1} should not be assigned to two symmetrical values, since two symmetric subtrees would be searched. For each value $v_i \in D(x_{k+1})$ that is symmetric to a value $v_j \in D(x_{k+1})$, only one state S_1 should be generated with the new constraint $x_{k+1} = v_i$.

A convenient way to calculate those symmetrical values uses the Schreier-Sims algorithm to obtain the sets $U_i = \{k \mid \exists\, \sigma \in Aut(G_t) : \sigma(i) = k \wedge \sigma(j) = j\, \forall\, j < i\}$. A set U_i gives the images of i by the automorphisms of G mapping $0, \ldots, i-1$ to themselves (the point-wise stabilizer of $\{0, \ldots, i-1\}$). We refer to the sets U_i as *U-structures.*

If values are assigned in an increasing order, assigning symmetrical values can be avoided by using those sets U_i [PUG 05a].

10.4. Experimental results

This section presents experiments for global variables and value symmetries.

The CSP model for subgraph monomorphism has been implemented in Gecode[1], using CP(Graph) [DOO 05] and CP(Map) [DEV 05]. The CP(Graph) framework provides graph domain variables and CP(Map) provides function domain variables. All the software is implemented in C++. The standard implementation of the NAUTY [MCK 81] algorithm is used. We also implemented the Schreier-Sims algorithm. The computation of the constraints for breaking injective problems is implemented, and the GE-Tree method is also incorporated.

We have evaluated global variable symmetry detection and breaking, global value symmetry detection and breaking, and global variable and value symmetry breaking.

The data graphs used to generate instances are from the GraphBase database containing different topologies and have been used in [LAR 02]. There is a directed and an undirected set of graphs. Experiments are performed on undirected and directed graphs, because automorphism groups are expected to be larger in undirected graphs than in directed graphs. We took the first 30 directed graphs and the first 50 undirected graphs from GraphBase. The directed set contains graphs ranging from 10 nodes to 462 nodes. The undirected set contains graphs ranging from 10 nodes to 138 nodes. Using those graphs, there are 405 instances for directed graphs and 1225 instances for undirected graphs. All runs were performed on a dual Intel(R) Xeon(TM) CPU 2.66GHz.

A major concern is how much time it takes to calculate the symmetries of the graphs. NAUTY processed each undirected graph in less than 0.02 second. For directed graphs, each graph was processed in less than 0.01 seconds,

1. http://www.gecode.org.

Undirected graphs				Directed graphs			
	solved	total time	mean time		solved	total time	mean time
CSP	58%	70 min.	5.95 sec.	CSP	67%	21 min.	4.31 sec.
Gen.	60.5%	172 min.	13.95 sec.	Gen.	74%	47 min.	8.87 sec.
FVS	61.8%	101 min.	8 sec.	FVS	74%	40 min.	7.64 sec.

Table 10.1. *Variable symmetries*

Undirected graphs				Directed graphs			
	solved	total time	mean time		solved	total time	mean time
CSP	53.7%	31 min.	20.1 sec.	CSP	67%	21 min.	4.31 sec.
GE-Tree	55.3%	6 min.	3.21 sec.	GE-Tree	68%	21 min.	4.39 sec.

Table 10.2. *Value symmetries*

with the exception of one which terminated after 0.8 seconds, and four for which processing did not terminate after five minutes. Note that we did not tune NAUTY. The Schreier-Sims algorithm calculated the sets U_i (described above) for each directed graph in less than one second, with the exception of three graphs for which the algorithm terminated after 0.5, 1.5 and 3.1 seconds respectively. All undirected graphs were processed by Schreier-Sims in less than one second, with the exception of two which took 4 and 8 seconds respectively to process.

In our tests, we look for all solutions. A run is solved if it finishes in less than 5 minutes, otherwise it is unsolved. We applied the basic CSP model, the model where constraints that break variable symmetries with generators (Gen.) are posted, and finally the full variable symmetry technique (FVS) that breaks all variable symmetries. Results are shown in Table 10.1. In those runs, the pre-processing time has not been considered.

Owing to variable symmetry breaking constraints more instances are solved, for the directed graphs as well as for the undirected graphs. On the other hand, the time for solved instances is increased because of the variable symmetry breaking constraints. Regarding the mean time, the full variable symmetry breaking constraint has a clear advantage over symmetry breaking with generators only.

Value symmetry breaking is evaluated on the set of directed graphs and undirected graphs. Table 10.2 shows that around one percent is gained. However the mean time for undirected graphs is decreased, even thought this is

Undirected graphs			
	solved	total time	mean time
CSP	53.7%	31 min.	20.1 sec.
GE-Tree	55.3%	6 min.	3.21 sec.
FVS	54.9 %	31 min.	19 sec.
GE-Tree and FVS	55.3 %	26 min.	8.68 sec.

Table 10.3. *Variable and value symmetries*

not the case for directed graphs. This may be due to the fact that there are less symmetries in directed graphs than in undirected graphs. For variable and value symmetries, a total of 233 undirected random instances were treated. We evaluated variable and value symmetries separately and then together in Table 10.3. This table shows that, as expected, value symmetries and variable symmetries each increase the number of solved instances. Notice here that value symmetry breaking with GE-Tree leads to new solved instances and a better performance, reducing mean time on solved instances. The full variable symmetry technique allows new instances to be solved, but does not significantly reduce mean time on solved instances. Moreover, the combination of value symmetry breaking and variable symmetry breaking does not combine the power of the two techniques. In fact the GE-Tree upper bound of the number of solved solutions is not increased by using the full variable symmetry technique. Moreover, its mean execution time is even increased.

From these experiments, we conclude that global variable and value symmetry techniques perform better and solve new instances. However they are not sufficient to solve a significantly higher percentage of instances. The next section shows how to detect and handle local value symmetries.

10.5. Local value symmetries

In subgraph monomorphism, the relations between values are explicitly represented in the target graph. This allows the detection of local values symmetries. Consider Figure 10.3. Only global value symmetries of the CSP P are in $Aut(G_t)$. There exists at least two local value symmetric solutions: $\{(x_1, 1), (x_2, 2), (x_3, 3), (x_4, 4)\}$ and $\{(x_1, 2), (x_2, 1), (x_3, 4), (x_4, 3)\}$ although $Aut(G_t) = \{id\}$.

Two techniques are presented in this section. The first one uses the target subgraph defined by the union of the current domains, called the dynamic target graph, and the second uses the graphs local to the current subproblem, called the partial dynamic graphs.

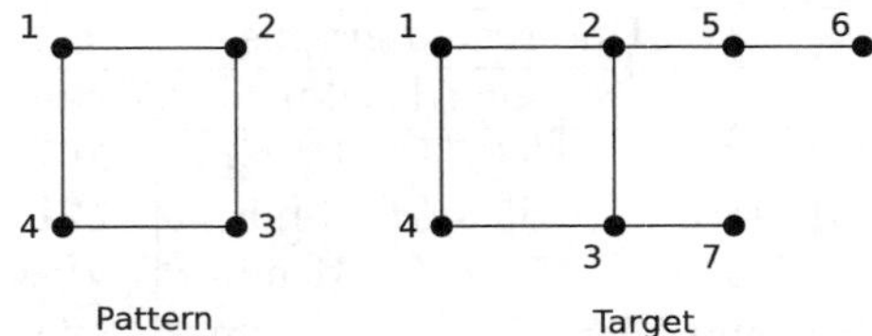

Figure 10.3. *Example of matching without value symmetries but with local value symmetries*

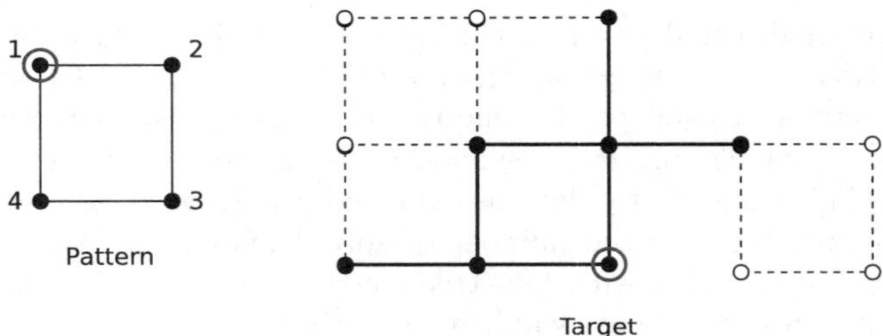

Figure 10.4. *Example of dynamic target subgraph*

10.5.1. *Dynamic target graph*

This first technique to detect local value symmetries considers the subgraph of the union of the current variable domains.

10.5.1.1. *Detection*

During the search, the target graph looses a node a whenever $a \notin \cup_{i \in N_p} D(x_i)$. This is interesting because the relationship between the values are known dynamically.

The set of values $\cup_{i \in N_p} D(x_i)$ denotes the nodes of the subgraph of G_t in which a solution is searched. For a given state S, such a subgraph can be calculated efficiently. We first define this subgraph of G_t.

DEFINITION.– *Let S be a state in the search where $x_1, \ldots, x_k$ are assigned, and $x_{k+1}, \ldots, x_n$ are not assigned. The* dynamic target graph $G_t^* = (N_t^*, E_t^*)$ *is a subgraph of G_t such that :*

– $N_t^* = \cup_{i \in [1,\ldots,n]} D(x_i)$

– $E_t^* = \{(a, b) \in E_t \mid a \in N_t^* \land b \in N_t^*\}$

Figure 10.4 shows an example of a dynamic target graph. In this figure, the circled nodes are mapped in the current assignment. The blank nodes are the nodes excluded from the union of the current domains, and the black nodes are the nodes included in this union. The plain edges are the selected edges for the dynamic target subgraph. The following theorem shows that each automorphism of G_t^* is a local value symmetry for the state S.

THEOREM.– *Suppose we have a subgraph monomorphism instance* (G_p, G_t), *its associated CSP* P, *and a state* S *in the search, each* $\sigma \in Aut(G_t^*)$ *is a local value symmetry of* P. *Moreover, the conditions of* σ *are* $x_1 = v_1, \ldots, x_k = v_k$.

Proof Suppose $Sol = (v_1, \ldots, v_k)$ is a partial solution. Consider the dynamic target subgraph G_t^*. The state S can be considered as a new CSP P' of an instance (G_p, G_t^*) with additional constraints $x_1 = v_1, \ldots, x_k = v_k$. From the theorem of section 10.3.1, the thesis follows. ■

The size of G_t^* is an important issue, as we will dynamically calculate symmetry information with it. The following theorem shows that, because of the *MC* constraints, the longest path in G_p is the same length as the longest path in G_t whenever at least one variable is assigned.

DEFINITION.– *Let* $G = (N, E)$ *be a graph. Then* $maxd(G)$ *denotes the size of the longest simple path between two nodes* $a, b \in N$.

THEOREM.– *Suppose we have a subgraph monomorphism instance* (G_p, G_t), *its associated CSP* P, *a state* S *in the search, and suppose the* MC_l *constraints are arc-consistent. Then if* $\exists\, i \in N_p$ *such that* $|D(x_i)| = 1$, *then* $maxd(G_p) = maxd(G_t^*)$.

This is a nice result for complexity issues, when $maxd(G_p)$ is small. In Figure 10.4, $maxd(G_p)$=2 and only nodes at shortest distance 2 from the image of node 1 in the target graph are included in G_t^*.

The dynamic target graph G can be calculated dynamically. In [DEV 05], we showed how subgraph matching can be modeled and implemented in an extension of CP, CP(Graph), with graph domain variables [DOO 05]. The domain of a graph variable is modeled by a lower bound and an upper bound graph, and represents all the graphs between the lower and upper bound. In this setting, a graph domain variable T represents the matched target subgraph. The initial lower bound of T is the empty graph, and the initial upper bound if G_t. When a solution is found, T is instantiated to the matched subgraph of G_t. Hence, during the search, the dynamic target graph G_t^* will be the upper bound of variable T and can be obtained in $O(1)$.

10.5.1.2. *Breaking*

In this subsection, we show how to modify the GE-Tree method to handle local value symmetries. Before distribution, the following actions are triggered:

1) Get G_t^*.

2) The NAUTY and Schreier-Sims algorithms are called. This returns the new U_i' sets.

3) The main problem is how to adapt the variable and value selection such that local value symmetries are broken.

a) a new state S_1 with a constraint $x_k = v_k$

b) a new state S_2 with constraints: $x_k \neq v_k$ and $x_k \neq v_j \ \forall\, j \in U_{k-1} \cup U'_{k-1}$.

The only difference with the original GE-Tree method is the addition of the U'_{k-1} during the creation of the second branch corresponding to the state S_2.

How to handle the global and local U-structures is an issue. In the Gecode system, in which the actual implementation is made, the states are copied and trailing is not needed. Thus the global structure U must not be updated because of backtracking. A single global copy is kept during the whole search process. In a state S where local value symmetries are discovered, structure U is copied into a new structure U'' and merged with U'. This structure U'' shall be used for all states S' having S in its predecessors.

10.5.2. *Partial dynamic graphs*

The second technique for detecting local value symmetries considers the subgraphs associated with the current state.

10.5.2.1. *Detection*

We first introduce partial dynamic graphs. Those graphs are associated to a state in the search and correspond to the unsolved part of the problem. This can be viewed as a new local problem to the current state.

DEFINITION.– *Let S be a state in the search whose variables $x_1, \dots, x_k$ are assigned to $v_1, \dots, v_k$ respectively, and $x_{k+1}, \dots, x_n$ are not yet assigned. The* partial dynamic pattern graph *$G_p^- = (N_p^-, E_p^-)$ is a subgraph of G_p such that:*

– $N_p^- = \{i \in [k+1, n]\}$

– $E_p^- = \{(i,j) \in E_p \mid i \in N_p^- \wedge j \in N_p^-\}$

The partial dynamic target graph *$G_t^- = (N_t^-, E_t^-)$ is a subgraph of G_t such that:*

– $N_t^- = \cup_{i \in [k+1,n]} D(x_i)$

– $E_t^- = \{(a,b) \in E_t \mid a \in N_t^- \wedge b \in N_t^-\}$

The following theorem states that value symmetries of the local CSP P' can be obtained by computing $Aut(G_t^-)$ and that these symmetries can be exploited without losing or adding solutions to the initial matching problem.

THEOREM.– *Let (G_p, G_t) be a subgraph monomorphism instance, P its associated CSP, and S a state of P during the search, where the assigned variables are $x_1, \ldots, x_k$ with values $v_1, \ldots, v_k$. Let P' be a new CSP of a subgraph monomorphism instance (G_p^-, G_t^-) with additional constraints $x'_{k+1} = D(x_{k+1}), \ldots, x'_n = D(x_n)$. Then:*

1) Each $\sigma \in Aut(G_t^-)$ is a value symmetry of P'.

2) Assuming we have the forward checking (FC) property, we have $((x_1, v_1), \ldots, (x_n, v_n)) \in Sol(S)$ if and only if $((x_{k+1}, v_{k+1}), \ldots, (x_n, v_n)) \in Sol(P')$.

Proof sketch When forward checking (FC) is used during the search, in any state in the search tree, every constraint involving *one* uninstantiated variable is arc consistent. In other words, every value in the domain of an uninstantiated variable is consistent with the partial solution. This FC property on a binary CSP ensures that one can focus on the uninstantiated variables and their associated constraints without losing or creating solutions to the initial problem. Such a property also holds when the search achieves stronger consistency in the search tree. ■

The calculation of G_t^- can be easily performed thanks to graph variables. If T is the graph variable representing the matched target subgraph (with initially $lub(T) = \emptyset$ and $glb(T) = G_t$), then during the computation G_t^- is $lub(T) \setminus glb(T)$.

10.5.2.2. *Breaking*

Breaking local value symmetries is equivalent to breaking value symmetries on the subproblem P'. Puget's method and the dynamic GE-Tree method can thus be applied to the local CSP P'.

10.6. Conclusion

In this work, we present techniques for symmetry breaking in subgraph matching. Specific detection techniques are developed for the variable symmetries and value symmetries. We show that global variable symmetries and value symmetries can be detected by computing the set of automorphisms on the pattern graph and on the target graph and how they can be broken. We also show that local value symmetries can be detected by computing the set of automorphisms on various subgraphs of the target graph. The GE-Tree method is extended to break these local symmetries. Experimental results illustrate the benefit of exploiting global variable and value symmetries. The results show that symmetry breaking is an effective way to increase the number of tractable instances of the graph matching problem. Ongoing work studies local variables as well as local value symmetries more specifically. Specific techniques are developed for this case [ZAM 07]. Another interesting research direction is the automatic detection of symmetries in graph domain variables.

Acknowledgment This research was supported by the Walloon Region, project BioMaze (WIST 315432).

10.7. References

[BEE 05] VAN BEEK P., Ed., *Proceedings of the 11th International Conference on Principles and Practice of Constraint Programming (CP-2005)*, Lecture Notes in Computer Science, Barcelona, Spain, Springer, October 2005.

[BEL 05] BELDICEANU N., FLENER P., LORCA X., "The Tree Constraint", BARTAK R., Ed., *Integration of AI and OR Techniques in Constraint Programming for Combinatorial Optimization Problems, Second International Conference, CPAIOR 2005, Prague, Czech Republic, Proceedings*, vol. 3524 of *Lecture Notes in Computer Science*, Springer, p. 64-78, June 2005.

[BEN 94] BENHAMOU B., "Study of Symmetry in Constraint Satisfaction Problems", BORNING A., Ed., *Second International Workshop on Principles and Practice of Constraint Programming, PPCP'94, Proceedings*, vol. 874 of *Lecture Notes in Computer Science*, Orcas Island, Seattle, USA, Springer, p. 246–254, May 1994.

[BEN 04] BENHAMOU B., "Symmetry in Not-equals Binary Constraint Networks", HARVEY W., KIZILTAN Z., Eds., *Fourth International Workshop on Symmetry and Constraint Satisfaction Problems, (in conjunction with the Tenth International Conference on Principles and Practice of Constraint Programming), Toronto, Canada, Proceedings*, p. 2–8, September 2004.

[BEN 06] BENHAMOU B., SAÏDI M. R., "Reasoning by Dominance in Not-Equals Binary Constraint Networks", BENHAMOU F., Ed., *Proceedings of the Twelfth International Conference on Principles and Practice of Constraint Programming, CP2006*, Lecture Notes in Computer Science, Cité des Congrès – Nantes, France, Springer, p. 670–674, September 2006.

[BUT 91] BUTLER G., *Fundamental Algorithms for Permutation Groups*, vol. 559 of *Lecture Notes in Computer Science*, Springer, 1991.

[CAM 04] CAMBAZARD H., BOURREAU E., "Conception d'une contrainte globale de chemin", *10e Journées nationales sur la résolution pratique de problèmes NP-complets (JNPC'04)*, Angers, France, p. 107–121, June 2004.

[COH 06] COHEN D., JEAVONS P., JEFFERSON C., PETRIE K. E., SMITH B. M., "Symmetry Definitions for Constraint Satisfaction Problems", *Constraints*, vol. 11, num. 2-3, p. 115–137, Kluwer Academic Publishers, 2006.

[CON 04] CONTE D., FOGGIA P., SANSONE C., VENTO M., "Thirty Years Of Graph Matching In Pattern Recognition.", *International Journal of Pattern Recognition and Artificial Intelligence*, vol. 18, num. 3, p. 265-298, World Scientific Publishing, 2004.

[CRA 96] CRAWFORD J., GINSBERG M. L., LUCK E., ROY A., "Symmetry-Breaking Predicates for Search Problems", AIELLO L. C., DOYLE J., SHAPIRO S., Eds., *KR'96: Principles of Knowledge Representation and Reasoning, Cambridge, Massachusetts, USA*, p. 148–159, Morgan Kaufmann, November 1996.

[DEV 05] DEVILLE Y., DOOMS G., ZAMPELLI S., DUPONT P., "CP(Graph+Map) for Approximate Graph Matching", AZEVEDO F., GERVET C., PONTELLI E., Eds., *1st International Workshop on Constraint Programming Beyond Finite Integer Domains (in conjunction with the Eleventh International Conference on Principles and Practice of Constraint Programming), CP2005, Sitges, Spain*, p. 33–47, October 2005.

[DOO 05] DOOMS G., DEVILLE Y., DUPONT P., "CP(Graph): Introducing a Graph Computation Domain in Constraint Programming", van Beek [BEE 05], p. 211–215, October 2005.

[GEN 01a] GENT I., "A Symmetry Breaking Constraint for Indistinguishable Values", FLENER P., PEARSON J., Eds., *First International Workshop on Symmetry and Constraint Satisfaction Problems (in conjunction with the Eighth International Conference on Principles and Practice of Constraint Programming)*, December 2001.

[GEN 01b] GENT I., SMITH B., "Symmetry Breaking during Search in Constraint Programming", VAN BEEK P., Ed., *Proceedings of the 7th International Conference on Principles and Practice of Constraint Programming, CP2001, Paphos, Cyprus*, vol. 2239 of *Lecture Notes in Computer Science*, Springer, p. 599-603, December 2001.

[GEN 03] GENT I., HARVEY W., KELSEY T., "Generic SBDD using Computational Group Theory", ROSSI F., Ed., *Proceedings of the 9th International Conference on Principles and Practice of Constraint Programming, CP2003, Kinsale, Ireland*, vol. 2833 of *Lecture Notes in Computer Science*, Springer, p. 333-346, 2003.

[GEN 05a] GENT I. P., KELSEY T., LINTON S., RONEY-DOUGAL C., "Symmetry and Consistency", van Beek [BEE 05], p. 271-285, October 2005.

[GEN 05b] GENT I. P., KELSEY T., LINTON S. A., MCDONALD I., MIGUEL I., SMITH B. M., "Conditional Symmetry Breaking", van Beek [BEE 05], p. 256-270, October 2005.

[LAR 02] LARROSA J., VALIENTE G., "Constraint Satisfaction Algorithms for Graph Pattern Matching", *Mathematical. Structures in Comp. Sci.*, vol. 12, num. 4, p. 403–422, Cambridge University Press, 2002.

[MAM 04] MAMOULIS N., STERGIOU K., "Constraint Satisfaction in Semi-structured Data Graphs.", WALLACE M., Ed., *Proceedings of the Tenth International Conference on Principles and Practice of Constraint Programming, CP2004, Toronto, Canada*, Lecture Notes in Computer Science, Springer, p. 393-407, October 2004.

[MCK 81] MCKAY B. D., "Pratical graph isomorphism", *Congressum Numerantium*, vol. 30, p. 35–87, 1981.

[MES 01] MESEGUER P., TORRAS C., "Exploiting Symmetries within the Constraint Satisfaction Search", *Artificial Intelligence*, vol. 129(1-2), p. 133–163, June 2001.

[PUG 05a] PUGET J.-F., "Automatic Detection of Variable and Value Symmetries", van Beek [BEE 05], p. 477-489, October 2005.

[PUG 05b] PUGET J.-F., "Élimination des symétries dans les problèmes injectifs", SOLNON C., Ed., *Journées Francophones de la Programmation par Contraintes, JFPC, Lens, France, Proceedings*, p. 259–266, June 2005.

[RON 04] RONAY-DOUGAL C., GENT I., KELSEY T., LINTON S., "Tractable Symmetry Breaking in Using Restricted Search Trees", DE MÁNTARAS R. L., SAITTA L., Eds., *16th European Conference on Artificial Intelligence, Proceedings, Valencia, Spain*, vol. 110, IOS Press, p. 211–215, 2004.

[RUD 98] RUDOLF M., "Utilizing Constraint Satisfaction Techniques for Efficient Graph Pattern Matching.", EHRIG H., ENGELS G., KREOWSKI H.-J., ROZENBERG G., Eds., *Sixth International Workshop on Theory and Application of Graph Transformations, TAGT'98, Paderborn, Germany*, vol. 1764 of *Lecture Notes in Computer Science*, Springer, p. 238-251, 1998.

[SEL 03] SELLMAN M., "Cost-based filtering for shorter path constraints", ROSSI F., Ed., *Nineth International Conference on Principles and Pratice of Constraint Programming, CP 2003, Kinsale, Ireland, Proceedings*, vol. 2833 of *Lecture Notes in Computer Science*, Springer-Verlag, p. 694–708, October 2003.

[SMI 01] SMITH B., "Reducing Symmetry in a Combinatorial Design Problem", GERVET C., WALLACE M., Eds., *Third International Workshop on Integration of AI and OR Techniques in Constraint Programming for Combinatorial Optimisation Problems, CP-AI-OR2001, Ashford, UK*, p. 351–359, April 2001.

[SOR 04] SORLIN S., SOLNON C., "A Global Constraint for Graph Isomorphism Problems", RÉGIN J.-C., RUEHER M., Eds., *International Conference on Integration of AI and OR Techniques in Constraint Programming for Combinatorial Optimisation Problems, Nice, France, Proceedings*, vol. 3011 of *Lecture Notes in Computer Science*, Springer, p. 287-302, 2004.

[SOR 06] SORLIN S., SOLNON C., "A New Filtering Algorithm for the Graph Isomorphism Problem", *Third International Workshop on Constraint Propagation and Implementation (in conjunction with the Twelth International Conference on Principles and Practice of Constraint Programming), Nantes, France*, p. 92–107, September 2006.

[ZAM 05] ZAMPELLI S., DEVILLE Y., DUPONT P., "Approximate Constrained Subgraph Matching", van Beek [BEE 05], p. 832–836, October 2005.

[ZAM 07] ZAMPELLI S., DEVILLE Y., SEDI M., BENHAMOU B., DUPONT P., "Breaking Local Symmetries in Subgraph Pattern Matching", GENT I., LINTON S., Eds., *Proceedings of International Symmetry Conference, Edinburgh*, January 2007.

PART IV

Interval Analysis, Constraint Propagation and Applications

Edited by Christophe JERMANN, Yahia LEBBAH and Djamila SAM-HAROUD

Introduction

This part of the book gathers a selection of papers from the third international workshop on INTerval analysis, constraint propagation and applications (IntCP 2006) held at Cité des Congrès, Nantes (France) on September 25th, 2006.

The two most appealing features of interval analysis and numerical constraint propagation, when used to solve numerical problems, are completeness and rigor. Completeness means the ability to find all solutions, whereas rigor is the ability to control the rounding errors due to floating-point computation. Completeness and rigor are essential in numerous applications such as engineering design, robotics, control, logistics, manufacturing, chemical and biological sciences and computer-aided design to name but a few. The problems in these domains involve equations, inequalities, differential equations and sometimes an objective function on variables taking their values in the set of real numbers.

The multidisciplinary nature of constraint propagation and the general framework offered by constraint programming give rise to a unique combination of theoretical and experimental research providing bridges between separate, but often complementary areas. However, while interval based constraint propagation solvers have proved particularly efficient in solving challenging instances of non-linear numerical problems, they do not yet have enough appeal in many practical areas. One of the reasons is that they generally provide representation of the solution set that are either prohibitively verbose or poorly informative. Another reason is that they are sometimes too inefficient, especially to address real-time applications like interactive control or animation. Recent advances have shown that these limitations are not intrinsic since constraint propagation can be considerably improved using techniques from interval analysis and local/global optimization.

The goal of IntCP 2006 was to emphasize the multidisciplinary nature of these researches and reach out to a number of communities which are increasingly interested in interval analysis and constraint propagation. Nine papers were accepted for presentation during the workshop[1]. Their content reflects the trends both towards the combination of techniques from different areas, and towards more demanding real life applications: non-linear differential equations, advanced relaxations for global optimization, interval disjunction for continuous shaving based reduction and for search, continuous MaxCSP, reduction methods for robotics, and hybrid systems. Our selection contains three representative papers chosen from these nine presentations. The first chapter on radio antenna deployment, introduces an interesting approach to model and solve a numerical sub-problem within a constraint programming framework. The second chapter shows that numerical injectivity can be handled rigorously via interval analysis. The third chapter presents an interval constraint propagation framework to handle hybrid systems where both discrete and continuous changes occur.

We hope that this workshop has helped to develop the maturity of interval analysis and constraint propagation. We would like to thank the program and referee committees who worked under tight deadlines.

Christophe Jermann,
Yahia Lebbah,
Djamila Sam-Haroud

Members of the program committee and referees

P. Barahona	D. Daney	S. Ratschan
M. Ceberio	L. Jaulin	N. Sahinidis
M. Christie	C. Jermann	D. Sam-Haroud
J. Cruz	Y. Lebbah	J. Vehi

1. See http://liawww.epfl.ch/Events/IntCP2006.

Chapter 11

Modeling and Solving of a Radio Antenna Deployment Support Application

The new theater of operations requires an ever growing number of telecommunications systems to share a limited frequency spectrum. As a consequence, the task of assigning frequencies becomes more and more difficult for operators taking care of the deployment of mobile units. Deployment support of radio antennas is a crossbreeding of traditional classical radio link frequency assignment problems [AAR 03] (RLFAP) and location analysis problems. In a standard RLFAP, the position of all antennas is known beforehand, and statically determines the set of constraints that apply on frequencies used for the communication links. This contrasts with our problem that we call LocRLFAP (for location and RLFAP), where the links to be established between different antennas are fixed, but the position of some antennas has to be found in a way that optimizes the overall frequency usage while respecting all physical constraints.

Outline of the chapter[1]

Section 11.1 gives two finite and mixed continuous domain models of the application, and compares their performance. Section 11.2 introduces a new continuous Euclidean distance global constraint. Section 11.3 presents how this

---

Chapter written by Michael HEUSCH.

1. This work has greatly benefited from discussions with Frédéric Benhamou, Frédéric Goualard and Juliette Mattioli.

constraint can fit into the model of the applications and what computational and qualitative improvements this global constraint enables.

11.1. Two simple models for the application

After having introduced a simple discrete model of our problem, we motivate why we wish to shift it to mixed domains. We then describe the search algorithm we use and analyze its performance on our experiments.

11.1.1. *A first finite domain model*

Call $S_0, \ldots, S_n$ the set of sites that host the antennas and f_{ij} the discrete frequency used to establish a link from S_i to S_j. For two sites S_i and S_j positioned at (x_i, y_i) and (x_j, y_j), the square of the Euclidean distance between them is given by $dist(S_i, S_j) = (x_i - x_j)^2 + (y_i - y_j)^2$.

The set of available frequencies is discrete and discontinuous. Discrete constraints applied solely to frequencies are the following:

– on each site, the frequency used by a transmitter must be at an absolute value distance from the frequencies of the receivers:

$$\forall (i, j, k) \ / \ i \neq j, i \neq k, \quad |f_{ij} - f_{ki}| > \Delta_{tr}$$

– an absolute value constraint applies on all bidirectional links:

$$\forall (i, j) \in E_d, \quad |f_{ij} - f_{ji}| = \Delta_b$$

We now list all Euclidean distance based constraints:

– for security and interference reasons, a minimum distance must be enforced between any two sites:

$$\forall (i, j) \ / \ i \neq j, \quad dist(S_i, S_j) \geq d_m \qquad [11.1]$$

– if there is a link from S_i to S_j, reachability of the link implies a maximum distance constraint:

$$\forall (i, j) \ / \ i \neq j, \quad dist(S_i, S_j) \leq d_M \qquad [11.2]$$

– two levels of compatibility are imposed between links established from remote or near sites $\forall (i, j, k, l)$, $i \neq j$, $i \neq k$, $j \neq l$:

$$dist(S_i, S_j) \geq d_l \ \vee \ |f_{ik} - f_{lj}| > \Delta_l \qquad [11.3]$$

$$dist(S_i, S_j) \geq d_L \ \vee \ |f_{ik} - f_{lj}| > \Delta_L \qquad [11.4]$$

The purpose of the optimization problem is to minimize the maximal frequency used by all links while respecting all operational constraints.

11.1.2. *Shifting the model to mixed domains*

Eclair [LAB 98], the finite domains constraint solver we use to tackle this problem, allows us to model all these discrete constraints with constructs that ensure equivalence with the mathematical model. Euclidean distance constraints can be discretized and decomposed using square and linear term constraints. Position variables are given by domain bounds, and the filtering algorithms that deal with the absolute value constraints take advantage of enumerated domain variables.

However, as Euclidean distance constraints are fundamentally continuous, it is interesting to see the advantage of reformulating this problem into a mixed model. When doing this with interval constraints, the mathematical model can be preserved and all that changes is the consistency algorithm used to solve the constraints on continuous variables. We achieve this with a generic HC4 [BEN 99] local consistency algorithm to propagate Euclidean distance constraints, whereas the other constraints remain handled by the discrete constraint solver. The only mixed discrete-continuous constraints of our model are disjunctions as in [11.4]. Both model components (discrete and continuous) obey a fixed point semantics which is governed by synchronization of these disjunctions.

11.1.3. *Description of the search algorithm*

After testing chronological order, minimum domain variable selection, and the heuristics proposed in [BES 96] we developed a new strategy. For frequency variables we chose the variable with the smallest domain and the greatest number of attached constraints (in case of ties); for positions we chose the variable with the largest domain first. This heuristic proved to perform the best on our examples. Also, as our model is mostly under-constrained on positions, the search algorithm can be improved slightly when exploring the positions subtree by using a heuristic introduced by Gelle [GEL 03]. This value selection heuristic refines the dichotomic search principle we used previously. In addition to splitting each domain in two parts at each choice point, it first explores the value at the middle of the domain. By orienting the search towards a point at the center of the box, we hope to select a region where a solution is most likely to be found.

	discrete model		hybrid model	
Instance	Time_{ms}	Fails	Time_{ms}	Fails
$L_9^{\emptyset}$	31,20	9,192	5,430	9,196
L_9^{0}	830	3,270	1,890	3,265
$L_9^{0..1}$	930	3,319	1,990	3,306
$L_9^{0..2}$	1,410	6,754	3,880	6,725
$L_9^{0..3}$	1,420	6,768	3,870	6,733
$L_9^{0..4}$	430	655	760	644
$L_9^{0..5}$	440	646	750	634
$L_9^{0..6}$	140	370	360	422
$L_9^{0..7}$	70	140	285,050	75,737
$L_9^{0..8}$	90	148	240	168

Table 11.1. *Analysis of the solving of the instance with 9 sites*

11.1.4. *Analysis of the performance on progressive deployment problems*

We compared the performance of both models on a set of six test instances[2] that represent networks with between 5 and 10 sites [3]. Those familiar with the RLFAP should notice that the LocRLFAP is much more difficult to solve: not only does it contain a great number of disjunctions, but the number of constraints also grows much faster for the same number of sites.

We consider scenarios where part of the site locations is relaxed. We did not study all 2^n possible cases but rather a chronological progressive relaxation from the problem where all sites are fixed. We first loosen up S_0, then S_0 and S_1, etc. up to the case where all sites are freed. When sites 0 to i out of 10 sites are relaxed we call the scenario $L_{10}^{0..i}$. We give the computational results of the instances with 9 and 10 sites in Tables 11.1 and 11.2. Remarkably, the difficulty of solving the LocRLFAP varies strongly and non-monotonously according to the number of relaxed site positions. On the example with 9 sites, differences of up to three orders of magnitude between the easiest and the most difficult instances can be observed. Except from $L_9^{0..7}$, the difficulty is generally analogous between the discrete and hybrid models. For this particular case, almost all backtracks (precisely 75,146 out of 75,737) take place in the continuous part of the search tree; this suggests that the local-consistency enforced by HC4 on the continuous distance constraints is not sufficient to efficiently solve the problem. In six instances out of ten, the hybrid model reaches optimum with

2. For confidentiality reasons, we could not use real numerical data. However, Thales has provided us with a slightly simplified testbed that it considers realistic and representative of the LocRLFAP's difficulty.

3. Experiments are performed on a 1.6Ghz Pentium M-735 laptop with 512Mb RAM.

Instance	discrete model		hybrid model	
	$Time_{ms}$	Fails	$Time_{ms}$	Fails
$L_{10}^{\emptyset}$	86,540	156,487	136,350	156,489
L_{10}^{0}	2,894,490	8,422,085	7,034,800	8,397,394
$L_{10}^{0..1}$	465,510	641,425	893,360	585,919
$L_{10}^{0..2}$	210,940	253,606	358,930	253,204
$L_{10}^{0..3}$	143,240	162,252	238,950	161,624
$L_{10}^{0..4}$	11,720	16,146	17,110	12,639
$L_{10}^{0..5}$	11,670	16,040	17,630	12,756
$L_{10}^{0..6}$	3,330	8,529	8,590	9,058
$L_{10}^{0..7}$	-	-	4,420	4,324
$L_{10}^{0..8}$	-	-	-	-
$L_{10}^{0..9}$	-	-	-	-

Table 11.2. *Analysis of the solving of the instance with 10 sites*

a few backtracks less, but the gap isn't sufficient to make the computations faster. This difference in the number of fails could be explained by the fact that in the discrete case, we sometimes get close to a real-number points solution which is necessarily rejected due to the restriction to integer solutions. With an equivalent number of backtracks, the hybrid resolution is between one and three times slower. If one excludes the outlier $L_9^{0..7}$ and the instance where all sites are fixed[4], solving times are on average 2.4 times slower. These experimentations generally show us that a naive hybridization of our application's model is of little help, as it allows only one additional test case to be solved while it basically always hampers the computation times.

11.2. Introducing the *distn* constraint

Euclidean distance constraints are of fundamental incidence in the core of our problem formulation. A constraint that considers all constraints of the problem globally rather than considering each member of a clique of distance constraints separately can therefore be advantageous to model our application more efficiently.

Euclidean distance constraints appear in many application domains of CP, ranging from deployment problems to robotics, spatial databases and chemistry. 2B-consistency type methods [BEN 99] attain a poor filtering [BAT 05] on Euclidean distance constraints, and stronger consistency techniques [LHO 93, FAL 94] not applicable on problems involving many such constraint instances. Different means have therefore been considered [PES 99, LEB 02, KRI 02,

4. For $L_9^{\emptyset}$, the LocRLFAP has no real justification and a model without disjunctions could just as well be chosen.

BAT 05, HEU 03] to enhance the usability of constraint solvers. However, none of these are adapted to variable distances.

We use a continuous n-ary global constraint proposed in [HEU 03, HEU 06] that considers the interdistance relations between n points. The syntax of this constraint is given by: $\texttt{distn}([\texttt{P}_1,\ldots,\texttt{P}_\texttt{n}],\texttt{V}_{\texttt{i},\texttt{j}})$ where the $P_i = (X_i, Y_i)$ is the Cartesian product of domain variables, $V_{i,j}$ is a symmetric $n \times n$ matrix of non-negative variables, constrained to be equal to the Euclidean distance between the P_i. Domains may be discrete or continuous. This constraint holds if, and only if, for all $p_i = (x_i, y_i)$, $p_j = (x_j, y_j)$ and $v_{i,j}$ we have $dist(p_i, p_j) = v_{i,j}$. To use this constraint to model plain (non-variable) minimal distance constraints, an upper bound equal to $+\infty$ can simply be used for all domains of the $V_{i,j}$. Conversely, it suffices to set a lower bound equal to 0 for all domains of the $V_{i,j}$ solely to model maximal distance constraints.

The continuous filtering of the constraints is done by an extension to an algorithm developed to solve circle packing problems [MAR 05]. It defines forbidden regions with a geometric reasoning and approximates them by representing domains with polygons. This allows us to reinforce the consistency level by considering n constraints simultaneously. Also, all computations are made reliable by using interval arithmetic [NEU 90] extensively, thus no feasible point is lost. An iteration of the algorithm considers each polygon in turn and operates in polynomial time. For efficiency reasons, we don't use a fixed point semantics and the algorithm is stopped after a fixed number of iterations. When working with discrete variables, floating point polygons are reduced to integer bounds and the algorithm is restarted until a fixed point is reached. See [HEU 06] for more details.

11.3. Modeling the application with the *distn* constraint

We show how we can use *distn* to improve both our simple discrete and hybrid constraint models. We then analyze the numerical results of our solving of the LocRLFAP on instances with 9 and 10 sites and finally we examine what qualitative improvements this further provides.

11.3.1. *Revised model of the application*

One weakness of the previous model is that distance constraints involved in the disjunctions [11.1] and [11.2] are disconnected from those appearing in the clique of inter-distance constraints [11.4]. For all $i \neq j$, $i \neq k$, $j \neq l$ we have:

$$\mathtt{dist}(\mathtt{S_i},\mathtt{S_j}) \geq \mathtt{d_L} \;\vee\; |\; \mathtt{f[i,k]} - \mathtt{f[l,j]} \;| > \Delta_\mathtt{L}$$

$$\mathtt{dist}(\mathtt{S_i},\mathtt{S_j}) \geq \mathtt{d_l} \;\vee\; |\; \mathtt{f[i,k]} - \mathtt{f[l,j]} \;| > \Delta_\mathtt{l}$$

$$\mathtt{dist}(\mathtt{S_i},\mathtt{S_j}) \geq \mathtt{m}$$

$$\mathtt{dist}(\mathtt{S_i},\mathtt{S_j}) \leq \mathtt{M} \quad \text{if there is a link from } \mathtt{S_i} \text{to } \mathtt{S_j}$$

Writing the whole deployment problem with a disconnected set of elementary Euclidean distance constraints does not deal with the domain's semantics. As a consequence, the filtering achieved on the variables giving the sites' positions is too low to enable an efficient solving of the given model. We address this problem by using the global constraint we introduced.

The *distn* constraint can be used for the application while maintaining a mathematical equivalence between the mathematical and the constraint model. This enables us to give a tighter formulation to both the reachability and minimal interdistance constraints. Moreover, it enhances the integration of the constraint in the disjunctive nature of the model, as it allows us to link the inter-distance constraints with the "distant compatibility" constraints.

For each couple (i, j), $i \neq j$ let us introduce a variable `v[i,j]` that expresses the Euclidean distance between S_i and S_j. The minimum and maximum distance constraints of [11.1] and [11.2] can be expressed simply by setting the distance variable's domain to $\mathtt{Domain}(\mathtt{v[i,j]}) = [\ \mathtt{m_{i,j}}, \mathtt{M_{i,j}}\ ]$ with for all $i \neq j$, $\mathtt{v[i,j]} = \mathtt{v[j,i]}$. It now remains to connect the distance constraints appearing in the hybrid disjunctions [11.4] to the global constraint. This can be done by gathering the whole set of distance constraints of the application and writing for all $i \neq j$, $i \neq k$, $j \neq l$:

$$\mathtt{v[i,j]} \geq \mathtt{d_l} \;\vee\; |\; \mathtt{f[i,k]} - \mathtt{f[l,j]} \;| > \Delta_\mathtt{l}$$

$$\mathtt{v[i,j]} \geq \mathtt{d_L} \;\vee\; |\; \mathtt{f[i,k]} - \mathtt{f[l,j]} \;| > \Delta_\mathtt{L}$$

$$\mathtt{distn}([\mathtt{S_1},\ldots,\mathtt{S_n}]\,,\ \mathtt{v[i,j]})$$

This allows us to have bidirectional communication between the distance constraints appearing in the distance constraints and those required by reachability and minimum distance constraints.

– If an absolute value constraint is violated, the new lower bound for the minimal inter-distance will directly influence all of the distance relations in *distn*.

	discrete model		hybrid model	
Instance	Time_{ms}	Fails	Time_{ms}	Fails
$L_9^{\emptyset}$	3,120	9,192	5,540	9,196
L_9^{0}	1,570	3,284	2,150	3,278
$L_9^{0..1}$	1,580	3,403	1,910	2,744
$L_9^{0..2}$	1,280	1,851	2,040	2,096
$L_9^{0..3}$	1,300	1,763	2,100	2,022
$L_9^{0..4}$	2,140	716	2,180	698
$L_9^{0..5}$	2,690	707	2,550	702
$L_9^{0..6}$	780	266	530	389
$L_9^{0..7}$	410	117	640	215
$L_9^{0..8}$	690	117	830	237

Table 11.3. *Solving of the 9 site instances with the discrete and hybrid models using distn*

	discrete model		hybrid model	
Instance	Time_{ms}	Fails	Time_{ms}	Fails
$L_{10}^{\emptyset}$	85,620	156,487	138,370	156,489
L_{10}^{0}	351,020	852,318	150,170	87,144
$L_{10}^{0..1}$	124,620	115,307	123,340	73,451
$L_{10}^{0..2}$	239,700	147,809	325,530	163,440
$L_{10}^{0..3}$	237,950	131,582	337,970	147,716
$L_{10}^{0..4}$	28,310	16,830	28,420	13,758
$L_{10}^{0..5}$	29,960	16,698	29,660	13,760
$L_{10}^{0..6}$	11,360	8,052	3,210	1,931
$L_{10}^{0..7}$	-	-	6,310	4,264
$L_{10}^{0..8}$	-	-	218,220	100,298
$L_{10}^{0..9}$	-	-	369,300	140,592

Table 11.4. *Solving of the 10 site instances with the discrete and hybrid models using distn*

– If the whole set of distance constraints considered globally in *distn* does not enable the left branch of a disjunction to be instantiated, the corresponding absolute value constraint is immediately enforced.

11.3.2. *Numerical results when solving the LocRLFAP with distn*

The solving times and number of backtracks obtained for instances with 9 and 10 sites using this new model are given in Tables 11.3 and 11.4.

In the example with 9 sites, when comparing these results with those obtained with elementary constraints, we can see that *distn* allows us to divide the number of backtracks by two on average for the nine deployment instances, both in the hybrid and discrete models, but the cost of calling the global constraint impedes that computations get 2 (resp. 1.2) slower on the discrete (resp. hybrid) models. The irregularity we had on $L_9^{0..7}$ can no longer be seen and we get a speedup of two orders of magnitude on this instance, therefore when totaling all the results for hybrid instances, the number of backtracks is divided by 8 and gains a time factor of 20.

In the examples with 10 sites, when we compare the seven instances of deployment that we manage to solve in both models, the hybrid model requires 63% fewer backtracks than the discrete model, but does solve only 3% faster. However, on three other instances, the hybrid model manages to solve the scenario in less than 10 minutes, whereas the discrete model doesn't manage to obtain even a feasible solution in more than one hour. Again, comparing these last results with those obtained with elementary constraints, we observe that *distn* allows the number of backtracks to be divided by 18.8 (resp. 7.4) in the hybrid case (resp. discrete) and the computation times to be divided by 8.6 (resp. 3.7) on an average of seven instances.

11.3.3. *Qualitative analysis of the results*

Although it requires greater computational effort, from a qualitative point of view, relaxing the problem from the RLFAP model to the LocRLFAP model enables us to save up to 63% of used frequencies. The most interesting conclusion on our new hybrid model is its twofold advantage:

– It allows us to obtain solutions which save frequencies compared to a discrete model: we get a result which is 15% better on L_{10}^0. We can not claim anything for the three last instances that we did not manage to solve in a discrete space.

– We manage to solve the whole of our instances with this model while no solution is found in more than one hour in a discrete search space.

11.4. Conclusion

We have defined a simple constraint model for a mobile radio antenna deployment support application and evaluated it on several test instances, both on discrete and on mixed finite and continuous domains. They enable the smallest models to be solved satisfactorily but are unable to scale to the larger ones, even with an improved search algorithm. We have remodeled the application by proposing a novel continuous global constraint maintaining variable Euclidean distance constraints. In particular we have seen how far this constraint addresses the disjunctive nature of the deployment problem. The association of a discrete-continuous hybrid search space with this advanced model and a new variable selection heuristic enable our complete set of test problems to be solved. More generally, these results have shown that both continuous global constraints and the hybridization of finite domain and interval constraints can improve the solving performance of complex combinatorial problems where a complete discretization is customarily used. Moreover, our tests have highlighted some scenarios where modeling using hybrid constraints enables a qualitative advantage in the sense that better optima become reachable than in a fully discretized model.

11.5. References

[AAR 03] AARDAL K. I., VAN HOESEL C. P. M., KOSTER A. M. C. A., MANNINO C., SASSANO A., "Models and Solution Techniques for the Frequency Assignment Problem", *4OR*, vol. 1, num. 4, p. 261–317, 2003.

[BAT 05] BATNINI H., Contraintes Globales et Techniques de Résolution pour les CSPs Continus, PhD thesis, University of Nice Sophia-Antipolis, December 2005, in French.

[BEN 99] BENHAMOU F., GOUALARD F., GRANVILLIERS L., PUGET J.-F., "Revising Hull and Box Consistency", *Proc. of ICLP-99*, 1999.

[BES 96] BESSIÈRE C., RÉGIN J.-C., "MAC and Combined Heuristics: Two Reasons to Forsake FC (and CBJ?) on Hard Problems", *Proc. of CP-96*, 1996.

[FAL 94] FALTINGS B., "Arc Consistency for Continuous Variables", *Artificial Intelligence*, vol. 65, num. 2, p. 363–376, 1994.

[GEL 03] GELLE E., FALTINGS B., "Solving Mixed and Conditional Constraint Satisfaction Problems", *Constraints*, vol. 8, num. 2, p. 107-141, Kluwer Academic Publishers, 2003.

[HEU 03] HEUSCH M., "distn: An Euclidean Distance Global Constraint", *Proc. of CP 2003*, Page975, 2003, Doctoral Program.

[HEU 06] HEUSCH M., Modeling and Solving of a Radio Antenna Deployment Support Application by Constraint Programming over Finite and Continuous Domains, PhD thesis, University of Nantes, January 2006, in French.

[KRI 02] KRIPPAHL L., BARAHONA P., "PSICO: Solving Protein Structures with Constraint Programming and Optimization", *Constraints*, vol. 7, num. 3-4, p. 317–331, Kluwer Academic Publishers, 2002.

[LAB 98] LABURTHE F., SAVÉANT P., DE GIVRY S., JOURDAN J., ECLAIR: A Library of Constraints over Finite Domains, Report num. ATS 98-2, Thomson-CSF LCR, 1998.

[LEB 02] LEBBAH Y., RUEHER M., MICHEL C., "A Global Filtering Algorithm for Handling Systems of Quadratic Equations and Inequations", *Proc. of CP-02*, 2002.

[LHO 93] LHOMME O., "Consistency Techniques for Numeric CSPs", *Proc. of IJCAI-93*, p. 232-238, 1993.

[MAR 05] MARKÓT M. C., CSENDES T., "A New Verified Optimization Technique for the "Packing Circles in a Unit Square" Problems", *SIAM J. Opt.*, vol. 16, p. 193-219, 2005.

[NEU 90] NEUMAIER A., *Interval Methods for Systems of Equations*, Camb. U. Press, 1990.

[PES 99] PESANT G., BOYER M., "Reasoning about Solids Using Constraint Logic Programming", *J. Autom. Reason.*, vol. 22, num. 3, p. 241–262, 1999.

Chapter 12

Guaranteed Numerical Injectivity Test via Interval Analysis

The purpose of this chapter is to present a new method based on guaranteed numerical computation able to verify that a function $f : \mathcal{X} \subset \mathbb{R}^n \to \mathbb{R}^m$ satisfies

$$\forall x_1 \in \mathcal{X}, \forall x_2 \in \mathcal{X}, x_1 \neq x_2 \Rightarrow f(x_1) \neq f(x_2). \qquad [12.1]$$

To our knowledge, there does not exist any numerical method able to perform this injectivity test and moreover, the complexity of the algebraic manipulations involved often makes the formal calculus (especially when the function is not polynomial) fail. Presently, in the context on structural identifiability, Braems and al. have presented in [BRA 01] an approximated method that verifies the injectivity around ε namely ε-injectivity. It consists of verifying the following condition

$$\forall x_1 \in \mathcal{X}, \forall x_2 \in \mathcal{X}, |x_1 - x_2| > \varepsilon \Rightarrow f(x_1) \neq f(x_2), \qquad [12.2]$$

which can be view as an approximation of condition [12.1].

Note that many problems could be formulated as the injectivity verification of a function. For example, concerning the identification of parametric models, the problem of proving the *structural identifiability* amounts to checking injectivity [WAL 90, BRA 01]. Other applications can be cited: for instance,

---

Chapter written by Sébastien LAGRANGE, Nicolas DELANOUE and Luc JAULIN.

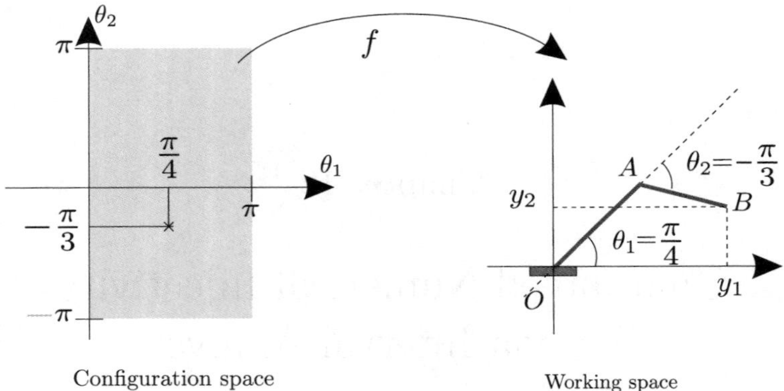

Figure 12.1. *A point in the configuration space and its corresponding robot configuration*

consider the robotic arm with two degrees of freedom ($\theta_1 \in [0, \frac{\pi}{2}], \theta_2 \in [-\pi, \pi]$) represented in the figure on the right of Figure 12.1. Each point (θ_1, θ_2) of the *configuration space* is associated with a robot position (y_1, y_2) by the function

$$f : (\theta_1, \theta_2) \rightarrow \begin{pmatrix} y_1 \\ y_2 \end{pmatrix} = \begin{pmatrix} 2cos(\theta_1) + 1.5cos(\theta_1 + \theta_2) \\ 2sin(\theta_1) + 1.5sin(\theta_1 + \theta_2) \end{pmatrix} \qquad [12.3]$$

(see Figure 12.1). Now, a basic question is to know whether several pairs (θ_1, θ_2) lead the robot ending to an identical position (y_1, y_2). This problem amounts to testing the function f (defined in [12.3]) for injectivity.

This chapter provides an efficient algorithm, based on interval analysis, able to check that a differentiable function is injective. The chapter is organized as follows. Section 12.1 presents interval analysis. In section 12.2, a new definition of partial injectivity makes it possible to use interval analysis techniques to test injectivity and to obtain a guaranteed answer. Section 12.3 presents an algorithm able to test a given differentiable function for injectivity. Finally, in order to show the efficiency of the algorithm, two illustrative examples are provided. A solver called ITVIA (injectivity test via interval analysis) implemented in C++ is made available at `http://www.istia.univ-angers.fr/~lagrange/`.

12.1. Interval analysis

This section introduces some notions of interval analysis to be used in this chapter. A vector interval or a *box* $[\mathbf{x}]$ of $\mathbb{R}^n$ is defined by

$$[x] = [\underline{x}, \overline{x}] = \{x \in \mathbb{R}^n \mid \underline{x} \leq x \leq \overline{x}\}, \qquad [12.4]$$

where $\underline{x}$ and $\overline{x}$ are two elements of $\mathbb{R}^n$ and the partial order $\leq$ is understood componentwise. The set of all bounded boxes of $\mathbb{R}^n$ is denoted by $\mathbb{IR}^n$ as in [JAU 01].

Note 1 *By extension, an* interval matrix $[M] = [\underline{M}, \overline{M}]$ *is defined as the set of the matrices of the form:*

$$[M] = \{M \in \mathbb{R}^{n \times m} \mid \underline{M} \leq M \leq \overline{M}\} \qquad [12.5]$$

and $\mathbb{IR}^{n \times m}$ *denoted the set of all interval matrices of* $\mathbb{R}^{n \times m}$*. The properties of punctual matrices can naturally be extended to interval matrices. For example,* $[M]$ *is full column rank if all the matrices* $M \in [M]$ *are full column rank.*

To *bisect* a box $[x]$ means to cut it along a symmetry plane normal to a side of maximal length. The length of this side is the *width* of $[x]$. A bisection of $[x]$ generates two non-overlapping boxes $[x_1]$ and $[x_2]$ such that $[x] = [x_1] \cup [x_2]$.

The *hull box* $[\mathcal{X}]$ of a bounded subset $\mathcal{X} \in \mathbb{R}^n$ is the smallest box of $\mathbb{IR}^n$ that contains $\mathcal{X}$.

Interval arithmetic defined in [MOO 66] provides an effective method to extend all concepts of vector arithmetic to boxes.
Let $f : \mathbb{R}^n \to \mathbb{R}^m$ be a vector function; the set-valued function $[f] : \mathbb{IR}^n \to \mathbb{IR}^m$ is a *inclusion function* of f if, for any box $[x]$ of $\mathbb{IR}^n$, it satisfies $f([x]) \subset [f]([x])$ (see Figure 12.2). Note that $f([x])$ is usually not a box contrary to $[f]([x])$. Moreover, since $[f([x])]$ is the hull box of $f([x])$, one has

$$f([x]) \subset [f([x])] \subset [f]([x]). \qquad [12.6]$$

The computation of an inclusion function $[f]$ for any analytical function f can be obtained by replacing each elementary operator and function by its interval counterpart [MOO 66, NEU 90].

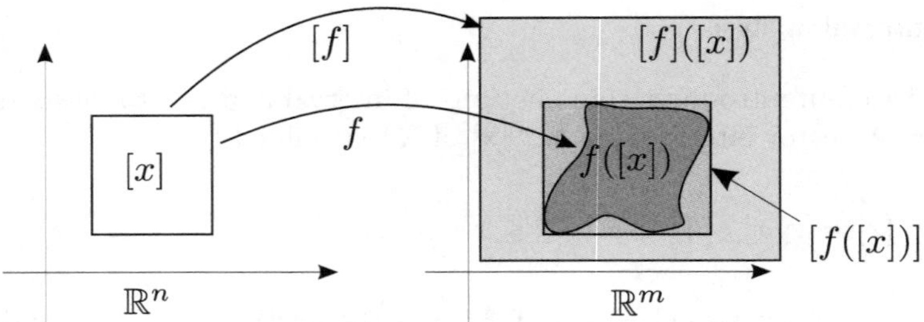

Figure 12.2. *Inclusion function $[f]$ of a function f*

Example 1 *An inclusion function for $f(x_1, x_2) = x_1^2+\cos(x_1x_2)$ is $[f]([x_1], [x_2]) = [x_1]^2+\cos([x_1][x_2])$. For instance, if $[x] = ([-1, 1], [0, \frac{\pi}{2}])$ then the box $[f]([x])$ is calculated as follows:*

$$\begin{aligned} [f]([-1,1],[0,\tfrac{\pi}{2}]) &= [-1,1]^2 + \cos([-1,1] \times [0,\tfrac{\pi}{2}]) &&= [0,1] + \cos([-\tfrac{\pi}{2},\tfrac{\pi}{2}]) \\ &= [0,1] + [-1,1] &&= [-1,2]. \end{aligned}$$

12.2. Injectivity

Let us recall that this chapter proposed to build an effective method to test the differentiable function $f : \mathcal{X} \subset \mathbb{R}^n \to \mathbb{R}^m$ for injectivity. The main idea of the divide-and-conquer algorithm to be proposed is to partition $\mathcal{X}$ into subsets $\mathcal{X}_i$ where f restricted to $\mathcal{X}_i$ (denoted $f_{|\mathcal{X}_i}$) is an injection. However, as illustrated in Figure 12.3, injectivity is not "preserved by the union operation" *i.e.* $\left(f_{|\mathcal{X}_1} \text{ is an injection and } f_{|\mathcal{X}_2} \text{ is an injection }\right) \not\Rightarrow f_{|\mathcal{X}_1\cup\mathcal{X}_2}$ is an injection. Thus, the injectivity cannot be used directly in our algorithm. That is why we are going to consider a concept akin to injectivity, namely *the partial injectivity*, that will be preserved by the union operation. The following subsections present the basic results that will be used in the algorithm able to test the function for injectivity.

First, we introduce the definition of the partial injectivity and give some illustrative examples. Then, we propose the theorem which gives a sufficient condition to test the function for partial injectivity.

12.2.1. *Partial injectivity*

Let us introduce the definition of *partial injectivity* of a function.

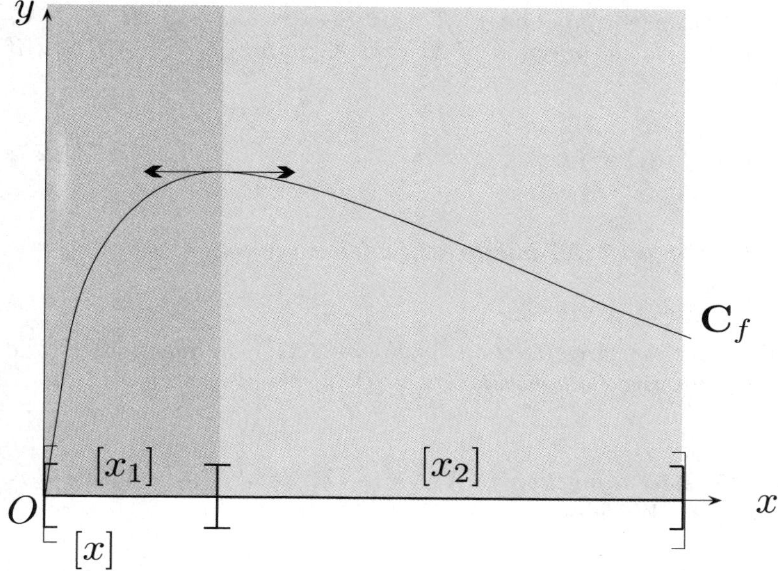

Figure 12.3. *Despite the fact that* $f_{|[x_1]}$ *and* $f_{|[x_2]}$ *are injections,* f *is not an injection*

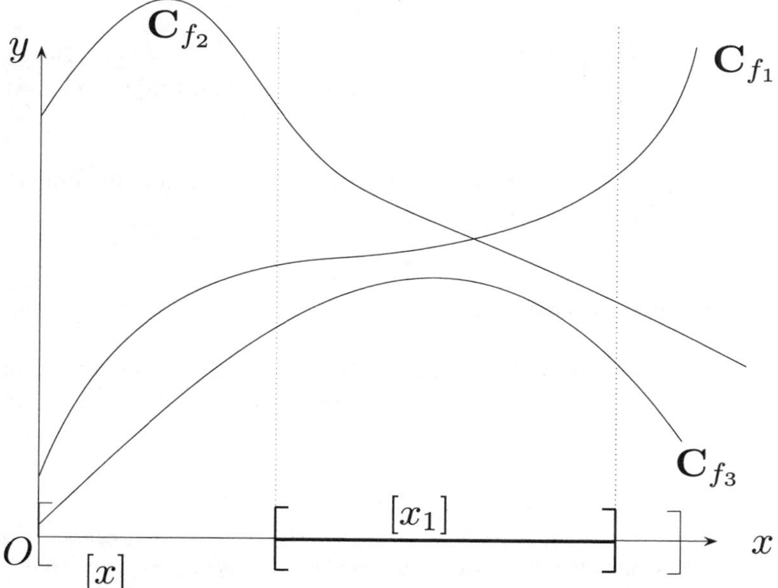

Figure 12.4. *Graphs of functions* f_1,f_2 *and* f_3

DEFINITION.– *Consider a function* f: $\mathcal{X} \subset \mathbb{R}^n \to \mathbb{R}^m$ *and any set* $\mathcal{X}_1 \subset \mathcal{X}$. *The function* f *is a partial injection of* $\mathcal{X}_1$ *over* $\mathcal{X}$, *noted* $(\mathcal{X}_1, \mathcal{X})$*-injective, if* $\forall x_1 \in \mathcal{X}_1, \forall x \in \mathcal{X}$,

$$x_1 \neq x \Rightarrow f(x_1) \neq f(x). \qquad [12.7]$$

Note 2 *Trivially, if* f *is* $(\mathcal{X}, \mathcal{X})$*-injective then* f *is an injection over* $\mathcal{X}$.

Example 2 *Consider the three functions of Figure 12.4. The functions* f_1 *and* f_2 *are* $([x_1], [x])$*-injective (although* f_2 *is not* $[x]$*-injective) whereas* f_3 *is not.*

Proposition 1 *Consider a function* $f : \mathcal{X} \subset \mathbb{R}^n \to \mathbb{R}^m$ *and* $\mathcal{X}_1, \ldots, \mathcal{X}_p$ *a collection of subsets of* $\mathcal{X}$. *We have:*

$$\forall i, 1 \leq i \leq p, f \text{ is } (\mathcal{X}_i, \mathcal{X}) - inj. \Leftrightarrow f \text{ is } \left(\bigcup_{i=1}^{p} \mathcal{X}_i, \mathcal{X}\right) - inj. \qquad [12.8]$$

Proof. $(\Rightarrow)$ We have $\forall x_i \in \mathcal{X}_i, \forall x \in \mathcal{X}$, $x_i \neq x \Rightarrow f(x_i) \neq f(x)$. Hence $\forall \breve{x} \in (\cup_i \mathcal{X}_i), \forall x \in \mathcal{X}$, $\breve{x} \neq x \Rightarrow f(\breve{x}) \neq f(x)$, i.e. f is $(\cup_i \mathcal{X}_i, \mathcal{X})$-injective. $(\Leftarrow)$ Trivial. ∎

Remark 2 and Proposition 1 ensure the correctness of the divide-and-conquer algorithm which is presented in section 12.3.

12.2.2. *Partial injectivity condition*

In this section, a fundamental theorem, which gives a sufficient condition of partial injectivity, is presented. First, let us introduce a generalization of the mean value theorem[1].

---

1. Let $f : \mathcal{X} \subset \mathbb{R}^n \to \mathbb{R}$, $f \in \mathcal{C}^1$. If $x_1, x_2 \in \mathcal{X}$ such that the segment between x_1 and x_2, noted $seg(x_1, x_2)$, is included in $\mathcal{X}$, then, there exists $\xi \in seg(x_1, x_2)$ such that

$$f(x_2) - f(x_1) = \nabla f(\xi) \cdot (x_2 - x_1).$$

Theorem 2 (generalized mean value theorem) *Consider a differentiable function $f\colon \mathcal{X} \subset \mathbb{R}^n \to \mathbb{R}^m$. Let ∇f be its Jacobian matrix and $[x] \subset \mathcal{X}$. We obtain:*

$$\forall x_1, x_2 \in [x], \exists J_f \in [\nabla f([x])] \ s.t. \ f(x_2) - f(x_1) = J_f \cdot (x_2 - x_1), \quad [12.9]$$

where $[\nabla f([x])]$ denotes the hull box of $\nabla f([x])$.

Proof. According to the mean value theorem applied on each component $f_i : \mathbb{R}^n \to \mathbb{R}$ of f $(1 \leq i \leq m)$ and as the segment $seg(x_1, x_2)$ belongs to $[x]$, we have:

$$\exists \xi_i \in [x] \ such \ that \ f_i(x_2) - f_i(x_1) = \nabla f_i(\xi_i) \cdot (x_2 - x_1).$$

Taking $J_{f_i} = \nabla f_i(\xi_i)$, we get:

$$\exists J_{f_i} \in \nabla f_i([x]) \ such \ that \ f_i(x_2) - f_i(x_1) = J_{f_i} \cdot (x_2 - x_1).$$

Thus

$$\exists J_f \in \left(\nabla f_1\left([x]\right), .., \nabla f_m\left([x]\right)\right)^T \ s.t. \ f(x_2) - f(x_1) = J_f \cdot (x_2 - x_1).$$

i.e., as $\left(\nabla f_1\left([x]\right), \ldots, \nabla f_m\left([x]\right)\right)^T \subset [\nabla f([x])]$ (see [12.6]),
$\exists J_f \in [\nabla f([x])]$ *such that* $f(x_2) - f(x_1) = J_f \cdot (x_2 - x_1)$. ■

Example 3 *Consider the function*

$$f : \left\{ \begin{array}{ccc} \mathbb{R} & \to & \mathbb{R}^2 \\ x & \to & (y_1, y_2)^T \end{array} \right. . \quad [12.10]$$

depicted in Figure 12.5. Figure 12.6 represents the set $\nabla f([x])$ of all derivatives of f (drawn as vectors) and its hull box $[\nabla f([x])]$. We can see that the vector J_f defined in [12.9] belongs to $[\nabla f([x])]$ (but $J_f \notin \nabla f([x])$) as forecasted by Theorem 2.

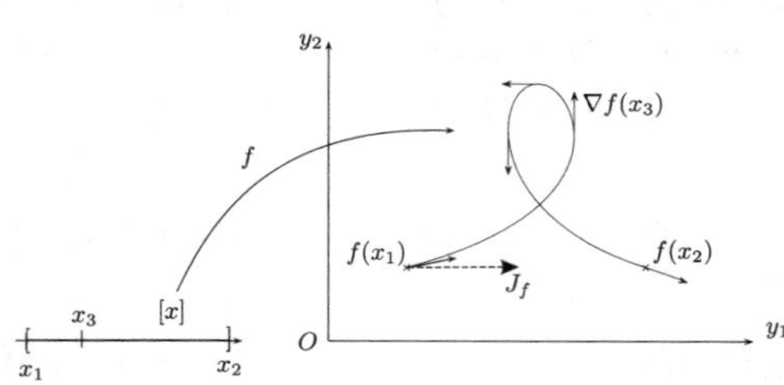

Figure 12.5. *Graph of* $f : \mathbb{R} \rightarrow \mathbb{R}^2$

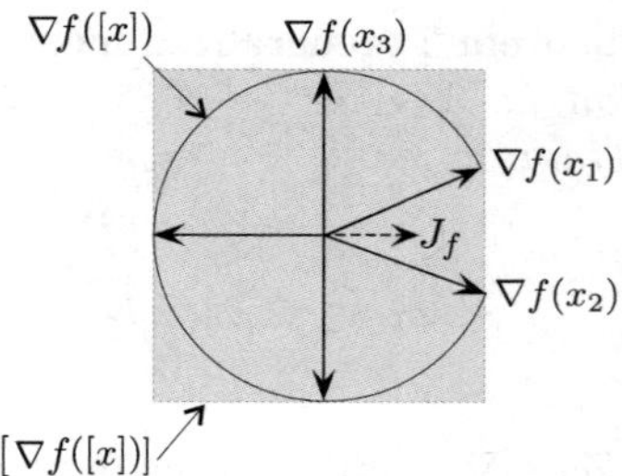

Figure 12.6. *Illustrating set* $[\nabla f([x])]$.

Now, the following theorem introduces a sufficient condition of partial injectivity. This condition will be exploited in next section in order to design a suitable algorithm that test injectivity.

Theorem 3 *Let* $f : \mathcal{X} \subset \mathbb{R}^n \rightarrow \mathbb{R}^m$ *be a differentiable function and* $[x_1] \subset [x] \subset \mathcal{X}$. *Set* $[\tilde{x}] = \left[f^{-1}\left(f\left([x_1]\right)\right) \cap [x]\right]$. *If the interval matrix* $[\nabla f\left([\tilde{x}]\right)]$ *is of full column rank then* f *is* $\left([x_1], [x]\right)$*-injective.*

Proof. The proof is by contradiction. Assume that f is not ($[x_1]$,$[x]$)-injective then

$$\exists x_1 \in [x_1], \exists x_2 \in [x] \ \textit{such that} \ x_1 \neq x_2 \ \textit{and} \ f\left(x_1\right) = f\left(x_2\right). \quad [12.11]$$

Now, since $f(x_1) = f(x_2)$, we have $x_2 \in f^{-1}\left(f\left([x_1]\right)\right) \cap [x]$ and trivially $x_1 \in f^{-1}\left(f\left([x_1]\right)\right) \cap [x]$. Therefore, since $(f^{-1}\left(f\left([x_1]\right)\right) \cap [x]) \subset \left[f^{-1}\left(f\left([x_1]\right)\right) \cap [x]\right] = [\tilde{x}]$ (see equation [12.6]), we obtain $x_1, x_2 \in [\tilde{x}]$.

Hence, (12.11) implies

$$\exists x_1, x_2 \in [\tilde{x}], \ \textit{such that} \ x_2 \neq x_1 \ \textit{and} \ f\left(x_1\right) = f\left(x_2\right).$$

To conclude, according to Theorem 2, $\exists x_1, x_2 \in [\tilde{x}]$, $\exists J_f \in [\nabla f\left([\tilde{x}]\right)]$ such that

$$x_1 \neq x_2 \ \textit{and} \ 0 = f(x_2) - f(x_1) = J_f \cdot (x_2 - x_1),$$

i.e. $\exists J_f \in [\nabla f\left([\tilde{x}]\right)]$ such that J_f is not full column rank and therefore the (interval) matrix $[\nabla f\left([\tilde{x}]\right)]$ is not full column rank. ■

12.3. ITVIA algorithm

This section presents the injectivity test via interval analysis (ITVIA) algorithm designed from Proposition 1 and Theorem 3. ITVIA (defined in Algorithm 2) uses the divide-and-conquer strategy to check a given differentiable function $f : [x] \subset \mathbb{R}^n \to \mathbb{R}^m$ for injectivity. Algorithm 1 is a sub-algorithm of 2 that checks (a sufficient condition of) partial injectivity.

– Algorithm 1 checks if the interval matrix $\left[\nabla f\left(\left[f^{-1}\left(f\left([x_1]\right)\right) \cap [x]\right]\right)\right]$ is full rank. In the positive case, according to Theorem 3, the function f is $([x_1], [x])$-injective. Therefore, Algorithm 1 can be viewed as a test for partial injectivity.

– Algorithm 2 divides the initial box $[x]$ into a paving $\{[x_i]\}_i$ such that, for all i, the function f is $([x_i], [x])$-injective. Then, since $[x] = (\cup_i [x_i])$ and according to Proposition 1, f is $[x]$-injective.

Algorithm 1 Partial_Injectivity_Test

Require: $f \in \mathcal{C}^1$, $[x]$ the initial box and $[x_1] \subset [x]$.
Ensure: A boolean :
- *true* : f *is* $([x_1], [x])$*-injective,*
- *false* : f *may or not be partially injective.*

Initialization : $\mathcal{L}_{stack} := \{[x]\}$, $[\tilde{x}] := \emptyset$.
while $\mathcal{L}_{stack} \neq \emptyset$ **do**
  Pop $\mathcal{L}_{stack}$ into $[w]$.
  if $[f]([w]) \cap [f]([x_1]) \neq \emptyset$ **then**
    if width($[w]$) $>$ width($[x_1]$) \\ To avoid useless splitting of $[w]$ *ad infinitum* **then**
      Bisect $[w]$ into $[w_1]$ and $[w_2]$.
      Stack $[w_1]$ and $[w_2]$ in $\mathcal{L}_{stack}$.
    else
      $[\tilde{x}] = [[\tilde{x}] \cup [w]]$.
    end if
  end if
end while
if $[\nabla f]([\tilde{x}])$ is full rank **then**
  Return true \\ "f is $([x_1], [x])$-injective"
else
  Return False \\ "Failure"
end if

In Algorithm 1, a set inversion technique [GOL 05, JAU 01] is first exploited to characterize a box $[\tilde{x}]$ that contains $[f^{-1}(f([x_1])) \cap [x]]$. Secondly,

Algorithm 2 Injectivity_Test_Via_Interval_Analysis

Require: f a $\mathcal{C}^1$ function and $[x]$ the initial box.

Initialization : $\mathcal{L} := \{[x]\}$.
while $\mathcal{L} \neq \emptyset$ **do**
  Pull $[w]$ in $\mathcal{L}$.
  if Partial_Injectivity_Test$(f, [x], [w])$ = False **then**
    Bisect $[w]$ into $[w_1]$ and $[w_2]$.
    Push $[w_1]$ and $[w_2]$ in $\mathcal{L}$.
  end if
end while
Return "f is injective over $[x]$".

an evaluation of $[\nabla f]([\tilde{x}])$ is performed in order to test its rank[2]. Thus, since $[\nabla f([\tilde{x}])] \subset [\nabla f]([\tilde{x}])$ and according to Theorem 3, we can test whether f is $([x_1], [x])$-injective.

Algorithm 2 creates a paving of the initial box $[x]$ such that, for all i, the function f is $([x_i], [x])$-injective. Therefore, if the algorithm terminates, then f is an injection.

By combination of these two algorithms, we can prove that a function is injective over a box $[x]$. A solver, called ITVIA, developed in C++ is made available and tests the injectivity of a given function $f : \mathbb{R}^2 \to \mathbb{R}^2$ (or $f : \mathbb{R} \to \mathbb{R}^2$) over a given box $[x]$.

12.4. Examples

In this section, two examples are provided in order to illustrate the efficiency of the solver ITVIA presented in the previous section. We are going to check the injectivity of two functions $f : \mathbb{R}^2 \to \mathbb{R}^2$ over a given box $[x]$.

2. Several techniques exist to test an interval matrix for full ranking. If it is square, the simplest way consists of verifying that the determinant (which is an interval) does not contain zero. Otherwise (i.e. $f : \mathbb{R}^n \to \mathbb{R}^m$), the interval Gauss algorithm could be used [NEU 90].

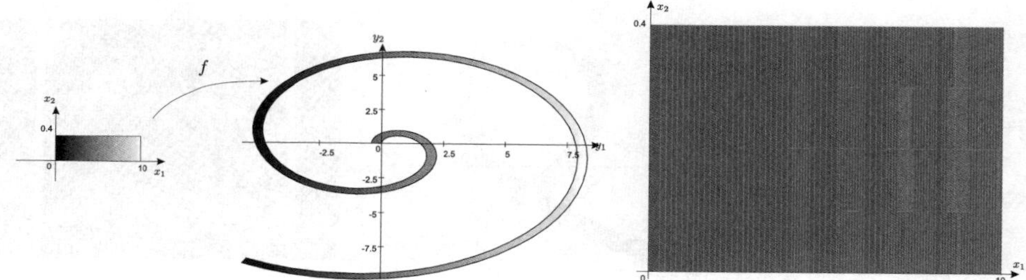

Figure 12.7. *Graph of the function f defined in [12.12]*

Figure 12.8. *Bisection of $[x]$ obtained by ITVIA for the function f defined in [12.12]. All the gray boxes have been proved partially injective*

12.4.1. *Spiral function*

Consider the function f, depicted in Figure 12.7, defined by

$$f : \begin{matrix} \mathbb{R}^2 & \rightarrow & \mathbb{R}^2 \\ \begin{pmatrix} x_1 \\ x_2 \end{pmatrix} & \rightarrow & \begin{pmatrix} y_1 \\ y_2 \end{pmatrix} = \begin{pmatrix} x_1 \sin(x_1) + x_2 \frac{x_1 \sin(x_1) - \cos(x_1)}{\sqrt{x_1^2+1}} \\ x_1 \cos(x_1) + x_2 \frac{\sin(x_1) + x_1 \cos(x_1)}{\sqrt{x_1^2+1}} \end{pmatrix} \end{matrix} \qquad [12.12]$$

and test its injectivity over the box $[x] = \left([0, 10], [0, \frac{4}{10}]\right)^T$. After less than 0.1 sec on a Pentium 1.7GHz, ITVIA proved that f is injective over $[x]$. The initial box $[x]$ has been divided in a set of sub-boxes where f is partially injective. Figure 12.8 shows the successive bisections of $[x]$ made by ITVIA.

12.4.2. *Ribbon function*

Consider the ribbon function f (depicted in Figure 12.9) defined by

$$f : \begin{matrix} \mathbb{R}^2 & \rightarrow & \mathbb{R}^2 \\ \begin{pmatrix} x_1 \\ x_2 \end{pmatrix} & \rightarrow & \begin{pmatrix} y_1 \\ y_2 \end{pmatrix} = \begin{pmatrix} \frac{x_1}{2} + (1 - x_2) \cos(x_1) \\ (1 - x_2) \sin(x_1) \end{pmatrix} \end{matrix} \qquad [12.13]$$

and get interest with its injectivity over the box $[x] = ([-1, 4], [0, \frac{1}{10}])^T$. Since the ribbon overlaps, one can see that f is not injective over $[x]$. After 3 seconds, the ITVIA solver is stopped (before going to end). It returns the solution presented in Figure 12.10. The function f has been proved to be a partial injection on the gray area over $[x]$, whereas the white area corresponds to the indeterminate area where ITVIA was not able to prove the partial injectivity. Indeed, the indeterminate area corresponds to the non-injective zone of f where all points are mapped in the overlapping zone of the ribbon.

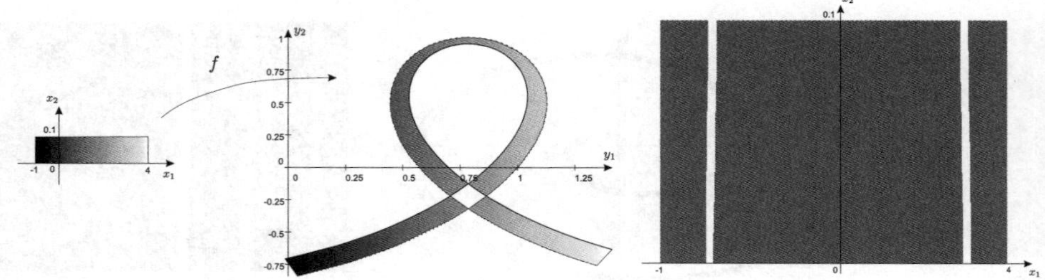

Figure 12.9. *Graph of the function f defined in [12.13]*

Figure 12.10. *Partition of the box $[x]$ obtained by ITVIA for the function f defined in [12.13]. In gray, the partial injectivity domain and, in white, the domain where the f is not proved partially injective*

12.5. Conclusion

In this chapter, we have presented a new algorithm, based on interval analysis, which is able to test differentiable functions for injectivity. In the case of functions $f\colon \mathbb{R} \to \mathbb{R}^2$ and $f : \mathbb{R}^2 \to \mathbb{R}^2$, a C++ solver is available. From a given function f and a given box $[x]$, the solver divides $[x]$ in two areas: a partially injective area and a indeterminate area (where the function may or may not be injective). Of course, when the indeterminate area is empty, the function is proved injective over $[x]$.

12.6. References

[BRA 01] Braems I., Jaulin L., Kieffer M., Walter E., "Guaranteed Numerical Alternatives to Structural Identifiability Testing", *Conference on Decision and Control.*, 2001.

[GOL 05] Goldsztejn A., "A Right-Preconditioning Process for the Formal-Algebraic Approach to Inner and Outer Estimation of AE-solution Set", *Reliable Computing*, 2005.

[JAU 01] Jaulin J., Kieffer M., Didrit D., Walter E., *Applied Interval Analysis*, Springer, 2001.

[MOO 66] Moore R., *Interval Analysis*, Prentice-Hall, Englewood Cliffs, 1966.

[NEU 90] Neumaier A., *Interval Methods for Systems of Equations*, Camb. Univ. Pres, 1990.

[WAL 90] Walter E., Pronzato L., "Qualitative and Quantitative Experiment Design for Phenomenological Models, a Survey", *Automatica*, vol. 26, p. 195-213, 1990.

Chapter 13

An Interval-based Approximation Method for Discrete Changes in Hybrid cc

Hybrid systems are systems consisting of continuous and discrete changes. Figure 13.1 (a) illustrates a simple hybrid system in which a particle falls down due to gravity and bounces off the ground. While the particle's falling is modeled by differential equations, the bouncing is governed by equations describing discrete changes.

Hybrid cc (*hybrid concurrent constraint programming*) [GUP 95], a compositional and declarative language based on constraint programming, has been proposed as a high-level development tool of hybrid systems for simulation, animation and design. Below is a description of the hybrid system in Figure 13.1(a) (see section 13.1 for the syntax and implementation):

```
y = 10, y' = 0,                  // initial conditions
hence {
    cont(y),                     // height is continuous
    if y > 0 then y'' = -10,     // free fall
    if y = 0 then
        y' = -0.5 * prev(y')     // bounce
}
```

However, in our experience of modeling a number of hybrid systems using Hybrid cc we have encountered several difficulties. Figure 13.1(b) shows

---

Chapter written by Daisuke ISHII, Kazunori UEDA and Hiroshi HOSOBE.

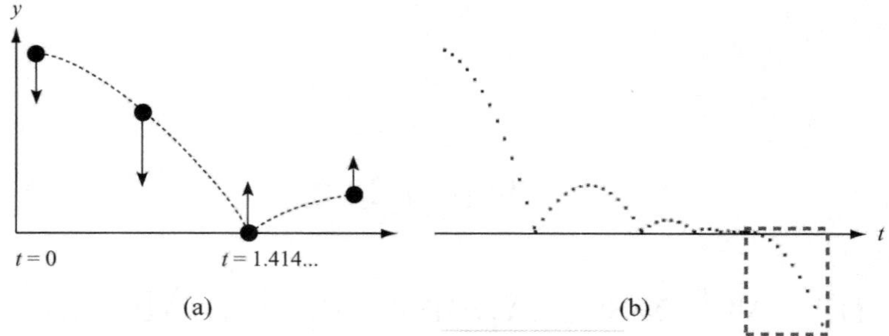

Figure 13.1. *(a) A bouncing particle and (b) an unexpected result*

a further execution result of the above example. As the distance between the particle and the ground gets closer, the particle moves in an unexpected way[1]. The problem is due to the computation of discrete changes in the current implementation of Hybrid cc (section 13.2). After the particle loses energy and its height stays within ϵ (to tolerate numerical errors), the implementation ignores discrete changes, and as a result the particle goes underground.

The contribution of this chapter is to develop a method for obtaining (guaranteed) approximate solutions for discrete changes in hybrid systems. As we discuss in section 13.2, our goal is to bring correct techniques to a number of issues such as reliable simulation, reachability analysis and backward computation in hybrid systems with Hybrid cc. Our approach is based on interval arithmetic (section 13.3). The proposed method detailed in section 13.4 aims to enclose trajectories of hybrid systems using tight intervals or boxes without losing any solutions. We have experimented and evaluated the effect of the method (section 13.5).

13.1. An overview of Hybrid cc

13.1.1. *The Hybrid cc language*

The formal operational semantics of Hybrid cc is described in [GUP 95]. The basic syntax for processes in Hybrid cc is shown in Table 13.1, where we denote processes by A and constraints by C. Computation in Hybrid cc is performed by processes interacting with the *constraint store*. A process *if C then A* triggers discrete changes when an *ask condition* C is entailed by

1. This kind of phenomenon that causes an infinite number of discrete changes in a finite length of time is known as *Zeno behavior*.

C	Add the constraint C
if C **then** A	If C holds, reduce to A
A, A	Parallel composition
hence A	Execute A at every instant after now
cont(C)	Declare that C is continuous over time
prev(C)	The value of C before entering a phase

Table 13.1. *The basic syntax of Hybrid cc processes*

the current constraint store. If C is entailed, the process is reduced to A. Otherwise, the process is ignored. If the entailment of C cannot be determined at the moment, the process is suspended.

13.1.2. *Implementation of Hybrid cc*

The implementation of the Hybrid cc interpreter is detailed in [CAR 98]. The interpreter handles a Hybrid cc process by alternating *point phases* and *interval phases* as follows:

Step 1 Computation starts from a point phase.

Step 2 In the point phase, the interpreter performs reductions of processes such as the propagation of arithmetic constraints. The computation of the point phase ends at a stable point, where all constraints have been propagated and all possible reductions have been completed.

Step 3 After the point phase, the computation proceeds to an interval phase. Each expression *hence A*, which is passed from Step 2, is reduced to A and processed. All the processes are reduced until a stable point is reached as in Step 2. The resulting constraint store consists of constraints on the derivatives of variables (i.e., ODEs), conditions for discrete changes and constraints to be reduced in the future.

Step 4 Integration of the arithmetic constraints that were given in the previous step is processed until one of the conditions changes its status.

Step 5 If there are no processes left in the constraint store, the computation terminates. Otherwise, go to Step 2.

The arithmetic constraint solvers in the implementation handle non-linear equations (NLEs) and ordinary differential equations (ODEs). In the implementation, the following approaches are adopted:

– the computation by the solvers is based on interval arithmetic to model uncertainty in the parameters;

– the NLE solver takes an arithmetic constraint which can be rewritten in the implicit form $f(x) = 0$. Solving of the constraint is done by interval pruning of each variable in the constraint. In the implementation, the following four pruning operators are adopted: (1) use of indexicals, (2) splitting of intervals, (3) the Newton-Raphson method, (4) the Simplex method (optional);

– the ODE solver uses the Runge-Kutta-Fehlberg method which numerically integrates with adaptive step-sizes. The solver reduces equations of arbitrary form to an explicit form by propagating equations in each step of integration;

– the ODE solver stops the integration at the *breakpoint* at which any state of constraints in the constraint store is changed. To take care of an overshoot from the breakpoint, the solver backtracks until an exact solution within a constant ϵ is found.

13.2. The objective of the chapter

We are developing systems for handling physical simulations and animations based on Hybrid cc. For example, we want to simulate a billiard table on which a number of balls roll and collide with other balls or table edges. The goal is to obtain trajectories of the balls from a description written in Hybrid cc that directly reflects the laws of elementary physics.

However, the current implementation of Hybrid cc has several limitations in the reliability aspect as follows:

– although the implementation supports interval arithmetic, it does not use interval arithmetic to handle discrete changes such as *if* C *then* A, based on interval arithmetic;

– the ODE solver detects discrete changes during the integration with an ad hoc method. To work around computation errors, the detection allows for a tolerance ϵ, but this may result in qualitatively different trajectories.

The goal of this chapter is to propose a reliable method for computing trajectories in Hybrid cc. Our method obtains valid and tight interval enclosures of discrete changes, corresponding to Step 4 in section 13.1.2. By combining the proposed method and other known techniques for reliable computing, we will be able to guarantee the accuracy of trajectories, as well as to verify the reachable area of objects. We also expect to apply the method to problems such as the backward computation of trajectories.

13.3. Background of interval arithmetic

To describe our method based on interval arithmetic [MOO 66], the following notions and definitions are used.

13.3.1. *Basic notions of interval arithmetic*

$\mathcal{F}$ denotes the set of machine-representable floating-point numbers, $\mathcal{I}$ denotes the set of intervals over $\mathbb{R}$ whose bounds are in $\mathcal{F}$, and I denotes an interval in $\mathcal{I}$. $\mathrm{lb}(I)$ denotes the lower bound, $\mathrm{ub}(I)$ denotes the upper bound, and $\mathrm{w}(I)$ denotes the width of I. $\mathcal{D}$ denotes the set of boxes over $\mathbb{R}^n$ whose bounds are in $\mathcal{F}$, and D denotes a box in $\mathcal{D}$. Given a real r and a subset A of $\mathbb{R}^n$, $\bar{r}$ denotes the smallest interval in $\mathcal{I}$ containing r, and $\Box A$ the smallest box in $\mathcal{D}$ containing A. If g is a function, G denotes the *interval extension* of g.

13.3.2. *ODE solving based on interval arithmetic*

There have been several techniques for solving ODEs based on interval arithmetic or constraint propagation; see [LOH 92, NED 99, DEV 98, CRU 03] for example. A *solution* of an ODE system $\mathcal{O}$ with the initial value $u(t_0) = u_0$ is a function $s^*(t) : \mathbb{R} \to \mathbb{R}^n$ satisfying $\mathcal{O}$ and the initial conditions $s^*(t_0) = u_0$. Also the solution of $\mathcal{O}$ is denoted as the function $s(t_0, u_0, t) : \mathbb{R} \times \mathbb{R}^n \times \mathbb{R} \to \mathbb{R}^n$ such that $s(t_0, u_0, t) = s^*(t)$. An *interval solution* of $\mathcal{O}$ is an interval extension S of s. A box B is an *a priori bound* of a solution s with respect to $\mathcal{O}$, $[t_0, t_1]$ and D, if for all t in $[t_0, t_1]$, $S(t_0, D, t) \subseteq B$.

LEMMA.– *(Continuity of the solution of ODEs) Let f be continuous over an open set E over $\mathbb{R} \times \mathbb{R}^n$ with the property that for every (t_0, u_0) in E, the initial value problem $\{u' = f(t, u), u(t_0) = u_0\}$ has a unique solution $u(t) = s(t_0, u_0, t)$. Let $T(t_0, u_0)$ be the maximal interval in which $u(t) = s(t_0, u_0, t)$ exists. Then s is continuous over $\{(t_0, u_0, t) \mid (t_0, u_0) \in E, t \in T(t_0, u_0)\}$.*

13.4. The proposed method

Our method is composed of two algorithms, TRACE and PRUNEANDMERGE. By processing Step 2 and Step 3 in section 13.1.2 using interval arithmetic, we obtain an ODE system $\mathcal{O}$, which has an initial value D_0 and an initial time T_0. The main TRACE algorithm calculates trajectories with respect to $\mathcal{O}$. TRACE simulates the continuous evolution of the system until an ask condition C is entailed. The PRUNEANDMERGE algorithm calculates the precise enclosure of the point of a discrete change.

13.4.1. *Assumptions on the proposed method*

We consider problems that satisfy the following assumptions:

– any ODE system $\mathcal{O}$ has the form $u' = f(t, u)$ (f is continuous) and a unique solution;

– any ask condition C is an arithmetic constraint of the form $f_d = 0$, where f_d is a continuous function $f_d : \mathbb{R}^n \rightarrow \mathbb{R}$ and is invariant over time.

Also, in this chapter, we investigate the method under the following additional assumptions that simplify the problems:

– we consider problems with a single variable and assume they cause only one discrete change at one time. It is a topic of future study to improve the method in this chapter to handle more general cases;

– the solution $s(t_0, u_0, t)$ of $\mathcal{O}$ either increases or decreases monotonically over any interval T_d whose width is equal to $\mathrm{w}(T_0)$ and which T_d includes t_d satisfying $f_d(s(t_0, u_0, t_d))$.

13.4.2. TRACE *algorithm*

We give the TRACE algorithm in Figure 13.2, and illustrate its basic idea in Figure 13.3. TRACE calculates a trajectory with respect to $\mathcal{O}$ and ensures a set of step solutions S. The main idea is to obtain the "lower bound" of the trajectory, which is calculated from the initial value D_0 at $\mathrm{lb}(T_0)$, and to shift it by $\mathrm{w}(T_0)$ over time. At the beginning of the loop (line 6), TRACE obtains the one-step solution of the trajectory consisting of an a priori bound $B_{t,h}$ and a tight solution D_{t+h}. Interval solutions of ODEs can be obtained using existing techniques, e.g. [NED 99]. TRACE preserves several a priori bounds of the width $\mathrm{w}(T_0)$ in a buffer Q (line 12), and obtains the step solution by taking the union of elements in Q (line 15). Figure 13.3(a) illustrates the idea. Note that we assume the step size h is equal to $\mathrm{w}(T_0)$. Although boundary trajectories do not enclose an envelope created by shifting an extremal value in a trajectory (consider Figure 13.3(b)), TRACE can safely enclose the envelope since a priori bounds are preserved in Q.

TRACE detects a time point of a discrete change by evaluating the ask condition C in each step of the loop (lines 7 and 9). We can use the existing interval-based methods such as [Van 97] to evaluate ask conditions. TRACE preserves step solutions in the buffer Q, from B_l in which C is first entailed to a step where C is overshot (line 8). Figure 13.3(c) illustrates the idea. As a result, Q encloses an area of a discrete change, and we obtain an output B_{result} by passing Q to the PRUNEANDMERGE algorithm. Below is a soundness theorem of the method:

THEOREM.– *Assume the assumptions in section 13.4.1 hold. Assume there exists $t \in \mathbb{R}$ such that for all $u \in D_0$, $f_d(s(t_0, u, t)) > 0$ holds. Assume there exists $t' \in \mathbb{R}$ such that for all $u \in D_0$, $f_d(s(t_0, u, t')) < 0$ holds. Then, for all $u \in D_0$, there exists $t_d \in \mathbb{R}$ between t and t' such that the ask condition $f_d(s(t_0, u, t_d)) = 0$ is entailed.*

Require: an ODE system $\mathcal{O}$, initial time T_0, initial value D_0, step size h, an ask condition C
Ensure: a set S of step solutions, an area of a discrete change B_{result}

$t := \mathrm{lb}(T_0)$
$D := D_0$
$Q :=$ a buffer to preserve a trajectory for several steps
$B_l := \emptyset$
loop
  $(B_{t,h}, D_{t+h}) :=$ do a step computation w.r.t. $\mathcal{O}$, t, D, h
  if $C(D_{t+h})$ is entailed **then**
    $B_l := B_{t,h}$
  else if $C(D_{t+h})$ is overshot **then**
    break
  end if
  put $(B_{t,h}, D_{t+h})$ to the tail of Q
  remove a redundant element from the top of Q
  $D := D_{t+h}$
  $S := S \cup \{$the sum of solutions in Q for $\mathrm{w}(T_0)\}$
  $t := t + h$
end loop
$B_{result} :=$ PRUNEANDMERGE$(Q, \mathcal{O}, C, \mathrm{w}(T_0))$
return B_{result}

Figure 13.2. TRACE *algorithm*

PROOF.– For each u in D_0, $f_d(s(t_0, u, t)) > 0$ and $f_d(s(t_0, u, t')) < 0$ hold. Since f_d is continuous, there exists a solution $s_d \in \mathbb{R}^n$ such that $f_d(s_d) = 0$ holds between $s(t_0, u, t)$ and $s(t_0, u, t')$. Since s is continuous by Lemma in section 13.3.2, and also since s increases or decreases monotonically, there exists a unique time t_d between t and t' such that $s(t_0, u, t_d) = s_d$ holds. ∎

13.4.3. PRUNEANDMERGE *algorithm*

We give the PRUNEANDMERGE algorithm in Figure 13.4. Figure 13.5 illustrates an application of the algorithm to an expanded example in which a 2-dimensional variable over the x and y axes and a non-linear condition C are used. Note that Figure 13.5(a) corresponds to Figure 13.3(c), and is overwritten by the computation result of PRUNEANDMERGE. We apply a *branch and prune* algorithm to the time component of an area of a discrete change based on the following hull consistency (line 1):

DEFINITION.– *(Hull consistency of a time interval of a discrete change) A time interval T_d of a discrete change with respect to an ODE system $\mathcal{O}$ and an ask*

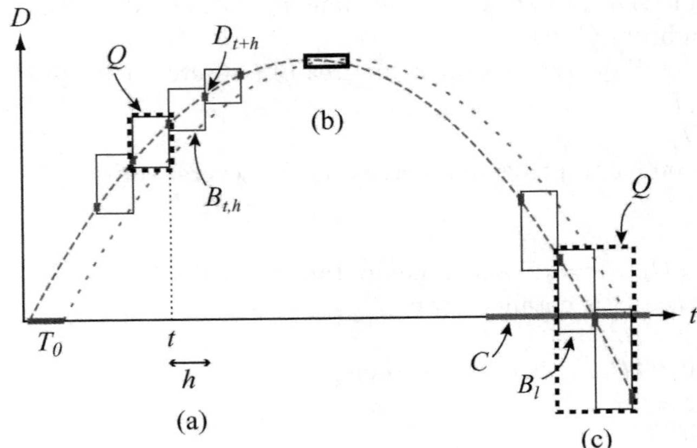

Figure 13.3. *Solving of an ODE system with an ask condition by* TRACE

Require: a buffer of solutions Q, an ODE system $\mathcal{O}$, an ask condition C, width w

Ensure: a box B_{result}

1: $B := \square\{\text{branch and prune } Q \text{ w.r.t. } \mathcal{O}, C\}$

2: $B' :=$ enlarge B for w

3: $B_{result} :=$ prune B'_D w.r.t. C

4: return B_{result}

Figure 13.4. PRUNEANDMERGE *algorithm*

condition $f_d = 0$ (F_d is an interval extension of f_d) is hull-consistent with respect to $T_d = [t_l, t_u]$, if the condition

$$(F_d(D_l) > \bar{0} \wedge F_d(D_u) < \bar{0}) \vee (F_d(D_l) < \bar{0} \wedge F_d(D_u) > \bar{0})$$

holds, where $D_l = S(t_0, D_0, t_l)$ and $D_u = S(t_0, D_0, t_u)$.

Figure 13.5(a) and (b) illustrates the result of the bisection method. The result is merged by obtaining the box enclosure (line 1). The algorithm enlarges B by w at line 2, as TRACE shifts trajectories for w(T_0) ($= w$). Moreover, we can prune B' by solving the condition C over the (x, y)-component (line 3, Figure 13.5(c)).

13.5. Experimental results

We evaluated the effect of the proposed method by simulating the example introduced at the beginning of this chapter. In the simulation, we used the

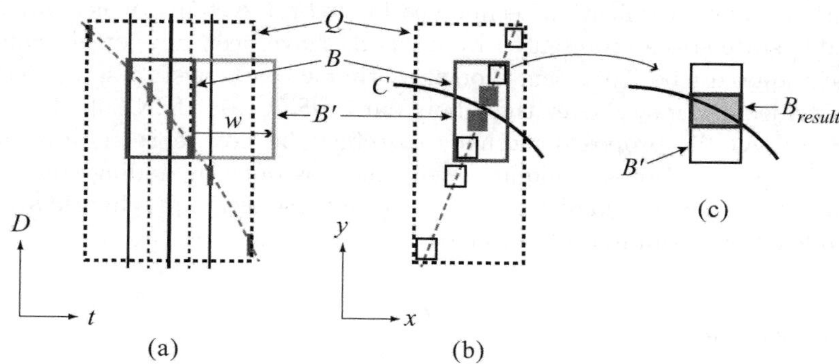

Figure 13.5. *Pruning of an area of a discrete change by* PRUNEANDMERGE

t	(a) Direct computation	(b) Proposed method	(c) Theoretical solution
0	[10.00000, 10.00000]	[10.00000, 10.00000]	10
2	[2.424746, 2.427454]	[2.426262, 2.426676]	2.426406...
3	[0.4398578, 0.4739294]	[0.4559554, 0.4613689]	0.4594154...

Table 13.2. *Experimental results*

existing interval-based solvers; VNODE-LP [NED 06] for ODEs and Elisa [GRA 05] for NLEs. Table 13.2 shows the initial value, the solution at $t = 2$ after the first bounce ($t = \sqrt{2}$), and the solution at $t = 3$ after the second bounce ($t = 2\sqrt{2}$). We solved ODEs with a step size of 0.0001. We can see an improvement in accuracy by comparing the results obtained by (a) direct interval computation without refinements and (b) our method. We can also make sure that the results enclose the theoretical solution (c).

13.6. Related work

Techniques for modeling and verification of hybrid systems based on constraint logic programming have been proposed. Hickey and Wittenberg [HIC 04] presented an approach using the CLP(F) language, which can describe analytical relationships between real variables and functions. CLP(F) supports interval arithmetic. However suppression of interval divergence in computing discrete changes is not considered. Urbina [URB 96] proposed a method using the CLP($\mathcal{R}$) language. Computations in the method are not based on intervals, and solutions are not accurate. Moreover, only linear numerical constraints are supported.

Various safety verification techniques for hybrid systems, which calculate reachable state space represented by intervals, have been developed. Some of the techniques use box representation of continuous parts of state space to check how a trajectory moves over their boundaries [STU 97, HEN 00]. Ratschan and She [RAT 05] proposed methods to refine the box representation using constraint propagation techniques. Refinement is done by adding constraints describing continuous and discrete changes. In these techniques hybrid systems are modeled based on hybrid automata.

13.7. Conclusion

We proposed a method for obtaining interval enclosures of discrete changes in hybrid systems. After relaxing the assumptions in section 13.4.1, we will next implement the proposed method in the Hybrid cc interpreter. The improved interpreter provides a reliable framework to model and control the variety of hybrid systems that occur in real-life applications.

Acknowledgements

The authors would like to thank Mitsuhiro Nishimura, Ryota Nishizawa, Yoshiyuki Ohno, Yui Sasajima, Shinichi Tobita and Satoshi Usami for helping the evaluation of the proposed method.

13.8. References

[CAR 98] CARLSON B., GUPTA V., "Hybrid cc with Interval Constraints", *HSCC 1998*, vol. 1386 of *LNCS*, Springer, 1998.

[CRU 03] CRUZ J., BARAHONA P., "Constraint Satisfaction Differential Problems", *CP 2003*, vol. 2833 of *LNCS*, Springer, p. 259–273, 2003.

[DEV 98] DEVILLE Y., JANSSEN M., HENTENRYCK P. V., "Consistency Techniques for Ordinary Differential Equations", *CP 1998*, vol. 1520 of *LNCS*, Springer, p. 162–176, 1998.

[GRA 05] GRANVILLIERS L., SORIN V., "Elisa", http://sourceforge.net/projects/elisa/, 2005.

[GUP 95] GUPTA V., JAGADEESAN R., SARASWAT V. A., BOBROW D., "Programming in Hybrid Constraint Languages", *Hybrid Systems 1994*, vol. 999 of *LNCS*, Springer, 1995.

[HEN 00] HENZINGER T. A., HOROWITZ B., MAJUMDAR R., WONG-TOI H., "Beyond HyTech: Hybrid Systems Analysis Using Interval Numerical Methods", *HSCC 2000*, vol. 1790 of *LNCS*, Springer, 2000.

[HIC 04] HICKEY T. J., WITTENBERG D. K., "Rigorous Modeling of Hybrid Systems using Interval Arithmetic Constraints", *HSCC 2004*, vol. 2993 of *LNCS*, p. 402–416, 2004.

[LOH 92] LOHNER R. J., "Computation of Guaranteed Enclosures for the Solutions of Ordinary Initial and Boundary Value Problems", *Computational Ordinary Differential Equations*, Oxford University Press, 1992.

[MOO 66] MOORE R. E., *Interval Analysis*, Prentice-Hall, 1966.

[NED 99] NEDIALKOV N. S., JACKSON K. R., CORLISS G. F., "Validated Solutions of Initial Value Problems for Ordinary Differential Equations", *Applied Mathematics and Computation*, vol. 105, num. 1, p. 21–68, 1999.

[NED 06] NEDIALKOV N. S., "VNODE-LP: A Validated Solver for Initial Value Problems in Ordinary Differential Equations,", *TR CAS-06-06-NN*, McMaster University, 2006.

[RAT 05] RATSCHAN S., SHE Z., "Safety Verification of Hybrid Systems by Constraint Propagation Based Abstraction Refinement", *HSCC 2005*, vol. 3414 of *LNCS*, Springer, 2005.

[STU 97] STURSBERG O., KOWALEWSKI S., HOFFMANN I., PREUSIG J., "Comparing Timed and Hybrid Automata as Approximations of Continuous Systems", *Hybrid Systems 1996*, vol. 1273 of *LNCS*, Springer, p. 361–377, 1997.

[URB 96] URBINA L., "Analysis of Hybrid Systems in CLP(R)", *CP 1996*, vol. 1118 of *LNCS*, Springer, 1996.

[Van 97] VAN HENTENRYCK P., MCALLESTER D., KAPUR D., "Solving Polynomial Systems Using a Branch and Prune Approach", *SIAM Journal on Numerical Analysis*, vol. 34, num. 2, p. 797–827, 1997.

PART V

Local Search Techniques in Constraint Satisfaction

Edited by Andrea ROLI and Yehuda NAVEH

Introduction

Constraint satisfaction plays an important role in theoretical and applied computer science. Constraint satisfaction problems (CSPs) are of particular interest to the constraint programming research community, as well as for many real world applications. Along with pure systematic techniques for solving CSPs, stochastic local search (SLS) and hybrid techniques have proved to be very effective on some classes of problems. One central goal of research in SLS for constraint satisfaction is the design and implementation of efficient algorithms to be used in stand-alone solvers or in conjunction with systematic techniques. As a result, there is a need to develop high-level SLS strategies that will lead to further progress and maturity of efficient and robust solvers for constraint satisfaction. Just some of the hot topics related to the field of SLS for CSP are modeling, global constraint handling, learning techniques, and hybrid stochastic-systematic search methods. On the more theoretical front, current interests include the mathematical properties of the search space and the probabilistic analysis of algorithm behavior. The design and analysis of SLS algorithms for constraint satisfaction involve a large number of issues related to algorithms, programming, statistics, probability and empirical analysis. A series of workshops called *Local Search Techniques in Constraint Satisfaction (LSCS)* was established to provide an open and informal environment for discussing all aspects of local search techniques and related areas, and to introduce recent results and ongoing research. This section is composed of the five contributions presented at LSCS 2006, the third occasion the workshop has taken place. The trends outlined by these chapters are among the most exciting in the field and emphasize the close relationship between theory and application.

Li *et al.* present a local search technique for the satisfiability problem (SAT). Their technique is an improvement of an adaptive WalkSAT, equipped with a new type of look-ahead for choosing the most promising variable to flip. The authors address the problem of making a local search more robust with respect to parameter tuning and propose a method that combines an adaptive parameter tuning mechanism with an effective deterministic heuristic for variable choice.

Prestwich's work focuses on one of the mainstream challenges in local search modeling. Today, SAT solvers are very well-designed and implemented; therefore, many constraint satisfaction problems can be efficiently tackled by modeling them as SAT instances. Nevertheless, the transformation into SAT clauses can hide important structural characteristics of the instance or increase the search space complexity. The chapter analyzes different models for solving the maximum clique problem through SAT local search, and shows the effectiveness of a new encoding for the at-most-one constraint.

The design of well-performing composite search techniques raises the need for an accurate experimental analysis that enables the designer to understand the reasons for good and bad performance of the different configurations of the algorithms. The chapter by Heckman and Beck relates to this theme and discusses an empirical study on the effect of varying the main components of the multi-point constructive search algorithm.

The chapter by Anbulagan *et al.* follows a similar direction. The authors undertake an extensive experimental analysis on the impact of resolution-based preprocessors, combined with local search for SAT. The chapter shows that resolution-based preprocessors enhance the performance of local search by enabling it to exploit the structure of the instance. They also show that choosing the best combination of preprocessor and solver is instance-dependent and suggest investigating the use of combinations of preprocessors.

This selection ends with the chapter by Van Hentenryck and Michel, who present a current overview of *COMET*, an object-oriented programming language that provides modeling and control abstractions for constraint-based local search. The chapter introduces the main concepts and aspects of *COMET* by describing its development process. The core concept of this system is that (local) search can be seen as orthogonal to modeling. The language provides constructs that support high-level local search programming, such as invariants, differentiable objects and abstract control structures.

Chapter 14

Combining Adaptive Noise and Look-Ahead in Local Search for SAT

The performance of a *Walksat* family algorithm crucially depends on noise parameter p and sometimes noise parameters wp or dp.[1] However, to find the optimal noise settings, extensive experiments on various values of p and sometimes wp or dp are needed because the optimal noise settings depend on the types and sizes of the instances. To deal with this problem, different approaches are proposed. The adaptive noise mechanism [HOO 02] is introduced in *Novelty+* to automatically adapt noise settings during the search, yielding the algorithm *adaptNovelty+*. This algorithm does not need any manual noise tuning. The local search algorithm G^2WSAT selects the best promising decreasing variable to flip if promising decreasing variables exist [LI 05]. Nevertheless, the performance of G^2WSAT still depends on static noise settings, since when there is no promising decreasing variable, a heuristic such as *Novelty++* is used to select a variable to flip, depending on p and dp. Furthermore, G^2WSAT does not favor those flips that can generate promising decreasing variables to minimize its dependance on noise settings.

Chapter written by Chu Min LI, Wanxia WEI and Harry ZHANG.

1. Noise parameters wp and dp are random walk probability and diversification probability respectively.

14.1. Implementation of the adaptive noise mechanism in G^2WSAT

We implement the adaptive noise mechanism [HOO 02] in G^2WSAT [LI 05] to obtain an algorithm *adapt*G^2WSAT.

Like *adaptNovelty+*, *adapt*G^2WSAT does not need any manual noise tuning to solve a new problem. In [LI 06], experimental results indicate that the deterministic exploitation of promising decreasing variables in *adapt*G^2WSAT probably enhances the adaptive noise mechanism. We thus expect that better exploitation of such variables will further enhance this mechanism.

14.2. Look-Ahead for promising decreasing variables

14.2.1. *Promising score of a variable*

Given a CNF formula $\mathcal{F}$ and an assignment A, let x be a variable, let B be obtained from A by flipping x, and let x' be the best promising decreasing variable with respect to B. We define the promising score of x with respect to A as

$$pscore_A(x) = score_A(x) + score_B(x')$$

where $score_A(x)$ is the score of x with respect to A and $score_B(x')$ is the score of x' with respect to B.[2]

If there are promising decreasing variables with respect to B, the promising score of x with respect to A represents the improvement in the number of unsatisfied clauses under A by flipping x and then x'. In this case, $pscore_A(x) > score_A(x)$. If there is no promising decreasing variable with respect to B

$$pscore_A(x) = score_A(x)$$

since *adapt*G^2WSAT does not know in advance which variable to flip for B [3].

The computation of $pscore_A(x)$ implies a look-ahead operation to calculate the highest score of all promising decreasing variables with respect to B. This computation takes time $O(L + \gamma)$, where L is the upper bound for the sum of the lengths of all clauses containing the flipped variable and γ is the upper bound for the number of the promising decreasing variables after flipping x.

2. x' has the highest $score_B(x')$ among all promising decreasing variables with respect to B.

3. The choice of the variable to flip is made randomly by using *Novelty++*.

14.2.2. *Integrating limited look-ahead in* $adaptG^2WSAT$

We improve $adaptG^2WSAT$ using the promising scores of variables. In practice, we limit the look-ahead computation in several ways. When there are promising decreasing variables with respect to assignment A, the improved $adaptG^2WSAT$ calculates the promising scores for only δ promising decreasing variables where δ is a parameter. Otherwise, the improved $adaptG^2WSAT$ selects a variable to flip from a randomly chosen unsatisfied clause, using heuristic $Novelty{+}{+}_P$ to exploit limited look-ahead. $Novelty{+}{+}_P$ is modified from $Novelty{+}{+}$ and is described as follows.

```
Function: Novelty++_P
Input: probabilities p and dp, clause c
Output: a variable in c

begin
  with probability dp do y← a variable in c whose flip will falsify the least recently satisfied clause;
  otherwise
      Determine best and second, breaking ties in favor of the least recently flipped variable;
       /* best and second are the best and second best variables in c according to the scores */
      if best is the most recently flipped variable in c
      then
          with probability p do y ← second;
          otherwise if pscore(second)>=pscore(best) then y ← second else y ← best;
      else
          if best is more recently flipped than second
          then if pscore(second)>=pscore(best) then y ← second else y ← best;
          else y ← best;
  return y;
end;
```

$Novelty{+}{+}_P$ uses limited look-ahead. Let *best* and *second* denote the best variable and the second best variable respectively, measured by the scores of variables in c. $Novelty{+}{+}_P$ calculates the promising scores for only *best* and *second*, only when *best* is more recently flipped than *second*,[4] in order to favor the less recently flipped *second*. In this case, $score(second) < score(best)$. As is suggested by the success of $HSAT$ [GEN 93] and $Novelty$ [MCA 97], a less recently flipped variable is generally better if it can improve the objective function at least as well as a more recently flipped variable does. Accordingly, $Novelty{+}{+}_P$ prefers *second* if *second* is less recently flipped than *best* and if $pscore(second) \geq pscore(best)$.

The improved $adaptG^2WSAT$ is called $adaptG^2WSAT_P$.[5] When there are promising decreasing variables, $adaptG^2WSAT_P$ first calculates the promising scores for $\min(|DecVar|, \delta)$ promising decreasing variables where $|DecVar|$ is

4. Including the case in which *best* is the most recently flipped one, where the computation is performed with probability $1-p$.

5. Both p and dp are automatically adjusted in $adaptG^2WSAT_P$ and $dp = p/10$.

the number of promising decreasing variables and δ is a parameter, and then flips the promising decreasing variable with the largest promising calculated score. Otherwise, it uses $Novelty{+}{+}_P$ to select a variable to flip from a randomly chosen unsatisfied clause.

Given a CNF formula $\mathcal{F}$ and an assignment A, the set of assignments obtained by flipping one variable of $\mathcal{F}$ is called the *1-flip neighborhood* of A, and the set of assignments obtained by flipping two variables of $\mathcal{F}$ is called the *2-flip neighborhood* of A. Algorithm $adaptG^2WSAT_P$ only exploits the 1-flip neighborhoods.

14.3. Evaluation

	$adaptG^2WSAT_P$			$adaptG^2WSAT$			G^2WSAT(optimal)			
	success	#flips	time	success	#flips	time	optimal	success	#flips	time
500vars	0.6489	32377	18457	0.5865	35465	15912	(.5 .05)	**0.6564**	29339	**13545**
Beijing	1	42046	**473**	0	0	> 36000	?	0	0	> 36000
bw_large.c	1	1547082	1975	0.8600	3636248	3720	(.2 0)	0.9320	2983209	1794
bw_large.d	**0.9960**	2326595	5656	0.5480	4636299	9152	(.2 0)	0.9520	3281619	4403
FLAT200	0.9559	154541	3014	0.9390	185721	2909	(.5 .06)	**0.9570**	150731	**2426**
GCP	0.8620	243672	12952	0.7750	225445	9755	(.3 .01)	**0.9320**	160942	**6967**
parity	1	137440504	89526	0.9936	175848492	90351	(.55 .01)	1	124133707	**68365**
QG	0.8524	94953	7286	0.8364	87576	4773	(.40 .03)	**0.8815**	26114	**4264**

Table 14.1. *Performance of $adaptG^2WSAT_P$, $adaptG^2WSAT$ and G^2WSAT*

We conduct experiments[6] on a number of benchmark SAT problems. Structured problems come from SATLIB[7]. These problems include 3bitadd_31 and 3bitadd_32 in Beijing, the 100 instances in the files Flat200-479, bw_large.c and bw_large.d in Blocksworld, the 4 satisfiable instances in GCP, par16-1, par16-2, par16-3, par16-4, and par16-5 in parity, and the 10 satisfiable instances in QG[8]. In addition, we generate 2,000 random 3-SAT formulas with 500 variables and 2,125 clauses and eliminate the 912 unsatisfiable ones. Each set of problems is considered as one group except that bw_large.c and bw_large.d are regarded as two groups. Each instance is executed 250 times[9]. In all tables, results in bold indicate the best performance for a group of instance(s).

---

6. All experiments reported in this chapter are performed on a computer with an Athlon 2000+ CPU under Linux.

7. http://www.satlib.org.

8. Since these QG instances contain unit clauses, we simplify them using the *my_compact* program, which is available at http://www.laria.u-picardie.fr/~cli, before running every algorithm.

9. The flip number, $cutoff$ ($Maxsteps$), is 10^5 for the random 3-SAT formulas, 10^7 for 3bitadd_31, 3bitadd_32, bw_large.c, and bw_large.d, 10^9 for the five instances in parity, and 10^6 for other instances.

We find that in *adaptG*^2WSAT and *adaptG*$^2WSAT_P$, which use the heuristics *Novelty++* and *Novelty++*$_P$ respectively, $\theta = 1/5$ and $\phi = 0.1$ give slightly better results on the above SAT instances than $\theta = 1/6$ and $\phi = 0.2$, their original default values in *adaptNovelty+*. In addition, after we run *adaptG*$^2WSAT_P$ with $\delta = 10, 20, 30, 40, 50, 60$, and $|DecVar|$ on these SAT instances, we find that all the constants are significantly better than $|DecVar|$ and that $\delta = 30$ is slightly better than other constants. So the default value of δ is 30 in *adaptG*$^2WSAT_P$.

	adaptG$^2WSAT_P$		*R + adaptNovelty+*		*VW*	
	success #flips	time time/per try	success #flips	time time/per try	success #flips	time time/per try
500vars	**0.6489**	18,457	0.4433	18,113	0.2825	21,447
	32,377	0.068	39,871	0.067	43,707	0.079
Beijing	1	473	1	1183	1	**192**
	42,046	0.946	14,984	2.366	40,013	**0.384**
bw_large.c	**1**	**1,975**	0.6200	5,808	0.9880	2,832
	1,547,082	**7.900**	4,303,455	23.232	2,319,761	11.328
bw_large.d	**0.9960**	**5,656**	0.2360	15,922	0.9720	7,397
	2,326,595	**22.624**	4,354,348	63.688	3,719,994	29.588
FLAT200	**0.9559**	**3,014**	0.8562	4,571	0.5292	8,534
	154,541	**0.121**	242,122	0.183	389,430	0.341
GCP	**0.8620**	12,952	0.7840	12,365	0.4950	30,611
	243,672	12.952	209,572	12.365	148,251	30.611
parity	**1**	**89,526**	0.9368	185,721	0.0056	663,668
	137,440,504	**71.621**	265,138,834	148.577	501,471,449	530.934
QG	**0.8524**	7,286	0.8124	**5,715**	0.7284	17,190
	94,953	2.914	104,398	**2.286**	111,858	6.876
total time	**139,339**		249,398		751,871	

Table 14.2. *Performance of adaptG*$^2WSAT_P$*, R+adaptNovelty+, and VW*

We compare *adaptG*$^2WSAT_P$ with *adaptG*^2WSAT, and *G*^2WSAT with approximately optimal noise settings in Table 14.1, where *adaptG*$^2WSAT_P$ uses *Novelty++*$_P$, and *adaptG*^2WSAT and *G*^2WSAT use *Novelty++*. Table 14.1[10] shows that *adaptG*$^2WSAT_P$ is generally better than *adaptG*^2WSAT in terms of success rate and successful run length. It is noticeable that the look-ahead approach makes *adaptG*$^2WSAT_P$ easily solve Beijing, which is hard for *adaptG*^2WSAT. Table 14.1 also shows that, in terms of success rate, *adaptG*$^2WSAT_P$ approaches *G*^2WSAT and sometimes is even better. As indicated in this table, *adaptG*$^2WSAT_P$ achieves higher success rates than

10. We report the success rate ("success"), the successful run length ("#flips"), which is the average flip number over all successful runs, and the total run time ("time") in seconds to execute all instances in the group 250 times (including successful and unsuccessful runs). The success rate and successful run length are averaged over the group.

G^2WSAT on 3 groups: Beijing, bw_large.c, and bw_large.d. The time performance of $adaptG^2WSAT_P$ is acceptable; it could be further improved by optimizing the computation of promising scores.

Finally, we compare $adaptG^2WSAT_P$ with *R+adaptNovelty+* [ANB 05] and *VW* [PRE 05][11] in Table 14.2. *R+adaptNovelty+* is *adaptNovelty+* with a preprocessing to add a set of resolvents of length ≤ 3 to the input formula [ANB 05]. *VW* takes variable weights into account when selecting a variable to flip, and adjusts and smoothes variable weights [PRE 05]. *R+adaptNovelty+*, G^2WSAT with *p*=0.50 and *dp*=0.05, and *VW* won the gold, silver, and bronze medal respectively in the satisfiable random formula category in the SAT 2005 competition.[12]

According to Table 14.2[13], $adaptG^2WSAT_P$ is better than *R+adaptNovelty+*[14] and *VW* in terms of success rate on all groups, except for Beijing, on which every algorithm has a success rate of 1. As for run time, $adaptG^2WSAT_P$ is faster on 5 out of the 8 groups than *R+adaptNovelty+*, and is comparable on other groups; $adaptG^2WSAT_P$ exhibits the shortest total run time. Algorithm $adaptG^2WSAT_P$ is faster than *VW* on 7 out of the 8 groups, whereas *VW* is faster on Beijing.

14.4. Conclusion

Without any manual noise or other parameter tuning, the resulting local search algorithm $adaptG^2WSAT_P$ approaches G^2WSAT with optimal static noise settings and is sometimes even better. Moreover, $adaptG^2WSAT_P$ compares favorably with state-of-the-art algorithms, such as *R+adaptNovelty+* and *VW*.

14.5. References

[ANB 05] ANBULAGAN, PHAM D. N., SLANEY J., SATTAR A., "Old Resolution Meets Modern SLS", *Proceedings of AAAI-05*, Pittsburgh, USA, July 9-13, 2005, AAAI Press, p. 354-359, 2005.

---

11. We download *R+adaptNovelty+* and *VW* from http://www.satcompetition.org.
12. http://www.satcompetition.org.
13. This table also reports the average time to execute an instance once in a group ("time/per try") and the total time to execute all groups 250 times ("total time").
14. We use the default value 0.01 for the random walk probability in *R+adaptNovelty+* when running *R+adaptNovelty+*.

[GEN 93] GENT I. P., WALSH T., "Towards an Understanding of Hill-Climbing Procedures for SAT.", *Proceedings of AAAI-93*, Washington, USA, July 11-15, 1993, AAAI Press, p. 28-33, 1993.

[HOO 02] HOOS H., "An Adaptive Noise Mechanism for WalkSAT", *Proceedings of AAAI-02*, Edmonton, Canada, July 28-August 1, 2002, AAAI Press, p. 655-660, 2002.

[LI 05] LI C. M., HUANG W. Q., "Diversification and Determinism in Local Search for Satisfiability", *Proceedings of SAT2005*, St. Andrews, UK, June 19-23, 2005, Springer, LNCS 3569, p. 158-172, 2005.

[LI 06] LI C. M., WEI W., ZHANG H., "Combining Adaptive Noise and Look-Ahead in Local Search for SAT", *Proceedings of LSCS06*, Nantes, France, September 24-29, 2006, p. 2-16, 2006.

[MCA 97] MCALLESTER D. A., SELMAN B., KAUTZ H., "Evidence for Invariant in Local Search", *Proceedings of AAAI-97*, Providence, Rhode Island, July 27-31, 1997, AAAI Press, p. 321-326, 1997.

[PRE 05] PRESTWICH S., "Random Walk with Continuously Smoothed Variable Weights", *Proceedings of SAT2005*, St. Andrews, UK, June 19-23, 2005, Springer, LNCS 3569, p. 203-215, 2005.

Chapter 15

Finding Large Cliques using SAT Local Search

Problem modeling is more of an art than a science, and the "best" model may depend partly upon the algorithm to be applied to the model. This is particularly true of local search vs backtrack search: quite different modeling aims and techniques have been shown to be necessary for the two types of algorithm. In this chapter we investigate methods for SAT-encoding clique problems, in such a way that large instances can be solved by local search algorithms. The work can be extended in several directions, as discussed in the conclusion[1].

The Maximum Clique Problem (MCP) has been the subject of four decades of research. It was one of the first problems shown to be NP-complete, and theoretical results indicate that even near-optimal solutions are hard to find. Its applications include computer vision, coding theory, tiling, fault diagnosis and the analysis of biological and archaeological data, and it provides a lower bound for the chromatic number of a graph. It was one of the three problems proposed in a DIMACS workshop [JOH 96] as a way of comparing algorithms (the other two being satisfiability and vertex coloring). Many algorithms have been applied to the MCP on a common benchmark set, and its history, applicability and rich set of available results make the MCP ideal for evaluating new approaches. The problem is defined as follows. A graph $G = (V, E)$ consists of a set V of vertices and a set E of edges between vertices. Two vertices connected by an edge are said to be *adjacent*. A *clique* is a subset of V whose vertices

---

Chapter written by Steven PRESTWICH.

1. This material is based in part upon works supported by the Science Foundation Ireland under Grant No. 00/PI.1/C075.

are pairwise adjacent. A *maximum clique* is a clique of maximum cardinality. Given a graph G the problem is to find a maximum clique, or a good approximation to one. We can reduce the MCP to a series of feasibility problems: finding a clique of k vertices (a *k-clique*) with k incremented iteratively. Each feasibility problem can be solved by constraint programming or SAT methods, and in this chapter we use the latter.

15.1. SAT-encoding the clique problem

The SAT problem is to determine whether a Boolean expression has a satisfying labeling (set of truth assignments). The problems are usually expressed in conjunctive normal form: a conjunction of clauses $c_1 \wedge \ldots \wedge c_m$ where each clause c is a disjunction of literals $l_1 \vee \ldots \vee l_n$ and each literal l is either a Boolean variable v or its negation $\bar{v}$. A Boolean variable can be labeled true (T) or false (F). We shall SAT-encode the problem of finding a k-clique in a graph with vertices $v_1 \ldots v_n$. Define SAT variables e_{ij} such that $e_{ij} = T$ if clique element j is vertex v_i, and m_i such that $m_i = T$ if v_i is in the clique. Each clique element must be assigned at least one vertex: $\bigvee_{i=1}^{n} e_{ij}$ $(j = 1 \ldots k)$. If a vertex is assigned to a clique element then it is in the clique: $\bar{e}_{ij} \vee m_i$. No non-adjacent vertices may be in the clique: $\bar{m}_i \vee \bar{m}_{i'}$ $(1 \le i < i' \le n$ and $v_i, v_{i'}$ are non-adjacent). There is a permutation symmetry on the assignments of vertices to clique elements, but we do not break this symmetry because symmetry breaking clauses often harm local search performance [PRE 03]. When modeling a problem for solution by local search, this point can be turned to our advantage: breaking symmetry can be complex and space-consuming.

There are two possible sets of at-most-one clauses in this model. Firstly, an optional set preventing more than one vertex from being assigned to a clique element: if we omit these then our model may represent a clique containing k vertices *or more*. Secondly, a mandatory set preventing a vertex from appearing more than once in the clique i.e. the number of e_{ij} that are true as $j = 1 \ldots k$ is at most one, for all $i = 1 \ldots n$. Without these clauses we could simply fill the clique with a single vertex (considering a vertex to be adjacent to itself does not prevent this because non-adjacency is only enforced on the m variables).

Several methods for SAT-encoding at-most-one constraints are known, and we shall present a new method. Leaving aside the clique model for a moment, suppose we wish to impose the constraint that at most one of a set of Boolean variables $x_1 \ldots x_s$ is T. There are several possibilities. Many SAT algorithms generalize naturally to linear pseudo-Boolean problems, in which at-most-one (and other cardinality constraints) are easy to express. But it is not always convenient to extend an existing SAT algorithm to such constraints, so we shall restrict ourselves to standard SAT. Another method treats the constraint as a special case of a cardinality constraint with $O(s \log s)$ new variables and $O(s^2)$ clauses. We shall not consider this method further, because for the at-most-one case it requires more variables and is no more compact than a common SAT method called the *pairwise encoding*, which simply adds $O(s^2)$ binary clauses $\bar{x}_i \vee \bar{x}_{i'}$ $(1 \leq i < i' \leq s)$. No new variables are necessary, and with the pairwise encoding the clique model has $O(nk)$ variables and $O(n^2 + nk^2)$ literals.

Another method described by [GEN 02] and others uses a *ladder* structure and has $O(s)$ new variables and $O(s)$ clauses of size no greater than three. Define new variables $l_1 \dots l_{s-1}$ and add *ladder validity clauses* $\bar{y}_{i+1} \vee y_i$ and *channeling clauses* derived from $x_i \leftrightarrow (y_{i-1} \wedge \bar{y}_i)$. The ladder adds only $O(n)$ new variables and $O(n)$ clauses. With this method the clique encoding has $O(nk)$ variables and $O(n^2 + nk)$ literals. We also consider a new variant of the ladder encoding for local search, formed by relaxing the equivalence $\leftrightarrow$ to an implication $x_i \rightarrow (y_{i-1} \wedge \bar{y}_i)$. These clauses are sufficient to ensure that no more than one of the x_i is true. The extra clauses in the original ladder encoding are useful for backtrack search but not necessarily for local search. The complexity is the same as for the original ladder encoding.

We now present a new *bitwise* encoding. Define $O(\log s)$ new Boolean variables b_k $(k = 1 \dots B_k = \lceil \log_2 s \rceil)$. Now add clauses $\bar{x}_i \vee b_k$ [or $\bar{b}_k$] if bit k of $i - 1$ is 1 [or 0] $(k = 1 \dots B_n)$. This encoding has $O(\log s)$ new variables and $O(s \log s)$ binary clauses, so the clique encoding has $O(nk)$ variables and $O(n^2 + nk \log k)$ literals. It has more literals than the ladder encoding, but is closer in space complexity to the ladder encoding than to the pairwise encoding. The correctness of the encoding can be shown as follows. Any single x_i can be T because any $i - 1$ has a binary representation. If no $x_i = T$ then the b_k may take any truth values so this is also permitted. To show that no more than one x_i can be true we use proof by contradiction. Suppose that $x_i = x_{i'} = T$ for some $i \neq i'$. Both these assignments force a pattern of truth values to be assigned to the b_k. But every integer $i - 1$ has a unique binary representation, so these patterns differ in at least one b_k. No b_k can be both T and F in any solution so $x_i = x_{i'} = T$ cannot occur in any solution. QED.

15.2. Notes on the bitwise at-most-one encoding

A motivation for the new encoding is as follows. The ladder encoding has lower space complexity than the pairwise encoding, and has been shown to perform well with backtrack search. But it has a potential drawback for local search: x_i and $x_{i'}$ can only interact with each other via a chain of $|i - i'| + 2$ flips (local moves). Such chains of dependent variables have been shown to harm local search performance [PRE 02, WEI 02] so we might expect the ladder encoding to perform poorly with local search (this is confirmed below).

encoding	variables	clauses	flips	seconds
pairwise/y	10100	1000100	8043	1.6
ladder/y	30100	89500	204043	10.6
rladder/y	30100	69700	80491	4.1
bitwise/y	11500	150100	12214	0.66
pairwise/n	10100	505100	5425	0.69
ladder/n	20100	49800	30617	1.35
rladder/n	20100	39900	29318	1.35
bitwise/n	10800	80100	6307	0.43

Table 15.1. *Comparison of 8 encodings*

The bitwise encoding does not require chains of flips to enforce the at-most-one constraint. Moreover, the ladder encoding roughly doubles the number of variables in our k-clique encoding, whereas the new encoding only slightly increases it.

Table 15.1 compares the pairwise, original ladder, relaxed ladder ("rladder") and bitwise encodings, each with and without the optional at-most-one clauses for clique elements (denoted by "y/n"). For this test we use a trivial problem: a totally connected graph with $n = k = 100$. All figures are medians over 100 runs and use the RSAPS local search algorithm [HUT 02] with default runtime parameters, which has been shown to be robust over a wide range of problems. The pairwise encoding is easily the largest in clause terms but has fewest variables. The ladder encodings have the most variables but fewest clauses. The bitwise encoding has slightly more variables than the pairwise encoding, and more clauses than the ladder encodings but fewer than the pairwise encoding. In the ladder encodings the optional clauses make the problem much harder to solve in both flips and seconds, especially the original ladder. In the pairwise and bitwise encodings they make the problem harder in both flips and time. The pairwise encoding is best in terms of flips, with or without the optional clauses, but because of its larger size it is not the fastest. The relaxed ladder encoding is better than the original ladder encoding in both flips and time. But the bitwise encoding is best in time, with or without the optional clauses. In further experiments the pairwise encoding was better than the bitwise encoding on graphs with small cliques, but we require a scalable encoding.

15.3. Experiments

In this section we evaluate our most scalable SAT model: no optional at-most-one clauses, and using the bitwise encoding of the mandatory at-most-one constraints. As our local search algorithm we use an ad hoc variant of WalkSAT that we call HWWSAT, which gave better results than several known algorithms we tried (but we do not necessarily recommend HWWSAT for other problems). HWWSAT randomly chooses a violated clause, then chooses the flip that minimises the number $x_v - c.a_v$ where x_v is the increase in the number of violated clauses that would occur if v were flipped, and a_v is the *age* of variable v (the number of flips since v was last flipped). This is similar to HWSAT [GEN 95] which breaks ties using variable age, but our use of the coefficient c forces a sufficiently old variable to be selected no matter what the effect on the number of violated clauses. HWWSAT has only one parameter c to be tuned by the user – it does not have a noise parameter which (on these problems) was found to be unnecessary.

We omit a table of results for space reasons, but summarize them here. We used the "snapshot" benchmarks of the DIMACS competition, with the exception of the three largest graphs C4000.5, MANN_a81 and keller6, which each have several million edges and yield rather large SAT files that slow down our machine. The largest problem we solved was C2000.9 which has 2,000 vertices and 1,799,532 edges. For most graphs we found either a maximum clique or a clique that is as large as those found by the algorithms we know of. Thus a simple SAT local search algorithm can find large cliques on a range of graph sizes and types *given the right model*. This shows the importance of choosing a good model: some SAT-encodings would either be too large or interact poorly with local search. Our clique sizes are not dominated by those found by any of the DIMACS stochastic algorithms, which include genetic algorithms, simulated annealing, neural networks, greedy local search, and Tabu search. Some of the cliques contain several hundred vertices.

However, some of our run times are not competitive with those of most other approaches. Recent local search algorithms such as RLS [BAT 01] and DLS-MC [PUL 06] find larger cliques in shorter times. A CP approach to finding cliques using ILOG Solver was described in [REG 03], and beats our approach except on some of the largest graphs (such as the 1500-vertex p_hat graphs). It is slightly disappointing that we have not made SAT a competitive approach to the MCP. But our results are (to the best of our knowledge) the first SAT results reported for large MCP instances, and we have improved SAT local search performance on problems with large at-most-one constraints.

15.4. Conclusion

We showed that SAT technology can be used to solve large clique problems with reasonable efficiency, compared with a variety of other methods. To achieve this we devised a new variant of the Walksat local search algorithm and experimented with several SAT-encodings of the problem. A key technique was the use of a new SAT-encoding for the at-most-one constraint, which out-performs other approaches as the number of variables becomes large. We believe that the reason for its superiority over another method (the ladder encoding) is that it avoids chains of dependent variables; though these may have no effect on backtrack search, they can have a very bad effect on local search. Previous bitwise encodings have performed rather poorly with both local and backtrack search. But our new bitwise at-most-one encoding performs very well. The aim of this work was not merely to solve clique problems, but to learn some general lessons on applying SAT local search algorithms to problems containing large at-most-one constraints. Using an appropriate SAT model was essential to success and we expect our approach to find further applications. For example, the very common `alldifferent` constraint can be encoded by limiting at most one variable to take any given value, so the new encoding provides a new way of SAT-encoding `alldifferent`. Our clique encoding can also be adapted to a new encoding for cardinality constraints, and in future work we will compare it to known encodings using local search algorithms.

15.5. References

[BAT 01] BATTITI R., PROTASI M., "Reactive Local Search for the Maximum Clique Problem", *Algorithmica*, vol. 29, num. 4, p. 610-637, 2001.

[GEN 95] GENT I. P., WALSH T., "Unsatisfied Variables in Local Search", *Hybrid Problems, Hybrid Solutions*, IOS Press, Amsterdam, the Netherlands, p. 73-85, 1995.

[GEN 02] GENT I. P., PROSSER P., SMITH B., "A 0/1 Encoding of the GACLex Constraint for Pairs of Vectors", *International Workshop on Modelling and Solving Problems With Constraints*, ECAI'02, 2002.

[HUT 02] HUTTER F., TOMPKINS D. A. D., HOOS H. H., "Scaling and Probabilistic Smoothing: Efficient Dynamic Local Search for SAT", *CP2002*, vol. 2470 of *LNCS*, p. 233-248, 2002.

[JOH 96] JOHNSON D. S., (EDS) M. A. T., "Cliques, Coloring and Satisfiability: Second DIMACS Implementation Challenge", *Second DIMACS Implementation Challenge*, vol. 26 of *DIMACS Series in Discrete Mathematics and Theoretical Computer Science*, American Mathematical Society, 1996.

[PRE 02] PRESTWICH S. D., "SAT Problems With Chains of Dependent Variables", *Discrete Applied Mathematics*, vol. 3037, p. 1-22, Elsevier, 2002.

[PRE 03] PRESTWICH S. D., "Negative Effects of Modeling Techniques on Search Performance", *Annals of Operations Research*, vol. 118, p. 137-150, Kluwer Academic Publishers, 2003.

[PUL 06] PULLAN W., HOOS H. H., "Dynamic Local Search for the Maximum Clique Problem", *Journal of Artificial Intelligence Research*, vol. 25, p. 159-185, 2006.

[REG 03] REGIN J.-C., "Using Constraint Programming to Solve the Maximum Clique Problem", *CP 2003*, vol. 2833 of *LNCS*, p. 634-648, 2003.

[WEI 02] WEI W., SELMAN B., "Accelerating Random Walks", *CP 2002*, vol. 2470 of *LNCS*, p. 216-230, 2002.

Chapter 16

Multi-Point Constructive Search for Constraint Satisfaction: An Overview

A number of metaheuristic and evolutionary approaches to optimization make use of multiple "viewpoints" by maintaining a set of promising solutions that are used to guide search. Multi-point constructive search (MPCS) [BEC 05a] is an algorithm framework designed to allow constructive search to exploit multiple viewpoints. As with randomized restart techniques [GOM 98], MPCS consists of a series of tree searches limited by a resource bound, (e.g., number of fails). When the resource bound is reached, search restarts. The difference from randomized restart is that MPCS keeps track of a small set of "elite" solutions: the best solutions it has found. Search is restarted either from an empty solution, as in randomized restart, or from one of the elite solutions. Restarting from an elite solution entails performing fail-limited backtracking search starting from the guiding elite solution with a randomized variable ordering. While preliminary experiments indicated that MPCS can significantly out-perform both standard chronological backtracking and randomized restart on optimization and satisfaction problems [BEC 05a, BEC 05b], the one systematic study addressed the former. Here we provide a summary of a similar systematic study of MPCS for three different constraint satisfaction problems.

Chapter written by Ivan HECKMAN and J. Christopher BECK.

Algorithm 1: MPCS: Multi-point constructive search

```
   MPCS():
1  initialize elite solution set e
2  while termination criteria unmet do
3      if rand[0, 1) < p then
4          set fail bound, b
5          s := search(∅, b)
6          if s is better than worst(e) then
7              replace worst(e) with s
       else
8          r := randomly chosen element of e
9          set fail bound, b
10         s := search(r, b)
11         if s is better than r then
12             replace r with s
```

16.1. Background

Pseudocode for the basic MPCS algorithm is shown in Algorithm 1. The algorithm initializes a set, e, of elite solutions and then enters a while-loop. In each iteration, with probability p, search is started from an empty solution (line 5) or from a randomly selected elite solution (line 10). In the former case, if the best partial solution found during the search, s, is better than the worst elite solution, s replaces the worst elite solution. In the latter case, s replaces the starting elite solution, r, if s is better than r. Each individual search is limited by a maximum number of fails that can be incurred. The entire algorithm ends when the problem is solved or proved insoluble within one of the iterations, or when some overall bound on the computational resources (e.g., CPU time, number of fails) is reached.

As the MPCS framework has been presented previously [BEC 06], we only briefly describe the algorithm details here. The elite solutions can be initialized by any search technique. We use independent runs of standard chronological backtracking with a randomized heuristic and a bound on the maximum number of fails for each run. Each individual search (lines 5 and 10) terminates, returning the best solution encountered, when it reaches a specified fail-bound. Searching from an empty solution (line 5) simply means using any standard constructive search with a randomized heuristic and a bound on the number of fails. When searching from an elite solution (line 10), we create a search tree using any variable ordering heuristic and specifying that the value assigned to a variable is the one in the elite solution, provided it is still in the domain of the variable. Otherwise, any other value ordering heuristic can be used to choose a value. Formally, given a constraint satisfaction problem with n variables, a solution, s, is a set of variable assignments, $\{\langle V_1 = x_1\rangle, \langle V_2 = x_2\rangle, \ldots, \langle V_m = x_m\rangle\}, m \leq n$. When $m = n$, the solution is complete; when $m < n$, s is a partial solution. A search tree is created by asserting a series of choice points of the form: $\langle V_i = x\rangle \vee \langle V_i \neq x\rangle$ where V_i is a variable and x the value that is assigned to V_i. The variable ordering heuristic has complete freedom to choose a variable, V_i, to be assigned. If $\langle V_i = x_i\rangle \in s$ and $x_i \in dom(V_i)$, the choice point is made with $x = x_i$. Otherwise any value ordering heuristic can be used to choose $x \in dom(V_i)$. Finally, in an optimization context, where a solution can be defined as a complete and feasible assignment of all variables, solutions can be compared based on their corresponding objective value or cost. To adapt MPCS for constraint satisfaction, we relax the need for a complete assignment and compare partial solutions based on the number of assigned variables: the more assigned variables, the "better" the partial solution.

While the core search technique in MPCS is the heuristic tree search, there are two ways in which MPCS can be viewed as a hybrid of constructive and local search. First, MPCS is based on a fundamental idea of local search: the use of sub-optimal solutions to guide search. Second, and more crucially, a single iteration of MPCS starting from an elite solution is an implicit neighborhood search. Given a variable ordering and a resource limit, chronological backtracking is only able to search through a small subtree before the resource bound is reached. That subtree is a neighborhood of the starting solution. From this perspective, heuristic tree search is used to implement the evaluation of neighboring solutions.

16.2. Empirical study

The experiments were performed on three different satisfaction problems: quasi-group-with-holes, magic squares, and a satisfaction version of multi-dimensional knapsack where the cost is set to the known optimal [REF 04]. These problems were chosen because benchmark sets exist and randomized restart shows an interesting pattern of performance: performing well on quasi-group problems [GOM 02] and poorly on multi-dimensional knapsack problems [REF 04]. Magic square problems appear to bear similarities to quasi-group-with-holes. Our reason for focusing on problems with an interesting performance of randomized restart is that MPCS can be interpreted as a form of guided randomized restart and therefore we are interested in its behavior as randomized restart behavior varies. For further details of the problems and experiments performed see Heckman and Beck [HEC 06].

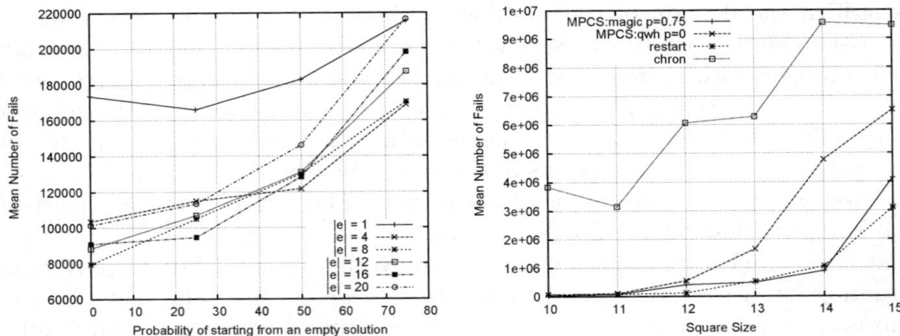

Figure 16.1. ***Left:*** *Mean fails to solve order-30 QWH problems for all values of* $|e|$ *and* p*.* ***Right:*** *Mean fails comparing different search techniques and MPCS on magic squares*

Our first set of experiments uses a set of order-30 QWH problems to examine the impact of the parameter settings. Due to space limitations only elite set size and the probability of searching from an empty solution are shown here. The results for varying both the number of elite solutions maintained $|e|$, and the probability p of starting from an empty solution, are shown in Figure 16.1 (Left). In contrast to previous results on scheduling problems [BEC 06], an elite size of one is worse than any of the other sizes. For any other setting of $|e|$ the best result is achieved by always guiding the search with an elite solution ($p = 0$) while the worst performance is achieved by always searching from an empty solution ($p = 1$).

Using the best parameter settings from the above QWH experiment, the results of comparing MPCS performance with standard chronological backtracking (*chron*) and randomized restart (*restart*) on an existing set of 24 QWH benchmarks instances are summarized in Table 16.1. MPCS achieves the lowest mean number of fails in 18 problem instances and the lowest mean run-time for 14. Furthermore, on 20 of the instances, all 10 runs of the algorithm found a solution within the global fail limit.[1] Exceptions to this pattern arise at higher orders and with no filled-in values. On such instances standard chronological search performed the best and MPCS the worst.

For magic squares, the performance of the MPCS algorithm is quite different. Results (not shown) find that varying the elite set size has little effect on the algorithm performance while varying the probability of starting from an

1. Each algorithm was run independently 10 times on each problem instance.

	chron	restart	MPCS-best
# best mean fails	3	3	18
# best mean time	10	2	14
# 100% solved	12	16	20

Table 16.1. *A summary of the QWH results on 24 benchmark problem instances*

empty solution has the opposite impact compared to QWH: $p = 1$ performs best, $p = 0$ worst.

Figure 16.1 (right) shows a comparison of other search algorithms with MPCS using the best settings found in the QWH (*MPCS:qwh*) and magic squares (*MPCS:magic*) experiments. For MPCS:magic the following parameters are used: $|e| = 8$, $p = 0.75$,[2] and the backtrack method is chronological. *Restart* and the MPCS variations are all better than chronological search however MPCS performs poorly compared to restart.

For the multi-dimensional knapsack problems, the best settings of $|e| = 8$ and $p = 0.5$ performed slightly better than other parameter settings. However, as shown in Table 16.2, both MPCS and randomized restart perform poorly in comparison to basic chronological search while MPCS performs about the same as restart.

	chron			restart			MPCS-qwh best			MPCS-knap best		
	%sol	fails	time	%sol	fails	time	%sol	fails	time	%sol	fails	time
mknap1-0	100	1	**0.0**	100	**0**	0.0	100	1	0.0	100	0	**0.0**
mknap1-2	100	26	0.0	100	**22**	**0.0**	100	24	0.0	100	23	**0.0**
mknap1-3	100	**363**	**0.0**	100	418	0.0	100	724	0.1	100	660	0.1
mknap1-4	100	**15551**	**1.1**	100	53938	4.8	100	30939	3.1	100	48219	4.4
mknap1-5	100	**2862059**	**148.3**	55	8141502	552.2	85	5035286	376.6	80	4156366	287.7
mknap1-6	0	10000000	**660.6**	0	10000000	843.7	0	10000000	938.5	0	10000000	857.8

Table 16.2. *Comparison of multi-dimensional knapsack results*

16.3. Conclusion

The goal of this work was to apply multi-point constructive search to constraint satisfaction problems. As the quasi-group-with-holes results indicate, MPCS is able to significantly out-perform both randomized restart and chronological backtracking on constraint satisfaction problems. The QWH results also showed that maintaining more than one elite solution improves search. This is an important result as previous scheduling experiments [BEC 06] found very good performance with $|e| = 1$.

---

2. The second best p is taken since it is not MPCS at $p = 1$.

However, when the results for the magic squares and multi-dimensional knapsack are considered, our conclusions are more nuanced. The significant change in the relative performance of randomized restart and MPCS when moving from the QWH to the magic squares problems is particularly interesting given the similarities in the problems. We hope that answering the reasons for this difference will lead us to an understanding of the reasons for MPCS performance. As a starting point, we believe it would be interesting to generate some magic-squares-with-holes problems to determine if the phase transition behavior of QWH is seen and to evaluate the performance of randomized restart and MPCS.

Multi-dimensional knapsack problems create a particular challenge for MPCS. From further examination of the knapsack runs, we speculate that MPCS gets poor heuristic guidance: there are many "solutions" with only the cost constraint broken and the elite set quickly stagnates to only those solutions.[3] Preliminary experiments using MPCS to solve the optimization version of the multi-dimensional knapsack problem show that it significantly out-performs all other techniques in finding the optimal solution implying that the actual cost of a solution provides a better criteria for inclusion in the elite set and much better heuristic guidance.

The types of problems that we experimented with revealed an interesting pattern. MPCS significantly out-performs chronological backtracking on the quasi-group-with-holes and magic squares problems but significantly underperforms on the multi-dimensional knapsack problems. Similarly, MPCS outperformed randomized restart on the quasi-group problems, performed slightly worse on the magic squares problems, and performed about the same on the multi-dimensional knapsack problems. This variety of results leads us to consider these three problem types as important for future work in understanding the reasons for the behavior of MPCS. If we can explain these varied results, we will be substantially closer to explaining the behavior of MPCS.

16.4. References

[BEC 05a] BECK J. C., "Multi-Point Constructive Search", *Proceedings of the Eleventh International Conference on Principles and Practice of Constraint Programming (CP05)*, 2005.

[BEC 05b] BECK J. C., "Multi-Point Constructive Search: Extended Remix", *Proceedings of the CP2005 Second International Workshop on Local Search Techniques for Constraint Satisfaction*, p. 17–31, 2005.

---

3. Recall that we made the multi-dimensional knapsack a satisfaction problem by requiring that the cost be equal to the (previously known) optimal cost.

[BEC 06] BECK J. C., "An Empirical Study of Multi-Point Constructive Search for Constraint-Based Scheduling", *Proceedings of the Sixteenth International Conference on Automated Planning and Scheduling (ICAPS'06)*, 2006.

[GOM 98] GOMES C. P., SELMAN B., KAUTZ H., "Boosting combinatorial search through randomization", *Proceedings of the Fifteenth National Conference on Artificial Intelligence (AAAI-98)*, p. 431–437, 1998.

[GOM 02] GOMES C., SHMOYS D., "Completing Quasigroups or Latin Squares: A Structured Graph Coloring Problem", *Proceedings of the Computational Symposium on Graph Coloring and Generalizations*, 2002.

[HEC 06] HECKMAN I., BECK J. C., "An Empirical Study of Multi-Point Constructive Search for Cosntraint Satisfaction", *Proceedings of the CP2006 Third International Workshop on Local Search Techniques for Constraint Satisfaction*, 2006.

[REF 04] REFALO P., "Impact-based Search Strategies for Constraint Programming", *Proceedings of the Tenth International Conference on the Principles and Practice of Constraint Programming (CP2004)*, p. 557–571, 2004.

Chapter 17

Boosting SLS Using Resolution

When stochastic local search (SLS) began to be seriously applied to propositional satisfiability problems, in the early 1990s, it seemed promising as the technique of choice wherever proofs of unsatisfiability or of strict optimality are not required. SLS brought within range problems previously thought inaccessible, solving randomly generated problems with thousands of variables. Unfortunately, despite many improvements in the algorithms, SLS solvers have generally failed to realize that early promise. For satisfiable random clause sets, they are indeed far more effective than any systematic reasoners, but on more realistic problems taken from practical applications they remain disappointing. By contrast, modern systematic solvers, based on clause learning or lookahead, can solve many highly structured problems with millions of clauses, in bounded model checking, for instance. The results of the International SAT competitions (http://www.satcompetition.org) are instructive: while SLS solvers occupied all the leading positions in the section on satisfiable random problems, the best solvers for hand-crafted and industrial problems were all clause learning DPLL variants. In outline, the explanation is clear: clause sets derived from real-world problems exhibit structure such as symmetries, variable dependencies and clustering. This enhances the effect of deduction at each node of the search tree by giving unit propagation more opportunities to "bite", while at the same time yielding detectable differences between clauses and between variables that assist the heuristics for choosing variables on which to branch. SLS solvers have no way to exploit this rich structure, because they have no propagation mechanisms and so do little or no reasoning.

Chapter written by ANBULAGAN, Duc Nghia PHAM, John SLANEY and Abdul SATTAR.

Combining systematic and local search, so that each may help the other, is a natural idea but hard to achieve: embedding either style of search in the other tends to incur prohibitive overheads. Consequently, there has been recent interest in the alternative of reasoning off-line, in a preprocessing phase, applying the SLS solver to the problem only after it has been refined, reduced or otherwise probed by some form of inference. Not all of the exploitable structure is detected by such a pre-search procedure, but the effects may nonetheless be enough to bring an important range of industrially relevant problems within the scope of SLS.

In previous work [ANB 05] we enhanced a number of contemporary SLS solvers with a resolution-based preprocessor. Our experiments were limited to a small problem set and only one preprocessor. Although powerful and complex preprocessors are important to the success of many systematic SAT solvers, to date there has been no systematic evaluation of the effects of these preprocessors on SAT solvers, especially on local search techniques. In the study, we attempt to address this deficiency by using problems, taken from SATLIB and SAT2005, known to be hard for SLS.

17.1. SLS solvers

Novelty [MCA 97], one of the best contemporary solvers in the WalkSAT family, may loop indefinitely due to its deterministic variable selection. To solve this problem, Hoos [HOO 99] added probabilistic random walks to Novelty, resulting in Novelty$^+$. As with other WalkSAT variants, the performance of Novelty$^+$ critically depends on the setting of its noise parameter, which controls the greediness of the search. AdaptNovelty$^+$ addresses this problem by adaptively tuning its noise level based on the detection of stagnation. Later, Li and Huang [LI 05] proposed a more diversified heuristic to weaken the determinism in Novelty: within a diversification probability, the recently least flipped variable is selected for the next move, otherwise the search performs as Novelty. They further improved this algorithm by reducing randomness: WalkSAT first randomly picks an unsatisfied clause and then flips a variable of this clause. Their solver g2wsat uses a sophisticated gradient-based greedy heuristic to choose a promising variable from among those of all unsatisfied clauses.

Recently, clause weighting-based SLS algorithms, PAWS [THO 04] and SAPS [HUT 02] most notably, have been very successfully applied to hard combinatorial SAT problems. These algorithms dynamically update the clause weights (or penalties) and hence modify the search landscape to effectively avoid or escape local minima during the search. The underlying weighting strategy of these solvers is based on two mechanisms: *increasing* (or *scaling*) and *reducing* (or *smoothing*). When the search encounters a local minimum, it increases the weights of the unsatisfied clauses, thus filling in the local minimum and forcing the search to move on. After a number of weight increases, the weights of all weighted clauses are reduced to forget about the high costs of violating clauses which are no longer helpful. These two mechanisms significantly increase the mobility of the search as well as helping to focus it on any "critical" clauses.

17.2. Preprocessors

SAT Preprocessors are introduced to exploit hidden structure in problems. They may either reduce or increase the size of the formula, as new clauses are deduced and old ones subsumed or otherwise removed. In the following empirical study, we consider five state of the art preprocessors:

1) 3-Resolution. This restricted resolution procedure, used in the systematic solver Satz [LI 97], calculates resolvents for all pairs of clauses of length ≤ 3. Any resolvent of length ≤ 3, is added to the formula. The procedure is repeated until saturation. Duplicates, subsumed clauses and tautologies are deleted.

2) 2-SIMPLIFY. This works on the implication graph of binary clauses in the formula, closing under transitive reduction, unit propagation and a restricted variant of hyper-resolution. The preprocessor was further enhanced by implementing subsumption and pure literal deduction rules [BRA 04].

3) HyPre. Like 2-SIMPLIFY, HyPre [BAC 04] reasons with binary clauses. It uses hyper-resolution to infer new binary clauses avoiding the space explosion of computing a full transitive closure. Unit and equality reductions are incrementally applied to infer more binary clauses, making the preprocessor more effective. It is more general and powerful than 2-SIMPLIFY.

4) NiVER. Variable Elimination Resolution (VER), used in the original Davis-Putnam (DP) procedure, replaces all clauses containing a chosen variable with their resolvents. Unfortunately, its space complexity is exponential. Non-increasing VER (NiVER) [SUB 05] restricts the variable elimination to the case in which there is no increase in the number of literals after elimination.

5) SatELite. This extends NiVER with a Variable Elimination by Substitution rule. Several additions including subsumption detection and improved data structures further improve performance in both space and time [EÉN 05]. SatELiteGTI (a combination of SatELite preprocessor with MiniSAT solver) dominated the SAT2005 competition on the crafted and industrial problem categories.

17.3. Empirical evaluation

We investigated the effect of preprocessing on SLS for 64 problem instances drawn from 12 classes of problems such as random 3-SAT, quasi-group existence and a wide range of industrial problems including job-shop scheduling, parity learning, and planning. Each of the five preprocessors was applied to each problem instance, resulting in 320 reduced problem instances. Each of these was solved 100 times with different random number seeds by each of the four SLS solvers, with a time limit of 1200 seconds on a Linux Pentium IV computer with 3.0GHz CPU and 1GB RAM.

All of the preprocessors reduce the size, in variables, clauses or literals, of most of the problems. In the case of random 3-SAT, the effect is small. No one preprocessor is best or worst across the whole range of problem classes, though for each problem class (except 3-SAT) some preprocessors are more effective than others. Overall, the most effective preprocessors appear to be HyPre, SatELite and 2-SIMPLIFY. This finding has to be set against the runtime cost – all three can be expensive in certain cases – and of course it is another question whether reductions in problem size translate into improvements in the behavior of SLS solvers.

17.3.1. *Clause weighting versus random walk*

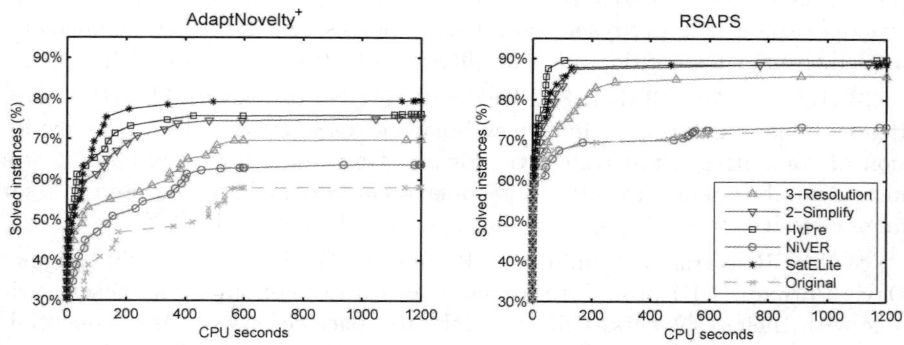

Figure 17.1. *Runtime performance of resolution-enhanced SLS solvers*

Figure 17.1 shows the runtime distributions (RTDs) of AdaptNovelty$^+$ and RSAPS over all industrial problems except bmc and vpn. The magnitude of improvement of solvers clearly depends on the heuristics employed in the solvers. For WalkSAT family solvers, e.g. AdaptNovelty$^+$, SatELite is the promising choice and clearly outperforms the second option, HyPre. However, this pattern is reversed when applied to the clause weighting solver RSAPS. The improvement provided by 2-SIMPLIFY to RSAPS is also very competitive to SatELite. Overall, the contribution of 3-Resolution and NiVER to SLS are smaller and less reliable than those of SatELite, HyPre and 2-SIMPLIFY. The poor performance of NiVER is expected, as it provides the least simplification on structured problem instances in our study.

17.3.2. *Matching preprocessors to solver-problem pairs*

Solvers\Problems	ais	bw	e*ddr	ferry	log	par16	qg	ssa	vmpc	3sat
AdaptNovelty$^+$	Sat	Sat	3-Res	Sat	HyP	Sat	HyP	Sat	HyP	NiV
g2wsat	Sat	HyP	Sat	Sat	HyP	Sat	HyP	Sat	Sat	Sat
PAWS_{10}	2-SIM	HyP	Sat	HyP	HyP	Sat	HyP	Sat	2-SIM	3-Res
RSAPS	HyP	HyP	Sat	HyP	HyP	Sat	HyP	Sat	2-SIM	n/a

Table 17.1. *The best preprocessor for SLS-problem pair*

In Table 17.1, where PAWS_{10} is PAWS with the parameter fixed to 10 and RSAPS is the reactive version of SAPS, we note the preprocessor that provides the most improvement on average for each solver on each benchmark problem domain. While there is no absolute "winner" among the preprocessors, it is clear that for most of the problem classes we examined, and for most of the solvers, SatELite is a good choice. This is perhaps not too surprising given that it is the most complex preprocessor. However, due to its novel implementation, SatELite records competitive running times in comparison with other preprocessors. HyPre is also valuable in most cases: it is the preferable choice of all four solvers to exploit the structures of the planning and quasi-group existence problems. It is worth noting that there is no uniform winner for the random 3-SAT problems. Indeed, each of the three solvers prefers a different preprocessor.

17.3.3. *Multiple preprocessing and preprocessor ordering*

Instances	Preprocessor	#Vars/#Cls/#Lits	Ptime	Succ. rate	CPU Time median	CPU Time mean	Flips median	Flips mean
ferry8-ks99i-4005	origin	2547/32525/66425	n/a	42	1, 200.00	910.38	302, 651, 507	229, 727, 514
	SatELite	1696/31589/74007	0.41	100	44.96	58.65	7, 563, 160	9, 812, 123
	HyPre	2473/48120/97601	0.29	100	9.50	19.61	1, 629, 417	3, 401, 913
	HyPre & Sat	1700/43296/116045	1.05	100	5.19	10.86	1, 077, 364	2, 264, 998
	Sat & HyPre	1680/92321/194966	0.90	100	2.23	3.62	252, 778	407, 258
par16-4	origin	1015/3324/8844	n/a	4	600.00	587.27	273, 700, 514	256, 388, 273
	HyPre	324/1352/3874	0.01	100	10.14	13.42	5, 230, 084	6, 833, 312
	SatELite	210/1201/4189	0.05	100	5.25	7.33	2, 230, 524	3, 153, 928
	Sat & HyPre	210/1210/4207	0.05	100	4.73	6.29	1, 987, 638	2, 655, 296
	HyPre & Sat	198/1232/4352	0.04	100	1.86	2.80	1, 333, 372	1, 995, 865

Table 17.2. *RSAPS performance on ferry planning and par16-4 instances*

The preprocessors in our study sometimes show quite different behavior on the same problem. One may increase the size of a given formula, while another decreases the number of clauses or number of variables or number of literals. It therefore seems reasonable to consider running multiple preprocessors on a hard formula before solving the preprocessed formula using an SLS solver. Table 17.2 shows preliminary results from an experiment with just one solver and two preprocessors on just two problems. We compare the effects of running each preprocessor separately, then of running SatELite after HyPre, and finally of running SatELite followed by HyPre.

These preliminary results show that the performance of an SLS solver such as RSAPS can be improved by several orders of magnitude, using multiple preprocessors and by selecting the right order of preprocessors. However, what the right combination is, as well as what the right order of preprocessors is remain unclear to us. This opens the way to a yet more complex study of preprocessor combinations and their use with different SLS and systematic solvers.

17.4. Conclusion

It emerges that while all the examined solvers do indeed benefit from preprocessing, the effect of each preprocessor is almost uniform across solvers and across problems. On most problems with a realistic structure, the right choice of preprocessor, combined with the right choice of solver, results in a performance superior to any previously achieved. However, what the right choice is requires an extensive empirical study to answer. For any of the solvers, the wrong preprocessor can make things worse. There is an interplay between problem structure (itself a poorly understood notion), preprocessor inference mechanism and SLS method.

17.5. References

[ANB 05] ANBULAGAN, PHAM D. N., SLANEY J., SATTAR A., "Old Resolution Meets Modern SLS", *Proceedings of 20th AAAI*, p. 354–359, 2005.

[BAC 04] BACCHUS F., WINTER J., "Effective Preprocessing with Hyper-Resolution and Equality Reduction", *Revised Selected Papers of SAT 2003, LNCS 2919 Springer*, p. 341–355, 2004.

[BRA 04] BRAFMAN R. I., "A Simplifier for Propositional Formulas with Many Binary Clauses", *IEEE Transactions on Systems, Man, and Cybernetics, Part B*, vol. 34, num. 1, p. 52–59, 2004.

[EÉN 05] EÉN N., BIERE A., "Effective Preprocessing in SAT through Variable and Clause Elimination", *Proceedings of 8th SAT, LNCS Springer*, 2005.

[HOO 99] HOOS H. H., "On the Run-time Behaviour of Stochastic Local Search Algorithms for SAT", *Proceedings of 16th AAAI*, p. 661–666, 1999.

[HUT 02] HUTTER F., TOMPKINS D. A. D., HOOS H. H., "Scaling and Probabilistic Smoothing: Efficient Dynamic Local Search for SAT", *Proceedings of 8th CP*, p. 233–248, 2002.

[LI 97] LI C. M., ANBULAGAN, "Look-Ahead Versus Look-Back for Satisfiability Problems", *Proceedings of 3rd CP*, p. 341–355, 1997.

[LI 05] LI C. M., HUANG W. Q., "Diversification and Determinism in Local Search for Satisfiability", *Proceedings of 8th SAT, LNCS Springer*, 2005.

[MCA 97] MCALLESTER D. A., SELMAN B., KAUTZ H. A., "Evidence for Invariants in Local Search", *Proceedings of 14th AAAI*, p. 321–326, 1997.

[SUB 05] SUBBARAYAN S., PRADHAN D. K., "NiVER: Non-Increasing Variable Elimination Resolution for Preprocessing SAT Instances", *Revised Selected Papers of SAT 2004, LNCS 3542 Springer*, p. 276–291, 2005.

[THO 04] THORNTON J., PHAM D. N., BAIN S., FERREIRA JR. V., "Additive Versus Multiplicative Clause Weighting for SAT", *Proceedings of 19th AAAI*, p. 191–196, 2004.

Chapter 18

Growing COMET

This chapter describes how COMET has grown since its inception, using a few abstractions that naturally combine to provide a rich modeling and search environment.[1]

18.1. Constraint-based local search

Local search is one of the main paradigms for solving hard combinatorial optimization problems and is often orthogonal and synergetic with other approaches such as constraint and integer programming. Local search algorithms approach the solving of combinatorial optimization problems by moving from solution to solution until a feasible solution or a high-quality solution is found. These algorithms typically maintain sophisticated data structures to evaluate or to propagate the effect of local moves quickly, and may rely on complex moves and neighborhoods.

Constraint-based local search is the idea of performing local search on high-level optimization models and is captured by the slogan

Local Search = Model + Search.

Chapter written by Pascal VAN HENTENRYCK and Laurent MICHEL.

1. The title of this chapter was inspired by an excellent article by Guy Steele.

Constraint-based local search thus transfers the expressiveness, flexibility, and compositionality of constraint programming to a fundamentally different computational paradigm. The goal of the COMET project is to study how to realize this vision.

18.2. COMET

The COMET system is centered around an object-oriented programming language with modeling and control abstractions to support advanced local search [VAN 05a]. The project started in 2001 and one of its goals was to design a language that could grow smoothly in order to solve increasingly complex problems and to accommodate novel technologies, algorithms, and abstractions as they are discovered. More precisely, the COMET system was based on a few design principles:

1) supporting a small number of basic concepts that can be composed naturally to provide complex functionalities;

2) building higher-level abstractions on top of the basic concepts using source-to-source transformations, thus reducing the implementation overhead;

3) allowing users to grow the language themselves by exposing the computational model through carefully chosen abstractions.

Examples of basic concepts in COMET include invariants [MIC 00], closures, and continuations. Higher-level abstractions include differentiable objects (constraints and objectives) [MIC 02], parallel loops [MIC 05, MIC 06], and nondeterministic instructions [VAN 05b]. In COMET, programmers can implement their own constraints and objectives in the language itself and may use controllers to implement their own search strategies and to manage their parallel and distributed executions efficiently. The abstractions in COMET are chosen and implemented to impose no runtime overhead when not used and to provide a reasonable tradeoff between their generality and efficiency.

Compositionality, reuse, and extensibility are the three main benefits of the COMET architecture. COMET makes it easy to combine constraints and objectives into more complex ones, to compose heterogenous neighborhoods, and to integrate modeling, search, and animation components. It is also possible to implement generic search procedures that can be applied to a variety of models. Finally, COMET provides multiple abstractions layers that greatly facilitate the growth of the language.

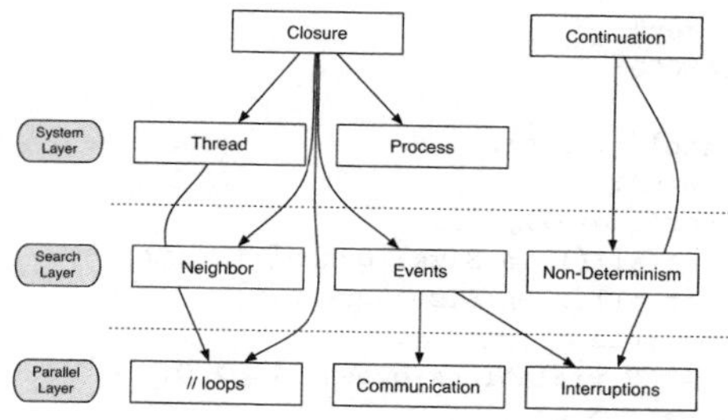

Figure 18.1. *The modeling abstractions of* COMET

18.3. Modeling

Figure 18.1 depicts (some of) the modeling abstractions of COMET that are mostly organized in three levels. The most basic abstractions are the concepts of invariants and differentiable objects. Once these are available, it becomes natural to introduce constraint-based combinators [VAN 05c] to combine constraints and objectives, as well as the concept of differentiable invariants [VAN 06]. These two layers provide significant help to programmers to implement their own constraints and objectives.

An invariant maintains the value of an expression under changes to its variables. Invariants can be defined over numerical, set, or graph variables. They specify which expression to maintain, not how to maintain it. Differentiable objects, the counterpart of global constraints for constraint-based local search, capture substructures that arise in many applications. Constraints and objectives are both differentiable objects. An objective not only maintains the value of an expression; it also provides variable gradients (how much the objective can increase or decrease by changing a specific variable) and differentiability (how much the objective changes for local moves). A constraint provides similar functionalities regarding its violations.

Figure 18.2 illustrates these concepts on the simple queens problem. Lines 1–4 specify the data and decision variables (line 4). Lines 5–8 specify the three *alldifferent* constraints that capture substructures of the applications. Lines 9-13 depict the search procedure which uses an invariant (line 9) to maintain the set of queens in conflict. The search selects a variable in the conflict set, selects the value for the selected queens minimizing the total number of violation, and assigns the value to the queens. Observe that the model (lines 1–8) is completely separated from the search (lines 9–13) textually, although they have complex interactions operationally. Indeed, line 12 queries the constraint system to

```
1.   include "LocalSolver";
2.   range Size = 1..65000;
3.   LocalSolver m();
4.   var{int} queen[Size](m,Size);
5.   ConstraintSystem S(m);
6.   S.post(alldifferent(queen));
7.   S.post(alldifferent(all(i in Size) queen[i] + i));
8.   S.post(alldifferent(all(i in Size) queen[i] - i));
9.   var{set{int}} Conflicts <-
        setof(i in Size) S.violations(queen[i]) > 0;
10.  while (S.violations() > 0)
11.     select(q in Conflicts)
12.        selectMin(v in Size)(S.getAssignDelta(queen[q],v))
13.           queen[q] := v;
```

Figure 18.2. *A program for the queens problem*

```
interface Objective {
   var{int} evaluation();
   var{int} increase(var{int} x);
   var{int} decrease(var{int} x);
   int getAssignDelta(var{int} x,int v);
   int getSwapDelta(var{int} x,var{int} y);
   int getAssignDelta(var{int}[] x,var[] v);
   var{int}[] getVariables();
}
```

Figure 18.3. *The interface of objective functions*

assess the impact of assigning value `v` to variable `queen[q]`, while line 13 must update the violations of all constraints due to the new assignment. Note also that the search can be made entirely generic, since it does not use any knowledge of the model but simply queries the constraint system as a whole.

This compositionality and clean separation of concerns is a consequence of the interface implemented by differentiable objects. The interface for objective functions is depicted in Figure 18.3. The interface for constraints is similar: there is no method `increase` (since it does not make sense to query how much a variable can increase the violations) and the `decrease` method is renamed `violations` which is more intuitive.

COMET uses invariants and differentiable objects to offer higher-level abstractions such as constraint-based combinators and differentiable invariables.

```
1. var{int} boat[Guests,Periods](m,Hosts);
2. ConstraintSystem S(m);
3. forall(g in Guests)
4.    S.post(2*alldifferent(all(p in Periods) boat[g,p]));
5. forall(p in Periods)
6.    S.post(2*knapsack(all(g in Guests) boat[g,p],crew,cap));
7. forall(i in Guests, j in Guests :  j > i)
8.    S.post(atmost(1,all(p in Periods)(boat[i,p]==boat[j,p])<=1);
```

Figure 18.4. *The model for the progressive party problem*

```
1.    var{int} S[1..n](m,{-1,1});
2.    ObjectiveExpr Obj =
         sum(k in 1..n-1) (sum(i in 1..n-k) x[i]*x[i+k])^2);
```

Figure 18.5. *The model for the low autocorrelation binary sequences*

Constraint-based combinators combine existing differentiable objects to produce more complex ones using traditional operators such as disjunctions, cardinalities, and weights. Figure 18.4 illustrates constraint-based combinators on the progressive party problem. Lines 4 and 6 show how to weight constraints, while line 8 depicts a cardinality constraint. Differentiable invariants automatically lift invariants into differentiable objects. Figure 18.5 shows a simple model for autocorrelation binary sequences. This model can be solved with tabu search, producing one of the most effective algorithms for this problem. The key functionality is that the expression (right side of line 2) is transformed into an objective function implementing the interface in Figure 18.3.

18.4. Search

Figure 18.6 depicts the search abstractions of COMET that are mostly organized into three layers. The system layer provides low-level abstractions such as closures and continuations, threads and processes. The search layer offers rich abstractions for implementing search procedures, including events, nondeterminism, and neighbors [VAN 05d, VAN 05b]. The parallel layer provides abstractions for parallel and distributed abstractions [MIC 05, MIC 06]. Space restrictions do not permit a detailed description of all these functionalities. Observe again how higher-level abstractions are naturally built from lower-level abstractions and how they encourage compositionality and separations of concerns. Figure 18.7 illustrates these benefits on the progressive party problem. It features an heterogenous neighborhood which selects the variable with the

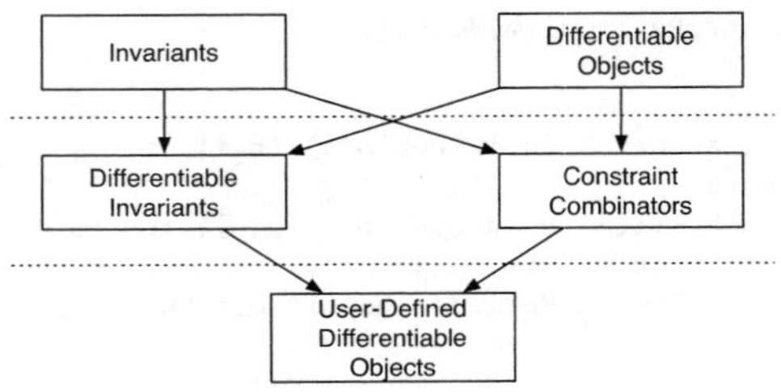

Figure 18.6. *Control abstractions of* COMET

```
1. MinNeighborSelector N();
2. while (S.violations() > 0) {
3.   selectMax(g in Guests, p in Periods)(S.violations(boat[g,p]))
4.     selectMin(h in Hosts,d=S.getAssignDelta(boat[g,p],h))(d)
5.       neighbor(d,N)
6.         boat[g,p] := h;
7.     selectMin(g1 in Guests,d=S.getSwapDelta(boat[g,p],boat[g1,p]))(d)
8.       neighbor(d,N)
9.         boat[g,p] :=: boat[g1,p];
10.  if (N.hasMove()) call(N.getMove()); }
```

Figure 18.7. *Search for the progressive party problem*

most violations (line 3) and explores two kinds of moves: those assigning a new value to the selected variable (lines 4–6) and those swapping the selected variable with another variable from the same period (line 7–9). The second move is motivated by the knapsack constraints which are best addressed by swaps than by sequences of assignments. The `neighbor` construct (lines 5–6 and lines 9–10) specifies, but does not execute, the moves. Its body (line 5 and line 9) is a closure, since it will be executed later on (line 10) or not at all. The neighbor selector declared in line 1 keeps the best neighbor, which is executed in line 10. The above code omits the management of the tabu-list for simplicity. Observe the elegance and simplicity of defining an heterogenous neighborhood and the possibilities for extensibility.

18.5. References

[MIC 00] MICHEL L., VAN HENTENRYCK P. Localizer *Constraints* 5: 41-82, 2000 – preliminary version in CP'97.

[MIC 02] MICHEL L., VAN HENTENRYCK P. A Constraint-Based Architecture for Local Search, *17th Annual ACM Conference on Object-Oriented Programming, Systems, Languages, and Applications (OOPSLA'2002)* Seattle, Wa, 2002

[MIC 05] MICHEL L., VAN HENTENRYCK P. Parallel Local Search in Comet *Proceedings of the 11th International Conference on Constraint Programming (CP-2005)* Stiges, Spain, September 2005.

[MIC 06] MICHEL L., SEE A., VAN HENTENRYCK, P. Distributed Constraint-Based Local Search *Proceedings of the 12th International Conference on Principles and Practice of Constraint Programming (CP'06)*, Nantes, France, September 2006.

[VAN 05a] VAN HENTENRYCK P., MICHEL L. *Constraint-Based Local Search.* The MIT Press, Cambridge, MA, 2005.

[VAN 05b] VAN HENTENRYCK P., MICHEL L. Nondeterministic Control for Hybrid Search. *Constraints,* forthcoming – preliminary version in CP'AI'OR'05.

[VAN 05c] VAN HENTENRYCK P., MICHEL L., LIU, L. Constraint-Based Combinators for Local Search *Constraints*, 10(4), 363–384, October 2005 – preliminary version in CP'04.

[VAN 05d] VAN HENTENRYCK P., MICHEL L. Control Abstractions for Local Search. *Constraints*, 10(2), 137–157, April 2005 – preliminary version in CP'03.

[VAN 06] VAN HENTENRYCK P., MICHEL L. Differentiable Invariants *Proceedings of the 12th International Conference on Principles and Practice of Constraint Programming (CP'06)*, Nantes, France, September 2006.

PART VI

Preferences and Soft Constraints

Edited by Thomas SCHIEX

Introduction

Constraints either separate feasible decisions from infeasible ones or capture the possible states of the world. In constraint networks, this is done in a concise and modular ways, by expressing information on partial decisions, using constraints involving few variables. The central problem is then to find an assignment of variables satisfying every constraint, an NP-hard problem. Often, beyond the crisp separation between feasible and unfeasible decisions, or between possible and impossible situations, more gradual information exists. Decisions may be more or less desirable and situations may be more or less likely to occur. Modeling such information using hard constraints may easily lead to "over-constrained" problems (without solutions).

Soft constraint frameworks [MES 06] have been defined to enable such gradual information to be captured. After several years of alternative definitions, two algebraic, related frameworks have been defined: the semiring constraint network [BIS 97] and the valued constraint network [SCH 95] formalisms. Very simply, these formalisms replace the essential notion of relations (underlying constraints) by the notion of cost functions (costs being combined using a dedicated operator, not necessarily addition). The resulting frameworks simply and directly generalize constraint networks since relations are just functions mapping partial decisions (tuples) to boolean costs (the relation is either satisfied or not). These generalizations enable information on forbidden decisions to be elegantly combined with information on authorized, but more or less undesirable decisions. This approach is very general, enabling basic problems to be captured simply, such as weighted MaxSat [LAR 05], most probable explanation in Bayesian nets, a variety of graph optimization problems (maximum clique,etc.) but also more practical problems from bioinformatics [GIV 05], combinatorial auctions, planning [COO 06] or resource allocation for example. An alternative view, the reified costs approach [PET 00], considers cost functions as specific "functional" relations involving one extra variable representing the cost. This enables existing constraint programming langages to be reused directly.

However, most existing results use the first cost function-based approach which enables costs and cost functions to be manipulated simply and explicitly. An important line of research is to generalize properties and algorithms defined on relations to cost functions: this includes inference mechanisms (local consistency, variable elimination) but also heuristics for variable and value selection, exploitation of specific constraint properties, tractable langages, etc. Much has been done along this line, with important theoretical and practical results, and much remains to be done[1]. The two papers selected use this cost function approach. The first shows how existing weighted inference mechanisms can be described at a very fine level using the signed MaxSAT formalism. The second shows how to exploit the structure of the problem solved to speed up the resolution.

References

[BIS 97] BISTARELLI S., MONTANARI U., ROSSI F., "Semiring-based Constraint Solving and Optimization", *Journal of the ACM*, vol. 44, num. 2, p. 201–236, 1997.

[COO 06] COOPER M., CUSSAT-BLANC S., ROQUEMAUREL M. D., RÉGNIER P., "Soft Arc Consistency Applied to Optimal Planning", *Proc. of CP'06*, num. 4204 LNCS, Nantes, France, Springer, p. 680-684, 2006.

[GIV 05] DE GIVRY S., PALHIERE I., VITEZICA Z., SCHIEX T., "Mendelian Error Detection in Complex Pedigree using Weighted Constraint Satisfaction Techniques", *Proc. of ICLP-05 workshop on Constraint Based Methods for Bioinformatics*, Sitges, Spain, 2005.

[LAR 05] LARROSA J., HERAS F., "Resolution in Max-SAT and its Relation to Local Consistency in Weighted CSPs", *Proc. of the 19th IJCAI*, p. 193-198, 2005.

[MES 06] MESEGUER P., ROSSI F., SCHIEX T., "Soft Constraints Processing", *Handbook of Constraint Programming*, Chapter 9, Elsevier, 2006.

[PET 00] PETIT T., RÉGIN J., BESSIÈRE C., "Meta Constraints on Violations for Over Constrained Problems", *Proceedings of IEEE ICTAI'2000*, p. 358–365, 2000.

[SCH 95] SCHIEX T., FARGIER H., VERFAILLIE G., "Valued Constraint Satisfaction Problems: Hard and Easy Problems", *Proc. of the 14th IJCAI*, p. 631-637, 1995.

1. The soft constraint wiki site (http://carlit.toulouse.inra.fr/cgi-bin/awki.cgi/SoftCSP) gathers implementations and benchmarks in a standardized format.

Chapter 19

The Logic Behind Weighted CSP

The weighted constraint satisfaction problem (WCSP) is a well-known soft constraint framework for modeling over-constrained problems with practical applications in domains such as resource allocation, combinatorial auctions and bioinformatics. WCSP is an optimization version of the CSP framework in which constraints are extended by associating *costs* with tuples. Solving a WCSP instance, which is NP-hard, consists of finding a complete assignment of minimal cost.

Global consistency WCSP algorithms such as bucket elimination [DEC 99] solve WCSP instances without search. They obtain an optimal solution by applying, to the original instance, transformations that preserve cost distributions. On the other hand, WCSP algorithms such as PFC [FRE 92], PFC-MRDAC [LAR 96], Russian Doll Search [VER 96], MAC* [LAR 04], MFDAC* [LAR 03], and MEDAC* [GIV 05] perform a systematic search in the space of all possible assignments following a branch and bound schema. They differ in the method of computing a lower bound at each node of the proof tree to prune some parts of the search space. Modern algorithms such as MAC*, MFDAC* and MEDAC* enforce some extension of arc consistency (AC) to WCSP – soft AC (AC*), full directional AC (FDAC*) or existential directional AC (EDAC*)– when computing that lower bound.

In this chapter we relate ideas from three different research communities – multiple-valued logic, satisfiability and constraint processing – with the aim of

Chapter written by Carlos Ansótegui, María L. Bonet, Jordi Levy and Felip Manyà.

describing the underlying logic of WCSP. Firstly, we define an encoding, called *signed encoding*, that transforms any WCSP instance to a *Signed Max-SAT* instance, where Signed Max-SAT is the Max-SAT problem of the multiple-valued clausal forms known as signed CNF formulae. Secondly, we define a complete resolution calculus for solving Signed Max-SAT. Thirdly, we devise an exact algorithm for solving WCSP from the completeness proof of the resolution calculus. Fourth, we define several sound inference rules for Signed Max-SAT that enforce some known arc consistency properties when applied to the signed encoding of any binary WCSP instance.

The connection between recent results for Boolean Max-SAT [BON 06] and the existing results for WCSP is established via the logic of signed CNF formulae. Signed CNF formulae are clausal forms based on a generalized notion of a literal, called a *signed literal*. A signed literal is an expression of the form $S{:}p$, where p is a propositional variable and S, its *sign*, is a subset of a domain N. The informal meaning of $S{:}p$ is "p takes one of the values in S". Signed CNF formulae have their origin in the community of automated theorem proving in many-valued logics, where they are used as a generic and flexible language for representing many-valued interpretations [BEC 00, HÄH 01]. Nevertheless, in this chapter we are interested in their use as a constraint programming language between CSP and SAT that offers a good trade-off between expressivity and efficiency [ANS 03, ANS 04, BÉJ 01, BEC 99].

The structure of the chapter is as follows. Section 19.1 contains preliminary definitions and the signed encoding. Section 19.2 defines the inference rule for signed Max-SAT and proves its soundness and completeness. Section 19.3 describes an exact algorithm for solving weighted CSP. Section 19.4 defines four derived rules that enforce soft local consistency properties. Finally, section 19.5 presents the conclusions of our work.

19.1. Preliminaries

In this section we define the syntax and semantics of signed CNF formulae, the concept of WCSP, and a reduction from WCSP to signed Max-SAT.

DEFINITION 19.1.– *A* truth value set, *or* domain, *N is a non-empty finite set $\{i_1, i_2, \ldots, i_n\}$ where n denotes its cardinality. A* sign *is a subset $S \subseteq N$ of truth values. A* signed literal *is an expression of the form $S{:}p$, where S is a sign and p is a propositional variable. The* complement *of a signed literal l of the form $S{:}p$, denoted by $\overline{l}$, is $\overline{S}{:}p = (N \setminus S){:}p$. A* signed clause *is a disjunction of signed literals. A* signed CNF formula *is a* multiset *of signed clauses.*

DEFINITION 19.2.– *An* assignment *for a signed CNF formula is a mapping that assigns to every propositional variable an element of the truth value set.*

An assignment I satisfies *a signed literal $S{:}p$ if, and only if, $I(p) \in S$,* satisfies *a signed clause C if, and only if, it satisfies at least one of the signed literals in C, and* satisfies *a signed CNF formula Γ if, and only if, it satisfies all clauses in Γ. A signed CNF formula is* satisfiable *if, and only if, it is satisfied by at least one assignment; otherwise it is* unsatisfiable.

DEFINITION 19.3.– *The* signed Max-SAT problem *for a signed CNF formula consists of finding an assignment that minimizes the number of falsified signed clauses.*

DEFINITION 19.4.– *A* constraint satisfaction problem (CSP) *instance is defined as a triple $\langle X, D, C\rangle$, where $X = \{x_1, \ldots, x_n\}$ is a set of variables, $D = \{d(x_1), \ldots, d(x_n)\}$ is a set of domains containing the values the variables may take, and $C = \{C_1, \ldots, C_m\}$ is a set of constraints. Each constraint $C_i = \langle S_i, R_i\rangle$ is defined as a relation R_i over a subset of variables $S_i = \{x_{i_1}, \ldots, x_{i_k}\}$, called the* constraint scope. *The relation R_i may be represented extensionally as a subset of the Cartesian product $d(x_{i_1}) \times \cdots \times d(x_{i_k})$.*

DEFINITION 19.5.– *An* assignment *v for a CSP instance $\langle X, D, C\rangle$ is a mapping that assigns to every variable $x_i \in X$ an element $v(x_i) \in d(x_i)$. An assignment v satisfies a constraint $\langle\{x_{i_1}, \ldots, x_{i_k}\}, R_i\rangle \in C$ if, and only if, $\langle v(x_{i_1}), \ldots, v(x_{i_k})\rangle \in R_i$.*

DEFINITION 19.6.– *A* weighted CSP (WCSP) *instance is defined as a triple $\langle X, D, C\rangle$, where X and D are variables and domains as in CSP. A constraint C_i is now defined as a pair $\langle S_i, f_i\rangle$, where $S_i = \{x_{i_1}, \ldots, x_{i_k}\}$ is the constraint scope and $f_i : d(x_{i_1}) \times \cdots \times d(x_{i_k}) \to \mathbb{N}$ is a* cost function. *The cost of a constraint C_i induced by an assignment v in which the variables of $S_i = \{x_{i_1}, \ldots, x_{i_k}\}$ take values $b_{i_1}, \ldots, b_{i_k}$ is $f_i(b_{i_1}, \ldots, b_{i_k})$. An optimal solution to a WCSP instance is a complete assignment in which the sum of the costs of the constraints is minimal.*

DEFINITION 19.7.– *The weighted constraint satisfaction problem (WCSP) for a WCSP instance consists of finding an optimal solution for that instance.*

DEFINITION 19.8.– *The* signed encoding *of a WCSP instance $\langle X, D, C\rangle$ is the signed CNF formula over the domain $N = \bigcup_{x_i \in D} d(x_i)$ that contains for every possible tuple $\langle b_{i_1}, \ldots, b_{i_k}\rangle \in d(x_{i_1}) \times \cdots \times d(x_{i_k})$ of every constraint $\langle\{x_{i_1}, \ldots, x_{i_k}\}, f_i\rangle \in C$, $f_i(b_{i_1}, \ldots, b_{i_k})$ copies of the signed clause:*

$$\overline{\{b_{i_1}\}}{:}x_{i_1} \vee \cdots \vee \overline{\{b_{i_k}\}}{:}x_{i_k}.$$

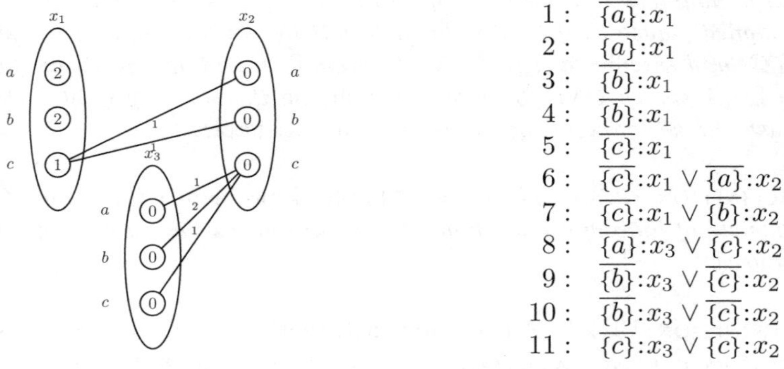

x_1
x_2
x_3
a
b
c
1 : $\overline{\{a\}}{:}x_1$
2 : $\overline{\{a\}}{:}x_1$
3 : $\overline{\{b\}}{:}x_1$
4 : $\overline{\{b\}}{:}x_1$
5 : $\overline{\{c\}}{:}x_1$
6 : $\overline{\{c\}}{:}x_1 \vee \overline{\{a\}}{:}x_2$
7 : $\overline{\{c\}}{:}x_1 \vee \overline{\{b\}}{:}x_2$
8 : $\overline{\{a\}}{:}x_3 \vee \overline{\{c\}}{:}x_2$
9 : $\overline{\{b\}}{:}x_3 \vee \overline{\{c\}}{:}x_2$
10 : $\overline{\{b\}}{:}x_3 \vee \overline{\{c\}}{:}x_2$
11 : $\overline{\{c\}}{:}x_3 \vee \overline{\{c\}}{:}x_2$

Figure 19.1. *A WCSP instance and its signed encoding*

An alternative encoding is to consider signed clauses with weights instead of allowing multiple copies of a clause. For the sake of clarity we use unweighted clauses. Nevertheless, any efficient implementation of the algorithms proposed should deal with weighted clauses. The extension of our theoretical results to weighted clauses is straightforward.

PROPOSITION 19.1.– *Solving a WCSP instance P is equivalent to solving the signed Max-SAT problem of its signed encoding; i.e., the optimal cost of P coincides with the minimal number of unsatisfied signed clauses of the signed encoding of P.*

PROOF.– *For every combination of values to the variables of the scope of a constraint $C_i = \langle S_i, f_i \rangle$, the signed encoding contains as many clauses as the cost associated with that combination. If an assignment of the signed encoding restricted to the variables of S_i coincides with a combination of C_i with cost 0, then all the clauses of the signed encoding introduced by C_i are satisfied because there is no clause forbidding that combination. If an assignment of the signed encoding restricted to the variables of S_i coincides with a combination $\langle b_{i_1}, \dots, b_{i_k} \rangle$ of C_i with cost u, where $u > 0$, then, by construction of the signed encoding, only the u clauses of the form $\overline{\{b_{i_1}\}}{:}x_{i_1} \vee \cdots \vee \overline{\{b_{i_k}\}}{:}x_{i_k}$ are falsified among the clauses introduced by C_i.*

EXAMPLE.– Figure 19.1 shows a WCSP instance $\langle X, D, C \rangle$ and its signed encoding. The WCSP has the set of variables $X = \{x_1, x_2, x_3\}$ with domains $d(x_1) = d(x_2) = d(x_3) = \{a, b, c\}$. There is a binary constraint between variables x_1 and x_2, a binary constraint between variables x_2 and x_3, and a unary constraint for every variable. Unary costs are depicted inside small circles. Binary costs are depicted as labeled edges connecting the corresponding pair of values. The label of each edge is the corresponding cost. If two values are not connected, the binary cost between them is 0. In this instance, the optimal cost is 2.

19.2. The inference rule – soundness and completeness

We define a resolution rule for solving signed Max-SAT, called *Signed Max-SAT Resolution*, and prove its soundness and completeness. This rule was inspired by previous works [LAR 05, BON 06] for Max-SAT. The completeness proof for signed CNF formulae is technically more involved than the proof for Boolean CNF formulae.

DEFINITION 19.9.– *The* Signed Max-SAT Resolution *rule is defined as follows*

$$\begin{array}{l}
S{:}x \vee a_1 \vee \cdots \vee a_s \\
S'{:}x \vee b_1 \vee \cdots \vee b_t \\
\hline\hline
S \cap S'{:}x \vee a_1 \vee \cdots \vee a_s \vee b_1 \vee \cdots \vee b_t \\
S \cup S'{:}x \vee a_1 \vee \cdots \vee a_s \vee b_1 \vee \cdots \vee b_t \\
S{:}x \vee a_1 \vee \cdots \vee a_s \vee \overline{b_1} \\
S{:}x \vee a_1 \vee \cdots \vee a_s \vee b_1 \vee \overline{b_2} \\
\cdots \\
S{:}x \vee a_1 \vee \cdots \vee a_s \vee b_1 \vee \cdots \vee b_{t-1} \vee \overline{b_t} \\
S'{:}x \vee b_1 \vee \cdots \vee b_t \vee \overline{a_1} \\
S'{:}x \vee b_1 \vee \cdots \vee b_t \vee a_1 \vee \overline{a_2} \\
\cdots \\
S'{:}x \vee b_1 \vee \cdots \vee b_t \vee a_1 \vee \cdots \vee a_{s-1} \vee \overline{a_s}
\end{array}$$

This inference rule is applied to multisets of clauses, and replaces *the premises of the rule by its conclusions. We say that the rule* resolves *the variable x. The tautologies concluded by the rule like $N{:}x \vee A$ are removed from the resulting multiset. In addition, we substitute clauses like $S{:}x \vee S'{:}x \vee A$ by $(S \cup S'){:}x \vee A$, and clauses like $\emptyset{:}x \vee A$ by A.*

DEFINITION 19.10.– *We write $\mathcal{C} \vdash \mathcal{D}$ when the multiset of clauses $\mathcal{D}$ can be obtained from the multiset $\mathcal{C}$ applying the rule finitely many times. We write $\mathcal{C} \vdash_x \mathcal{C}'$ when this sequence of applications only resolves the variable x.*

In the context of Max-SAT problems, an inference rule is *sound* if, and only if, the number of falsified clauses in the premise is equal to the number of falsified clauses in the conclusions for any complete assignment.

THEOREM 19.1.– *[Soundness] The signed Max-SAT resolution rule is sound.*

PROOF.– *Let I be an arbitrary assignment. There are four cases:*
1. *If I falsifies the two premises, then I only falsifies the first two conclusions.*
2. *If I satisfies the two premises, then it also trivially satisfies the last $s+t$ clauses of the conclusion, because they are either implied by one or the other premise. The second clause of the conclusion is implied by each one of the premises. Therefore, it is also satisfied by I. The first clause of the conclusion is not implied by the premises. However, if both premises are satisfied then we have two cases. If $S{:}x$ and $S'{:}x$ are both satisfied, then it is thus $(S \cap S'){:}x$. Otherwise, either some a_i or some b_j are satisfied, thus the first clause of the conclusion is also satisfied.*
3. *If I satisfies the first premise, but not the second one, then the second clause of the conclusion as well as the t following clauses are satisfied, because all them are implied by the first premise. For the rest of the conclusions, there are two cases: If some of the a_i are satisfied, then let i be the index of such a. The assignment will satisfy the first clause of the conclusion and the last s conclusions, except for $S'{:}x \vee b_1 \vee \cdots \vee b_t \vee a_1 \vee \cdots \vee a_{i-1} \vee \overline{a_i}$, which is falsified. Otherwise none of the a_i are satisfied, and therefore, $S{:}x$ is satisfied. Hence, the first conclusion is falsified, and the last s conclusions are satisfied.*
4. *If I satisfies the second premise, but not the first one, the situation is analogous to the previous case.*

DEFINITION 19.11.– *A multiset of clauses $\mathcal{C}$ is said to be* saturated w.r.t. x *if, for every pair of clauses $C_1 = S{:}x \vee A$ and $C_2 = S'{:}x \vee B$ of $\mathcal{C}$, it holds (i) there are literals $S_1{:}y$ in A and $S_2{:}y$ in B such that $S_1 \cup S_2 = N$, or (ii) $S \cap S' = S$ or $S \cap S' = S'$.*

A multiset of clauses $\mathcal{C}'$ is a saturation of $\mathcal{C}$ *w.r.t. x if $\mathcal{C}'$ is saturated w.r.t. x and $\mathcal{C} \vdash_x \mathcal{C}'$, i.e. $\mathcal{C}'$ can be obtained from $\mathcal{C}$ applying the inference rule resolving x finitely many times.*

We assign to every clause C a score $s(C)$ equal to the number of assignments to the variables that falsify C. The score of a multiset of clauses is the sum of scores of the clauses contained in it.

LEMMA 19.1.– *For every multiset of clauses $\mathcal{C}$ and variable x, there exists a multiset $\mathcal{C}'$ such that $\mathcal{C}'$ is a saturation of $\mathcal{C}$ w.r.t. x.*

PROOF.– *We proceed by applying non-deterministically the inference rule resolving x, until we obtain a saturated multiset. We only need to prove that this process terminates in finitely many inference steps, i.e that there does not exist infinite sequences $\mathcal{C} = \mathcal{C}_0 \vdash \mathcal{C}_1 \vdash \ldots$, where at every inference we resolve the variable x and none of the sets $\mathcal{C}_i$ are saturated. Let M be the score of $\mathcal{C}$.*

Let us partition the multiset $\mathcal{C}$ of clauses into n multisets (n is the size of the domain), $\{B_0, B_1, \ldots, B_{n-1}\}$, where B_i contains the clauses where the cardinality of the support of x is i. Notice that B_0 is the multiset of clauses that do not contain the variable x. Let us denote by $s(B_i)$ the score of the multiset B_i. We will look at these n multisets as a word of length n and base $M + 1$. So our multiset will be represented by the number $s(B_0)\, s(B_1) \cdots s(B_{n-1})$, taking $s(B_0)$ as the most significant digit. Since B_i is a subset of $\mathcal{C}$, for $i = 0, \ldots, n-1$, $s(B_i) \leq M$.

When we apply our inference rule, we take two clauses, say one from B_i and one from B_j and substitute them by a set of clauses that we will distribute among the different B_k. Now we have a new multiset of clauses and by the soundness of our rule the score of the new multiset is the same. But, if we again look at the multiset as a number in base M, the number will be different. We will argue that for each inference step, the number increases. Say that the clauses used for the inference step are $S{:}x \vee A \in B_{|S|}$ and $S'{:}x \vee B \in B_{|S'|}$. Through the inference step we remove these clauses and add some clauses in $B_{|S \cap S'|}$, and possibly also some clauses in $B_{|S|}$, $B_{|S'|}$ and $B_{|S \cup S'|}$. Since, by definition of saturation $S \cap S' \neq S$ and $S \cap S' \neq S'$, we know that $|S \cap S'| < |S|, |S'| < |S \cup S'|$, hence the digit of $B_{|S \cap S'|}$ is more significant than the digits of $B_{|S|}$, $B_{|S'|}$ and $B_{|S \cup S'|}$. We have to conclude that the new M-base number after the inference step is larger than before. As the largest possible number we can obtain is the one represented as $s(B_0)s(B_1) \cdots s(B_{n-1}) = M0 \cdots 0$, the saturation procedure for x has to finish before M^n steps.

LEMMA 19.2.– *Let $\mathcal{E}$ be a saturated multiset of clauses w.r.t. x. Let $\mathcal{E}'$ be the subset of clauses of $\mathcal{E}$ not containing x. Then, any assignment I satisfying $\mathcal{E}'$ (and not assigning x) can be extended to an assignment satisfying $\mathcal{E}$.*

PROOF.– *We have to extend I to satisfy the whole $\mathcal{E}$. In fact we only need to set the value of x. Let us partition the multiset $(\mathcal{E} - \mathcal{E}')$ (multiset of clauses that contain the variable x) into two multisets: $(\mathcal{E} - \mathcal{E}')_T$ the multiset already satisfied by I, and $(\mathcal{E} - \mathcal{E}')_F$ the multiset such that the partial assignment I doesn't satisfy any of the clauses. Our aim is to show that the intersection of all the supports of x in $(\mathcal{E} - \mathcal{E}')_F$ is non-empty. This way we will extend I by assigning x to a value in the intersection of all the supports.*

Since $\mathcal{E}$ is saturated, for every pair of clauses $C_1 = S{:}x \vee A$ and $C_2 = S'{:}x \vee B$ in $(\mathcal{E} - \mathcal{E}')_F$ either condition i) or ii) of the definition happens. Condition i) cannot happen because C_1 and C_2 cannot both be in $(\mathcal{E} - \mathcal{E}')_F$. Therefore, for every pair of clauses, $C_1 = S{:}x \vee A$ and $C_2 = S'{:}x \vee B$ in $(\mathcal{E} - \mathcal{E}')_F$, $S \cap S' = S$ or $S \cap S' = S'$. Now, we order all the supports of x appearing in $(\mathcal{E} - \mathcal{E}')_F$ in decreasing order of their cardinality. It is straightforward to see that every support is contained or equal to its predecessor. In particular, the last support is equal to the intersection of all the supports, and it is non-empty.

THEOREM 19.2.– *[Completeness] For any multiset of clauses $\mathcal{C}$, we have*

$$\mathcal{C} \vdash \underbrace{\square, \ldots, \square}_{m}, \mathcal{D}$$

where $\mathcal{D}$ is a satisfiable multiset of clauses, and m is the minimum number of unsatisfied clauses of $\mathcal{C}$.

PROOF.– *Let $x_1, \ldots, x_n$ be any list of the variables of $\mathcal{C}$. We construct two sequences of multisets $\mathcal{C}_0, \ldots, \mathcal{C}_n$ and $\mathcal{D}_1, \ldots, \mathcal{D}_n$ such that (1) $\mathcal{C} = \mathcal{C}_0$, (2) for $i = 1, \ldots, n$, $\mathcal{C}_i \cup \mathcal{D}_i$ is a saturation of $\mathcal{C}_{i-1}$ w.r.t. x_i, and (3) for $i = 1, \ldots, n$, $\mathcal{C}_i$ is a multiset of clauses not containing $x_1, \ldots, x_i$, and $\mathcal{D}_i$ is a multiset of clauses containing the variable x_i. Using Lemma 19.1, these sequences can be effectively calculated: for $i = 1, \ldots, n$, we saturate $\mathcal{C}_{i-1}$ w.r.t. x_i, and then we partition the resulting multiset into a subset $\mathcal{D}_i$ containing x_i, and another $\mathcal{C}_i$ not containing this variable. Notice that, since $\mathcal{C}_n$ does not contain any variable, it is either the empty multiset $\emptyset$, or it only contains (some) empty clauses $\{\square, \ldots, \square\}$.*

Now we are going to prove that the multiset $\mathcal{D} = \bigcup_{i=1}^{n} \mathcal{D}_i$ is satisfiable by constructing an assignment satisfying it. For $i = 1, \ldots, n$, let $\mathcal{E}_i = \mathcal{D}_i \cup \cdots \cup \mathcal{D}_n$, and let $\mathcal{E}_{n+1} = \emptyset$. Notice that, for $i = 1, \ldots, n$, (1) the multiset $\mathcal{E}_i$ only contains the variables $\{x_i, \ldots, x_n\}$, (2) $\mathcal{E}_i$ is saturated w.r.t. x_i, and (3) $\mathcal{E}_i$ decomposes as $\mathcal{E}_i = \mathcal{D}_i \cup \mathcal{E}_{i+1}$, where all the clauses of $\mathcal{D}_i$ contain x_i and none of $\mathcal{E}_{i+1}$ contains x_i.

Now, we construct a sequence of assignments $I_1, \ldots, I_{n+1}$, where I_{n+1} is the empty assignment, hence satisfies $\mathcal{E}_{n+1} = \emptyset$. Now, I_i is constructed from I_{i+1} as follows. Assume by induction hypothesis that I_{i+1} satisfies $\mathcal{E}_{i+1}$. Since $\mathcal{E}_i$ is saturated w.r.t. x_i, and decomposes into $\mathcal{D}_i$ and $\mathcal{E}_{i+1}$, using Lemma 19.2, we can extend I_{i+1} with an assignment for x_i to obtain I_i which satisfies $\mathcal{E}_i$. Iterating, we get that I_1 satisfies $\mathcal{E}_1 = \mathcal{D} = \bigcup_{i=1}^{n} \mathcal{D}_i$. In conclusion, since by the soundness of the rule (theorem 19.1) the inference preserves the number of falsified clauses for every assignment, $m = |\mathcal{C}_n|$ is the minimum number of unsatisfied clauses of $\mathcal{C}$.

19.3. Global consistency in WCSP

From the proof of Theorem 19.2, we can extract an exact algorithm for solving WCSP. Given an initial WCSP instance P with k variables, the algorithm in Figure 19.2 returns the minimal cost m of P and an optimal solution I.

The function *saturation*(C_{i-1}, x_i) calculates a saturation of C_{i-1} w.r.t. x_i applying the resolution rule resolving x until it obtains a saturated set.

```
input: A WCSP instance P
C_0 := signed_encoding(P)
for i := 1 to k
        C := saturation(C_{i-1}, x_i)
        ⟨C_i, D_i⟩ := partition(C, x_i)
endfor
m := |C_k|
I := ∅
for i := k downto 1
        I := I ∪ [x_i ↦ extension(x_i, I, D_i)]
output: m, I
```

Figure 19.2. *Exact algorithm for solving WCSP*

Lemma 19.1 ensures that this process terminates, in particular that it does not cycle. As we have already said, the saturation of a multiset is not unique, but the proof of Theorem 19.2 does not depend on which particular saturation we take.

The function $partition(C, x_i)$ calculates a partition of C, already saturated, into the subset of clauses containing x_i and the subset of clauses not containing x_i.

The function $extension(x_i, I, D_i)$ calculates an assignment for x_i extending the assignment I, to satisfy the clauses of D_i according to Lemma 19.2. The function filters all clauses of D_i that are not satisfied by I. Then it calculates the intersection of the supports for x_i of all of them, and returns one of the values of such an intersection. It returns a value from $\cap\{S \mid S{:}x_i \vee A \in D_i \text{ and } I \text{ falsifies } A\}$. The argumentation of the proof of Lemma 19.2 ensures that this intersection is not empty. The order on the saturation of the variables can be freely chosen, i.e. the sequence $x_1, \ldots x_n$ can be any enumeration of the variables.

A similar approach to this algorithm was defined using bucket elimination [DEC 99]. Even though both procedures have the same exponential worst-case complexity, we believe that our algorithm can give rise to a better performance profile, in the sense that our computation of the joint operation is incremental.

19.4. Local consistency in WCSP

In WCSP a number of local consistency properties have been proposed. These local properties do not ensure the global consistency of a set of constraints. However, they can be enforced very efficiently and used to find a lower bound of the cost.

In this section we focus on binary WCSP instances as in [LAR 03, GIV 05]. We assume the existence of a unary constraint for every variable x_i. If no such constraint is defined, we can always define a dummy constraint as $f(a_k) = 0$ for every $a_k \in d(x_i)$. We will use the standard notation for binary WCSP in the literature: C_i will denote a unary constraint over a variable x_i, and C_{ij} will denote a binary constraint between variables x_i and x_j; $C_i(a_k)$, where $a_k \in d(x_i)$, will denote $f(a_k)$, and $C_{ij}(a_k, b_l)$, where $a_k \in d(x_i)$ and $b_l \in d(x_j)$, will denote $f(a_k, b_k)$.

DEFINITION 19.12.– *Variable x_i is* node consistent *if there exists a value $a_k \in d(x_i)$ such that $C_i(a_k) = 0$. A WCSP is node consistent (NC*) if every variable is node consistent.*

DEFINITION 19.13.– *Given a binary constraint C_{ij}, the value $b \in d(x_j)$ is a* simple support *for $a \in d(x_i)$ if $C_{ij}(a, b) = 0$, and is a* full support *if $C_{ij}(a, b) + C_j(b) = 0$. Variable x_i is* arc consistent *if every value $a \in d(x_i)$ has a simple support in every constraint C_{ij}. A WCSP is arc consistent (AC*) if every variable is node and arc consistent.*

DEFINITION 19.14.– *Variable x_i is* full arc consistent *if every value $a \in d(x_i)$ has a full support in every constraint C_{ij}. A WCSP is full arc consistent (FAC*) if every variable is node and full arc consistent.*

DEFINITION 19.15.– *Let $>$ be a total ordering over the variables of a WCSP. Variable x_i is* directional arc consistent *(DAC) if every value $a \in d(x_i)$ has a full support in every constraint C_{ij} such that $x_j > x_i$. It is* full directional arc consistent *(FDAC) if, in addition, every value $a \in d(x_i)$ has a simple support in every constraint C_{ij} such that $x_j < x_i$. A WCSP is full directional arc consistent (FDAC*) if every variable is node and full directional arc consistent.*

DEFINITION 19.16.– *Let $>$ be a total ordering over the variables of a WCSP. Variable x_i is* existential arc consistent *if there is at least one value $a \in d(x_i)$ such that $C_i(a) = 0$ and has a full support in every constraint C_{ij}. A WCSP is existential arc consistent (EAC*) if every variable is node and existential arc consistent. A WCSP is* existential directional arc consistent *(EDAC*) if it is FDAC* and EAC*.*

In what follows we define four sound inference rules for a sub-language of signed formulae. We only consider clauses with at most two literals and whose signs are complements of singletons. This language captures binary WCSP instances. As we will see below, the rules enforce some known local consistency properties. In the next rules we assume that $N = \{i_1, \ldots, i_n\} = \{j_1, \ldots, j_n\}$ and $j \in N$.

Rule 1:

$$\frac{\begin{array}{l}\overline{\{i_1\}}{:}x\\ \cdots\\ \overline{\{i_n\}}{:}x\end{array}}{\Box}$$

Rule 2:

$$\frac{\begin{array}{l}\overline{\{i_1\}}{:}x \vee \overline{\{j\}}{:}y\\ \cdots\\ \overline{\{i_n\}}{:}x \vee \overline{\{j\}}{:}y\end{array}}{\overline{\{j\}}{:}y}$$

Rule 3:

$$\frac{\begin{array}{l}\overline{\{i_1\}}{:}x \vee \overline{\{j_1\}}{:}y\\ \cdots\\ \overline{\{i_s\}}{:}x \vee \overline{\{j_1\}}{:}y\\ \overline{\{i_{s+1}\}}{:}x\\ \cdots\\ \overline{\{i_n\}}{:}x\end{array}}{\begin{array}{l}\overline{\{j_1\}}{:}y\\ \overline{\{i_{s+1}\}}{:}x \vee \overline{\{j_2\}}{:}y\\ \cdots\\ \overline{\{i_{s+1}\}}{:}x \vee \overline{\{j_n\}}{:}y\\ \cdots\\ \overline{\{i_n\}}{:}x \vee \overline{\{j_2\}}{:}y\\ \cdots\\ \overline{\{i_n\}}{:}x \vee \overline{\{j_n\}}{:}y\end{array}}$$

Rule 4:

$$\frac{\begin{array}{l}\overline{\{i_1\}}{:}x \vee \overline{\{j_1\}}{:}y\\ \cdots\\ \overline{\{i_s\}}{:}x \vee \overline{\{j_1\}}{:}y\\ \overline{\{i_{s+1}\}}{:}x\\ \cdots\\ \overline{\{i_n\}}{:}x\\ \overline{\{j_2\}}{:}y\\ \cdots\\ \overline{\{j_n\}}{:}y\end{array}}{\begin{array}{l}\Box\\ \overline{\{i_{s+1}\}}{:}x \vee \overline{\{j_2\}}{:}y\\ \cdots\\ \overline{\{i_{s+1}\}}{:}x \vee \overline{\{j_n\}}{:}y\\ \cdots\\ \overline{\{i_n\}}{:}x \vee \overline{\{j_2\}}{:}y\\ \cdots\\ \overline{\{i_n\}}{:}x \vee \overline{\{j_n\}}{:}y\end{array}}$$

LEMMA 19.3.– *Star node consistency (NC*) can be enforced applying rule 1.*

PROOF.– *Say x_i is a variable of a WCSP that is not star node consistent. Then for every $j \in N$, $C_i(j) > 0$. Let $w = \min\{C_i(j) \mid j \in N\}$ and k be such that $C_i(k) = w$. This means that in the corresponding signed encoding we have $C_i(j)$ copies of $\overline{\{j\}}{:}x_i$, for all $j \in N$. Rule 1 applied to the encoding w times will remove w copies of $\overline{\{j\}}{:}x_i$, for all $j \in N$, hence all the copies of $\overline{\{k\}}{:}x_i$. Therefore, the WCSP equivalent to the new encoding has the star node consistency property of the variable x_i.*

LEMMA 19.4.– *Arc consistency (AC*) can be enforced applying rule 2.*

PROOF.– *Say x_i is a variable that is not arc consistent with respect to a constraint C_{ij}, for variable x_j. This means that there is a value $a \in N$ such that for all $b \in N$, $C_{ij}(a,b) > 0$. Let be $w = \min\{C_{ij}(a,b) \mid b \in N\}$. The constrain C_{ij} will generate among others $C_{ij}(a,b)$ copies of $\overline{\{a\}}{:}x_i \vee \overline{\{b\}}{:}x_j$, for every $b \in N$. Applying rule 2 w times, we substitute these clauses by w copies of $\overline{\{a\}}{:}x_i$ and $C_{ij}(a,b) - w$ copies of $\overline{\{a\}}{:}x_i \vee \overline{\{b\}}{:}x_j$, for every $b \in N$. Since there is one value k such that $C_{ij}(a,k) - w = 0$, this new set of clauses indicates that variable x_i is now arc consistent with respect to C_{ij}, for value a. Arc consistency for other values would be obtained in the same way.*

The previous two lemmas where proved for domains of size two in [LAR 05].

LEMMA 19.5.– *A total ordering $>$ fixed on the variables, directional arc consistency (DAC) can be enforced from rule 3 applied with the restriction $x > y$.*

PROOF.– *Let $>$ be a total ordering on the variables. Say x_i is a variable that is not directional arc consistent with respect to a restriction C_{ij} for some variable x_j where $x_j > x_i$. This means that there is a value $a \in N$ such that for all $b \in N$, $C_{ij}(a,b) + C_j(b) > 0$. Suppose that there is some b such that $C_{ij}(a,b) = 0$, otherwise we can use rule 2 to enforce arc consistency. W.l.o.g. suppose that, for $s \in \{k \dots n\}$, $C_{ij}(a,s) = 0$. So, for the same subdomain, $C_j(s) > 0$. This ensures that we have the following subset of clauses $\{\overline{\{a\}}{:}x_i \vee \overline{\{1\}}{:}x_j, \dots, \overline{\{a\}}{:}x_i \vee \overline{\{k-1\}}{:}x_j, \overline{\{k\}}{:}x_j, \dots, \overline{\{n\}}{:}x_j\}$. Rule 2 allows us to substitute this set of clauses by $\{\overline{\{a\}}{:}x_i\} \cup \bigcup_{c \neq a, b \in \{1 \dots k-1\}} \{\overline{\{c\}}{:}x_i \vee \overline{\{b\}}{:}x_j\}$. Applying rule 3 repeatedly the values $\{k \dots n\}$ of x_j become the full support for x_i.*

Rule 4 enforces DAC*, as it combines DAC and NC*. Rule 3 also enforces full arc consistency (FAC*), but then it must be applied without the limitation $x > y$. Existential arc consistency (EAC*) can also be obtained from rule 3 but with different limitations than DAC* (in order to avoid cycles).

EXAMPLE.– Figure 19.3 shows a sequence of equivalent signed Max-SAT instances obtained by applying rules 1, 2 and 3. The sequence of transformations is: a) original formula, b) application of rule 1 to clauses 1, 3 and 5, c) application of rule 2 substituting clauses 8, 9 and 10 by clause 12, d) application of rule 3 substituting clauses 6, 7 and 12 by 13, 14 and 15, and e) application of rule 1 to clauses 2, 4 and 13. The minimal cost is 2. The corresponding sequence of WCSP instances is: a) original instance, b) is NC* but not AC*, c) is AC* but not DAC*, d) is DAC* but not NC* and e) is DAC* and NC*.

19.5. Conclusions

We have proved that the logic of signed CNF formulae provides the underlying logic of WCSP. On the one hand, this language allows a compact and natural representation of WCSP with not only binary but n-ary constraints. On the other hand, the inference system we have defined captures and formalizes the local consistency properties that have been described in the WCSP community, and provides a new exact algorithm for solving WCSP.

Signed CNF formulae have been used here to extend a Max-SAT result [BON 06] to WCSP, but they can also be used to bridge the gap between CSP and SAT. On the one hand, the solving techniques developed for SAT can be

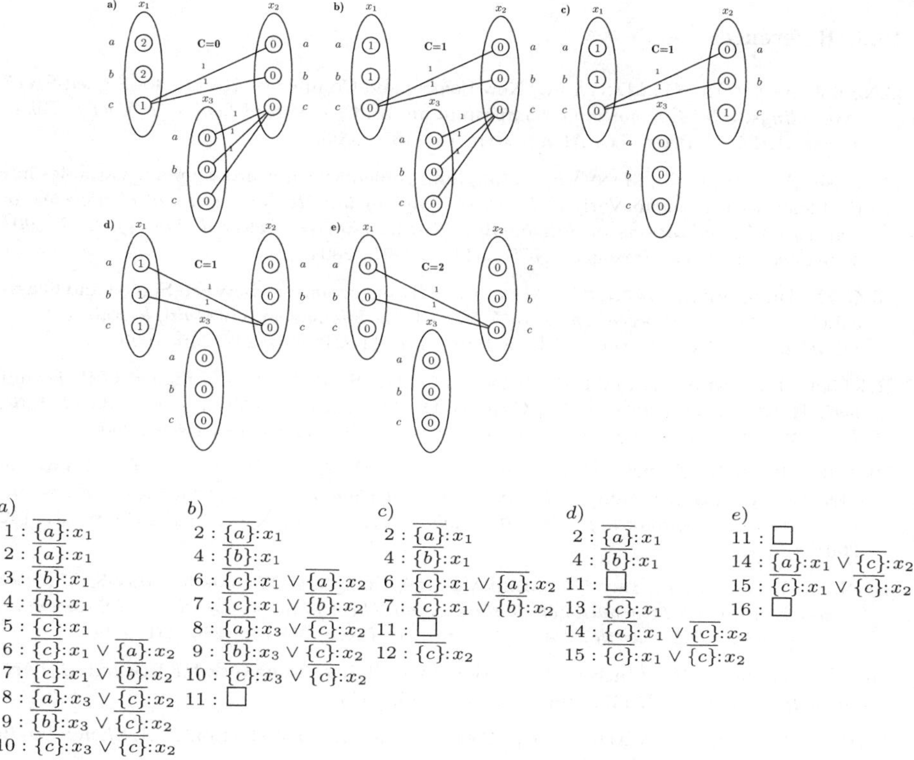

Figure 19.3. *Example of the application of the rules*

extended to signed SAT in a natural way with a low overhead. On the other hand, the problem structure exploited in CSP encodings can also be exploited in signed SAT encodings. While the structure of the domains of the variables is hidden in SAT encodings of CSPs, it is made explicit in signed SAT encodings. It is an open problem to know whether the logic of signed CNF formulae can give new insights to devise CSP solving techniques with better performance profiles.

Acknowledgements This research was founded by the MEC research projects iDEAS (TIN2004-04343), and Mulog (TIN2004-07933-C03-01/03).

19.6. References

[ANS 03] ANSÓTEGUI C., MANYÀ F., "New Logical and Complexity Results for Signed-SAT", *Proceedings, 33rd International Symposium on Multiple-Valued Logics (ISMVL), Tokyo, Japan*, IEEE CS Press, Los Alamitos, p. 181–187, 2003.

[ANS 04] ANSÓTEGUI C., MANYÀ F., "Mapping Problems with Finite Domain Variables into Problems with Boolean Variables", *Proceedings of the 7th International Conference on Theory and Applications of Satisfiability Testing (Revised Selected Papers), SAT-2004, Vancouver, Canada*, Springer LNCS 3542, p. 1–15, 2004.

[BEC 99] BECKERT B., HÄHNLE R., MANYÀ F., "Transformations between Signed and Classical Clause Logic", *Proceedings, 29th International Symposium on Multiple-Valued Logics (ISMVL), Freiburg, Germany*, IEEE Press, Los Alamitos, p. 248–255, 1999.

[BEC 00] BECKERT B., HÄHNLE R., MANYÀ F., "The SAT Problem of Signed CNF Formulas", BASIN D., D'AGOSTINO M., GABBAY D., MATTHEWS S., VIGANÒ L., Eds., *Labelled Deduction*, vol. 17 of *Applied Logic Series*, p. 61–82, Kluwer, Dordrecht, 2000.

[BÉJ 01] BÉJAR R., CABISCOL A., FERNÁNDEZ C., MANYÀ F., GOMES C. P., "Capturing Structure with Satisfiability", *7th International Conference on Principles and Practice of Constraint Programming, CP-2001,Paphos, Cyprus*, Springer LNCS 2239, p. 137–152, 2001.

[BON 06] BONET M. L., LEVY J., MANYÀ F., "A Complete Calculus for Max-SAT", *Proceedings of the 9th International Conference on Theory and Applications of Satisfiability Testing, SAT-2006, Seattle/WA, USA*, Springer LNCS 3569, p. 240–251, 2006.

[DEC 99] DECHTER R., "Bucket Elimination: A Unifying Framework for Reasoning", *Artificial Intelligence*, vol. 113, num. 1–2, p. 41–85, 1999.

[FRE 92] FREUDER E., WALLACE R., "Partial Constraint Satisfaction", *Artificial Intelligence*, vol. 58, p. 21–71, 1992.

[GIV 05] DE GIVRY S., HERAS F., LARROSA J., ZYTNICKI M., "Existencial Arc Consistency: Getting Closer to Full Arc Consistency in Weighted CSPs", *Proceedings of the International Joint Conference on Artificial Intelligence, IJCAI-2005, Edinburgh, Scotland*, Morgan Kaufmann, p. 84–89, 2005.

[HÄH 01] HÄHNLE R., "Advanced Many-Valued Logic", GABBAY D., GUENTHNER F., Eds., *Handbook of Philosophical Logic*, vol. 2, Kluwer, second edition, 2001.

[LAR 96] LARROSA J., MESEGUER P., "Exploiting the use of DAC in Max-CSP", *Proceedings of CP'96*, p. 308–322, 1996.

[LAR 03] LARROSA J., SCHIEX T., "In the Quest of the Best Form of Local Consistency for Weighted CSP", *Proceedings of the International Joint Conference on Artificial Intelligence, IJCAI'03, Acapulco, México*, p. 239–244, 2003.

[LAR 04] LARROSA J., SCHIEX T., "Solving Weighted CSP by Maintaining Arc-Consistency", *Artificial Intelligence*, vol. 159, num. 1–2, p. 1–26, 2004.

[LAR 05] LARROSA J., HERAS F., "Resolution in Max-SAT and its Relation to Local Consistency in Weighted CSPs", *Proceedings of the International Joint Conference on Artificial Intelligence, IJCAI-2005, Edinburgh, Scotland*, Morgan Kaufmann, p. 193–198, 2005.

[VER 96] VERFAILLIE G., LEMAITRE M., SCHIEX T., "Russian Doll Search", *Proceedings of the 14th National Conference on Artificial Intelligence, AAAI'96, Portland/OR, USA*, AAAI Press, p. 181–187, 1996.

Chapter 20

Dynamic Heuristics for Branch and Bound on Tree-Decomposition of Weighted CSPs

This chapter deals with methods exploiting tree-decomposition approaches for solving weighted constraint networks. We consider here the practical efficiency of these approaches by defining three classes of variable orders more and more dynamic which preserve the time complexity bound. Then, we extend this theoretical time complexity bound to increase the dynamic aspect of these orders. For that, we define a constant k allowing us to extend the classical bound from $O(exp(w+1))$ firstly to $O(exp(w+k+1))$, and finally to $O(exp(2(w+k+1)-s^-))$, with w the "tree-width" of a Weighted CSP and s^- the minimum size of its separators. Finally, we empirically assess the defined theoretical extensions of the time complexity bound.

20.1. Introduction

The CSP formalism (constraint satisfaction problem) offers a powerful framework for representing and solving efficiently many problems. Modeling a problem as a CSP consists of defining a set X of variables $x_1, x_2, \dots x_n$, which must be assigned in their respective finite domain, by satisfying a set C of constraints which express restrictions between the different possible assignments. A solution is an assignment of every variable which satisfies all the constraints. Determining if a solution exists is a NP-complete problem. This framework has been extended in order to capture notions like preference or possibility or,

---

Chapter written by Philippe JÉGOU, Samba Ndojh NDIAYE and Cyril TERRIOUX.

when there is no solution, to produce an assignment minimizing a given criterion on constraint satisfaction. Hence, recently, many extensions of the CSP framework have been proposed (e.g. [FRE 92, BIS 95, SCH 95]).

In this chapter, we focus our study on weighted CSPs (WCSPs) which is a well known framework for soft constraints. In this extension, a weight (or a cost) is associated with each tuple of each constraint. So, each assignment has a cost defined by the sum of the costs of all the tuples included in the considered assignment. Solving a WCSP instance requires finding an assignment whose cost is minimum. This task is NP-hard. Many algorithms have been defined in the past years for solving this problem. On the one hand, the usual complete method for solving WCSPs is based on branch and bound search, which, in order to be efficient, must use both filtering techniques and heuristics for choosing the next variable or value. This approach, often efficient in practice, has an exponential theoretical time complexity in $O(exp(n))$ for an instance having n variables. On the other hand, some other methods are based on the dynamic programming approach (e.g. [VER 96, KOS 99, MES 00, MES 01, MES 02, LAR 03]). Some of them exploit the problem structure such as [KOS 99, MES 00, LAR 02, LAR 03]. Exploiting the structure often leads to an improvement in the solving methods and, in particular, to the provision for better theoretical time complexity bounds. Several bounds exist like the induced width [DEC 99] or the tree-height [FRE 85, MAR 04]. Yet, the best known complexity bounds are given by the "tree-width" of a WCSP (often denoted w). This parameter is related to some topological properties of the constraint graph which represents the interactions between variables via the constraints. It leads to a time complexity in $O(exp(w+1))$. Different methods have been proposed to reach this bound (see [GOT 00] for a survey and a theoretical comparison of these methods). They rely on the notion of tree-decomposition of the constraint graph. They aim to cluster variables so that the cluster arrangement is a tree. Depending on the instances, we can expect a significant gain w.r.t. enumerative approaches. Most of these works only present theoretical results. Few practical results have been provided (e.g. [GOT 02, JÉG 04]). So, we study these approaches by focusing on the BTD method (for backtracking with tree-decomposition [JÉG 03]) which seems to be one of the most effective structural method.

The problem of finding the best decomposition (w.r.t. the tree-width) was originally studied in the literature from a theoretical viewpoint. More recently, some studies (e.g. [JÉG 05]) have been realized in the field of CSP, integrating, as quality parameter for a decomposition, its efficiency for solving the considered CSP. Yet, these studies do not consider the questions related to an efficient use of the considered decomposition. This chapter deals with this question. Given a tree-decomposition, we study the problem of finding good orders on variables for exploiting this decomposition in a branch and bound search such as that achieved by BTD. Similar works have been already performed for SAT or CSP (e.g. [HUA 03, JÉG 06]). As presented in [TER 03, JÉG 04], the order on the variables is static and compatible with a depth first traversal of the associated cluster tree. Since enumerative methods highlight the efficiency of dynamic variable orders, we give conditions which allow the tree-decomposition to be exploited in a more dynamic way and guarantee the time complexity bound. We propose five classes of orders respecting these conditions, two of them giving more freedom to order variables dynamically. Consequently, their time complexity possesses larger bounds: $O(exp(w+k+1))$ and $O(exp(2(w+k+1)-s^-))$, where s^- is the minimum size of the separators and k is a constant to be parameterized. Based on the properties of these classes, we define several heuristics which aim to calculate a good order on clusters and more generally on variables. They rely on topological and semantic properties of the WCSP instance. Heuristics based on a dynamic variable ordering and those based on the expected number of solutions significantly enhance the performances of BTD. Finally, we report here experiments to assess the interest of our propositions.

This chapter is organized as follows. Section 20.2 provides basic notions about WCSPs and BTD. Then, in section 20.3, we define several classes of variable orders which preserve the traditional time complexity bound. Section 20.4 introduces two extensions giving new time complexity bounds. Section 20.5 presents the different heuristics we use for guiding the exploration of the cluster tree. Then, section 20.6 is devoted to empirical results. Finally, in section 20.7, we conclude and outline some future works.

20.2. Preliminaries

A *constraint satisfaction problem* (CSP) is defined by a tuple (X, D, C). X is a set $\{x_1, \ldots, x_n\}$ of n variables. Each variable x_i takes its values in the finite domain d_{x_i} from D. The variables are subject to the constraints from C. Given an instance (X, D, C), the CSP problem consists of determining if there is a solution (i.e. an assignment of each variable which satisfies each constraint). This problem is NP-complete. In this chapter, we focus our study on an extension of CSPs, namely weighted CSPs (WCSPs). In this extension, a weight (or a cost) is associated with each tuple of each constraint. The cost of a tuple allowed by a constraint is 0, while a forbidden one has a cost greater than 0. Then, each assignment has a cost defined by the sum of the costs of all the tuples included in the considered assignment. Solving a WCSP instance requires to find an assignment whose cost is minimum. This task is NP-hard. In this chapter, without loss of generality, we only consider binary constraints (i.e. constraints which involve two variables). So, the structure of a WCSP can be represented by the graph (X, C), called the *constraint graph*. The vertices of this graph are the variables of X and an edge joins two vertices if the corresponding variables share a constraint.

Methods providing interesting theoretical time complexity bounds often rely on the structure of the constraint graph, and in particular the notion of tree-decomposition of graphs [ROB 86]. Let $G = (X, C)$ be a graph, a *tree-decomposition* of G is a pair (E, T) where $T = (I, F)$ is a tree with nodes I and edges F and $E = \{E_i : i \in I\}$ a family of subsets of X, such that each subset (called cluster) E_i is associated with a node of T and verifies:

1) $\cup_{i \in I} E_i = X$;

2) for each edge $\{x, y\} \in C$, there exists $i \in I$ with $\{x, y\} \subseteq E_i$;

3) for all $i, j, k \in I$, if k is in a path from i to j in T, then $E_i \cap E_j \subseteq E_k$.

The width of a tree-decomposition (E, T) is equal to $max_{i \in I} |E_i| - 1$. The *tree-width* w of G is the minimal width over all the tree-decompositions of G.

Assume that we have a tree-decomposition of minimal width w, the reference structural method, tree-clustering [DEC 89], has a time complexity in $O(exp(w + 1))$ while its space complexity can be reduced to $O(n.s.d^s)$ with s the size of the largest minimal separators of the graph [DEC 01]. Note that tree-clustering does not provide interesting results in practical cases. Thus, an alternative approach, also based on a tree-decomposition of graphs was proposed in [TER 03]. This method, called BTD, seems to provide empirical results which are among the best obtained by structural methods.

BTD proceeds using a branch and bound search guided by a static pre-established partial order induced by a tree-decomposition of the constraint network. So, the first step of BTD consists of computing a tree-decomposition of the constraint graph. The calculated tree-decomposition induces a partial variable ordering which allows BTD to exploit some structural properties of the graph and so to prune some parts of the search tree. In fact, variables are assigned according to a depth-first traversal of the rooted tree. In other words, we first assign the variables of the root cluster E_1, then we assign the variables of E_2, then the variables of E_3, and so on. For example, $(x_1, x_2, \ldots, x_{14})$ or $(x_2, x_1, x_4, x_3, x_6, x_5, x_7, x_8, x_9, x_{11}, x_{10}, x_{12}, x_{13}, x_{14})$ are possible variable orderings for the problem whose constraint graph is presented in Figure 20.1. Furthermore, the tree-decomposition and the variable ordering allow BTD to divide the problem $\mathcal{P}$ into several subproblems. Given two clusters E_i and E_j (with E_j a E_i's son), the subproblem rooted in E_j depends on the current assignment $\mathcal{A}$ on the separator $E_i \cap E_j$. It is denoted $\mathcal{P}_{\mathcal{A}, E_i/E_j}$. Its variable set is equal to $Desc(E_j)$ where $Desc(E_j)$ denotes the set of variables belonging to the cluster E_j or to any descendant E_k of E_j in the cluster tree rooted in E_j.

The domain of each variable in $E_i \cap E_j$ is restricted to its value in $\mathcal{A}$. Regarding the constraint set, it contains the constraints which involve at least one variable which exclusively appears in E_j or in a descendant of E_j. For instance, let us consider the WCSP whose constraint graph and a possible tree-decomposition are provided in Figure 20.1. Given an assignment $\mathcal{A}$ on $E_2 \cap E_3$, the variable set of $\mathcal{P}_{\mathcal{A},E_2/E_3}$ is $Desc(E_3) = \{x_5, x_6, x_7, x_8, x_9\}$, and its constraint set is $\{c_{57}, c_{58}, c_{67}, c_{68}, c_{78}, c_{79}, c_{89}\}$ (where c_{ij} is the constraint involving the variables x_i and x_j). Note that c_{56} does not belong to this constraint set since both x_5 and x_6 appear in E_2. Finally, the tree-decomposition notion enables the *valued structural good* notion to be defined. A valued structural good of E_i w.r.t. a son E_j is a pair $(\mathcal{A}, v)$ with $\mathcal{A}$ an assignment on $E_i \cap E_j$ and v the optimal cost of the subproblem $\mathcal{P}_{\mathcal{A},E_i/E_j}$.

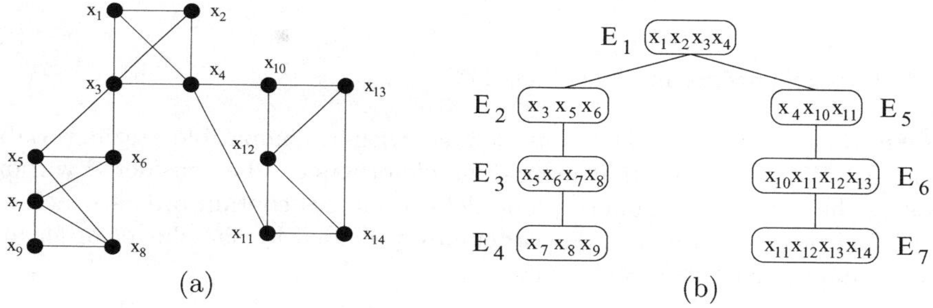

Figure 20.1. *(a) A graph and (b) a possible tree-decomposition*

To satisfy the bounds of complexity, the variable ordering exploited in BTD is related to the cluster ordering. Formally, we consider a tree-decomposition (E, T) of the WCSP. We suppose that the elements of $E = \{E_i : i \in I\}$ are indexed w.r.t. the notion of *compatible numeration*. A numeration on E compatible with a prefix numeration of the tree T with E_1 the root is called compatible numeration. An order $\preceq_X$ of variables of X such that $\forall x \in E_i$, $\forall y \in E_j$, with $i < j$, $x \preceq_X y$ is a compatible enumeration order. The cluster numeration gives a partial order on the variables as the variables in E_i are assigned before those in E_j if $i < j$, except variables encountered when computing a good, namely those located in the subproblem rooted on the cluster containing the good. In fact, using goods enables us not to have to explore subproblems twice if their optimal cost is known. If we use a good $(\mathcal{A}, v)$ to avoid visiting a subtree again, we know that the variables in it can be optimally assigned with a cost v. So BTD does not assign them effectively, but they are considered done. They are named *assignable variables* thanks to a good. Of course, if we are interested in providing an optimal assignment, additional work must be performed to assign these variables at the end of the search [JÉG 04]. Thus the variables in E_j are assigned if the variables in E_i are either already assigned or assignable thanks to a good. To complete this order, we have to choose variable ordering heuristics inside a cluster. Finally, a compatible enumeration order on the variables is given by a compatible numeration on clusters and a variable order in each cluster.

In [JÉG 04], the results were presented without heuristics for the choice of the clusters and thus the choice of the variables, except on the level of the order used inside the cluster which corresponded to a traditional dynamic order. Obviously, the variable ordering has a tremendous impact on the efficiency of enumerative methods. Thus, we study here how the benefits of variable orderings can be fully exploited in BTD. However, to guarantee the time complexity bound, it is necessary to respect some conditions. So, in the next section, we define classes of orders guaranteeing the complexity bounds.

20.3. Dynamic orders in $O(exp(w+1))$

The first version of BTD was defined with a compatible static variable ordering. We prove here that more dynamic orders can be considered without loosing the complexity bounds. The defined classes contain orders which are more and more dynamic. These orders are provided by the cluster order and the variable order inside each cluster.

Let $\mathcal{P} = (X, D, C)$ be a WCSP and (E, T) a tree-decomposition of the graph (X, C), we exploit an order σ_i on the subproblems $\mathcal{P}_{i_1}, \ldots, \mathcal{P}_{i_k}$ rooted on the sons E_{i_j} of E_i and an order γ_i on the variables in E_i. We recursively define the following classes of orders. In the three next classes, we choose the first cluster to assign (the root): E_1 among all the clusters and we consider $\mathcal{P}_1$ the subproblem rooted on E_1 (i.e. $\mathcal{P}$).

DEFINITION.– *We begin the search in E_1 and we try to extend the current assignment on the subproblem rooted on E_i recursively by assigning first the variables in E_i according to γ_i and then on $\mathcal{P}_{i_1}, \ldots, \mathcal{P}_{i_k}$ according to σ_i.*

– ***Class 1.** σ_i **and** γ_i **are static**. We calculate σ_i and γ_i statically (before starting the search).*

– ***Class 2.** σ_i **is static and** γ_i **is dynamic**. We calculate σ_i statically, while γ_i is calculated during the search.*

– ***Class 3.** σ_i **and** γ_i **are dynamic**. Both, σ_i and γ_i are calculated during the search. σ_i is calculated w.r.t. the current assignment as soon as all the variables in E_i are assigned.*

– ***Class ++. Enumerative dynamic order**. The variable ordering is completely dynamic. Thus, the assignment order is not necessarily a compatible enumeration order. There is no restriction due to the cluster tree.*

The defined classes form a hierarchy since we have: *Class 1* $\subset$ *Class 2* $\subset$ *Class 3* $\subset$ *Class ++*.

Property of *Class 3* Let Y be an assignment, $x \in E_j - (E_i \cap E_j)$ with E_i the parent of E_j: $x \in Y$ if, and only if: i)$\forall v \in E_i$, $v \in Y$; ii) let $E_{i_p} = E_j$, $\forall \mathcal{P}_{i_u}$ s.t. $\sigma_i(\mathcal{P}_{i_u}) \leq \sigma_i(\mathcal{P}_{i_p})$, $\forall v \in \mathcal{P}_{i_u}$, $v \in Y$; iii) $\forall v \in E_j$ s.t. $\gamma_j(v) \leq \gamma_j(x)$, $v \in Y$.

In [JÉG 04], the experiments use *Class 2* orders. Formally, only the orders of *Class 1* are compatible. Nevertheless, for an order o_3 in *Class 3* and a given assignment $\mathcal{A}$, we can find an order o_1 in *Class 1* that assigns the variables in $\mathcal{A}$ in the same way as the same order o_3 does. This property gives to *Class 3* (thus *Class 2*) orders the ability to record goods and use them to prune branches in the same way *Class 1* orders do. *Class ++* gives a complete freedom. Yet, it does not guarantee the time complexity bound because sometimes it is impossible to record goods. Indeed an order of *Class ++* may lead to assigning some variables of a cluster E_j (with E_j a son of a cluster E_i) without having assigned the variables of the separator $E_i \cap E_j$. By so doing, we cannot safely calculate the optimal solution of the subproblem rooted in E_j and so it is impossible to record a good on $E_i \cap E_j$. Hence, a subproblem may be solved several times and thus the time complexity bound is not guaranteed anymore. Meanwhile, *Class 3* orders guarantee this bound.

THEOREM.– *The time complexity of BTD with a Class 3 order is* $O(exp(w+1))$.

PROOF.– *We consider a cluster E_j in the cluster tree, and we must prove that any assignment on E_j is calculated only once. Let E_i be the cluster parent of E_j and suppose that all the variables in E_i are assigned and those in $E_j - (E_i \cap E_j)$ are not. Since the order belongs to Class 3, the variables of the clusters on the path from the root to E_i are already assigned and those exclusively in the subtree rooted on E_j are not yet assigned. An assignment $\mathcal{A}$ on $E_i \cap E_j$ is calculated at the latest when the variables in E_i are assigned (before those in the subproblem rooted on E_j). Solving the subproblem rooted on E_j leads to the computation of its optimal cost v. Then, $(\mathcal{A}, v)$ is recorded as a good. Let $\mathcal{A}'$ be an assignment on E_j compatible with $\mathcal{A}$. The next assignment of variables in E_i leading to $\mathcal{A}$ on $E_i \cap E_j$ will not be pursued on the subproblem rooted on E_j thanks to $(\mathcal{A}, v)$. $\mathcal{A}'$ is not calculated twice, only the variables in $E_i \cap E_j$ are assigned again. So the time complexity is $O(exp(w+1))$.*

The properties of *Class 3* offer more possibilities in the variable ordering. Thus, it is possible to choose any cluster to visit next among the sons of the current cluster. And in each cluster, the variable ordering is totally free. In the next section, we propose two natural extensions of the complexity bound.

20.4. Bounded extensions of dynamic orders

We propose two extensions based on the ability given to the heuristics to choose the next variable to assign not only in one cluster, but also among k variables in a path rooted on the cluster that verifies some properties. So, we define two new classes of orders extending *Class 3*. First, we propose a generalization of the tree-decomposition definition before providing the definition of *Class 4*.

DEFINITION.– *Let $G = (X, C)$ be a graph and k a positive integer, the set of directed k-covering tree-decompositions of a tree-decomposition (E, T) of G with E_1 its root cluster, is defined by the set of tree-decompositions (E', T') of G that verify:*

– $E_1 \subseteq E'_1$, *E'_1 the root cluster of (E', T')*

– $\forall E'_i \in E'$, $E'_i \subseteq E_{i_1} \cup E_{i_2} \cup \ldots \cup E_{i_R}$ *and* $E_{i_1} \cup E_{i_2} \cup \ldots \cup E_{i_{R-1}} \subset E'_i$, *with $E_{i_1} \ldots E_{i_R}$ a path in T*

– $|E'_i| \leq w + k + 1$, *where* $w = max_{E_i \in E}|E_i| - 1$

DEFINITION.– *Let (X, D, C) be a WCSP, (E, T) a tree-decomposition of the graph (X,C) and k a positive integer. A variable order is in* ***Class 4****, if this order is in Class 3 for one directed k-covering tree-decomposition of (E, T).*

We derive a natural theorem:

THEOREM.– *The time complexity of BTD with a Class 4 order is $O(exp(w + k + 1))$.*

PROOF.– *This proof is similar to the one given for Class 3 as we can consider that BTD runs on a tree-decomposition (E', T') of width at most $w + k + 1$.*

A second extension is possible in exploiting during the search, a dynamic computing of the tree-decomposition (we can use several directed k-covering tree-decompositions during the search). Then, the time complexity bound changes because sometimes it would be impossible to record goods.

DEFINITION.– *Let (X, D, C) be a WCSP, (E, T) a tree-decomposition of the graph (X,C) and k a positive integer. A variable order o_5 is in* ***Class 5****, if for a given assignment $\mathcal{A}$, one can find one directed k-covering tree-decomposition (E', T') of (E, T) such that $\forall E'_i \in E'$, $E'_i = E_{i_1} \cup E_{i_2} \cup \ldots \cup E_{i_R}$, with $E_{i_1} \ldots E_{i_R}$ a path in T and an order o_3 on (E', T') in Class 3 that assigns the variables in $\mathcal{A}$ in the same way and the same order that o_5 does.*

THEOREM.– *The time complexity of BTD with a Class 5 order is $O(exp(2(w + k + 1) - s^-))$.*

PROOF.– *We have to prove that any assignment on a set V of $2(w + k + 1) - s^-$ variables on a path of the tree T is calculated only once. Let $\mathcal{A}$ be an assignment containing V. The order in which the variables of $\mathcal{A}$ were assigned is in the Class 3 for a directed k-covering tree-decomposition (E', T') of (E, T) that verifies $\forall E'_i \in E'$, $E'_i = E_{i_1} \cup E_{i_2} \cup \ldots \cup E_{i_R}$, with $E_{i_1} \ldots E_{i_R}$ a path in T. The size of the clusters in (E', T') is bound by $w + k + 1$, so the set V is covered by at least two clusters since s^- is the minimum size of the separators. Let $E'_{i_1} \ldots E'_{i_q}$ be a path on (E', T') covering V. The solving of the subproblem rooted on E'_{i_1} with the assignment $\mathcal{A}$ leads to the recording of goods on the separators of these clusters. If E'_{i_1} is the root cluster of (E', T'), then V contains the root cluster E_1 of (E, T). Thus $\mathcal{A}$ will not be calculated again because it contains the first variables in the search. We suppose that E'_{i_1} is not the root cluster of (E', T'). Since $q \geq 2$, we record a good on the separator of E'_{i_1} and its parent and at least another one on the separator $E'_{i_1} \cap E'_{i_2}$. Let $\mathcal{B}$ be a new assignment that we try to extend on V with the same values in $\mathcal{A}$. One of the goods will be calculated first. Thus before all the variables in V are assigned, the search is stopped thanks to this good. So $\mathcal{A}$ is not calculated again. We prove that any assignment on V is calculated only once.*

Note that the newly defined classes are included in the hierarchy presented in section 20.3: *Class 3* $\subset$ *Class 4* $\subset$ *Class ++* and *Class 3* $\subset$ *Class 5* $\subset$ *Class ++*.

To define the value of k, we have several approaches to choose variables to group. A good one consists of trying to reduce the value of the parameter s (the minimum size of the tree-decomposition separators) and, in this way, enhancing the space complexity bound. Then, we can observe that grouping clusters with large separators enables a significant reduction of s to be achieved.

20.5. Heuristics

Here we propose several heuristics in order to improve the performances of BTD.

20.5.1. *Cluster orders*

Firstly we define several heuristics for computing the order the clusters are visited for *Classes 1, 2* and *3*. They are static for *Class 1* and dynamic for the *Classes 2* and *3*. They consist of choosing the first visited cluster (called the root cluster) and ordering the sons of each cluster. These orders are used by assuming that the early use of goods does not enforce another order. Indeed, this early use of goods greatly improves the method, by increasing the lower bound more quickly. In fact, as soon as all the variables in the separator between the current cluster and one of its sons are assigned, we check whether this assignment is a good. If so, we do not explore the subtree rooted on this son cluster and the cost related to this good is added to the lower bound.

Static orders A static order is defined before the search begins. We propose criteria for the choice of the root cluster:

– *minexp*: this heuristic is based on the expected number of partial solutions of clusters [SMI 94] and on their size. Exploiting the expected number of solutions may appear surprising in the WCSP framework. However, some subproblems may have solutions while the whole problem has none. If so, it could be interesting to begin the search with the subproblems having no solution since they have a positive cost, which may result in quickly increasing the lower bound. The heuristic chooses a root cluster which minimizes the ratio between the expected number of solutions and the size of the cluster. This allows the exploration to be started with a large cluster having few solutions or no solution;

– *size*: this local criterion chooses the cluster of maximum size as root cluster;

– *bary*: it is a global criterion based on the location of the cluster in the tree. For this criterion, we use the notion of distance, denoted $dist(x, y)$, between two vertices x and y of a graph G, which is defined by the length of a shortest path between x and y. A *barycenter* of G is a vertex x s.t. x minimizes $\Sigma_{y \in X} dist(x, y)$. The *bary* heuristic chooses a barycenter cluster as a root cluster.

Likewise, we propose heuristics for ordering cluster sons:

– $minexp_s$: this heuristic is similar to *minexp* and orders the son clusters according to the increasing value of their ratio;

– $minsep_s$: this heuristic orders the son clusters according to the increasing size of their separator with their parent.

Dynamic orders A dynamic order is defined during the search. But, the choice of the root cluster is done at the beginning of the search. Thus only static heuristics can be used to choose the root. We also propose a new heuristic: *nv*. The dynamic variable-ordering heuristics improve the runtime of enumerative methods very significantly. To derive benefit from this property, we choose a dynamic variable-ordering heuristic and the root cluster is one containing the first variable w.r.t. the chosen variable order. The dynamic aspect of the cluster orders is in the son cluster ordering:

– $minexp_{sdyn}$: the next cluster to be visited minimizes the ratio between the current expected number of solutions and the size of the cluster. The current expected number of solutions of a cluster is modified by filtering the domains of unassigned variables. Thus, we calculate this number for unordered clusters as soon as their parent is fully assigned. Thus, the choice of the next cluster is more precise;

– nv_{sdyn}: this heuristic is similar to nv. First we visit the son cluster where the next variable in the variable order appears among the variables of the unvisited son clusters.

20.5.2. *Variable orders*

Here we define static and dynamic variable orders according to which the variables inside a cluster are assigned.

Static orders A static order is defined before the search begins.

– mdd: the variables are ordered according to the increasing value of the ratio domain/degree. This heuristic gives good results compared to other static ones.

Dynamic orders A dynamic order is defined during the search.

– mdd_{dyn}: the next variable to be assigned minimizes the ratio domain/degree. The current ratio of a variable is modified by the domain filtering. So we calculate this number again each time the domain is filtered. This heuristic gives very good results.

20.5.3. *Heuristics for grouping variables in Classes 4 and 5*

Grouping variables gives more freedom for dynamic variable ordering heuristics which may improve the enumerative methods runtime significantly. Furthermore, it is necessary to find a good value of the parameter k besides which BTD does not profit sufficiently of the problem structure and therefore its time complexity increases a lot. We propose several criteria for grouping variables. For *Class 4* orders, these criteria are exploited as a preliminary step before computing the order.

– sep: this heuristic has one parameter which is the maximum size of separators. We merge clusters $< parent, son >$ if their separator size exceeds the value of the parameter;

– pv: this heuristic has one parameter which is the minimum number of proper variables in a cluster. A proper variable of a cluster is a variable of a cluster which does not belong to the parent cluster. We merge a cluster with its parent if its number of proper variables is less than the value of the parameter.

All the heuristics we have defined, try to satisfy the first-fail principle, first performing the most constrained choices.

20.6. Experimental study

Applying a structural method on an instance generally assumes that this instance presents some particular topological features. So, our study is performed on instances having a structure which can be exploited by structural methods. In practice, we assess the proposed strategies on particular random WCSPs and real-world instances in order to point out the best ones w.r.t. the WCSP solving. Regarding the random instances, we exploit partially structured instances. A randomly structured instance of a class (n, d, w, t, s, n_c) is built according to the model described in [JÉG 03]. This structured instance consists of n variables having d values in their domain. Its constraint graph is a clique tree with n_c cliques whose size is at most w and whose separator size does not exceed s. Each constraint forbids t tuples. For each forbidden tuple, a weight between 1 and 10 is associated randomly. Then, for building a partial structured instance of a class (n, d, w, t, s, n_c, p), we randomly remove $p\%$ edges from a structured instance of a class (n, d, w, t, s, n_c). Secondly, we test the proposed heuristics on some real-world instances, namely radio-link frequency assignment problems from the FullRLFAP archive (for more details, see [CAB 99]).

All these experimentations are performed on a Linux-based PC with a Pentium IV 3.2GHz and 1GB of memory. For each random partially structured instance class considered, the presented results are the average over 30 solved instances. In the following tables, the letter M means that at least one instance cannot be solved because it requires more than 1GB of memory.

In [JÉG 05], a study was performed on triangulation algorithms to find out the best way to calculate a good tree-decomposition w.r.t. the solving. As MCS [TAR 84] obtains the best results, we use it to calculate tree-decompositions in this study.

In the following, the results for *Class 5* are not presented since we cannot get good results. Table 20.1 shows the runtime of BTD based on FC with several heuristics of *Classes 1, 2* and *3* on random partial structured instances. Clearly, we observe that the choice of the root cluster seems more important than the son ordering. Indeed, the obtained results appear to be similar as soon as we choose the root cluster with the same heuristic. Moreover, the main difference between the heuristics are observed for different choices of root cluster. The son cluster ordering has a limited effect because the considered instances have a few son clusters reducing the possible choices and so their

Instance	Class 1	Class 2			Class 3		
	size $minsep_s$	*bary* $minsep_s$	*minexp* $minexp_s$	*size* $minsep_s$	*minexp* $minexp_{sdyn}$	*size* nv_{sdyn}	*nv* nv_{sdyn}
(75,10,15,30,5,8,10)	M	22.31	M	M	M	M	M
(75,10,15,30,5,8,20)	3.27	4.77	6.13	3.34	6.24	2.88	M
(75,10,15,33,3,8,10)	8.30	6.16	7.90	8.67	7.87	8.82	5.36
(75,10,15,34,3,8,20)	2.75	2.29	3.42	2.82	3.52	2.84	2.14
(75,10,10,40,3,10,10)	11.81	1.33	3.02	11.89	4.73	11.87	1.43
(75,10,10,42,3,10,20)	1.02	0.67	0.76	1.02	0.83	1.03	0.79
(75,15,10,102,3,10,10)	11.76	3.74	12.10	12.07	12.09	11.70	4.93
(100,5,15,13,5,10,10)	M	M	M	M	M	M	M

Table 20.1. *Runtime (in s) on random partially structured CSPs with mdd for Class 1 and* mdd_{dyn} *for Classes 2 and 3*

Instance	Class 4				
	minexp $minexp_s$	*size* $minsep_s$	*minexp* $minexp_{sdyn}$	*size* nv_{sdyn}	*nv* nv_{sdyn}
(75,10,15,30,5,8,10)	9.42	18.99	8.69	18.30	16.77
(75,10,15,30,5,8,20)	1.65	1.67	1.56	1.53	2.32
(75,10,15,33,3,8,10)	5.22	4.31	5.26	4.18	3.24
(75,10,15,34,3,8,20)	1.50	1.61	1.48	1.58	1.40
(75,10,10,40,3,10,10)	0.58	0.81	0.58	0.85	0.52
(75,10,10,42,3,10,20)	0.41	0.42	0.51	0.41	0.38
(75,15,10,102,3,10,10)	5.50	4.73	5.41	4.63	3.13
(100,5,15,13,5,10,10)	9.40	9.05	9.60	9.10	11.71

Table 20.2. *Runtime (in s) on random partial structured CSPs with* mdd_{dyn} *for Class 4 orders and sep heuristic (the separator size is bounded to 5)*

impact. We can expect a more important improvement for instances with more son clusters. The heuristics *size* and *minexp* often provide interesting results but sometimes make bad choices. The heuristic *nv* leads to promising results except for one instance class which cannot be solved due to the required amount of memory. The heuristic *bary* seems the more robust heuristic: it obtains good results and succeeds in solving the instances of class $(75, 10, 15, 30, 5, 8, 10)$ while BTD with any other heuristics requires too much memory space. This memory problem can be solved by exploiting a *Class 4* order with the *sep* heuristic for grouping variables. Table 20.2 gives the runtime of BTD for this class with a separator size bounded to 5. When we analyze the value of the parameter k, we observe that in general, its value is limited (between 1 to 3). The results of *Class 4* orders improve significantly ones obtained for *Classes 2* and *3*. Like previously, the results are mostly influenced by the choice of the root cluster. The best results are obtained by $nv + nv_{sdyn}$, but $minexp + minexp_s$

Instance	Class 1	Class 2			Class 3		
	size	*bary*	*minexp*	*size*	*minexp*	*size*	*nv*
	$minsep_s$	$minsep_s$	$minexp_s$	$minsep_s$	$minexp_{sdyn}$	nv_{sdyn}	nv_{sdyn}
SUB_0	9.48	5.71	9.65	9.57	9.62	9.64	9.52
SUB_1	448	511	516	515	516	518	520
SUB_2	520	703	705	701	702	700	702
SUB_3	5,575	-	6,596	6,553	6,640	6,595	6,570
SUB_4	8,146	-	9,677	9,693	9,780	9,672	9,694

Table 20.3. *Runtime (in s) on some instances from the FullRLFAP archive with mdd for Class 1 and mdd_{dyn} for Classes 2 and 3*

and *minexp* + $minexp_{sdyn}$ have very close performances. For most of instance classes, the other heuristics obtain similar results. Unfortunately, for some other classes, some bad choices for the root cluster significantly increase the runtime.

Finally, in Table 20.3, we assess the behavior of the proposed heuristics on some real-world instances. Surprisingly, the considered *Class 1* order obtains the best results. This result can be explained by the weak size of the considered instances (between 16 and 22 variables). It ensures that the cost of computing the variable ordering or the son ordering dynamically is not compensated. The same reason explains the close results obtained for *Class 2* and *3* orders. Whereas it obtains the more promising results on random instances, the heuristic *bary* requires more than 8 hours for solving the SUB_3 and SUB_4.

20.7. Discussion and conclusion

In this article, we have studied the WCSP solving methods based on tree-decompositions in order to improve their practical interest. This study was done both theoretically and empirically. The analysis of the variable orders allows us to define more dynamic heuristics without losing the time complexity bound. Thus, we have defined classes of variable orders which allow a more and more dynamic ordering of variables and preserve the theoretical time complexity bound. This bound has been extended to enforce the dynamic aspect of orders that has an important impact on the efficiency of enumerative methods. Even though these new bounds are theoretically less interesting than the initial bound, it allows us to define more efficient heuristics which improve the runtime of BTD significantly. This study, which could not be achieved previously, is now more important for solving hard instances with suitable structural properties.

We have compared the classes of variable orders with relevant heuristics w.r.t. WCSP solving. This comparison highlights the promising results obtained by *Class 4* orders. These orders give more freedom to the variable order heuristic while their time complexity is $O(exp(w+k+1))$ where k is a constant to be parameterized. For *Class 5* (which is the most dynamic), we get a time complexity in $O(exp(2(w+k+1)-s^-))$.

The experimental study presented in this chapter is a preliminary step. We only assess the interest of some heuristics. Other variable heuristics must be studied (e.g. the Jeroslow-like heuristic [GIV 03]). Likewise, for the choice of a root cluster or the son cluster ordering, we must propose heuristics which are well-adapted to the WCSP problem. For instance, the heuristic based on the expected number of solutions must be extended by taking into account the weights associated to each tuple. Then, for *Class 4*, we aim to improve the criteria used to calculate the value of k and to define more general values by better exploiting the problem features. Finally, these experiments must be performed by exploiting BTD jointly with local consistency techniques [GIV 06].

Acknowledgments This work is supported by an ANR grant (STAL-DEC-OPT project).

20.8. References

[BIS 95] BISTARELLI S., MONTANARI U., ROSSI F., "Constraint Solving over Semirings", *Proceedings of IJCAI*, p. 624-630, 1995.

[CAB 99] CABON C., DE GIVRY S., LOBJOIS L., SCHIEX T., WARNERS J. P., "Radio Link Frequency Assignment", *Constraints*, vol. 4, p. 79-89, 1999.

[DEC 89] DECHTER R., PEARL J., "Tree-Clustering for Constraint Networks", *Artificial Intelligence*, vol. 38, p. 353-366, 1989.

[DEC 99] DECHTER R., "Bucket Elimination: A Unifying Framework for Reasoning", *Artificial Intelligence*, vol. 113, p. 41-85, 1999.

[DEC 01] DECHTER R., FATTAH Y. E., "Topological Parameters for Time-Space Tradeoff", *Artificial Intelligence*, vol. 125, p. 93-118, 2001.

[FRE 85] FREUDER E., QUINN M., "Taking Advantage of Stable Sets of Variables in Constraint Satisfaction Problems", *Proceedings of IJCAI*, p. 1076-1078, 1985.

[FRE 92] FREUDER E., WALLACE R., "Partial Constraint Satisfaction", *Artificial Intelligence*, vol. 58, p. 21-70, 1992.

[GIV 03] DE GIVRY S., LARROSA J., MESEGUER P., SCHIEX T., "Solving Max-SAT as Weighted CSP", *Proceedings of CP*, 2003.

[GIV 06] DE GIVRY S., SCHIEX T., VERFAILLIE G., "Exploiting Tree Decomposition and Soft Local Consistency in Weighted CSP", *Proceedings of AAAI*, 2006.

[GOT 00] Gottlob G., Leone N., Scarcello F., "A Comparison of Structural CSP Decomposition Methods", *Artificial Intelligence*, vol. 124, p. 343-282, 2000.

[GOT 02] Gottlob G., Hutle M., Wotawa F., "Combining Hypertree, Bicomp and Hinge Decomposition", *Proceedings of ECAI*, p. 161-165, 2002.

[HUA 03] Huang J., Darwiche A., "A Structure-Based Variable Ordering Heuristic for SAT", *Proceedings of IJCAI*, p. 1167-1172, 2003.

[JÉG 03] Jégou P., Terrioux C., "Hybrid Backtracking Bounded by Tree-Decomposition of Constraint Networks", *Artificial Intelligence*, vol. 146, p. 43-75, 2003.

[JÉG 04] Jégou P., Terrioux C., "Decomposition and Good Recording for Solving Max-CSPs", *Proceedings of ECAI*, p. 196-200, 2004.

[JÉG 05] Jégou P., Ndiaye S. N., Terrioux C., "Computing and Exploiting Tree-Decompositions for Solving Constraint Networks", *Proceedings of CP*, p. 777-781, 2005.

[JÉG 06] Jégou P., Ndiaye S. N., Terrioux C., "An Extension of Complexity Bounds and Dynamic Heuristics for Tree-Decompositions of CSP", *Proceedings of CP*, 2006.

[KOS 99] Koster A., Frequency Assignment – Models and Algorithms, PhD thesis, University of Maastricht, November 1999.

[LAR 02] Larrosa J., Meseguer P., Sánchez M., "Pseudo-Tree Search with Soft Constraints", *Proceedings of ECAI*, p. 131-135, 2002.

[LAR 03] Larrosa J., Dechter R., "Boosting Search with Variable Elimination in Constraint Optimization and Constraint Satisfaction Problems", *Constraints*, vol. 8, num. 3, p. 303-326, 2003.

[MAR 04] Marinescu R., Dechter R., "AND/OR Tree Search for Constraint Optimization", *Proceedings of CP workshop on Soft Constraints and Preferences*, 2004.

[MES 00] Meseguer P., Sánchez M., "Tree-based Russian Doll Search", *Proceedings of CP Workshop on soft constraint*, 2000.

[MES 01] Meseguer P., Sánchez M., "Specializing Russian Doll Search", *Proceedings of CP*, p. 464–478, 2001.

[MES 02] Meseguer P., Sánchez M., Verfaillie G., "Opportunistic Specialization in Russian Doll Search", *Proceedings of CP*, p. 264-279, 2002.

[ROB 86] Robertson N., Seymour P., "Graph minors II: Algorithmic Aspects of Tree-Width", *Algorithms*, vol. 7, p. 309-322, 1986.

[SCH 95] Schiex T., Fargier H., Verfaillie G., "Valued Constraint Satisfaction Problems: hard and easy problems", *Proceedings of IJCAI*, p. 631-637, 1995.

[SMI 94] Smith B., "The Phase Transition and the Mushy Region in Constraint Satisfaction Problems", *Proceedings of ECAI*, p. 100-104, 1994.

[TAR 84] Tarjan R., Yannakakis M., "Simple Linear-time Algorithms to Test Chordality of Graphs, Test Acyclicity of Hypergraphs, and Selectively Reduce Acyclic Hypergraphs", *SIAM Journal on Computing*, vol. 13 (3), p. 566-579, 1984.

[TER 03] Terrioux C., Jégou P., "Bounded Backtracking for the Valued Constraint Satisfaction Problems", *Proceedings of CP*, p. 709-723, 2003.

[VER 96] Verfaillie G., Lemaître M., Schiex T., "Russian Doll Search for Solving Constraint Optimization Problems", *Proceedings of AAAI*, p. 181-187, 1996.

PART VII

Constraints in Software Testing, Verification and Analysis

Edited by Benjamin BLANC, Arnaud GOTLIEB and Claude MICHEL

Introduction

Recent years have seen an increasing interest in the application of constraint-solving techniques to the field of verification, testing and analysis of software systems. A significant body of constraint-based techniques have been proposed and investigated in program verification, software model checking, static program analysis, structural and model-based testing, computer security, etc. These applications also introduced specific issues which were at the root of dedicated constraint-solving techniques. Among these issues, we may cite the requirement for heterogenous type handling, the ability to deal with control structures, or the need to solve constraints over specific domains such as floating-point numbers. Thus, we initiated this workshop with the hope that people coming from these communities could meet to exchange experiences and fruitful ideas which could enhance their current and future work.

This part of the book contains a selection of refereed papers from participants of the workshop on Constraints in Software Testing, Verification and Analysis, held on the 25th September 2006 in Nantes, France. This year, the organizers of the CPsec workshop[1], Giampaolo Bella, Stefano Bistarelli, Simon N. Foley and Fred Spiessens contacted us to propose transferring some of their papers to CSTVA, as CPsec shared significant interests with the CSTVA workshop. The workshop was attended by nearly 25 participants and included two sessions, six regular presentations, an invited presentation by Andy King "On Modular-Reduction Vulnerabilities", and a presentation of the French ACI's V3F project. This project, from which the workshop originated, started three years ago with the aim of addressing the specific features of floating-point computations in critical software verification and validation.

1. CPsec is a workshop dedicated to the applications of constraint programming to computer security.

After a careful reviewing process, we selected four papers addressing issues of program analysis and constraint programming as well as computer security:

– Michel Leconte and Bruno Berstel propose to extend a CP solver with congruence domains to avoid the slow convergence phenomenon due to the large domains that program analysis often has to handle;

– Erwan Jahier and Pascal Raymond describe algorithms to solve Boolean and numerical constraints, and to draw values among the set of solutions;

– Yannick Chevalier and Mounira Kourjieh present a method relying on the reduction of constraint solving to take into account, at the symbolic level, that an intruder actively attacking a protocol execution may use some collision algorithms in reasonable time during an attack;

– Najah Chridi and Laurent Vigneron investigate a strategy, based on both a service-driven model for group protocols and constraint solving for flaw detection for group protocol properties.

We wish to thank the speakers and participants who made the workshop a stimulating event, as well as the program committee and the reviewers for their thorough evaluations of submissions.

Benjamin Blanc, Arnaud Gotlieb, Claude Michel
co-organizers of CSTVA'06

Program Committee

Benjamin Blanc,
Fabrice Bouquet,
Arnaud Gotlieb,
Andy King,
Bruno Legeard,
Bruno Marre,
Fred Mesnard,
Christophe Meudec,
Claude Michel,
Andreas Podelski,
Jean-Charles Régin,
Michel Rueher,
Pascal Van Hentenryck.

Additional reviewers

Frédéric Besson, Martine Ceberio, Yannick Chevalier, Tristan Denmat, Katy Dobson, Patricia Hill, Bruno Martin, Matthieu Petit, Michael Rusinowitch, Fred Spiessens.

Chapter 21

Extending a CP Solver with Congruences as Domains for Program Verification

Constraints generated for program verification tasks very often involve integer variables ranging over all the machine-representable integer values. Thus, if the propagation takes a time that is linear in the size of the domains, it will not reach a fix point in practical time. Consider a simple constraint such as $2x + 2y = 1$ where x and y are integer variables with values ranging from $-d$ to d, for a particular integer d. Obviously, there is no solution to this constraint, and the "usual" interval reduction will find this out, by reducing the domains of x and y down to empty sets. However, to achieve this, the interval reduction will have to step through all the domains $[-d, d]$, then $[-d + 1, d - 1]$, etc. converging onto the empty interval.

We stress that this *slow convergence* phenomenon occurs during the propagation of constraints: the time taken to reach a fix point is proportional to the width of the domains. Propagation occurs both initially and during labeling; as a result, slow convergence may happen when searching for a solution. In addition, because program verification often works by refutation, verification problems tend to produce unsatisfiable constraint problems. If the time needed to conclude to unsatisfiability is proportional to the size of the domains of the variables, this results in inefficiency in some cases, and especially on bug-free programs, for which the constraint problems are unsatisfiable.

Chapter written by Michel LECONTE and Bruno BERSTEL.

To avoid this slow convergence phenomenon, we propose to enrich a constraint programming solver (CP solver) with *congruence domains*. Using a CP solver to solve such problems has the advantage of genericity, that is, being able to address a large class of formulas. This comes at the price of completeness, but practical experience shows that it is effective most of the time [COL 06]. Congruences are about the division of an integer by another, and the remainder in this division. Congruence analysis comes from the static analysis community. It was introduced by Granger in [GRA 89]. As shown in that paper [GRA 89], congruence analysis is not restricted to linear equations, but can also handle general multiplicative expressions. We extend its scope to other non-linear expressions such as absolute value or minimum expressions.

As an example of program verification problems that lead to proving that a conjunction of integer equalities is unsatisfiable, consider the problem of overlapping conditions in guarded integer programs. The original motivation for the work presented in this chapter comes from the verification of business rules programs, but the overlapping conditions problem may arise in any context that involves guarded commands. The program below returns the number of days in a Gregorian calendar year.

```
function nbOfDays (y : int) : int is
   y === 0 mod 4  ->  366  |
   y === 1 mod 4  ->  365  |
   y === 2 mod 4  ->  365  |
   y === 3 mod 4  ->  365
end
```

The guards in this program do not overlap. To prove it, we shall first translate the guards into constraints, which gives the four constraints $y = 4x_i + i$, for $i = 0, 1, 2, 3$. In these constraints y and x_i are integer variables lying in $[-d-1, d]$ for some integer d (potentially $2^{31} - 1$). Then we shall prove that for any two distinct i and j between 0 and 3, the conjunction $y = 4x_i + i \wedge y = 4x_j + j$ is unsatisfiable. As previously seen in this section, interval reduction can achieve this, but will need d steps. The rest of this chapter shows that using congruences as domains allows a CP solver to prove the unsatisfiability in a fixed number of steps.

In this chapter, all variables are elements of $\mathbb{Z}$, the set of the integers. We will denote $a\mathbb{Z} + b$ for the set $\{az + b \mid z \in \mathbb{Z}\}$. For $x \in a\mathbb{Z} + b$, we will also denote $x \equiv b\,[a]$. We will use $a \wedge b$ for the greatest common divisor of a and b, and $a \vee b$ for the least common multiplier of a and b.

21.1. Related work

Congruence analysis was introduced by Granger [GRA 89, GRA 91] with applications for automatic vectorization. Today congruence analysis is an important technique, especially for verifying pointer alignment properties [BAL 04, VEN 05]. Congruence domains have been extended to constraints of the form $x - y \equiv b\,[c]$ [MIN 02, BAG 97, TOM 94]. Grids [BAG 06, MÜL 05] are another extension which addresses *relational* congruence domains. [GRA 97] proposes an extension of the congruence analysis by considering sets of rationals of the form $a\mathbb{Z} + b$, where $a, b \in \mathbb{Q}$.

In this chapter, we extend the finite domain CP solver ILOG JSOLVER with congruence as domains for variables. Very few CP solvers reason with congruence. The ALICE system [LAU 78] and its successor RABBIT [LAU 96] implement some congruence reasoning capabilities as part of formal constraint handling. As we will see, interval and congruence domains interact smoothly [GRA 89, BAL 04, VEN 05]. Numerical domains, such as intervals, are available in static analysis systems such as ASTRÉE [COU 05] or PPL [BAG 05, PPL 06], which also provides congruences.

21.2. Congruences as domains

The scope of constraints that we consider here extends to any equality constraint over integer variables and expressions. The integer expressions are built using the usual $+$, $-$, $\times$, $\div$ arithmetic operators, as well as the absolute value, minimum, and maximum ones. We also consider *element expressions* in the form $\mathbf{t}[i]$, where $\mathbf{t}$ is an array of integer variables, and i is an integer variable. An *element constraint* is a constraint of the form $z \in \{\mathbf{t}[i]\}$, which amounts to the disjunction $\bigvee_i z = \mathbf{t}[i]$. Finally, we also consider *if-then-else expressions* in the form $\mathsf{if}(c, e_1, e_2)$, where c is a constraint, and the e_i are integer expressions. The if-then-else expression denotes the expression e_1 if the constraint c is true, and the expression e_2 if the constraint c is false. Although the whole range of integer constraints is covered, congruence analysis alone will not always detect the unsatisfiability of a set of integer constraints. And this does not harm, since it is simply meant to strengthen the constraint propagation.

Let us first consider the equation $2x + 4y + 6z = 1$. When looking for integer solutions, the interval-based constraint propagation will perform no bound reduction at all. In particular, the unsatisfiability of the constraint will not be detected by constraint propagation. A congruence reasoning shows that the expression $2x + 4y + 6z$ is even, and thus cannot equal 1. Remember that a constraint $\sum_i a_i x_i = c$ has no solution if the greatest common divisor $\bigwedge_i a_i$ does not divide the constant c. We can use this property in the propagators of integer linear constraints in a *passive* way: we calculate the greatest common divisor of the coefficients of uninstantiated variables, and check if it divides the constant minus the sum of the $a_i x_i$ for instantiated variables.

Let us now consider the system $2x+4y+3z = 1$ and $z = 2t+12$. The passive use of congruence information will not detect that z cannot be even in $2x+4y+3z = 1$. Thus the unsatisfiability of the two constraints will be not detected. However, it would be a bad idea to use such a congruence constraint in an *active* way without caution. Imagine for example that the congruence constraint not only checks for the constants dividing the greatest common divisor, but also *adjusts* the bounds of the domains of variables accordingly. Let us say that propagating $2x + 4y + 3z = 1$ would lead to adjusting the bounds of z in such a way that these bounds are not even. Coming back to the example above, an empty domain will be found for z, as the constraints will eventually lead to a domain with both odd and even bounds. Unfortunately, this would exhibit a slow convergence behavior since the bounds would change by one unit at a time.

The way to solve this last problem is to share the congruence information between constraints, that is to say to equip variables with congruence information, as opposed to hiding it in the actual values of their bounds. Consequently, in the very same way we associate a point-wise finite domain with each integer variable, we associate with each of them a congruence domain in the form of a pair (a, b) that represents the set $a\mathbb{Z}+b$. Then for each expression, the congruence domain of the expression can be calculated from the congruence domains of the sub-expressions, using the formulas detailed in next section. Similarly the calculated congruence domains are propagated by equality constraints to reduce the congruence domains of the variables. This active use of congruence information, where domains are reduced, subsumes the passive use described previously, which only performs divisibility checks.

21.3. Propagation of congruences as domains

Each integer variable has a congruence domain, noted $a\mathbb{Z} + b$, which represents all possible values for this variable. We use $0\mathbb{Z} + b$ to represent the constant b, and $1\mathbb{Z} + 0$ as the domain of a variable with all integers as possible values.

We now define how to propagate the congruences through *operations*. Given $x \in a\mathbb{Z}+b$ and $y \in a'\mathbb{Z}+b'$, the congruence domain for $x+y$ is $(a \wedge a')\mathbb{Z}+(b + b')$, and the one for $x \times y$ is $(aa' \wedge a'b \wedge ab')\mathbb{Z} + bb'$. These formulas, and those for subtraction and division, can be found in [GRA 89].

As for union expressions, if $z \in \{x, y\}$ then the congruence domain of z is $(a \wedge a' \wedge |b - b'|)\mathbb{Z} + b$. This last formula gives the formula for *if-then-else* expressions, denoted $\mathsf{if}(c, e_1, e_2)$. If the constraint c is known to be true (resp. false), then the congruence domain for *if-then-else* is the congruence domain of e_1 (resp. e_2). However if the truth value of the constraint is unknown, then the expression has a congruence domain which is the union of the congruence domains of the two expressions. (This unifies an over-approximation of *if-then-else* expressions.) Given $x \in a\mathbb{Z} + b$, $y \in a'\mathbb{Z} + b'$, and a constraint c:

$$\mathsf{if}(c, x, y) \in \begin{cases} a\mathbb{Z} + b & \text{if } c \text{ is known to be true} \\ a'\mathbb{Z} + b' & \text{if } c \text{ is known to be false} \\ (a \wedge a' \wedge |b - b'|)\mathbb{Z} + b & \text{otherwise} \end{cases}$$

This also leads to the formula for a min expression, as $\min(x, y)$ is equivalent to $\mathsf{if}(x < y, x, y)$, as well as for the absolute value since $|x| = \mathsf{if}(x < 0, -x, x)$. Finally, for an array $\mathbf{t}$ of integer variables and an integer variable i, the congruence domain of the expression $z = \mathbf{t}[i]$ can be calculated from the one of $z \in \{\mathbf{t}[j]\}$ for all legal indices j.

We now indicate how to deal with *equality* constraints. As usual when propagating through equality, we just have to calculate the intersection of the domains. Given $x \in a\mathbb{Z} + b$ and $y \in a'\mathbb{Z} + b'$:

$$\text{if } x = y \text{ then } x \in \begin{cases} (a \vee a')\mathbb{Z} + b'' & \text{if } (a \wedge a') \text{ divides } (b - b') \\ \emptyset & \text{otherwise} \end{cases}$$

The number b'' can be calculated using the Generalized Euclid's algorithm [KNU 81]. If the equality constraint involves expressions instead of variables, then the congruence domains of the expressions are used to calculate the intersection. This resulting domain is then downward propagated to the sub-expressions of the expressions until it reaches the variables.

Let us illustrate how the propagation of congruence domains proceeds on the equation $4x = 3|y| + 2$. In the absence of further information, we have $x, y \in 1\mathbb{Z}+0$. The formulas for addition, multiplication, and absolute value give that $4x \in 4\mathbb{Z}+0$ and $3|y|+2 \in 3\mathbb{Z}+2$. The formula for the equality constraint gives that both expressions belong to $12\mathbb{Z} + 8$. Since $4x \in 12\mathbb{Z} + 8, x \in 3\mathbb{Z} + 2$. Since $3|y| + 2 \in 12\mathbb{Z} + 8, |y| \in 4\mathbb{Z} + 2$. The absolute value can be decomposed into the case where $y \in 4\mathbb{Z} + 2$, and the case where $-y \in 4\mathbb{Z} + 2$. This latter case gives $y \in 4\mathbb{Z} - 2$, which is the same as $4\mathbb{Z} + 2$. Eventually $y \in 4\mathbb{Z} + 2$. The domains cannot be further reduced: a fix point is reached with $x \in 3\mathbb{Z} + 2$ and $y \in 4\mathbb{Z} + 2$.

21.4. Cooperation of congruences and intervals

The idea here is to merge the two notions and to consider domains of the form $a\mathbb{Z} + b \cap [min, max]$. It is called reduced interval congruence (RIC) in [BAL 04, VEN 05]. By combining the two domains, information coming from interval domains will be used by the congruence domain and vice-versa.

To communicate information from interval domains to congruence domains, three techniques are applicable. When a variable is bound, as for instance in $x = b$, this can be formulated in congruences as $x \in 0\mathbb{Z} + b$. When it is found that $x \in \{b_i\}$ for some constants b_i, this implies that $x \in (\bigwedge_{i>0} |b_i - b_0|)\mathbb{Z} + b_0$. For an element constraint $z \in \{\mathbf{t}[i]\}$, the range of the variable i restricts the elements of $\mathbf{t}$ that are to be taken into account to calculate the congruence domain of z.

To communicate information from congruence domains to interval domains, we will use the fact that the bounds of a variable must lie in the same congruence domain as the variable itself. That is, if $x \in [min, max]$ and $x \in a\mathbb{Z} + b$, then min and max must be adjusted in order to belong to $a\mathbb{Z} + b$. When $a \neq 0$, the adjusted min is $a\lceil(min-b)/a\rceil+b$ and the adjusted max is $a\lfloor(max-b)/a\rfloor+b$. If the diameter $max-min$ is less than a, the variable will have a singleton or empty domain. For instance if the interval domain was reduced to $[0, a-1]$, then the variable could be instantiated to b, which is the only element of $a\mathbb{Z}+b\cap[0, a-1]$. For an element constraint $z \in \{\mathbf{t}[i]\}$, the congruence domain of z is to be taken into account to remove from the index variable domain the values i_0 for which $z = \mathbf{t}[i_0]$ cannot be satisfied. Also, for an *if-then-else* expression $z = \mathsf{if}(c, x, y)$, we can deduce that c is true (resp. false) if the domains of z and y (resp. x) do not intersect.

Let us close this section with a example showing non-trivial reductions. Consider the two constraints $4x = 3y + 2$ and $|x| - 12z = 2$. We have already seen that the first constraint leads to $x \in 3\mathbb{Z}+2$ and $y \in 4\mathbb{Z}+2$. Now, looking at the second constraint, we deduce that $|x| \in 12\mathbb{Z}+2$. Since $|x| = \mathsf{if}(x < 0, -x, x)$, we deduce that $x \in 12\mathbb{Z} + 10$ (if $x < 0$) or $x \in 12\mathbb{Z} + 2$ (if $x \geq 0$). Because $12\mathbb{Z} + 10 \cap 3\mathbb{Z} + 2 = \emptyset$, we are left with $x \in 12\mathbb{Z} + 2$ and $x \geq 0$.

21.5. Conclusion

Integer constraint propagation exhibits a *slow convergence* phenomenon when the time to reach a fix point or to fail is proportional to the size of the domains of the variables. To avoid this phenomenon for some integer equality constraints, we added some congruence reasoning capabilities to a CP solver. We took the idea of equipping the variables with congruence domains from the abstract interpretation community [GRA 89], as it leads to efficient and scalable implementations. We have shown how a CP solver can benefit from these congruence domains with several examples, concluding with illustrations on the interaction of interval and congruence domains.

21.6. References

[BAG 97] BAGNARA R., Data-Flow Analysis for Constraint Logic-Based Languages, PhD thesis, Dipartimento di Informatica, University of Pisa, March 1997.

[BAG 05] BAGNARA R., HILL P. M., ZAFFANELLA E., "Not Necessarily Closed Convex Polyhedra and the Double Description Method", *Formal Asp. Comput.*, vol. 17, num. 2, p. 222-257, 2005.

[BAG 06] BAGNARA R., DOBSON K., HILL P. M., MUNDELL M., ZAFANELLA E., "Grids: A Domain for Analyzing the Distribution of Numerical Values", *LOPSTR*, 2006.

[BAL 04] BALAKRISHNAN G., REPS T. W., "Analyzing Memory Accesses in x86 Executables", DUESTERWALD E., Ed., *CC*, vol. 2985 of *LNCS*, Springer, p. 5-23, 2004.

[COL 06] COLLAVIZZA H., RUEHER M., "Exploration of the Capabilities of Constraint Programming for Software Verification", HERMANNS H., PALSBERG J., Eds., *TACAS*, vol. 3920 of *LNCS*, Springer, p. 182-196, 2006.

[COU 05] COUSOT P., COUSOT R., FERET J., MAUBORGNE L., MINÉ A., MONNIAUX D., RIVAL X., "The ASTRÉE Analyzer", *ESOP'05*, 2005.

[GRA 89] GRANGER P., "Static Analysis of Arithmetic Congruences", *International Journal of Computer Math*, p. 165-199, 1989.

[GRA 91] GRANGER P., "Static Analysis of Linear Congruence Equalities among Variables of a Program", ABRAMSKY S., MAIBAUM T. S. E., Eds., *TAPSOFT, Vol.1*, vol. 493 of *LNCS*, Springer, p. 169-192, 1991.

[GRA 97] GRANGER P., "Static Analyses of Congruence Properties on Rational Numbers (Extended Abstract)", HENTENRYCK P. V., Ed., *SAS*, vol. 1302 of *LNCS*, Springer, p. 278-292, 1997.

[KNU 81] KNUTH D. E., *Seminumerical Algorithms*, vol. 2 of *The Art of Computer Programming*, Addison-Wesley, Reading, Massachusetts, second edition, 1981.

[LAU 78] LAURIÈRE J.-L., "A Language and a Program for Stating and Solving Combinatorial Problems", *Artif. Intell.*, vol. 10, num. 1, p. 29-127, 1978.

[LAU 96] LAURIÈRE J.-L., Programmation de contraintes ou programmation automatique, Report , L.I.T.P., 1996, `http://www.lri.fr/~sebag/Slides/Lauriere/Rabbit.pdf`.

[MIN 02] MINÉ A., "A Few Graph-Based Relational Numerical Abstract Domains", HERMENEGILDO M. V., PUEBLA G., Eds., *SAS*, vol. 2477 of *LNCS*, Springer, p. 117-132, 2002.

[MÜL 05] MÜLLER-OLM M., SEIDL H., "A Generic Framework for Interprocedural Analysis of Numerical Properties", HANKIN C., SIVERONI I., Eds., *SAS*, vol. 3672 of *LNCS*, Springer, p. 235-250, 2005.

[PPL 06] PPL, Parma Polyhedra Library, 2006, `http://www.cs.unipr.it/ppl`.

[TOM 94] Toman D., Chomicki J., Rogers D. S., "Datalog with Integer Periodicity Constraints", *SLP*, p. 189-203, 1994.

[VEN 05] Venable M., Chouchane M. R., Karim M. E., Lakhotia A., "Analyzing Memory Accesses in Obfuscated x86 Executables", Julisch K., Krügel C., Eds., *DIMVA*, vol. 3548 of *LNCS*, Springer, p. 1-18, 2005.

Chapter 22

Generating Random Values Using Binary Decision Diagrams and Convex Polyhedra

Reactive embedded programs are often critical, and therefore need to be verified. Formal verification methods face both theoretical (undecidability) and practical (state explosion) problems. Test and simulation, that do not explore the whole state space, remain the only tractable method for complex systems, in particular when numeric variables are involved.

Reactive systems are not supposed to behave correctly in a chaotic environment, and thus a completely random test generation is likely to produce irrelevant executions. As a matter of fact, the environment, while non-deterministic, is generally far from random: it satisfies known properties that must be taken into account to generate realistic test sequences. Hence, we defined a testing framework which includes languages for describing constrained random scenarios [RAY 06]. More precisely, an atomic step is described by a constraint on the current values of the variables. Those steps are then combined with control structures describing possible behaviors (sequence, loop, choice). Here, we focus on the basic problem of solving a constraint in order to generate a single step.

This chapter describes algorithms for solving Boolean and numerical constraints, and for randomly selecting values among the set of solutions. We chose a solving technology that allowed a fine control in the way solutions are elected.

Chapter written by Erwan JAHIER and Pascal RAYMOND.

Indeed, a fair selection is sometimes required, while favoring limit cases is often interesting for testing.

22.1. BDD and convex polyhedra

The constraints we want to solve are a mixture of Boolean and linear numerical constraints. Basically, the formers are handled with BDD (Binary Decision Diagram), and the latter with convex polyhedra. We briefly review these representations before explaining how we use them.

Binary Decision Diagram. A Binary Decision Diagram is a concise representation of Boolean expressions [BRY 86]. The BDD of a formula f is a Directed Acyclic graph (DAG) (1) with two leaves labeled by *true* and *false* (2) where non-leaf nodes have two successors, and (3) where non-leaf nodes are labeled by variables of f. All solutions of a formula can be obtained by enumerating in its BDD all paths from the top-level node to the true leaf. For such a path, when a node is traversed using its *left* branch (resp. *right* branch), it means that the corresponding variable is true (resp. false).

Convex polyhedra, convex polytopes. The objective is to solve linear inequations, namely, to solve systems of the form $P = \{X|AX \leq B\}$, where A is a $n \times m$-matrix of constants, and B a m-vector of constants. A system such as this defines a convex polyhedron. If all variables are bounded, the polyhedron is called a *polytope*[1]. Solving such systems requires the set of the polytope *generators*, namely, the vertices $v_1, \ldots, v_k$ such that $P = \{\sum_{i=1,k} \alpha_i.v_i | \sum_{i=1,k} \alpha_i = 1\}$ to be calculated. Reasonably efficient algorithms exist for that purpose, and several convex polyhedron libraries are freely available on the web [JEA 02, BAG 02, WIL 93]. They are all based on an algorithm from Chernikova [CHE 68].

22.2. The resolution algorithm

The input constraint language combines Boolean and numeric linear variables, constants, and operators. It is described by the following syntax rules, where $\mathcal{N}$, V_b, and $V_n$stand for numeric constants, Boolean and numeric variables respectively:

$$\begin{array}{lll} \langle e_b \rangle & \rightarrow & V_b \mid \text{true} \mid \text{false} \mid \text{not } \langle e_b \rangle \mid \langle e_b \rangle \star_b \langle e_b \rangle \mid \langle e_n \rangle \star_n \langle e_n \rangle \mid (\langle e_b \rangle) \\ \langle e_n \rangle & \rightarrow & V_n \mid \mathcal{N} \mid \mathcal{N}.\langle e_n \rangle \mid \langle e_n \rangle \star_\pm \langle e_n \rangle \mid \text{if } \langle e_b \rangle \text{ then } \langle e_n \rangle \text{ else } \langle e_n \rangle \mid (\langle e_n \rangle) \\ \star_b & \rightarrow & \vee \mid \wedge \mid \text{xor} \mid \ldots \qquad \star_n \rightarrow \; > \mid \geq \mid = \mid \leq \mid < \qquad \star_\pm \rightarrow + \mid - \end{array}$$

1. Existing libraries are not restricted to bounded polyhedron, but for software testing purposes, we are only interested in these.

Get rid of if-then-else. The first step is to transform constraints to remove if-then-else constructs. Indeed, together with the comparison operators, the "if-then-else" construct allows us to combine numeric and Boolean arbitrarily deeply. In addition, this does not fit in the resolution scheme we propose later.

If $t(e_1) = \{(c_1^i, e_1^i)\}_{i=1,n}$ and $t(e_2) = \{(c_2^j, e_2^j)\}_{j=1,m}$, then we have:

- $t(e_1 + e_2) = \{c_1^i \wedge c_2^j, e_1^i + e_2^j\}_{i=1,n}^{j=1,m}$ (ditto for "$-$", "$*$", etc.)
- $t(if\ c\ then\ e_1\ else\ e_2) = \{(t_{\mathbb{B}}(c) \wedge c_1^i, e_1^i)\}_{i=1,n} \cup \{(\overline{t_{\mathbb{B}}(c)} \wedge c_2^j, e_2^j)\}_{j=1,m}$
- $t_{\mathbb{B}}(e_1 \leq e_2) = t_{\mathbb{B}}(e_1 - e_2 \leq 0)$
- $t_{\mathbb{B}}(e_1 \leq 0) = \vee_{i=1,n}(e_1^i \leq 0 \wedge c_1^i)$ (ditto for "$\geq$", "$<$", "$>$", "$=$", "$\neq$")

Figure 22.1. *Remove "if-then-else" from constraints. t transforms numeric expressions, and $t_{\mathbb{B}}$ transforms Boolean expressions*

The key idea of the transformation is to put the formula into the normalized form: $if\ c_1\ then\ e_1\ else\ if\ c_2\ then\ e_2\ else\ \ldots\ else\ if\ c_n\ then\ e_n$, where the Boolean expressions $c_1, \ldots, c_n$ do not contain "if-then-else". This transformation can be done recursively on the constraint syntax structure, as described in Figure 22.1. This transformation has the property to produce a set of conditions $\{c_1, \ldots, c_n\}$ that forms a partition ($i \neq j \implies c_i \wedge c_j = false$, and $\vee_{i=1,n} c_i = true$). Therefore, for the sake of conciseness, we note such expressions as a set of couples made of a condition and a numeric expression: $\{(c_i, num\_expr_i)\}_{i=1,n}$. During this transformation, one can simplify the resulting set by merging conditions corresponding to the same numeric expressions, and by removing couples where the condition is false. However, the transformation into BDD performed later will automatically do that.

Solving Booleans. We first replace numeric constraints with new intermediary Boolean variables: $\alpha_i = n_1 \star_n n_2$. The resulting expression contains only Boolean variables and operators, and can therefore be translated into a BDD. This BDD provides the set all the Boolean solutions of the constraint.

Solving numerics. For each of the Boolean solution, namely, for each path in the BDD, we obtain a set of linear numeric constraints $\{\alpha_i\}_i$. Those constraints are sent to a numeric constraint *solver* that is based on a convex polyhedra library. On demand, the solver can return the set of generators corresponding to the convex polytope defined by the sent constraints. In the end, each constraint is translated into a BDD that represents a union of (possibly empty) convex polytopes.

22.3. Choosing solutions

In order to generate test sequences, once the set of solutions is calculated, one of them has to be chosen. Using convex polytopes, this set of solutions is represented by a set of generators, which makes it very easy to favor limit cases. A slightly more complex task is to perform a fair choice efficiently. However, as we discuss later, being fair sometimes costs too much. We present in the following some heuristics leading to reasonable trade-offs.

Random choice of Boolean values. The first step consists of selecting a Boolean solution. Once the constraint has been translated into a BDD, we have a (hopefully compact) representation of the set of solutions. We first need to randomly choose a path into the BDD that leads to a true leaf. But if we naively perform a fair toss at each branch of the BDD during this traversal, we would be very unfair. Indeed, a BDD branch that contains very few solutions compared to the other one would have the same probabilities to be taken. That is the reason why counting the solutions before drawing them is necessary. Once each branch of the BDD is decorated with its solution number, performing a fair choice among Boolean solutions is straightforward.

Random choice of numeric values. In order to generate value sequences for feeding a program under test, it is often useful to try to limit values at domain boundaries. Since convex polyhedron libraries return the set of polytope generators, choosing randomly among vertices, or edges, or faces, is easy. One heuristic we use that is computationally cheap and that appears to be quite effective is the following. Consider a set of n generators $\{\gamma_i\}_{i=1,n}$ of a polytope of dimension k. Then: (1) draw one generator p; (2) draw another generator γ_j in $\{\gamma_i\}_{i=1,n}$; (3) draw a point p' between p and γ_j; (4) go back to step 2 with $p = p'$, $k - 1$ times. The advantage of this heuristic is that, since at step 2 the same γ_j can be chosen several times, vertices are favored, and then edges, and then faces, and so on, whatever the dimension of the polytope is.

Drawing numerics uniformly. At the end of the process, we have a valuation for each of the Boolean variables, plus a set of generators representing several possible valuations for the numeric variables. In order to complete the random selection process, one needs to randomly choose such a numeric valuation using the generators. The only method we are aware of to perform this choice uniformly is to draw inside the smallest parallelepiped parallel to the origin axes containing the polytope until a point inside the polytope is found. That parallelepiped can be obtained by computing the minimum and the maximum values of generators for each of their components.

Fairness versus efficiency. The algorithm proposed above suffers from a major performance problem. Indeed, drawing into the smallest parallelepiped parallel to the axes is not that expensive: O(n.d), where d is the polytope dimension, and n is the number of generators (the draw is O(d) by itself, but obtaining the parallelepiped is O(n.d)). But the number of necessary draws depends on the ratio between the volume of the polytope and the volume of the parallelepiped. And this ratio can be very small. For example, when the dimension of the polytope is smaller than that of the parallelepiped, the theoretical ratio is 0. It is not always true for the numeric values effectively representable on a machine, but still, the ratio is very small. By changing the base using a Gauss method, this ratio can be augmented. But as the dimension increases, doing that is not sufficient.

A solution would be to calculate the smallest surrounding parallelepiped (via rotations), but this ought to be very costly. We have also considered performing a random walk in the polytope: but in order to know when to stop the walk, we need to know the volume of polytope, which is also very expensive [LOV 93].

A rather efficient algorithm to draw inside a convex polytope is to use a variant of the algorithm of section 22.3, choosing a different generator each time at step 2. But this leads to a distribution that is not uniform: points tend to concentrate close to vertices. To our knowledge, there is no computationally simple way to perform such a uniform draw. However, for high dimensions, this seems to be a reasonable trade-off, especially for testing purposes. Even if it means completely losing control over the distribution, another thing that could be done would be to use enumerative techniques based on Simplex.

22.4. Available tools

All the tools presented in the sequel are freely available on the web at the URL: `http://www-verimag.imag.fr/ synchron/index.php?page=tools`

LuckyDraw. The solving and drawing algorithms presented here are provided under the form of an Ocaml and a C API [2]. Both the underlying BDD and polyhedra library have been developed at Verimag and are available separately.

This library is used in Rennes by the STG tool (symbolic test generation). STG aims at generating and executing test cases using symbolic techniques [JEA 05]. LuckyDraw is used at the final stage in order to generate a concrete trace sequence from a symbolic automaton describing several scenarios.

2. Many thanks to B. Jeannet for the C-Ocaml interfacing work.

Lucky, Lutin, Lurette. The LuckyDraw library is one of the main building-blocks of Lutin and Lucky[3], which are languages dedicated to the programming of stochastic reactive systems. Basically, the constraint language presented here is extended with (1) an explicit control structure, (2) a mechanism to instantiate input and memory variables, (3) and external function calls (to be applied on input and memory variables only). Those languages were originally designed to model reactive program environments in the Lurette testing tool [JAH 06].

22.5. Related work

Quite a lot of related work (e.g [GOT 98, BOT 02, MAR 00]) deals with how to generate random-based test sequences using constraint logic programming (CLP) or other external constraint solvers. Constraint-based techniques tackle quite general constraints, whereas we focus on linear constraints. Moreover, most authors use enumerative techniques such as SAT for Booleans and Simplex for numerics, whereas we use more constructive techniques (BDD and convex polyhedron). The main advantage of constructive techniques is to provide a finer-grained control over the distribution of the values to be generated. Besides, very few authors describe the drawing heuristics they use precisely, in particular with respect to numeric values.

Several works describe constraints-based methods [DEN 04] and heuristics [PRE 01] to generate random test values using graphs. But as already mentioned above and in section 22.4, we also have an explicit control structure in order to control finely the distribution [RAY 06] (although we hardly describe this in this article).

Other work uses constraint solvers to generate test sequences for B and Z specifications [LEG 02]. Their test objective is to generate values that exercise their boundaries. A finite state automation (FSA) that represents a set of abstract executions is obtained via a reachability analysis. Then, they try to find a concrete path in the abstract FSA to reach desired states. The way they concretize a trace from FSA is comparable to what we do with Lucky [RAY 06], the difference being that their FSA are automatically generated, whereas we provide a language to program them.

Another difference with most works using constraint solvers to generate tests is that they use finite domain solvers, whereas we more specifically deal with floating-point numbers or rationals. The domain of floating-point numbers is also finite, but it is much bigger and finite domain solvers are quite inefficient with floats.

3. www-verimag.imag.fr/~synchron/tools.html.

22.6. Conclusion

We have presented algorithms to solve linear constraints combining Boolean and numeric variables, as well as several heuristics to choose data values among the constraint solutions. Although they sometimes handle non-linear constraints, other constraint based techniques for generating test sequences generally target finite domain variables (integers). Moreover, they are based on enumerative techniques (SAT, Simplex) that make it difficult to provide a fine-grained control over the distribution of the generated values. The algorithms and the associated library presented in this article are used as one of the main component of automatic test generation tools [RAY 98, JAH 06].

22.7. References

[BAG 02] BAGNARA R., RICCI E., ZAFFANELLA E., HILL P. M., "Possibly Not Closed Convex Polyhedra and the Parma Polyhedra Library", *SAS*, vol. 2477 of *LNCS*, Springer, p. 213-229, 2002.

[BOT 02] BOTELLA B., GOTLIEB A., MICHEL C., RUEHER M., TAILLIBERT P., "Utilisation des contraintes pour la génération automatique de cas de test structurels", *Technique et Science Informatiques*, vol. 21, num. 9, p. 1163-1187, 2002.

[BRY 86] BRYANT R. E., "Graph-Based Algorithms for Boolean Function Manipulation", *IEEE Trans. Computers*, vol. 35, num. 8, p. 677-691, 1986.

[CHE 68] CHERNIKOVA N. V., "Algorithm for Discovering the Set of all Solutions of a Linear Programming Problem", *U.S.S.R. Computational Mathematics and Mathematical Physics*, vol. 8, num. 6, 1968.

[DEN 04] DENISE A., GAUDEL M.-C., GOURAUD S.-D., "A Generic Method for Statistical Testing", *ISSRE*, IEEE Computer Society, p. 25-34, 2004.

[GOT 98] GOTLIEB A., BOTELLA B., RUEHER M., "Automatic Test Data Generation Using Constraint Solving Techniques", *ISSTA*, p. 53-62, 1998.

[JAH 06] JAHIER E., RAYMOND P., BAUFRETON P., "Case Studies with Lurette V2", *International Journal on Software Tools for Technology Transfer (STTT)*, vol. Special Section on Leveraging Applications of Formal Methods, 2006.

[JEA 02] JEANNET B., The Polka Convex Polyhedra library Edition 2.0, May 2002, www.irisa.fr/prive/bjeannet/newpolka.html.

[JEA 05] JEANNET B., JÉRON T., RUSU V., ZINOVIEVA E., "Symbolic Test Selection Based on Approximate Analysis", HALBWACHS N., ZUCK L. D., Eds., *TACAS*, vol. 3440 of *LNCS*, Springer, p. 349-364, 2005.

[LEG 02] LEGEARD B., PEUREUX F., UTTING M., "Automated Boundary Testing from Z and B", ERIKSSON L., LINDSAY P. A., Eds., *FME*, vol. 2391 of *LNCS*, Springer, p. 21-40, 2002.

[LOV 93] LOVÁSZ L., SIMONOVITS M., "Random walks in a convex body and an improved volume algorithm", *Random Structures and Algorithms*, vol. 4, num. 4, p. 359–412, 1993.

[MAR 00] MARRE B., ARNOULD A., "Test Sequences Generation from LUSTRE Descriptions: GATeL", *ASE*, p. 229-, 2000.

[PRE 01] PRETSCHNER A., "Classical Search Strategies for Test Case Generation with Constraint Logic Programming", BRICS, Ed., *Proceedings of the Workshop on Formal Approaches to Testing of Software (FATES'01)*, Aalborg, Denmark, p. 47-60, 2001.

[RAY 98] RAYMOND P., WEBER D., NICOLLIN X., HALBWACHS N., "Automatic Testing of Reactive Systems", *19th IEEE Real-Time Systems Symposium*, Madrid, Spain, 1998.

[RAY 06] RAYMOND P., JAHIER E., ROUX Y., "Describing and Executing Random Reactive Systems", *4th IEEE International Conference on Software Engineering and Formal Methods*, Pune, India, September 11-15 2006.

[WIL 93] WILDE D., "A Library for Doing Polyhedral Operations", 1993.

Chapter 23

A Symbolic Model for Hash-Collision Attacks

Cryptographic hash functions play a fundamental role in modern cryptography. They are used as cryptographic primitive for data integrity, authentication, key agreement, e-cash and many other cryptographic schemes and protocols. Cryptographic hash functions (or simply hash functions) map from larger domains to smaller ranges, they take a message as input and produce an output referred to as a *hash-value.* A hash function is many-to-one, implying that the existence of collisions (pairs of inputs with identical output) is unavoidable. However, only a few years ago, it was intractable to calculate collisions on hash functions, so they were considered to be collision-free by cryptographers, and protocols were built upon this assumption. From the 1990s onwards, several authors have proved the tractability of finding pseudo-collision and collision attacks over several hash functions. Examples of collision-vulnerable hash functions are MD5 [BOE 93, WAN 04], MD4 [DOB 96, WAN 05a], RIPE-MD [WAN 05a], SHA-0 [BIH 04] and SHA-1 hash functions [WAN 05b]. Taking this into account, we consider that cryptographic hash functions have the following properties:

– the input can be of any length, the output has a fixed length, $\mathrm{h}(x)$ is relatively easy to calculate for any given x;

– pre-image resistance: given y, it is computationally infeasible to find any x such that $y = \mathrm{h}(x)$;

– 2nd-pre-image resistance: it is computationally infeasible, given x , to find x' different from x such that $\mathrm{h}(x) = \mathrm{h}(x')$;

Chapter written by Yannick CHEVALIER and Mounira KOURJIEH.

– hash collision: it is computationally *feasible* to calculate two distinct inputs x and x' which hash to the same output, i.e., $\mathrm{h}(x) = \mathrm{h}(x')$ provided that x and x' are created at the same time and independently of one another.

In other words, a collision-vulnerable hash function h is one for which an intruder can find two different messages x and x' with the same hash value. To mount a collision attack, an adversary would typically begin by constructing two messages with the same hash where one message appears legitimate or innocuous while the other serves the intruder's purposes. For example, consider the following simple protocol:

$$A \rightarrow B : M, \sigma_A(M)$$

where $\sigma_A(M)$ denotes A's digital signature on message M using the DAS digital signature scheme in which only the hash-value of M by a function h is considered. The following attack:

$$A \rightarrow B : M', \sigma_A(M)$$

can be launched successfully if the intruder first calculates two different messages M and M' having the same hash value and then can lead A into executing the protocol with message M.

In this chapter we propose a decision procedure to decide on the insecurity of cryptographic protocols when a hash function for which collisions may be found is employed. Relying on the result [CHE 05] we do not consider here other cryptographic primitives such as public key encryption, signature or symmetric key encryption, and assume that a protocol execution has already been split into the views of the different equational theories. The decidability proof presented here heavily relies on a recent result [CHE 06b] that enables constraint-solving problems to be reduced with respect to a given intruder to constraint-solving problems for a simpler one. In our case, we reduce constraint solving for an intruder exploiting the collision properties of hash functions to constraint solving for an intruder operating on words, that is with an associative symbol of concatenation.

23.1. Terms and subterms

We consider an infinite set of free constants C and an infinite set of variables $\mathcal{X}$. For any signature $\mathcal{G}$ (i.e. sets of function symbols not in C with arities) we denote $\mathrm{T}(\mathcal{G})$ (resp. $\mathrm{T}(\mathcal{G}, \mathcal{X})$) the set of terms over $\mathcal{G} \cup \mathrm{C}$ (resp. $\mathcal{G} \cup \mathrm{C} \cup \mathcal{X}$). The former is called the set of ground terms over $\mathcal{G}$, while the latter is simply called the set of terms over $\mathcal{G}$.

Given a signature $\mathcal{G}$, a *constant* is either a free constant or a function symbol of arity 0 in $\mathcal{G}$. Given a term t we denote by $\mathrm{Var}(t)$ the set of variables occurring in t. A substitution σ is an involutive mapping from $\mathcal{X}$ to $\mathrm{T}(\mathcal{G},\mathcal{X})$ such that $\mathrm{Supp}(\sigma) = \{x|\sigma(x) \neq x\}$, the *support* of σ, is a finite set. The application of a substitution σ to a term t (resp. a set of terms E) is denoted $t\sigma$ (resp. $E\sigma$) and is equal to the term t (resp. E) where all variables x have been replaced by the term $\sigma(x)$. A substitution σ is *ground* w.r.t. $\mathcal{G}$ if the image of $\mathrm{Supp}(\sigma)$ is included in $\mathrm{T}(\mathcal{G})$.

An *equational presentation* $\mathcal{H} = (\mathcal{G}, A)$ is defined by a set A of equations $u = v$ with $u, v \in \mathrm{T}(\mathcal{G},\mathcal{X})$ and u, v without free constants. For any equational presentation $\mathcal{H}$ the relation $=_{\mathcal{H}}$ denotes the equational theory generated by $(\mathcal{G}, A)$ on $\mathrm{T}(\mathcal{G},\mathcal{X})$, that is the smallest congruence containing all instances of axioms of A. We will also often refer to $\mathcal{H}$ as an equational theory. An equational theory $\mathcal{H}$ is said to be *consistent* if two free constants are not equal modulo $\mathcal{H}$ or, equivalently, if it has a model with more than one element modulo $\mathcal{H}$.

The *subterms* of a term t are denoted $\mathrm{Sub}(t)$ and are defined recursively as usual. If t is an atom then $\mathrm{Sub}(t) = \{t\}$. If $t = f(t_1, \ldots, t_n)$ then $\mathrm{Sub}(t) = \{t\} \cup \bigcup_{i=1}^{n} \mathrm{Sub}(t_i)$.

Unification systems. We recall here the definition of unification systems and their satisfaction.

DEFINITION.– *(Unification systems) Let $\mathcal{H}$ be a set of equational axioms on $\mathrm{T}(\mathcal{G},\mathcal{X})$. An $\mathcal{H}$-*unification system* $\mathcal{S}$ is a finite set of couples of terms in $\mathrm{T}(\mathcal{G},\mathcal{X})$ denoted by $\{u_i \stackrel{?}{=} v_i\}_{i\in\{1,\ldots,n\}}$. It is satisfied by a ground substitution σ, and we note $\sigma \models_{\mathcal{H}} \mathcal{S}$, if for all $i \in \{1, \ldots, n\}$ we have $u_i\sigma =_{\mathcal{H}} v_i\sigma$.*

In the rest of this chapter, unification problems are denoted with the symbol $\stackrel{?}{=}$, and we reserve $=$ for equality or equality modulo. We will consider only satisfiability of unification systems with ordering constraints, i.e. we consider the following decision problem:

Ordered Unifiability

Input: A $\mathcal{H}$-unification system $\mathcal{S}$ and an ordering $\prec$ on the variables X and constants C of $\mathcal{S}$.

Output: SAT if, and only if, there exists a substitution σ such that $\sigma \models_{\mathcal{H}} \mathcal{S}$ and for all $x \in X$ and $c \in C$, $x \prec c$ implies $c \notin \mathrm{Sub}(x\sigma)$

23.2. Analysis of reachability properties of cryptographic protocols

We recall in this section the definitions of [CHE 05] concerning our model of an intruder actively attacking a protocol, and of the simultaneous constraint satisfaction problems employed to model a finite execution of a protocol.

DEFINITION.– *An* intruder system $\mathcal{I}$ *is given by a triple* $\langle \mathcal{G}, \mathcal{S}, \mathcal{H} \rangle$ *where* $\mathcal{G}$ *is a signature,* $S \subseteq \mathrm{T}(\mathcal{G}, \mathcal{X})$ *and* $\mathcal{H}$ *is a set of equations between terms in* $\mathrm{T}(\mathcal{G}, \mathcal{X})$. *With each* $t \in S$ *we associate a* deduction rule $\mathrm{L}^t : \mathrm{Var}(t) \to t$ *and* $\mathrm{L}^{t,\mathrm{g}}$ *denotes the set of ground instances of the rule* L^t modulo $\mathcal{H}$*:*

$$\mathrm{L}^{t,\mathrm{g}} = \{l \to r \mid \exists \sigma, \textit{ground substitution on } \mathcal{G},\ l = \mathrm{Var}(t)\sigma \text{ and } r =_{\mathcal{H}} t\sigma.\}$$

The set of rules $\mathrm{L}_{\mathcal{I}}$ *is defined as the union of the sets* $\mathrm{L}^{t,\mathrm{g}}$ *for all* $t \in \mathcal{S}$.

Each rule $l \to r$ in $\mathrm{L}_{\mathcal{I}}$ defines an intruder deduction relation $\to_{l\to r}$ between finite sets of terms. Given two finite sets of terms E and F we define $E \to_{l\to r} F$ if and only if $l \subseteq E$ and $F = E \cup \{r\}$. We denote $\to_{\mathcal{I}}$ the union of the relations $\to_{l\to r}$ for all $l \to r$ in $L_{\mathcal{I}}$ and by $\to_{\mathcal{I}}^{*}$ the transitive closure of $\to_{\mathcal{I}}$. Given an initial set of terms E, we denote $\overline{E}^{\mathcal{I}}$ the (infinite) set of terms deducible from E by the intruder theory $\mathcal{I}$. When $\mathcal{I}$ is clear from context, we simply denote it $\overline{E}$. We capture the fact that the intruder first has to build a message m_1, then send it to an honest agent, receive the response and add it to its knowledge, and iterates using the following constraint systems.

DEFINITION.– *(Constraint systems) – Let* $\mathcal{I} = \langle \mathcal{G}, S, \mathcal{H} \rangle$ *be an intruder system. An* $\mathcal{I}$-constraint system $\mathcal{C}$ *is denoted:* $((E_i \rhd v_i)_{i\in\{1,\ldots,n\}}, \mathcal{S})$ *and is defined by a sequence of couples* $(E_i, v_i)_{i\in\{1,\ldots,n\}}$ *with* $v_i \in \mathcal{X}$ *and* $E_i \subseteq \mathrm{T}(\mathcal{G}, \mathcal{X})$ *for* $i \in \{1, \ldots, n\}$*, and* $E_{i-1} \subseteq E_i$ *for* $i \in \{2, \ldots, n\}$ *and by an* $\mathcal{H}$*-unification system* $\mathcal{S}$.
An $\mathcal{I}$-constraint system $\mathcal{C}$ *is satisfied by a ground substitution* σ *if for all* $i \in \{1, \ldots, n\}$ *we have* $v_i\sigma \in \overline{E_i\sigma}$ *and if* $\sigma \models_{\mathcal{H}} \mathcal{S}$. *If a ground substitution* σ *satisfies a constraint system* $\mathcal{C}$ *we denote it by* $\sigma \models_{\mathcal{I}} \mathcal{C}$.

We are not interested in general constraint systems but only in those related to protocols. In particular we need to express that a message to be sent at a particular step i should be built from previously received messages recorded in the variables $v_j, j < i$, and from the initial knowledge. To this end we define:

DEFINITION.– *(Deterministic constraint systems) – We say that an* $\mathcal{I}$*-constraint system* $((E_i \rhd v_i)_{i\in\{1,\ldots,n\}}, \mathcal{S})$ *is* deterministic *if, and only if, for all* i *in* $\{1, \ldots, n\}$ *we have* $\mathrm{Var}(E_i) \subseteq \{v_1, \ldots, v_{i-1}\}$.

In order to be able to combine solutions of constraints for the intruder theory $\mathcal{I}$ with solutions of constraint systems for intruders defined on a disjoint signature we have, as for unification, to introduce some ordering constraints to be satisfied by the solution (see [CHE 05] for details on this construction).

Ordered Satisfiability

Input: an $\mathcal{I}$-constraint system $\mathcal{C}$, $X = \mathrm{Var}(\mathcal{C})$, $C = \mathrm{Const}(\mathcal{C})$ and a linear ordering $\prec$ on $X \cup C$.

Output: SAT if, and only if, there exists a substitution σ such that $\sigma \models_{\mathcal{I}} \mathcal{C}$ and
for all $x \in X$ and $c \in C$, $x \prec c$ implies $c \notin \mathrm{Sub}(x\sigma)$

23.3. Model of a collision-aware intruder

We define in this section intruder systems to model the way an active intruder may deliberately create collisions for the application of hash functions. Note that our model doesn't take into account the time for finding collisions, which is significantly greater than the time necessary for other operations.

23.3.1. *Intruder on words*

We first define our goal intruder, that is an intruder only able to concatenate messages and extract *prefixes* and *suffixes*. We denote by $\mathcal{I}_{\mathrm{AU}} = \langle \mathcal{F}_{AU}, S_{AU}, \mathcal{E}_{AU} \rangle$ an intruder system that operates on words, such that, if $\_\cdot\_$ denotes the concatenation and ϵ denotes the empty word, the intruder has at its disposal all ground instances of the following deduction rules:

$$\begin{cases} x, y \to x \cdot y \\ x \cdot y \to x \\ x \cdot y \to y \\ \to \epsilon \end{cases}$$

Moreover we assume that the concatenation and empty word operations satisfy the following equations:

$$\begin{cases} x \cdot (y \cdot z) & = & (x \cdot y) \cdot z & & & \\ x \cdot \epsilon & = & x & \qquad \epsilon \cdot x & = & x \end{cases}$$

Pitfall. Notice that this intruder model does not fit into the intruder systems definition of [CHE 05, CHE 06b]. The rationale for this is that, in the notation given here, the application of the rules is non-deterministic, and thus cannot be modeled easily into our "deduction by normalization" model. We however believe that a deterministic and still associative model of message concatenation by means of an "element" unary operator, associative operator "·" and head and tail operations may be introduced. This means that we also assume that unification problems are only among words of this underlying theory, disregarding equations that may involve these extra operators. Another direction would be to extend the current definition of intruder systems to take these deductions directly into account. We leave the exact soundness of our model for further analysis and concentrate on the treatment of collision discovery for hash functions.

23.3.2. *Intruder on words with free function symbols*

We extend the $\mathcal{I}_{\mathrm{AU}}$ intruder with two free function symbols g and f. We denote by $\mathcal{I}_{\mathrm{g}} = \langle \{\mathrm{g}\}, \{\mathrm{g}(x_1, x_2, y_1, y_2)\}, \emptyset \rangle$ the intruder which has at its disposal all ground instances of the rule:

$$x_1, x_2, y_1, y_2 \rightarrow \mathrm{g}(x_1, x_2, y_1, y_2).$$

We denote by $\mathcal{I}_{\mathrm{f}} = \langle \{\mathrm{f}\}, \{\mathrm{f}(x_1, x_2, y_1, y_2)\}, \emptyset \rangle$ the intruder which has at its disposal all ground instances of the rule:

$$x_1, x_2, y_1, y_2 \rightarrow \mathrm{f}(x_1, x_2, y_1, y_2).$$

Finally, we denote by $\mathcal{I}_{\mathrm{free}}$ the intruder which is the disjoint union of $\mathcal{I}_{\mathrm{AU}}$, $\mathcal{I}_{\mathrm{f}}$ and $\mathcal{I}_{\mathrm{g}}$, and we have:

$$\mathcal{I}_{\mathrm{free}} = \langle \mathcal{F}_{\mathrm{AU}} \cup \{\mathrm{g}, \mathrm{f}\}, S_{\mathrm{AU}} \cup \{\mathrm{f}(x_1, x_2, y_1, y_2), \mathrm{g}(x_1, x_2, y_1, y_2)\}, \mathcal{E}_{\mathrm{AU}} \rangle .$$

23.3.3. *Hash-colliding intruder*

We assume that the algorithm followed by the intruder to find collisions starting from two messages m and m' proceeds as follows:

1) first the intruder splits both messages into two parts, thus choosing m_1, m_2, m'_1, m'_2 such that $m = m_1 \cdot m_2$ and $m' = m'_1 \cdot m'_2$;

2) then, in order to find collisions, the intruder calculates two messages $\mathrm{g}(m_1, m_2, m'_1, m'_2)$ and $\mathrm{f}(m_1, m_2, m'_1, m'_2)$ such that:

$$(\mathrm{HC})\ \mathrm{h}(m_1 \cdot \mathrm{g}(m_1, m_2, m'_1, m'_2) \cdot m_2) = \mathrm{h}(m'_1 \cdot \mathrm{f}(m_1, m_2, m'_1, m'_2) \cdot m'_2).$$

Given $S_{\mathrm{h}} = \{\mathrm{f}(x_1, x_2, y_1, y_2), \mathrm{g}(x_1, x_2, y_1, y_2), \mathrm{h}(x)\}$, we denote:

$$\mathcal{I}_{\mathrm{h}} = \langle \mathcal{F}_{\mathrm{AU}} \cup \{\mathrm{f}, \mathrm{g}, \mathrm{h}\}, S_{\mathrm{AU}} \cup S_{\mathrm{h}}, \mathcal{E}_{\mathrm{AU}} \cup \{(HC)\} \rangle$$

the intruder system which may create collisions for the application of hash functions. Our main theorem is that insecurity of protocols employing weak hash functions is decidable.

THEOREM.– *Ordered satisfiability for the $\mathcal{I}_h$ intruder is decidable.* **Sketch of the proof.** In [CHE 06a], we give an algorithm that reduces $\mathcal{I}_h$ intruder system to $\mathcal{I}_{free}$ intruder system. We then reduce the decidability problems of ordered reachability for $\mathcal{I}_{free}$ deterministic constraint problems to the decidability problems of ordered reachability for deterministic constraint problems for $\mathcal{I}_g$, $\mathcal{I}_f$ and $\mathcal{I}_{AU}$. As $\mathcal{I}_{free}$ is the disjoint union of $\mathcal{I}_g$, $\mathcal{I}_f$ and $\mathcal{I}_{AU}$, ordered satisfiability for the last three intruder systems is decidable [CHE 06a, DEL 04], and using the result obtained in [CHE 05], we prove that ordered satisfiability for $\mathcal{I}_{free}$ intruder is decidable [CHE 06a] and, thus, ordered satisfiability for $\mathcal{I}_h$ is decidable.

23.4. Conclusion

We have presented here a novel decision procedure for the search for attacks on protocols employing hash functions subject to collision attacks. Since this procedure is of practical interest for the analysis of the already normalized protocols relying on these weak functions, we plan to implement it into an already existing tool, CL-Atse [M. 06]. Alternatively an implementation may be carried out in OFMC [BAS 05], though the support of associative operators is still partial. In order to model hash functions we have introduced new symbols to denote the ability to create messages with the same hash value. This introduction amounts to the skolemization of the equational property describing the existence of collisions. We believe that this construction can be extended to model the more complex and game-based properties that appear when relating a symbolic and a concrete model of cryptographic primitives.

23.5. References

[BAS 05] BASIN D. A., MÖDERSHEIM S., VIGANÒ L., "OFMC: A Symbolic Model Checker for Security Protocols", *Int. J. Inf. Sec.*, vol. 4, num. 3, p. 181-208, 2005.

[BIH 04] BIHAM E., CHEN R., "Near-Collisions of SHA-0", FRANKLIN M. K., Ed., *CRYPTO*, vol. 3152 of *Lecture Notes in Computer Science*, Springer, p. 290-305, 2004.

[BOE 93] DEN BOER B., BOSSELAERS A., "Collisions for the Compression Function of MD5", *EUROCRYPT*, p. 293-304, 1993.

[CHE 05] CHEVALIER Y., RUSINOWITCH M., "Combining Intruder Theories", CAIRES L., ITALIANO G. F., MONTEIRO L., PALAMIDESSI C., YUNG M., Eds., *ICALP*, vol. 3580 of *LNCS*, Springer, p. 639-651, 2005.

[CHE 06a] CHEVALIER Y., KOURJIEH M., A Symbolic Intruder Model for Hash-Collision Attacks, Report , IRIT, Dec 2006, Available at `ftp://ftp.irit.fr/IRIT/LILAC/HashCollisions-CK.pdf`.

[CHE 06b] CHEVALIER Y., RUSINOWITCH M., "Hierarchical Combination of Intruder Theories", *Proceedings of the 17th International Conference on Rewriting Techniques and Applications (RTA'05)*, Lecture Notes in Computer Science, Seattle, USA, Springer, August 2006.

[DEL 04] DELAUNE S., JACQUEMARD F., "Narrowing-Based Constraint Solving for the Verification of Security Protocols", *Proceedings of the 18th International Workshop of Unification (UNIF'04)*, Cork, Ireland, July 2004.

[DOB 96] DOBBERTIN H., "Cryptanalysis of MD4.", GOLLMANN D., Ed., *Fast Software Encryption*, vol. 1039 of *Lecture Notes in Computer Science*, Springer, p. 53-69, 1996.

[M. 06] M. T., "The CL-Atse Protocol Analyser, 17th International Conference on Term Rewriting and Applications – RTA 2006, Seattle, WA/USA, July, 12, 2006,", *RTA*, vol. 4098 of *Lecture Notes in Computer Science*, Springer, p. 277–286, 2006.

[WAN 04] WANG X., FENG D., LAI X., YU H., Collisions for Hash Functions MD4, MD5, HAVAL-128 and RIPEMD, `http://eprint.iacr.org/`, 2004.

[WAN 05a] WANG X., LAI X., FENG D., CHEN H., YU X., "Cryptanalysis of the Hash Functions MD4 and RIPEMD.", CRAMER R., Ed., *EUROCRYPT*, vol. 3494 of *Lecture Notes in Computer Science*, Springer, p. 1-18, 2005.

[WAN 05b] WANG X., YIN Y. L., YU H., "Finding Collisions in the Full SHA-1.", SHOUP V., Ed., *CRYPTO*, vol. 3621 of *Lecture Notes in Computer Science*, Springer, p. 17-36, 2005.

Chapter 24

Strategy for Flaw Detection Based on a Service-driven Model for Group Protocols

In recent years, applications requiring an unbounded number of participants have received increasing attention from both public and dedicated domains. As such, the design of secure group protocols [WON 98] continues to be one of the most challenging areas of security research. To make their communication secure, group members need to use a shared key, known as group key, which has to be updated following changes in the dynamics of the group (join or leave operations, etc.). Therefore, several protocols dedicated to key establishment and updates have been proposed [RAG 05]. Among them, we are particularly interested in group key agreement protocols [PER 03]. These protocols enable a group of participants to share a common key over insecure public networks, even when adversaries completely control all the communications.

Research into formal verification of cryptographic protocols has so far mainly concentrated on reachability properties such as secrecy and authentication. It has given such successful and interesting results in recent years that this field could be considered saturated. As such, many fully automatic tools have been developed and successfully applied to find flaws in published protocols, where many of these tools employ so-called *constraint solving* (see e.g., [CHE 04]). Nowadays, dealing with the verification of group protocols brings several problems to light. Indeed, such protocols highlight new requirements and consider some complicated security properties other than secrecy and authentication. In fact, most of the verification approaches can only tackle specific models of

---

Chapter written by Najah CHRIDI and Laurent VIGNERON.

protocol, and usually require the size of the group to be set in advance. This leads to a lower probability of discovering attacks. In addition, because of the dynamics of group membership, security requirements are more complicated to satisfy.

The main contribution of the present work is a strategy for flaw detection for the security properties of group protocols. Our approach is based both on the service-driven model described in [CHR 05] and on constraint solving. As already mentioned, in the past constraint solving has been successfully employed for reachability properties and proved to be a good basis for practical implementations. The service-driven model is a model for group key agreement protocols that require a service from each participant, a contribution to the group key. It enables security properties to be specified for group protocols as sets of constraints. This model specifies both group protocols and a large class of their intended properties, varying from standard secrecy and authentication properties to much more difficult properties, such as key integrity, and backward and forward secrecy. Hence, our strategy paves the way for extending existing tools to deal with security properties of group protocols. In this chapter, we focus on group key establishment protocols, but it is worth mentioning that our method also deals with contributing protocols.

The chapter is structured as follows. In section 24.1, we present the input required by our method and show how this model can be used to search for attacks. The management of Intruder knowledge and constraints is explained in sections 24.1.3 and 24.1.4. Several attacks have been found by applying our strategy to some protocols; they are briefly summarized in section 24.2.

24.1. Protocol modeling and attack search

24.1.1. *Input of the method*

As with any communication protocol, a group protocol can be seen as an exchange of messages between several participants. This exchange is usually described by the set of actions executed by each participant in a normal protocol execution, i.e. without intervention of an Intruder.

Formally speaking, we define an instance of the protocol as the union of instances of roles and Intruder knowledge. An instance of a protocol is then given by $(\{\mathcal{R}_p \rightarrow \mathcal{S}_p\}_{p \in \mathcal{P}}, <_{\mathcal{P}}, IK_0)$ where, $\mathcal{P}$ is a finite set and:

– $\{\mathcal{R}_p \rightarrow \mathcal{S}_p\}_{p \in \mathcal{P}}$ denotes the set of rules of receive-send messages exchanged between honest participants. Each rule defines one step of the protocol: the messages sent by a honest participant ($\mathcal{R}_p$) and the expected response ($\mathcal{S}_p$).

– $<_{\mathcal{P}}$ is a partial order over $\mathcal{P}$, such that for each variable x of a $\mathcal{S}_j$, there is a $i <_{\mathcal{P}} j$ such that x is a variable of $\mathcal{R}_i$.

– IK_0 is a set of terms representing the initial Intruder knowledge.

We illustrate our method's input using the Asokan-Ginzboorg [ASO 00] protocol. Messages exchanged throughout this protocol are expressed as follows:

$$\begin{array}{lcl} 1.A_n \longrightarrow \text{ALL} & : & A_n, \{E\}_P \\ 2.A_i \longrightarrow A_n & : & A_i, \{R_i, S_i\}_E,\ \text{i=1,...,n-1} \\ 3.A_n \longrightarrow A_i & : & \{\{S_j, \text{j=1,...,n}\}\}_{R_i},\ \text{i=1,...,n-1} \\ 4.A_i \longrightarrow A_n & : & A_i, \{S_i, H(S_1, \ldots, S_n)\}_k \text{ some } i, k = F(S_1, \ldots, S_n). \end{array}$$

In this message exchange, P is a short group password that is known by the n participants, H is a hash function and F is a commonly known function. E is a public key generated by the leader A_n and used to encrypt the contribution (S_i) of each participant A_i. R_i denotes a fresh symmetric key generated by the participant A_i, sent to the leader with the contribution S_i. The leader will use it to encrypt all contributions (including S_n) in order to send the whole message to the participant A_i.

Having tested our method over several scenarios of this protocol, we have found an interesting result in the case of two parallel sessions. In the first session, we have two participants: a leader A_1 and a normal member A_2 of the group. In the second session, the roles are exchanged. Due to limited space, we are only modeling the first session which is expressed by the following steps:

$$\begin{array}{lll} \mathbf{p_{111}}: & Init \longrightarrow A_1, \{E_1\}_P & \\ \mathbf{p_{121}}: & x_1, \{x_2, x_3\}_{E_1} \longrightarrow \{x_3, S_{11}\}_{x_2} & \\ \mathbf{p_{131}}: & x_1, \{x_3, H(x_3, S_{11})\}_{F(x_3, S_{11})} \longrightarrow End & Alg_{11} = F(x_3, S_{11}) \\ \mathbf{p_{211}}: & x_4, \{x_5\}_P \longrightarrow A_2, \{R_1, S_{21}\}_{x_5} & \\ \mathbf{p_{221}}: & \{x_6, x_7\}_{R_1} \longrightarrow A_2, \{S_{21}, H(x_6, x_7)\}_{F(x_6, x_7)} & Alg_{21} = F(x_6, x_7) \end{array}$$

p_{ijk} denotes the j-th step of the protocol played by the i-th participant in the k-th session. Alg_{ij} is the point of view of the group key of the i-th participant during the j-th session. S_{ij} denotes the contribution to the group key of the i-th participant in the j-th session. Variables are written in small letters, and constants start with a capital letter.
The second session can be specified in a similar way. Thus, the set of steps specifying both sessions is: $\mathcal{P} = \{p_{111}, p_{121}, p_{131}, p_{211}, p_{221}, p_{212}, p_{222}, p_{232}, p_{112}, p_{122}\}$.

The partial order $<_{\mathcal{P}}$ over its elements is defined by: $p_{111} <_{\mathcal{P}} p_{121} <_{\mathcal{P}} p_{131}$, $p_{211} <_{\mathcal{P}} p_{221}$, $p_{212} <_{\mathcal{P}} p_{222} <_{\mathcal{P}} p_{232}$ and $p_{112} <_{\mathcal{P}} p_{122}$.

24.1.2. *Searching for attacks in group protocols*

We present in this section the algorithm of searching for attacks. This algorithm takes as parameters the security property (denoted by *ppty*) to verify and the instance of the protocol. It analyzes all possible executions of the protocol, looking for one that contradicts the given security property.

```
Algorithm AttackSearch(ppty, instance)
    execCorrect = True
    SC_P = ConstraintsPpty(ppty, instance)
    Exec = BuildAllPossibleExecs(instance)
    While execCorrect And Exec ≠ ∅ Do
        choose (ST, STT, IK, SC) ∈ Exec
        canCompose = True
        While canCompose And STT ≠ ∅ Do
            choose R_p → S_p ∈ STT such that p is minimal
            If Compose(R_p, IK) Then
                Treat(R_p → S_p, IK, SC)
                remove R_p → S_p from STT
                add R_p → S_p to ST
            Else
                canCompose = False
            EndIf
        End
        If STT = ∅ And Attack(SC, SC_P) Then
            execCorrect = False
        EndIf
    End
```

An execution is represented by a 4-tuple (ST,STT,IK,SC): ST is the set of steps already done; STT is the totally ordered set of steps that have not been considered yet; IK is the Intruder knowledge; SC is the tree of constraints built from the beginning of the execution.

The initialization of the algorithm starts with the generation of the constraints SC_P that represent the violation of the security property (function *ConstraintsPpty*). Then, the function *BuildAllPossibleExecs* generates all the possible executions, i.e. all possible sequences of receive-send steps according to the partial order given in the protocol instance to be considered; in each of them, ST is empty, IK is the Intruder initial knowledge and SC is empty.

Then, for each possible execution, we try to take several steps forward: we first select the minimal step $\mathcal{R}_p \rightarrow \mathcal{S}_p$ in STT; we check if the Intruder can compose messages matching $\mathcal{R}_p$ from his current knowledge IK (*Compose* function); the *Treat* function considers each solution: for each composed message, it generates the constraints that link variables of $\mathcal{R}_p$ with it; the new knowledge brought by $\mathcal{S}_p$ is given to the Intruder (see section 24.1.3). The tree that corresponds to the disjunction of all those sets of constraints is combined with SC (see section 24.1.4).

If an execution is completed, we check if it corresponds to an attack, that is if the new value of SC is coherent with SC_P. If this is the case, the resolution of SC and SC_P, applied to the steps in ST, generates the trace of an attack. This method is rather efficient since the search for flaws is static and it corresponds to a resolution of two constraint systems. Nevertheless, it may happen

Operation	Composition Rules	Decomposition Rules
Fresh	$\frac{}{k}$ (k is new)	
Concatenation	$\frac{m1 \quad m2}{< m1, m2 >}$	$\frac{< m1, m2 >}{m1}, \frac{< m1, m2 >}{m2}$
Asymmetric Encryption	$\frac{m \quad k}{\{m\}_k}$	$\frac{\{m\}_k \quad inv(k)}{m}$
Symmetric Encryption	$\frac{m \quad b}{\{m\}_b}$	$\frac{\{m\}_b \quad b}{m}$
Product	$\frac{x \quad y}{x.y}$	$\frac{x.y \quad y^{-1}}{x}$
Inverse	$\frac{y}{y^{-1}}$	$\frac{y^{-1}}{y = \{y^{-1}\}^{-1}}$
Exponentiation	$\frac{t \quad \alpha}{\alpha^t}$	$\frac{\alpha^{x.y} \quad y^{-1}}{\alpha^x}$

Table 24.1. *Rules of composition and decomposition of the Intruder*

that for an execution step, generating the constraints matching all possible composed messages to the expected message leads to a huge tree of constraints. In order to minimize this set, we propose to combine the construction of the constraints tree of the protocol SC and the test of coherence of the two trees of constraints SC and SC_P. Indeed, while generating the constraints of the protocol related to one step, we test the coherence of this subset of constraints with all the constraints built before. This makes it possible to eliminate unnecessary constraints. This can be done by simply initializing SC in each execution with SC_P.

24.1.3. *Intruder knowledge management*

In our method for flaw detection we assume that the Intruder follows the most referred to Intruder's model: the Dolev-Yao model [DOL 83]. In this model, the Intruder has complete control of the communications network: he can intercept, record, modify, compose, send, encrypt and decrypt (if he has the appropriate key) each message. He also has the possibility of sending faked messages in the name of another participant. As he has these capabilities, the Intruder has to manage the information that he can acquire at each step.

By Intruder knowledge (written IK), we mean all the information he can extract from the messages that have been sent over the network. The Intruder is able to decompose messages and to compose new ones, according to the rules given in Table 24.1. So, for a step $\mathcal{R}_p \rightarrow \mathcal{S}_p$, the Intruder has to compose messages that can match $\mathcal{R}_p$; if he can do this, honest participants will answer using the corresponding $\mathcal{S}_p$. The Intruder knowledge can then be enriched with the information resulting from the maximal decomposition of that $\mathcal{S}_p$. Note that the Intruder knowledge IK may contain some information that was not decomposable at a particular step, but that will be able to be decomposed at a further step thanks to some newly acquired information. Thus, decomposition may also apply to old information in IK.

24.1.4. *Constraint management*

Constraints generated by our algorithm are equalities ($x = y$) and disequalities ($x \neq y$) over constants, variables and terms. They are represented by a tree, where a path represents the conjunction of constraints (i.e. a partial execution), and the successors of a node the different alternatives. The initial constraint tree of an execution corresponds to the violation of the security property to be tested.

This tree is updated after each new step: at level i in the tree, the extension to level $i + 1$ is performed when a step $\mathcal{R}_p \rightarrow \mathcal{S}_p$ is possible, i.e. when the Intruder is able to compose messages matching $\mathcal{R}_p$. In this case, the constraints linking the composed message to $\mathcal{R}_p$ are generated. As there may be several solutions for composing messages that will be accepted by honest participants, a tree of constraints is built. Then, we connect the new constraint tree to each leaf at level i. The resulting tree is then simplified in different ways. First, constraints at level $i+1$ that are not coherent with those at parent levels (from the root to the level i) are removed. Then, if these constraints (at level $i + 1$) contain one constraint that already exists in previous levels or may be deduced then we may omit it in order to get rid of redundancy. Moreover, if a constraint at level $i + 1$ manages variables that already exist in previous levels and are now related to some new variables then this constraint is replaced by a new one connecting the new variables to their value (by transitivity). For variables appearing for the first time at level $i + 1$, and not linked to older variables, we have to remember that they can be assigned with information that is built with the Intruder knowledge of that level.

24.2. Verification results

By applying the strategy described in previous sections, we have found an attack of key agreement in the Asokan-Ginzboorg protocol [ASO 00]. We have also found two authentication attacks for the GDH.2 protocol [PER 03] with 4 participants (attacking resp. participants A_3 and A_4). The first attack is illustrated in Figure 24.1: it displays the normal execution of the protocol, plus the message change that leads to an attack; indeed, if $\alpha^{R_1 R_2 R_3}$ is replaced by $\alpha^{R_2 R_3}$, A_4 will then calculate $\alpha^{R_2 R_3 R_4}$ as the group key which is different

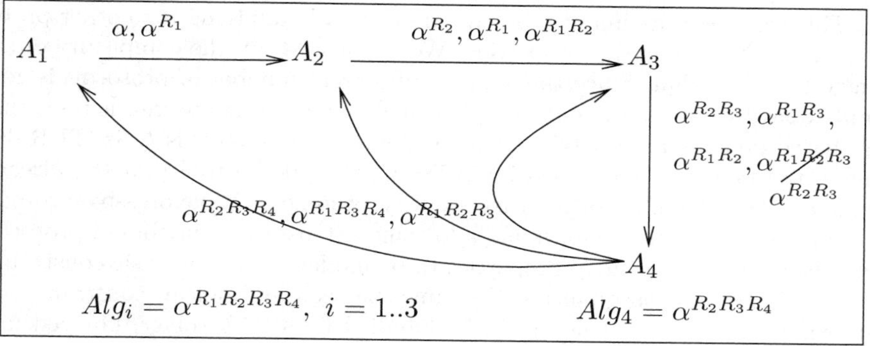

Figure 24.1. *First authentication attack for the GDH.2 protocol with 4 participants*

from the correct one ($\alpha^{R_1R_2R_3R_4}$). We describe below how this attack can be generalized to n participants.

Consider the GDH.2 protocol with n participants ($A_1, ..., A_n$). The Intruder can have the point of view of the group key of the last member A_n. Indeed, he intercepts the last message intended for A_n $(x_1, ..., x_{n-1}, x_n)$ and replaces the last component (x_n) with any other component of the message (x_1 or... or x_{n-1}). The Intruder will get components of the form ${x_i}^{R_n}$ where $i \in \{1, \ldots, n-1\}$ (sent by A_n). In addition, A_n deduces $Alg_n = {x_n}^{R_n}$ as the group key. However, this information is already available on the network as $x_n = x_i, i \in \{1, \ldots, n-1\}$.

The second attack on GHD.2 and its generalization to n participants, together with an attack on A-GDH.2 [PER 03] and the key agreement attack on Asokan-Ginzboorg can be found in [CHR 06].

24.3. Summary and future work

Throughout this chapter, we have presented a new strategy for dealing with group protocols and, more generally, contributed protocols. The approach hinges upon the use of the service-driven model to deduce constraints related to the violation of the security property to be verified. These constraints are used with the constraints of the protocol execution to obtain a trace of attack if it exists. This strategy enables new attacks to be pinpointed in three different protocols. From these attacks, we have generalized the result to two protocols with n participants.

This work is in its infancy, but we are currently applying it to other protocols and to other security properties. We will also study the complexity of the suggested algorithm. Since the analysis of a great number of protocols is generally done by automatic tools, we plan to extend existing automatic tools that are based on constraint solving. One of the best candidates is AtSe [TUR 06], one of the four back-ends used in AVISPA [ARM 05], a tool that has already treated a large number of internet security protocols. Its expressive protocol specification language enables, modulo some extensions, contributed protocols and their intended security properties to be modeled. As our basic constraints are equalities and disequalities, they may be seen as Boolean constraints, so the whole set of constraints could be handled by a SAT solver, plugged into AtSe. The suggested approach can also be developed to consider other kinds of group protocols such as hierarchical protocols that present additional verification constraints. For this, we will have to extend the service-driven model to deal with this type of protocols.

24.4. References

[ARM 05] Armando A., Basin D., Boichut Y., et al., "The AVISPA Tool for the Automated Validation of Internet Security Protocols and Applications", *17th Int. Conf. on Computer Aided Verification, CAV*, vol. 3576 of *LNCS*, Springer, p. 281-285, 2005.

[ASO 00] Asokan N., Ginzboorg P., "Key Agreement in Ad Hoc Networks", *Computer Communications*, vol. 23, num. 17, p. 1627–1637, 2000.

[CHE 04] Chevalier Y., Vigneron L., "Strategy for Verifying Security Protocols with Unbounded Message Size", *Journal of Automated Software Engineering*, vol. 11, num. 2, p. 141-166, Kluwer Academic Publishers, April 2004.

[CHR 05] Chridi N., Vigneron L., "Modélisation des propriétés de sécurité de protocoles de groupe", *Actes du 1er Colloque sur les Risques et la Sécurité d'Internet et des Systèmes, CRiSIS*, Bourges, France, p. 119-132, October 2005.

[CHR 06] Chridi N., Vigneron L., "Strategy for Flaws Detection based on a Services-driven Model for Group Protocols", *Proc. of the 1st Workshop on Constraints in Software Testing, Verification and Analysis, CSTVA*, p. 88-99, 2006.

[DOL 83] Dolev D., Yao A., "On the Security of Public Key Protocols", *IEEE Transactions on Information Theory*, vol. 29, num. 2, p. 198-207, 1983.

[PER 03] Pereira O., Modelling and Security Analysis of Authenticated Group Key Agreement Protocols, PhD thesis, Université catholique de Louvain, May 2003.

[RAG 05] Ragab Hassan H., Bouabdallah A., Bettahar H., Challal Y., "HI-KD: Hash-Based Hierarchical Key Distribution for Group Communication", Poster in IEEE-INFOCOM, Miami, FL, USA, 2005.

[TUR 06] Turuani M., "The CL-Atse Protocol Analyser", *Proc. of 17th Int. Conf. on Term Rewriting and Applications, RTA*, vol. 4098 of *LNCS*, p. 277-286, 2006.

[WON 98] Wong C., Gouda M., Lam S., "Secure Group Communications Using Key Graphs", *Proc. of the ACM SIGCOMM Conf. on Applications, Technologies, Architectures, and Protocols for Computer Communication*, p. 68–79, 1998.

PART VIII

Constraint Programming for Graphical Applications

Edited by Marc CHRISTIE, Hiroshi HOSOBE and Kim MARRIOTT

Chapter 25

Trends and Issues in using Constraint Programming for Graphical Applications

Since 1963, which witnessed the marriage between constraint techniques and graphical applications with Sutherland's Sketchpad system [SUT 63], a number of successful applications have emerged which demonstrate the strengths of this alliance and the usefulness of constraint solving for graphical layout and design. Traditionally, the main application areas have been:

– Diagram authoring tools: the use of constraint-solving techniques to preserve geometric relationships specified by the author during subsequent manipulation of the diagram is an obvious application of constraint-based graphics and, starting with Sketchpad, many experimental systems have been built that demonstrate the success of this alliance.

– Computer-aided design (CAD): in the field of engineering, it is often necessary to design two- or three-dimensional models of physical components. Such components involve geometric constraints that describe their geometric relationships as well as their shapes. CAD tools assist designers in geometric modeling by automatic maintenance of geometric constraints on physical components.

– Automated/assisted layout: in information visualization, for example, an important application of contraints has been visualization of abstract relational data and networks, such as biological networks, social networks, organization structure. Layout of graphs and related diagrams can be couched as a constrained optimization problem and a wide variety of specialized algorithms have

---

Chapter written by Marc Christie, Hiroshi Hosobe and Kim Marriott.

been developed to find "good" layouts [BAT 99]. In a more general way, this encompasses all applications that need to establish and maintain layout relations, e.g. widget layout in GUIs, advertisement placement or image labeling.

– Animation: to set and maintain properties on objects over time is a natural way of thinking and designing complex dynamic systems. Animation applications share a common problem in which the number of degrees of freedom are too important to be simultaneously manipulated easily by the user (e.g. path-planning, simulation and assisted manipulation).

However successful these applications are, there are still a number of significant problems which need to be overcome before the full potential of constraint-based approaches in graphical applications can be realized. Though recent advances in many aspects of constraint programming (CP) such as meta-heuristics, symmetry breaking and hybridizations open new possibilities, the current state-of-the-art is far from providing adequate support for graphical applications. In this chapter we identify and detail the particular characteristics of graphical applications that make it difficult to apply standard CP techniques directly. These fall into three broad categories.

The first is the development of more powerful constraint-solving techniques. One of the potential benefits of a constraint-based approach is that it allows the user to tailor the constraints and layout objectives to their particular application. Currently many applications utilize specialized algorithms for constraint solving which are quite brittle, and do not adequately support user customization. The problem is that the kind of constraint solving required in graphical applications is very difficult. They generally require the solving of heterogenous contraints (linear, polynomial, non-linear) over heterogenous domains (Boolean, symbolic, integer and numeric). Preferences need to be supported to handle over-constrained systems and performance has to be fast enough to support real-time interaction.

The second main issue is the user interface issues raised by providing constraints in the graphical application. This covers modeling the problem: authoring the constraints and determining strengths, priorities or controls on preferential constraints and representation of the constraints. It also covers user understand the solving process and constraint interaction such as unexpected failure due to inconsistent constraints.

The third issue is how to help the application programmer bridge the gap between the user interface and the underlying constraint solver. Problems here are the large gap between the high-level semantics of the application and the low-level constraints provided by current solvers. Another problem is the inadequacy of a black-box view of constraint solving when the solver needs to support interaction and understand constraint solving. Thus this third issue gives rise to a number of questions on the design of expressive, extensible, specific or generic modeling languages, libraries or APIs for constraint solvers.

The remainder of this chapter discusses these three issues in more detail while demonstrating how this field covers many of the most challenging and active problems in the constraint programming community.

25.1. More powerful constraint-solving techniques

Graphical applications typically have a number of characteristics that mean that standard constraint-solving algorithms and software cannot be directly used. As identified by G.J. Badros [BAD 00], graphical systems make strong demands on the underlying solving techniques: expressiveness, reliability, performance and predictability of the solutions from the point of view of the user. Traditionally, techniques range from simple one-way local propagation to multi-way propagation, iterative optimization, linear programming-based methods and backtracking. We identify in the following some of the demands on solving techniques.

25.1.1. *Mixture of discrete and continuous constraints*

Most graphical applications require a mixture of discrete and continuous constraint solving. Examples of common discrete constraints are determining which page a particular floating figure occurs on, topological relationships between diagram and document components, such as whether an object is to the left of another object, or the route of a connector. Continuous constraint solving arises because in many graphical applications positions and sizes naturally range over the reals and so constraints such as alignment and distribution require continuous constraint solving. Continuous solvers typically abstract discrete values in continuous specific operators (e.g. Numerica [HEN 97]), and little effort has been spent in devising adequate mixed contracting operators.

25.1.2. *Mixture of linear, polynomial, geometric and non-linear constraints*

Whereas the very first graphical applications only considered linear problems (due to limitations of available techniques), obvious relations such as distances (in layout applications) and geometric relations (in CAD) give rise to quadratic and non-linear constraints. Although the CP community, and more generally applied mathematics, have found adequate techniques for specific subclasses of problems considered separately, more general combinations of linear, polynomial, geometric and non-linear systems are not currently handled. Decompositions of mixed systems, as well as hybridizations of solving techniques are still active-open research topics. Actual graphical applications must either embed ad hoc techniques or restrict the functionalities to a limited subset of constraints.

25.1.3. *Managing user interaction*

One key characteristic of most graphical applications is user interaction. This gives rise to three specific challenges: efficient re-computation, dynamic constraint solving and stability of solutions:

– *Efficiency in re-computation:* interactive applications that support direct manipulation require close to real-time solving techniques that update the current solution given new values for some of the variables. Related solving techniques rely on any-time computation by currently maintaining a local best optimum. Linearization of the problem around the current configuration is generally a solution of choice to guarantee efficiency, at the price of accuracy and sometimes consistency.

– *Dynamic constraint solver:* interactive applications require the constraint solver to efficiently support insertion/deletion of constraints. The underlying solving techniques need to recalculate consistent (or close to consistent) solutions for each insertion/retreival, e.g. built on repairing or incremental solving techniques [MIG 99]. Reactive methods have been proposed and implemented to manage these systems when minimizing change, however these are generally restricted in their use for graphical applications (e.g. finite domains, linear systems, scheduling problems).

– *Stability in re-computation:* interactive processes recalculate solutions that are close to the previous configurations both for reasons of efficiency and to follow the *"principle of least astonishment"*. One issue is that similarity in terms of the underlying variable assignments does not necessarily imply similarity from the user point of view. Another issue is handling non-convex solution spaces. For example when the interactive process leads to a local inconsistency and the system must jump to a new solution, such as for instance when a non-overlap constraint forces an object to "tunnel" through an obstacle.

25.1.4. *Managing preferences*

In many graphical applications there are a number of geometric relations that any valid solution must satisfy and there are a large number of desirable, often conflicting, properties that the solution should have. These might arise from aesthetic preferences. For example, a layout for a graph should preferably have no edge crossings and edges should be straight. Another reason for conflicting preferences is stability. As discussed above, in an interactive system objects should not move or change shape unnecessarily. One standard approach is to place a weak preference on each variable that its value does not change unless forced to. Thus, the constraint problems arising in graphical applications are over-constrained, i.e. involve conflicting constraints. And since no solutions satisfy all of the constraints at the same time, it is necessary to find solutions that "best" satisfy the constraints in the over-constrained problem.

One approach to modeling these over-constrained systems is to use an objective function that captures the preferences and then use constrained optimization techniques. The other approach to handling over-constrained problems is to associate preferences with constraints. With this approach, the best (or optimal) solutions better satisfy more preferable constraints. A simple method for realizing this approach is to use the least-squares method, where preferences are represented as weights assigned to constraints, and the weighted sum of the squares of constraint violations is minimized (which can be done with known algorithms typically developed in the numerical analysis and operations research communities). A more sophisticated method is the constraint hierarchy [BOR 92] framework, which allows multiple preference levels called strengths. In this framework, strengths are different from weights, in that strengths represent "absolute" preferences (as opposed to "relative" preferences indicated by weights); that is, strong constraints are never relaxed due to weaker constraints that are inconsistent with the strong ones. Although good algorithms have been proposed for the case of linear constraints [BAD 01, MAR 02], research on non-linear constraint hierarchy solvers is still under way. In practice the two approaches are closely related and often "soft" constraints are translated into an objective function.

25.1.5. *Generic techniques*

The above requirements have meant that standard off-the-shelf constraint-solving techniques such as MIP or CP, meta-heuristic approaches are either not expressive enough or are too slow and so special purpose algorithms have been developed. The downside of this is that often these algorithms are specialized to a particular application and class of constraints and layout aesthetic. This is unfortunate because it means that one of the great potential benefits of using constraint solving, genericity and the ability to handle new constraints and user-defined aesthetic criteria is lost.

Thus there is a clear need to develop generic constraint solving techniques that can support interaction and preferences over different classes of constraints and domains. A possible approach is to express interaction and preferences in a unique hierarchical framework (e.g. as an optimization problem where user inputs, stability and dynamicity are expressed as preferences of different levels).

In the application areas of diagram authoring, network layout and adaptive document layout one promising approach is linear constraint-solving systems augmented with one-way constraints to handle text, dynamic linear approximation of disjunctive constraints such as non-overlap [HUR 02], and stress majorization to handle desired distances between objects. However, currently such systems have difficulty handling non-linear constraints such as tangents.

25.2. Better modeling and understanding of constraint systems by the end-user

One of the hardest issues facing constraint-based graphics is how to bridge the gap between the underlying constraint solver and the typical user of a graphics application who almost certainly has little knowledge of computer science or mathematics much less constraint programming. In this section we consider both the modeling from the user's point of view (i.e. constraint specification through the interface) and in the next section from the application programmer's point of view (i.e. interfacing the user's need with the underlying constraint modeling language). We shall focus on interactive graphical applications since the problems associated with non-interactive applications are similar to those found in other more traditional application areas.

25.2.1. *Model specification*

Constraint specification in non-interactive graphical systems raises similar problems to constraint modeling in most other non-interactive application domains. The standard approach is to use an application specific modeling language.

Constraint specification in interactive systems is more difficult and a number of approaches have been investigated. The most common approach is that the author explicitly imposes constraints using, for example, placement tools such as alignment or distribution on objects. The disadvantage of this is that in a diagram with a large amount of structure the author may need to impose a large number of constraints. Thus, there has been interest in systems in which constraints are inferred either from the current placement of objects or from a series of snapshots [KUR 93].

Another difficult problem is how to assign levels and weights to constraints in over-constrained systems or the relative weighting for terms in an objective function if the constraints are under-constrained. Requiring the end-application user to set these weights means the application becomes difficult to use, while if the application programmer programs the weight then it is quite difficult to find values that accord with the users intuition. For instance, most users expect objects to change location in preference to changing their size or aspect ratio.

25.2.2. *Extensibility*

One of the great strengths of constraints for graphical applications is that they allow the user to extend and tailor the constraints provided by the underlying system to their specific application. For instance the user might want to define a new re-usable widget and use constraints to specify its behavior, or they might want to define a new constraint such as "below-and-to-the-right". Even more ambitiously they might want to define a new layout style for a particular kind of network. A key feature for developers and users is certainly the declarative aspect of constraints: describing what the solution should be without having to specify how to calculate it.

One possibility is to force the user to write a textual description of the new components, or even worse write code, but clearly a more intuitive graphical interface would be better. There has been some research into this problem but it is still not solved.

25.2.3. *Constraint representation*

One seemingly trivial issue is how to represent the constraints in an interactive system. One approach is to represent the constraints in a separate view typically as a constraint graph. The obvious disadvantages of this approach are that the constraint graph is a rather abstract representation of the constraints and that the user finds it difficult to link the objects in the view with the actual objects in the layout.

Thus the more standard approach is to present the constraints as graphical objects in the application view. For example, an alignment constraint is represented by a guideline. This has the problem that the constraints can clutter the view and obscure the "real" objects and not all constraints have a natural graphical representation. For instance, what is a natural visual representation for a non-overlap constraint?

25.2.4. *Understanding constraint interaction during solving*

One of the most challenging issues in usability of constraint-based graphical applications is how the system allows the user to understand what has gone wrong when it does not behave in the way the user expects. This is difficult because constraints can combine in unexpected and non-local ways, especially once preferences are allowed. In interactive systems immediate feedback during direct manipulation can provide some support. For non-interactive systems the problem is even more difficult.

Major causes of unexpected solutions are under- and over-constrainedness of systems. Under-constrained systems on continuous domains essentially have an infinite number of solutions. However, in graphical applications, since only a single solution is typically used for displaying the resulting graphics, inherent under-constrainedness may not always be apparent. Therefore, it is necessary to support the user in identifying under-constrained parts of a system if they exist.

Over-constrainedness causes difficulties in several ways. If the traditional approach (without preferences) is used, an over-constrained system simply results in no solutions; in such a situation, no graphics can be displayed, which makes it difficult for the user to identify the cause of the problem. On the other hand, constraint preferences are useful as the user can obtain a solution from an over-constrained system. Nevertheless, they are not perfect. A simple problem is that the treatment of constraint preferences might be done in an unexpected way for the user. A more complex problem is that there might be several alternatives in processing constraint preferences that would result in different equally valid solutions, which might become a potential problem.

To tackle such problems with under- and over-constrained systems, "debugging" techniques have been proposed [SAN 94, TAK 03] in the context of constraint-based GUIs, but they support only simple constraints. Though explanation aspects of CP have recently received some attention [JUS 01], they are not compatible with constraints in graphical applications.

25.3. Bridging the gap between the solver and the application semantics

As we have discussed, the application user requires constraint specification and constraint solving to be presented in terms of the graphical objects and semantics of the high-level application domain. However, most existing constraint-solving tools require this high-level view to be translated into simpler flat systems of constraints in which the high-level semantics and structure of the initial problem is lost. This means that the application programmer has a considerable task mapping between the two representations, especially if the constraint-solving process operating on the low-level constraint solver is to be presented to the user in terms of the high-level application view. Better support for bridging the gap would make it easier to develop graphical applications. Indeed this problem is not restricted only to graphical applications: in most applications there is a large gap between the two views.

25.3.1. *High-level modeling*

Given that the standard approach for modeling graphical entities is the object-oriented paradigm, an obvious way for high-level modeling of constraint systems in graphical applications is to extend the object-oriented paradigm by allowing constraints to establish and automatically maintain relations between the graphical entities. Each graphical entity stands for an object with its variables (attributes) and its constraints (behavior) and has the possibility of setting constraints between objects. Many graphical problems have a hierarchical structure that could be translated into the constraint model, authorizing the setting of constraints in and between the different hierarchical levels. Hierarchical structuring is a good candidate for managing scalability issues (solving at higher levels of abstraction and then refining). These approaches have been explored in ThingLab [BOR 81]. Though both straightforward, such structured object-based systems have received little attention from the CP community both in terms of modeling and adequate solving techniques.

25.3.2. *Support for interaction*

The standard interface for off-the-shelf solvers can usually be easily integrated into non-interactive graphical applications typically in a master-slave architecture. But, as we have discussed previously, most graphical applications are interactive and so require a more sophisticated solver interface which supports incremental construction of the problem and end-user understanding of the constraint-solving process.

Constraint solver API for declaring constraints are rich and complex. They thus require the programmer to have a good knowledge of the underlying notions and techniques which prevents the wider use of CP in many graphical applications. Providing tools with better higher-level abstract representation of the constraints and of the solving process is required.

25.4. Conclusion

This chapter has presented problems and issues of graphical applications *w.r.t.* contraint programming techniques. Interestingly, many of the issues we have identified as particularly relevant to graphical applications – for instance hybrid constraint-solving methods, handling preferences, high-level modeling, and debugging – are currently hot topics in the CP community.

One major issue that has emerged from this study is that constraint-based graphical applications are still limited in their usability due to the lack of expressiveness and performance of the underlying solving techniques. Expressiveness and functionalities of constraint-based graphical applications are more a consequence of the underlying solving technique than of the software designer's will or the application needs.

Another major issue is that more effort needs to be devoted to the user-interface aspects of graphical applications. No matter how powerful the underlying constraint-solving techniques, constraint-based graphical applications will not be accepted until they can be used by people who do not have a background in CP.

The third major issue is that more research is required to design better, glass box, interfaces to constraint-solving tools that allow a finer level of interaction between the application and the solving process so that the application can support incremental construction of the problem and provide information about interaction, over and under-constrained problems to the end-user.

A fourth issue confounding research in this field is that the mainstream graphics community are not always aware of the latest constraint programming softwares and techniques. Better communication and exchanges between the two communities would benefit both: for the CP community it would provide interesting applications and generally challenging problems, while for the graphics community they could utilize more powerful constraint-solving technology.

25.5. References

[BAD 00] BADROS G. J., Extending Interactive Graphical Applications with Constraints, PhD thesis, University of Washington Department of Computer Science and Engineering, May 2000.

[BAD 01] BADROS G. J., BORNING A., STUCKEY P. J., "The Cassowary Linear Arithmetic Constraint Solving Algorithm", *ACM Trans. Comput.-Human Interact.*, vol. 8, num. 4, p. 267–306, 2001.

[BAT 99] BATTISTA G. D., EADES P., TAMASSIA R., TOLLIS I., *Graph Drawing, Algorithms for the Visualization of Graphs*, Prentice Hall, 1999.

[BOR 81] BORNING A., "The Programming Language Aspects of ThingLab, A Constraint-Oriented Simulation Laboratory", *ACM Transactions on Programming Languages and Systems*, vol. 3, num. 4, p. 353–387, October 1981.

[BOR 92] BORNING A., FREEMAN-BENSON B., WILSON M., "Constraint Hierarchies", *Lisp Symbolic Comput.*, vol. 5, num. 3, p. 223–270, 1992.

[HEN 97] HENTENRYCK P. V., MICHEL L., DEVILLE Y., *Numerica: A Modeling Language for Global Optimization*, The MIT Press, Cambridge, MA, USA, 1997.

[HUR 02] HURST N., MARRIOTT K., MOULDER P., "Dynamic Approximation of Complex Graphical Constraints by Linear Constraints", *UIST '02: Proceedings of the 15th Annual ACM Symposium on User Interface Software and Technology*, New York, NY, USA, ACM Press, p. 191–200, 2002.

[JUS 01] JUSSIEN N., OUIS S., "User-friendly Explanations for Constraint Programming", *ICLP'01 11th Workshop on on Logic Programming Environments*, Paphos, Cyprus, 1 December 2001.

[KUR 93] KURLANDER D., FEINER S., "Inferring Constraints from Multiple Snapshots", *ACM Transactions on Graphics*, vol. 12, num. 4, p. 277–304, October 1993.

[MAR 02] MARRIOTT K., CHOK S. S., "QOCA: A Constraint Solving Toolkit for Interactive Graphical Applications", *Constraints*, vol. 7, num. 3–4, p. 229–254, 2002.

[MIG 99] MIGUEL I., SHEN Q., "Hard, Flexible and Dynamic Constraint Satisfaction", *Knowl. Eng. Rev.*, vol. 14, num. 3, p. 199–220, Cambridge University Press, 1999.

[SAN 94] SANNELLA M., "Analyzing and Debugging Hierarchies of Multi-way Local Propagation Constraints", *Principles and Practice of Constraint Programming – PPCP'94*, vol. 874 of *LNCS*, Springer, p. 63–77, 1994.

[SUT 63] SUTHERLAND I. E., "Sketchpad: A Man-machine Graphical Communication System", *Proceedings of the AFIPS Spring Joint Computer Conference*, p. 329-346, 1963.

[TAK 03] TAKAHASHI S., "A Browsing Interface for Exploring Constraints in Visualization Rules", *Proc. IEEE Symposia on Human Centric Computing Languages and Environments*, p. 108–110, 2003.

Chapter 26

A Constraint Satisfaction Framework for Visual Problem Solving

AI models problem solving as a search for a path to a goal state from an initial state. Traditionally, the underlying representations have been in the so-called symbolic framework, i.e. the goal, the states and the operators that transform the states are all represented as compositions of predicate-symbolic structures, similar to natural language. However, in real-world problem solving, states and operators often have perceptual components, such as when diagrams are used in problem solving. In diagrammatic reasoning (DR), problem solving proceeds opportunistically. In addition to the traditional symbolic state transformations, perception may be called upon to extract certain information from the diagram, or actions may be taken on the diagram to create or modify parts of it to satisfy a given description. For example, a problem solving episode might need the information whether there is a school within five miles of the agent's home. The agent has to solve appropriate visual problems – abstract his home and all schools in a given map as points, calculate the distances of schools from his home, and compare them to five miles – to extract the required information.

The ability to obtain information about spatial properties and relations from a diagram and to modify or create diagrammatic objects have been referred to as routines, as in humans with repeated applications they eventually become so hardwired that they can be performed as a prescribed sequence of operations with limited problem solving. However, synthesizing routines from their

---

Chapter written by Bonny BANERJEE and Balakrishnan CHANDRASEKARAN.

specifications requires problem solving. In this chapter, we concentrate on the following research issues – is there a high-level language that is finite, extensible, human-usable, and expressive enough to precisely describe the properties of a wide variety of visual problems relevant to DR, and is there a general framework for solving the visual problems specified in the language and storing them as routines? We approach the problem by designing a visual problem solver that can synthesize and store solutions of visual problems from their specifications in a language at the behest of the DR system. For an artificial problem-solving agent, a diagram is an abstract data-structure consisting of a set of labeled objects whose spatiality is relevant to reasoning, along with their spatial information.

26.1. The framework

Our framework for visual problem solving consists of two components – a high-level specification language for describing the visual problems as a quantified logical combination of constraints which are well-defined mathematical functions and/or predefined visual properties/relations, and a visual problem solver for computing the solutions of visual problems from their specification in the language, along with a memory for storing visual problems and their solutions as routines. In the rest of this section, we describe each of these components in detail.

26.1.1. *A language for expressing visual problems*

The act of perceiving properties of, relations among or emergence of objects from their specifications is what we refer to as solving visual problems. We have developed a general ontology of objects, properties and relations that are widely used in expressing complicated problems. We allow addition of new objects/properties/relations when a problem cannot be expressed using the existing ones.

26.1.1.1. *The specification language*

The specification language is the language in which a diagrammatic reasoner describes a problem to the visual problem solver. The goal is to hide the internal representations of objects, properties and relations and the problem-solving strategies from the diagrammatic reasoner and let him deal with them in terms of their labels only. If the underlying representation or problem-solving strategy is changed, the specification language should remain unchanged. Our specification language is a functional constraint logic programming language. It recognizes an ontology of objects, properties, relations and a large set of mathematical/logical operators, such as $\leq$, $\neq$, $\cup$, $\forall$, $\vee$, $\Rightarrow$, etc. Formally, a visual problem ϕ is defined as a mapping from a set of diagrammatic objects O satisfying a set of constraints C to a set of booleans $\{True, False\}$ or real numbers $\Re$ or diagrammatic objects O'.

Diagrammatic objects. A point is the basic diagrammatic object defined as a pair $\{x, y\}$, $x, y \in \Re$. Any other object is defined as a set of points satisfying certain constraints. A line segment ls, for example, is specified by its pair of terminal points $\{p, q\}$. The x- and y-coordinates of ls are represented as

$$f_x(ls, t) = ls[1].x + t(ls[2].x - ls[1].x)$$
$$f_y(ls, t) = ls[1].y + t(ls[2].y - ls[1].y)$$

where t is a parameter, $0 \leq t \leq 1$, $ls[1] == p$ and $ls[2] == q$. A curve c, when piecewise linear, is specified as a sequence of points $\{p_1, p_2, ...p_n\}$ where the ith line segment $ls_i == \{p_i, p_{i+1}\}$. When not piecewise linear, c is represented as the tuple $\{f_x(c,t), f_y(c,t), t_0(c), t_1(c)\}$ where t is the parameter, $t_0 \leq t \leq t_1$, $f_x(c,t)$ and $f_y(c,t)$ represent the x- and y-coordinates respectively. To reduce computational costs, we restrict the domain of arbitrary curves to piecewise linear. A region is specified as the set of all points inside a closed curve which forms its periphery.

Visual problems. We are interested in a wide variety of properties of and relations relevant to DR. Some of them are more fundamental than others as they are used more often in expressing other properties/relations. For example, relations such as $Collinear(p_1, p_2, p_3)$ where p_1, p_2, p_3 are points, $Intersect(c_1, c_2)$ where c_1, c_2 are curves, $On(p, c)$ where p is a point and c a curve, $Inside(p, r)$ where p is a point and r a region, etc. are more fundamental than others. Similarly, properties such as $Distance(p_1, p_2)$ where p_1, p_2 are points, $Area(r)$ where r is a region, $Closed(c)$ where c is a curve, etc. are more fundamental than others. After using our framework for DR in a number of different domains, we have identified a small number of object properties and relations that are fundamental to DR, which are provided as part of the ontology. We provide a few examples of problems specified using our ontology. $BehindCurve(p, c)$, where p is a point and c is a curve, is specified as the set of all points that lie behind c with respect to p (see Figure 26.1(a)), i.e.

$$BehindCurve(p, c) = \{q : isaPoint(q) \wedge Intersect(c, \{p, q\})\}$$

Many problems in DR not only require constraint solving but also constraint optimization. For example, a bunch of points in a plot is abstracted as a curve to understand the nature of how a variable depends on another. Given a set of points S and a set of models of curves M, the problem $AbstractCurve(S, M)$ calculates the parameters for the model that minimizes the regression error, i.e.

$$AbstractCurve(S, M) = \{Q : Q \in M \wedge Minimize(\sum_{i=1}^{\#(S)} Q(S[i])^2)\}$$

where $\#(S)$ denotes the cardinality of S and $S[i]$ represents the ith element of S. A curve obtained by solving *AbstractCurve* for a given S and M is shown in Figure 26.1(b). Another example is the abstraction of a set of points S as an annular region depicting the notion of "surrounded". The problem *AbstractAnnulus*(S) is defined as the region between the smallest circle containing S and the largest circle not containing S but placed entirely inside the points in S (see Figure 26.1(c)). Thus,

$AbstractSmallestOuterCircle(S) = \{\{a, b, r\} : r \geq 0 \wedge_{i=1}^{\#(S)} (Distance^2(S[i], \{a, b\}) \leq r^2) \wedge Minimize(r)\}$

$AbstractLargestInnerCircle(S) = \{\{a, b, r\} : Min(\{S[i].x : 1 \leq i \leq \#(S)\}) \leq a \leq Max(\{S[i].x : 1 \leq i \leq \#(S)\}) \wedge Min(\{S[i].y : 1 \leq i \leq \#(S)\}) \leq b \leq Max(\{S[i].y : 1 \leq i \leq \#(S)\}) \wedge_{i=1}^{\#(S)} (Distance^2(S[i], \{a, b\}) \geq r^2) \wedge Maximize(r)\}$

$AbstractAnnulus(S) = \{\{a_1, b_1, r_1, a_2, b_2, r_2\} : \{a_1, b_1, r_1\} == AbstractSmallestOuterCircle(S) \wedge \{a_2, b_2, r_2\} == AbstractLargestInnerCircle(S)\}$

Perhaps one of the most widely used abstractions is grouping. We define the problem *AbstractnGroups*(S, n) as partitioning the set S of points into n groups such that the total variance is minimized. The problem *Partition*(S, P, i), where P is a set of points, calculates the set of points in S that are nearer to the ith point in P than to any other point in P. Thus,

$Partition(S, P, i) = \{Q : Q \subseteq S \wedge_{j=1}^{\#(Q)} (\forall k, 1 \leq k \leq \#(P), i \neq k \Rightarrow Distance(Q[j], P[i]) < Distance(Q[j], P[k]))\}$

$AbstractnGroups(S, n) = \{Q : Q \subseteq S \wedge \#(Q) == n \wedge Minimize(\sum_{i=1}^{n} Variance(Partition(S, Q, i)))\}$

Grouping is a NP-hard problem. *AbstractnGroups* requires searching through a space of $O(C_n^{\#(S)})$ possible solutions. The optimum number of groups is obtained by partitioning S into 1, 2,...$\#(S)$ groups and by minimizing the product of number of groups and total variance. The problem is specified as

$AbstractOptGroups(S) = \{Q : Q \subseteq \{AbstractnGroups(S, i) : 1 \leq i \leq \#(S)\} \wedge Minimize(i \times \sum_{j=1}^{i} Variance(Partition(S, Q, j)))\}$

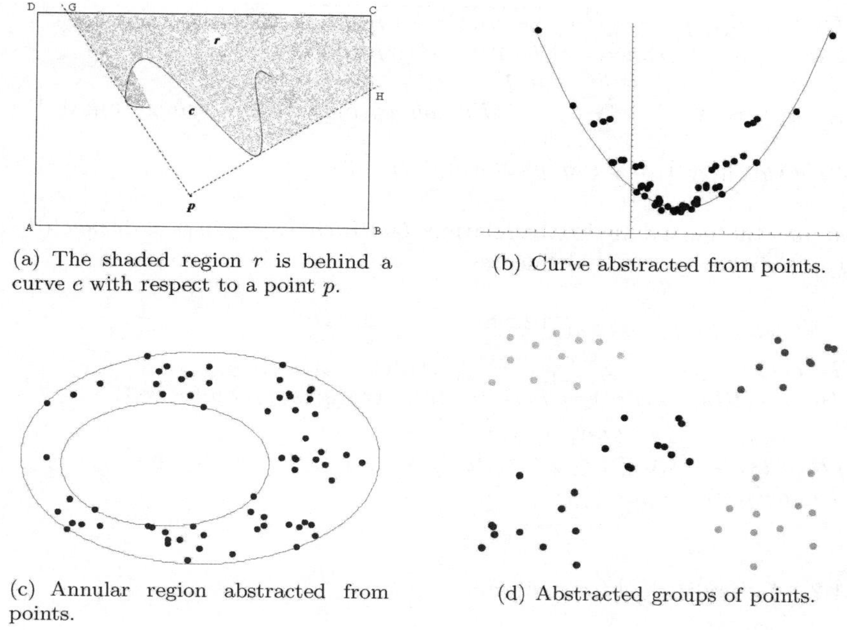

(a) The shaded region r is behind a curve c with respect to a point p.

(b) Curve abstracted from points.

(c) Annular region abstracted from points.

(d) Abstracted groups of points.

Figure 26.1. *Examples of visual problems relevant to DR*

Figure 26.1(d) shows an optimum grouping obtained by solving *AbstractOptGroups*, which requires searching through a space of $O(2^{\#(S)})$ possible solutions.

26.1.1.2. *The modeling language*

It is the language in which a problem is described in terms of the underlying representations. The goal is to transform the problem from the specification language using the internal representations of objects/properties/relations to a form that can be readily subjected to syntactic treatment. Beyond this stage, the visual problem solver does not have any recognition of any object/property/relation and no knowledge except those that come from the general principles of mathematics and logic can be applied. If the underlying representation or problem-solving strategy is changed, the modeling language should change.

Many of the fundamental properties and relations in our ontology are defined internally in the modeling language. Here we provide a few examples. Assuming the domain to be piecewise linear, the properties $Distance(p_1, p_2)$, $Closed(c)$, $Area(r)$ are defined as:

$$Distance(p_1, p_2) = \sqrt{(p_1.x - p_2.x)^2 + (p_1.y - p_2.y)^2}$$
$$Closed(c) = (c[1].x == c[\#(c)].x \wedge c[1].y == c[\#(c)].y)$$
$$Area(r) = \frac{1}{2} \sum_{i=1}^{\#(Periphery(r))-1} (Periphery(r)[i].x \times Periphery(r)[i+1].y - Periphery(r)[i+1].x \times Periphery(r)[i].y)$$

Assuming the same domain, the relations $Collinear(p_1, p_2, p_3)$, $Intersect(c_1, c_2)$, $On(p, c)$, $Inside(p, r)$ are defined as

$$Collinear(p_1, p_2, p_3) = (\frac{p_1.x - p_2.x}{p_3.x - p_2.x} == \frac{p_1.y - p_2.y}{p_3.y - p_2.y})$$
$$Intersect(c_1, c_2) = \vee_{i=1,\quad j=1}^{\#(c_1)-1, \#(c_2)-1} Intersect(ls_{1i}, ls_{2j})$$
$$Intersect(ls_1, ls_2) = (\exists q, isaPoint(q) \wedge On(q, ls_1) \wedge On(q, ls_2))$$
$$On(p, c) = \vee_{i=1}^{\#(c)-1} On(p, ls_i)$$
$$On(p, ls) = (\exists t, 0 \leq t \leq 1 \wedge f_x(ls, t) == p.x \wedge f_y(ls, t) == p.y)$$
$$Inside(p, r) = r(p.x, p.y)$$

26.1.2. *A visual problem solver*

In this section, we describe the visual problem solver which incorporates a number of constraint solvers with the primary goals of maintaining generality (i.e. being able to solve a wide variety of visual problems) and minimizing time complexity. A problem ϕ is transformed from the specification language into the modeling language by replacing ontological terms in the specification with their internal definitions. If a definition cannot be found, an error is flagged and problem solving halts until it is provided. From ϕ in the modeling language, the first step in the problem solving process is to decompose ϕ into disjunctions of subproblems, i.e. $\phi = \phi_1 \vee \phi_2 \vee ...\phi_n$. Each subproblem ϕ_i is now treated as an independent problem and further decomposed into disjunctions of subproblems. This process continues in a depth-first manner until no further decomposition is possible. From a subproblem, e.g. ϕ_i, the next step is to check the memory for similar problems. The memory contains relatively simple symbolic problems and their corresponding quantifier-free symbolic solutions. These problems may not have any visual semantics in DR. If ϕ_i can be mapped to one of these problems, its solution can be readily obtained by reverse-mapping from the corresponding symbolic solution in memory. Obtaining a solution in such a way completely bypasses the quantifier elimination and constraint-solving processes, thereby reducing the computational costs considerably. If ϕ_i cannot be mapped to any problem in memory, it is sent to a problem classifier that classifies and sends it to the appropriate constraint solver. The problem classifier and combination of constraint solvers have been developed in line with the ideas mentioned in [HOF 00]. If a problem with quantified constraints cannot be classified, it is sent by default to the quantifier elimination algorithm. The computational bottleneck of our problem solving process is quantifier elimination, the complexity of which is $O(s^{(l+1)\Pi(k_i+1)}d^{(l+1)\Pi k_i})$ where s is the number of polynomials, their maximum degree is d and coefficients are real, l is the number of free variables while $k = \sum k_i$ is the number of quantified variables [BAS 03]. Once a subproblem occurring at a leaf of the depth-first tree is solved by constraint solving or quantifier elimination, the subproblem in the modeling language and its solution are stored in memory so that the solution can be used when a similar problem is encountered in future. Thus, our visual problem solver grows smarter as it solves more and more problems. Finally, the solution of the given problem is obtained by combining the solutions of all its subproblems.

To illustrate the problem solving process, we consider the $BehindCurve(p, c)$ problem, specified in section 26.1.1.1. For a point $p = \{a, b\}$ and a curve $c = \{p_1, p_2, ...p_n\}$ where $p_i = \{x_i, y_i\}$ is a point, transformation of the problem to the modeling language occurs as follows:

$$\phi = \vee_{i=1}^{n-1} Intersect(\{p_i, p_{i+1}\}, \{\{a, b\}, \{x, y\}\})$$
$$= \vee_{i=1}^{n-1}(\exists q, isaPoint(q) \wedge On(q, \{\{x_i, y_i\}, \{x_{i+1}, y_{i+1}\}\}) \wedge On(q, \{\{a, b\}, \{x, y\}\}))$$
$$= \vee_{i=1}^{n-1}(\exists\{u, v\}, (\exists t, 0 \leq t \leq 1 \wedge x_i + t(x_{i+1} - x_i) == u \wedge y_i + t(y_{i+1} - y_i) == v) \wedge (\exists t, 0 \leq t \leq 1 \wedge a + t(x - a) == u \wedge b + t(y - b) == v))$$

Thus we have disjunctions of n-1 subproblems. It is interesting to note that for this particular problem, each subproblem corresponds to the visual problem of computing the set of all points that are behind a line segment with respect to a given point. The set of all points behind a curve, represented piecewise linearly, with respect to a given point is the union of all points behind each line segment of the curve with respect to that point. This rule, though not stated explicitly anywhere in our system, was appropriately applied due to the underlying representation and mathematical/logical principles. This is a huge advantage for visual problem solving as it does not require much of the desired knowledge to be stored explicitly.

If a problem similar to the first subproblem ϕ_1 is not found in memory, it is sent to the problem classifier which sends it to the quantifier elimination algorithm. The problem and its solution are stored in memory as follows:

$$\phi_1(x_1, y_1, x_2, y_2, a, b, x, y) = (\exists\{u, v\}, (\exists t, 0 \leq t \leq 1 \wedge x_1 + t(x_2 - x_1) == u \wedge y_1 + t(y_2 - y_1) == v) \wedge (\exists t, 0 \leq t \leq 1 \wedge a + t(x - a) == u \wedge b + t(y - b) == v))$$
$$= (a - x == 0 \wedge a - x_1 == 0 \wedge x_1 - x_2 == 0 \wedge b - y_1 == 0) \vee (a - x == 0 \wedge a - x_1 == 0 \wedge x_1 - x_2 == 0 \wedge y - y_1 == 0) \vee (a - x == 0 \wedge a - x_1 == 0 \wedge ...$$

where the arguments of ϕ_1 are the free variables not in any particular order. When the second subproblem ϕ_2 is encountered, a problem similar to it is found in memory which is ϕ_1. Two problems are considered to be similar if they have the same number of free variables and they are structurally equivalent. While determining structural equivalence, we calculate a correspondence between the free variables of two problems. Then, if similar, the variables in the solution of the first problem can be replaced by the corresponding variables of the second problem to obtain its solution. In the *BehindCurve*(p, c) problem, all the subproblems are found to be similar to ϕ_1 which might not be the case in general. The solutions of all subproblems are combined to obtain the final solution, which is shown in Figure 26.1(a) for an instance of c and p. Also, ϕ_1 in the modeling language and its solution are stored in memory.

26.2. Applications

The proposed framework has been used for a number of applications, including domains that require arbitrary objects with a wide variety of properties and relations. In this section, we will solve visual problems for entity re-identification and ambush analysis in the military domain and theorem proving in geometry.

Entity re-identification. The problem is to decide if a newly cited entity, given its time and location, is one of the entities identified earlier or a new entity. The first visual problem is to decide whether there exists a contiguous region avoiding a set of obstacles $\{r_1, r_2, r_3, r_4\}$ and containing two points T_1, T_3 of interest (see Figure 26.2(a)). The safe region avoiding the obstacles is specified as:

$$isaSafeRegion(\{r_1, r_2, r_3, r_4\}, d) = \{q : isaPoint(q) \wedge_{i=1}^{4} \sim Inside(q, r_i) \wedge_{i=1}^{4} (\forall a, isaPoint(a) \wedge Inside(a, r_i) \Rightarrow Distance(q, a) \geq d)\}$$

where d is the shooting range of the obstacles. In order to decide whether the safe region is contiguous or not, we resort to the adjacency algorithm in [ARN 84]. The other visual problem of interest is computing the shortest path between two points avoiding obstacles. Since our domain is piecewise linear, the shortest path will either be a line segment or be passing through some points lying on the periphery of the safe region. So the problem reduces to finding a sequence of points from the periphery such that the total length of the path between two points s, e is minimized. Thus,

$$FindnPointsonShortestPath(s, e, U, n) = \{Q : Q \in \{Permutations(Subsets(U, n), i) : 1 \leq i \leq C_n^m\} \wedge Minimize(Distance(s, Q[1]) + \sum_{i=1}^{n-1} Distance(Q[i], Q[i+1]) + Distance(Q[n], e))\}$$

where $U = \{u_1, u_2, ...u_m\}$ is the set of all points on the periphery of the safe region, the function $Subsets(S, n)$ creates all subsets of S that are of size n, and $Permutations(\{S_1, S_2, ...S_k\}, i)$ creates all permutations of the elements of set S_i. Thus, $FindnPointsonShortestPath$ calculates the shortest path that passes through exactly n points on the periphery of the safe region. This requires searching through a space of $O(n!C_n^m)$ possible solutions. The absolute shortest path is obtained by comparing the lengths of shortest paths that pass through 1, 2,...m points. Thus,

$$FindPointsonShortestPath(s, e, U) = \{Q : Q \in \{FindnPointsonShortestPath(s, e, U, i) : 1 \leq i \leq m\} \wedge Minimize(Distance(s, Q[1]) + \sum_{i=1}^{\#(Q)} Distance(Q[i], Q[i+1]) + Distance(Q[\#(Q)], e))\}$$

This requires searching through a space of $O(\sum_{i=1}^{m} i!C_i^m)$ possible solutions. The shortest paths from T_1 and T_2 to T_3 lying within the safe region as obtained by solving $FindPointsonShortestPath$ are shown in Figure 26.2(c). The lengths of the shortest paths eventually determine whether T_3 is T_1 or T_2.

Ambush analysis. Given a curve c (or region) as a hiding place and the firepower and sight range d, the problem is to determine the regions and portions of path prone to ambush. We specify the problem $RiskyRegion(c, d)$ as the region covered by range d from c. Thus,

$$RiskyRegion(c, d) = \{q : isaPoint(q) \wedge \exists a, isaPoint(a) \wedge On(a, c) \wedge Distance(a, q) \leq d\}$$

The solution is the shaded region in Figure 26.2(d) for curve c_2 and a particular value of d. The problem $RiskyRegion(r, d)$ for a region r can be defined by replacing the relation $On(a, c)$ by $Inside(a, r)$. Given a path c_1, the problem $RiskyPath(c_1, c_2, d)$ is specified as the set of all points on c_1 and inside the risky region.

$$RiskyPath(c_1, c_2, d) = \{q : isaPoint(q) \wedge On(q, c_1) \wedge Inside(q, RiskyRegion(c_2, d))\}$$

Theorem proving in geometry. Proving theorems in geometry requires making constructions and perceiving information from diagrams. For example, in order to prove Pythagoras' theorem, we make constructions such as (see Figure 26.2(e)):

$$DrawLineSegment(p_3, p_4) = \{p_4 : isaPoint(p_4) \wedge Collinear(p_2, p_3, p_4) \wedge Distance(p_3, p_4) == a\}$$

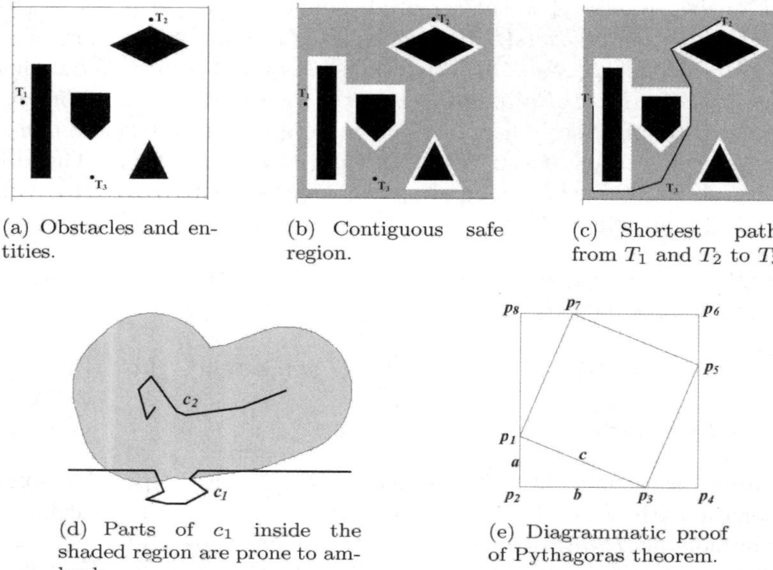

(a) Obstacles and entities.

(b) Contiguous safe region.

(c) Shortest paths from T_1 and T_2 to T_3.

(d) Parts of c_1 inside the shaded region are prone to ambush.

(e) Diagrammatic proof of Pythagoras theorem.

Figure 26.2. *Applications of the visual problem solving framework*

$DrawLineSegment(p_8, p_6) = \{p_6 : isaPoint(p_6) \wedge Angle(p_1, p_8, p_6) == 90^o \wedge Distance(p_8, p_6) == a + b\}$

We also need to perceive information, such as $Area(p_2p_4p_6p_8) == Area(p_1p_2 p_3) + Area(p_3p_4p_5) + Area(p_5p_6p_7) + Area(p_7p_8p_1) + Area(p_1p_3p_5p_7)$, which can be obtained by computing the existence of a point that lies inside one of the smaller regions and but not inside the largest region, or lies inside the largest region and not inside any of the smaller regions. If such a point exists, then the above expression is false; otherwise true. Thus, the visual problem is specified as

$\exists q, isaPoint(q) \wedge (((Inside(q, p_1p_2p_3) \vee Inside(q, p_3p_4p_5) \vee Inside(q, p_5p_6p_7) \vee Inside(q, p_7p_8p_1) \vee Inside(q, p_1p_3p_5p_7)) \wedge \sim Inside(q, p_2p_4p_6p_8)) \vee (Inside(q, p_2p_4p_6p_8) \wedge \sim Inside(q, p_1p_2p_3) \wedge \sim Inside(q, p_3p_4p_5) \wedge \sim Inside(q, p_5p_6p_7) \wedge \sim Inside(q, p_7p_8p_1) \wedge \sim Inside(q, p_1p_3p_5p_7)))$

26.3. Conclusion

We proposed and implemented a constraint satisfaction framework for solving visual problems relevant to DR. The specification language is set-theoretic with constraints specified in first order logic. We have expressed and solved a number of problems including those that require constraint solving as well as constraint optimization, with discrete as well as continuous domains. Though most of the problems were solved efficiently, there were two problems – grouping and computing the shortest path – that required searching through a combinatorially large set of solutions. We also illustrated how our problem solver grows smarter by solving more problems.

26.4. References

[ARN 84] Arnon D. S., Collins G. E., McCallum S., "Cylindrical Algebraic Decomposition II: An Adjacency Algorithm for the Plane", *SIAM Journal on Computing*, vol. 13, num. 4, p. 878–889, 1984.

[BAS 03] Basu S., Pollack R., Roy M.-F., *Algorithms in real algebraic geometry*, Springer-Verlag, 2003.

[HOF 00] Hofstedt P., "Better Communication for Tighter Cooperation", *Lecture Notes in Computer Science*, vol. 1861, p. 342–356, 2000.

Chapter 27

Computer Graphics and Constraint Solving: An Application to Virtual Camera Control

Modeling, animation and rendering have dominated research in computer graphics yielding increasingly rich and complex virtual worlds. In order to manage the complexity of these new worlds, some applications have successfully relied on the use of *CSPs* (constraint satisfaction problems) and their associated constraint-solving techniques. Indeed such techniques seem highly appropriate to solve difficult problems (such as computer graphics applications) thanks to their declarative properties as well as the whole set of methods available that will ensure the efficiency of constraint-solving approaches.

However, actual constraint-based techniques are somehow limited in the interaction offered to the user. This is especially true when considering that the modeling stage actually looses the semantics pertaining to the properties given by the user when transforming them into algebraic constraints. Indeed the constraints obtained by this step are solved without any consideration with respect to their membership to one property or another. Some *semantic* decomposition involving geometric constraints involve a semantic dimension and are able to give explanations in case of failures (for a broad overview of these decompositions see [JER 06]).

Nevertheless, this is restricted to geometric constraints and cannot be seen as a very general method. When solving the CSP, information that could be gathered from the knowledge of the violated constraints is lost and nothing is

---

Chapter written by Jean-Marie NORMAND.

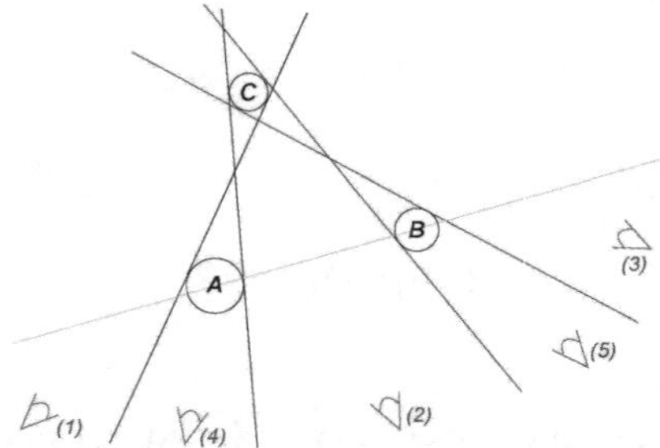

Figure 27.1. *Possible distinct areas for viewing a couple of objects A and B (resp. on the left and right of the screen) w.r.t. C*

provided for the user regarding the inconsistency of the problem. The main difficulties arise when the nature of a CSP (over, under or well constrained) cannot be determined before solving it, and that the solving methods should be chosen according to this nature. This would also lead to the usual measure of similarity between two solutions (usually the Euclidean distance) being replaced by a closeness *w.r.t.* constraints satisfaction which would more accurately capture the difference among solutions.

In this chapter, we rely on the problem of virtual camera composition (VCC) that consists of positioning a camera in a virtual world such that the resulting image satisfies a set of visual cinematographic properties, in order to illustrate the integration of semantics in the whole solving process.

The virtual camera composition task is generally achieved through a tedious and time-consuming process requiring a succession of "place the camera" and "check the result" operations. Current 3D modelers surprisingly lack integration of tools to assist the user in this task, despite the fact that cinema, in more than a hundred years, has provided a rich grammar that allows a director to unambiguously describe shots.

The chapter is organized as follows, we next present a brief overview of our method before detailing the semantic space partitioning approach *w.r.t.* to visual properties on the image. Section 27.3 will address the description of our numeric algorithm which is based on a continuous extension of a local search algorithm. The interpretation and reasoning with the semantic volumes is presented in section 27.4. Finally results are presented in section 27.5 before drawing a conclusion.

27.1. Overview

Most camera positioning methods rely upon optimization processes to calculate satisfactory camera placements and therefore lead to a unique solution closely related to the objective function (see [CHR 06] for an overview).

However, the description of a cinematic shot can possibly yield different visual solutions. Therefore, by computing the set of semantically distinct solutions *w.r.t.* cinematographic properties, we can provide the user with meaningful results. Figure 27.1 presents a top view of a simple scene containing three objects A, B and C. Whenever the user describes a shot in which he constrains A and B respectively to lay on the left and on the right sides of the screen, it clearly yields three possible classes of camera configurations: area (1) object C is on the left of A and B on the screen, (2) object C is between A and B, and (3) object C is on the right of A and B. Moreover, when considering possible occlusions, two classes can be added (4) A occludes C and (5) B occludes C. In such cases, classical optimization and incomplete CSP-based approaches fail in that a unique solution [DRU 95, OLI 99, PIC 02], or a reduced subset [JAR 98, CHR 02] of solutions is proposed, whereas all classes of solutions should be equally considered. These approaches actually lose the semantics of the problem while relying upon pure numerical approaches.

In this chapter, we propose to integrate a semantic dimension in the solving and interaction processes to assist the user in his camera placement tasks. We follow a threefold declarative approach: (1) describe the desired solution with a set of cinematographic-based properties, (2) calculate distinct classes of solutions satisfying the description with related cinematographic properties and (3) explore and interact with the classes of possible solutions.

In the description phase, as in previous approaches ([OLI 99, DRU 95]), a high-level grammar is offered including composition properties (framing objects on screen surface, relative object orientation and size) and shot properties (close up, establishing shot, etc.). The geometry of the scene (locations and orientation of objects) is considered as an input provided by the user.

In the computational phase, two processes are combined. The first process partitions the search space according to cinematographic properties (e.g. area such that A occludes B on the screen) and builds the intersection of the space partitions (indeed the conjunction of the visual properties will correspond to an intersection of the *semantic volumes*). The second process calculates a *nice* representative of each possible class of solutions via a continuous domain implementation of a local search meta-heuristic algorithm.

Finally, in a third phase, the user navigates in the possible solution sets and interacts with the semantic information provided in each area. This chapter concentrates on the first two phases and offers solid foundations for high-level interactions with the user.

27.2. A semantic space partitioning approach

Our approach to virtual camera composition (VCC) is based on the primary idea of *visual aspects* [KOE 79]. The idea behind *visual aspects* is to gather all the viewpoints of a single polyhedron that share similar topological characteristics on the image. A change of appearance of the polyhedron with changing viewpoint, gives rise to boundaries in the search space. Computing all the boundaries enables the construction of regions of constant aspect, namely *viewpoint space partitions.*

In this chapter, we propose an extension of viewpoint space partitions to multiple objects and replace the topological characteristics of a polyhedron by cinematographic properties such as occlusions, relative viewing angles, distance shots and relative object locations.

We introduce the notion of *semantic volume* as a volume of possible camera locations that give rise to qualitatively equivalent shots *w.r.t.* cinematographic properties, i.e. semantically equivalent shots. Each volume is characterized by a set of semantic tags issued from film grammar [ARI 76] and each tag is associated with a satisfied property in the volume. The entire space of possible camera locations is thoroughly partitioned for each object, and each pair of objects.

We then derive from the user's description the subset of volumes to be considered and intersect them. This process leads to a set of non-connected regions of which each represents a different class of solutions in terms of visual aspect.

27.2.1. *Projection property*

The projection property is based on the notion of scale shots in cinematography. It allows the artist to specify a viewing shot for an object. There are basically six different kinds of shots : the *Extreme Close-Up*, the *Close-Up*, the *Medium Close-Up*, the *Medium Long Shot* (or *Plan Américain*), the *Long Shot*, the *Extreme Long Shot.* Related semantic tags reflect all six kinds of shots (ExtremeCloseUp(Object) to ExtremeLongShot(Object)).

The underlying *semantic volume* is calculated given the position of an object and a cinematographic scale shot specified by the user. An optimal size can

Figure 27.2. *Distances between the camera and a character according to Arijon [ARI 76]*

be deduced corresponding to each scale shot presented in Figure 27.2. The object's bounding sphere and desired area in the frame are used to determine the range of camera distances. The minimum and maximum bounds of the interval correspond to two distances defining the inner and outer radii of an hollow sphere that includes the set of consistent positions for the camera.

27.2.2. *Orientation property*

The orientation property lets the virtual cinematographer specify the viewing angle required to shoot an object or a character. A common set of 8 viewing angles is offered (e.g. relative to object A, there are IsLeftProfileOf(A), IsRightProfileOf(A),..., IsThreeQuarterFrontLeft(A) up to IsThreeQuarterBackRight(A)) and each can be composed with high and low relative angles IsHighAngle(A) and IsLowAngle(A).

Computing orientation *semantic volumes* consists of building a prism-shaped volume of possible camera locations (see Figure 27.3 left), *w.r.t.* the vector to be considered (front, back, left, etc.).

27.2.3. *Occlusion property*

The occlusion property gives the user the opportunity to specify some visibility constraints between two objects of the scene. The cinematographer can characterize a total, partial or non-occlusion of an object by another. The *semantic volumes* induced by an occlusion property are calculated given characteristic cones defined with respect to the positions of the two objects involved

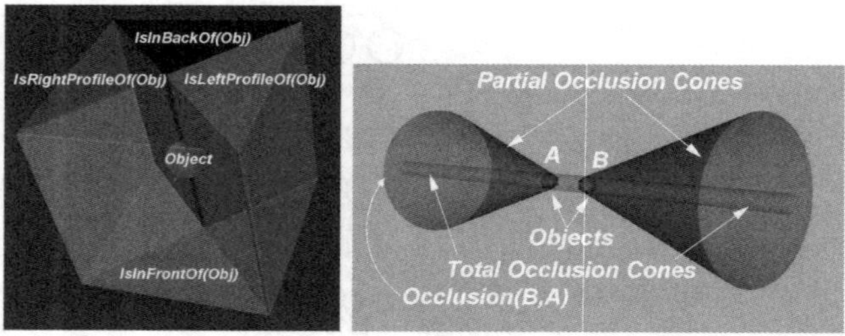

Figure 27.3. *Four common relative viewing angles and related semantic tags (left) and occlusion cones computation (right)*

in the occlusion property. The inside bounds of the cones define the volumes of partial occlusion. The outside bounds of the cones define the volumes where no possible occlusion can occur (see Figure 27.3 right).

27.3. Numerical solving stage

The output of the space partitioning approach consists of a semantic volume $s_v = \langle \mathcal{S}, \mathcal{V} \rangle$ containing possible camera locations. From there, the numerical stage calculates a *nice* representative of each disjoint volume in $\mathcal{V}$. This consists of choosing in $\mathcal{V}$ a consistent camera configuration (location, orientation and focal distance) that maximizes each property p_i corresponding to a semantic tag of S (i.e. minimizing a cost function).

The problem therefore comes down to determining a septet of variables c, such that:

$$\begin{cases} \min \sum_i \mathsf{cost}_{p_i}(c) \\ c \in \mathcal{V} \end{cases}$$

where $\mathsf{cost}_{p_i}(c)$ stands for the function cost associated with property p_i.

Traditional optimization and constrained optimization techniques require a differentiable objective function (e.g. general gradient descent algorithm). In order to manage our constraints we rely on stochastic-based *Local Search* techniques.

The algorithm relies on the exploration of the search space – here a *semantic volume* $\langle \mathcal{S}, \mathcal{V} \rangle$ – starting from an initial set-up, and exploring the neighborhood around the current configuration. A neighborhood function randomly selects a number of neighbors in $\mathcal{V}$, each is evaluated, and the best one is kept as the new current configuration. *Diversification* and intensification techniques are provided to respectively prevent being stuck in local minima and concentrate on promising regions.

27.4. Exploitation of semantic volumes

The main contribution of this chapter is to offer a semantic basis for exploring and interacting with the volumes. We illustrate two possible interactions: making requests on the calculated *semantic volumes* and making requests on the whole 3D scene *w.r.t.* the calculated volumes.

27.4.1. *Making requests on the volumes*

For a given description, each calculated volume provided by the geometric solver stores some knowledge related to the satisfaction of the properties. From here, the characterization of each distinct volume can be semantically augmented according to properties the user has not mentioned. For example, if a semantic volume s_v is characterized by the relative location $\mathsf{IsLeftOf}(A, B)$ tag, some further characterization of s_v can be calculated by considering the orientation properties related to A and B (e.g. $\mathsf{IsInFrontOf}(A) \wedge \mathsf{IsInBackOf}(B)$). As a consequence, the user can select two semantically augmented volumes s_{v1} and s_{v2} from the same description and request the differences between them. This request boils down to computing all tags in s_{v1} and in s_{v2} that do not belong to $s_{v1} \cap s_{v2}$.

27.4.2. *Making requests on the scene*

As each object and pair of objects in the scene generate their respective *semantic volumes*, it is trivial to make requests on a calculated volume s_v against any possible object or property. The request comes down to computing a new geometric intersection and checking the number of connected volumes calculated by tessellation.

27.5. Results

Two examples illustrate our approach. First the traditional over-the-shoulder shot implying two characters and then a framing shot with 7 possible classes of solutions.

The traditional over-the-shoulder shot is commonly encountered when filming a dialog between two or more actors and consists of laying the camera behind one actor while framing the other. Figure 27.4 illustrates the related *semantic volume* and a result is presented in Figure 27.5.

In the next problem, the geometry of the scene is composed of 5 coplanar objects (see top-view Figure 27.6). The user frames objects A, B and C respectively in the left, middle and right of the screen, and constrains D and E

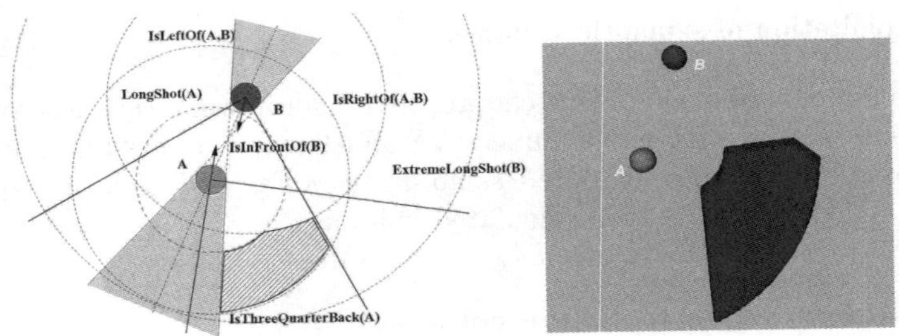

Figure 27.4. *Top view of the search space calculated by the* over-the-shoulder *shot (left) and tessellation of the implicit volume (right)*

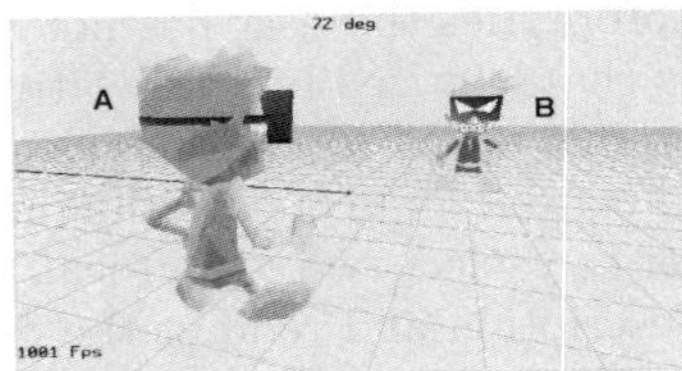

Figure 27.5. *A result of the over-the-shoulder shot*

to belong to the screen without any occlusion. All three shots satisfy the users description and illustrate different classes of solutions. Table 27.1 presents the time spent during the geometrical (T_G) and numerical (T_N) steps in computation of one representative of each semantic volume. T_G is directly related to the granularity of the tessellation (examples 1 and 2 generate 240 and 4036 polygons respectively). T_N is the time spent in the local search with nbSteps $= 25$ and nbTries $= 25$. Values such as these provide a very good time-to-quality ratio. Although the total time to calculate all representatives seems quite high ($7 \times 0.67 = 4.69$ seconds), time per representative is around 0.7 seconds which is quite acceptable for interaction purposes.

Example	Nb Vol	T_G	T_N	Total time
1	1	0.21	0.60	0.81
2	7	0.53	0.67	5.22 *(0.53+7×0.67)*

Table 27.1. *Time for computing a representative of each volume. T_G and T_N represents the time spend in the geometrical and numerical processes (Time in seconds on Linux OS, Pentium M 2GHz, 512Mo)*

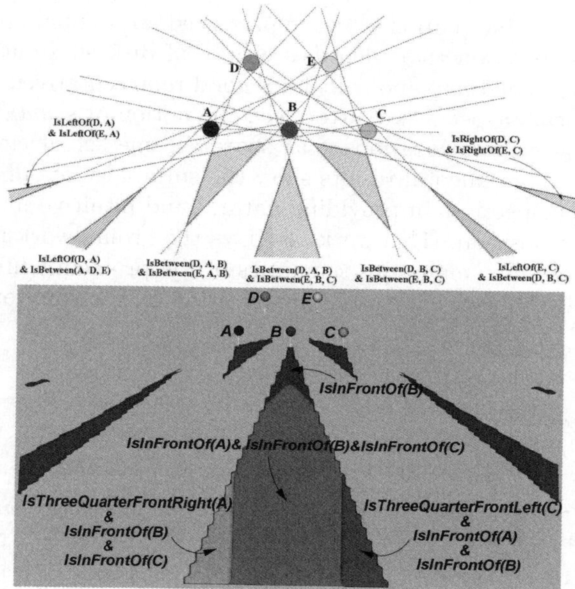

Figure 27.6. *Top view of the* five-framing *shot (top) and tessellation related to possible camera locations (bottom) with further semantic information related to orientations of A, B and C*

27.6. Discussion

The semantic space-partitioning approach offers the following features: cinematographic properties provide semantic volumes containing the possible solutions of the problem through a geometric process that filters non-satisfactory areas of the world. Whenever the intersection process leads to an empty result, there is a guarantee of contradiction in the user's specification. The numerical process offers a *good* representative of each volume at relatively low computational cost.

The main interest of maintaining semantics throughout the whole solving process (as shown is the case of positioning a virtual camera), is that the user gains meaningful and interesting information on the solutions of his problem. Unlike other approaches we offer solutions as well as additional knowledge on the different classes of solutions (if existing). This allows the user to reason on the problem instead of "only" being given a solution. Additional information could also be provided on constraints the user has not modeled (see section 27.4).

To conclude, in this chapter we have presented an original approach to virtual camera composition that identifies classes of distinct solutions, provides means to characterize them and calculates good representatives. By extending the notion of visual aspects, we introduced the notion of *semantic volumes* as a set of possible camera locations that share a same set of cinematographic characteristics. Experimental results show the suitability of our approach and open exciting perspectives in providing natural and intuitive interfaces to virtual camera composition. This work also lays the groundwork for a new type of solving process that maintains semantics of the problem while solving it in order to provide the user with useful information on the solutions (or pseudo-solutions).

27.7. References

[ARI 76] ARIJON D., *Grammar of the Film Language*, Silman-James Press, 1976.

[CHR 02] CHRISTIE M., LANGUÉNOU E., GRANVILLIERS L., "Modeling Camera Control with Constrained Hypertubes", *Procs of CP 2002*, September 9-13 2002.

[CHR 06] CHRISTIE M., OLIVIER P., "Camera Control", *Eurographics 2006, State of the Art Reports*, September 2006.

[DRU 95] DRUCKER S. M., ZELTZER D., "CamDroid: a System for Implementing Intelligent Camera Control", *Procs of the 1995 Symposium on Interactive 3D graphics*, p. 139–144, 1995.

[JAR 98] JARDILLIER F., LANGUÉNOU E., "Screen-Space Constraints for Camera Movements: the Virtual Cameraman", *Procs. of EUROGRAPHICS-98*, vol. 17, p. 175–186, 1998.

[JER 06] JERMANN C., TROMBETTONI G., NEVEU B., MATHIS P., "Decomposition of Geometric Constraint Systems: a Survey", *Internation Journal of Computational Geometry and Applications (IJCGA)*, vol. to appear, 2006.

[KOE 79] KOENDERINK J., VAN DOORN J., "The Internal Representation of Solid Shape with Respect to Vision", *Biological Cybernetics*, vol. 32, p. 211–216, 1979.

[OLI 99] OLIVIER P., HALPER N., PICKERING J., LUNA P., "Visual Composition as Optimisation", *AISB Symposium on AI and Creativity in Entertainment and Visual Art*, p. 22–30, 1999.

[PIC 02] PICKERING J. H., Intelligent Camera Planning for Computer Graphics, PhD thesis, Department of Computer Science, University of York, September 2002.

Index

D, E, F

G, H

I, J, K, L